EXPERT SYSTEMS

The Technology of Knowledge Management and Decision Making for the 21st Century

VOLUME I

EXPERT SYSTEMS

The Technology of Knowledge Management and Decision Making for the 21st Century

VOLUME I

Edited by

Cornelius T. Leondes

Professor Emeritus
University of California
Los Angeles, California

ACADEMIC PRESS

A Harcourt Science and Technology Company

San Diego San Francisco New York Boston London Sydney Tokyo

This book is printed on acid-free paper. ♾

Academic Press
A Harcourt Science and Technology Company
525 B Street, Suite 1900, San Diego, California 92101-4495, USA
http://www.academicpress.com

Academic Press
Harcourt Place, 32 Jamestown Road, London NW1 7BY, UK
http://www.academicpress.com

Library of Congress Catalog Card Number: 00-2001089412

Set International Standard Book Number: 0-12-443880-6
Volume 1 International Standard Book Number: 0-12-443881-4

PRINTED IN THE UNITED STATES OF AMERICA
01 02 03 04 05 06 HP 9 8 7 6 5 4 3 2 1

CONTENTS

CONTENTS OF VOLUME I

5 Experimental Design and Decision Support

TAY KIANG MENG

6 A Model-Based Expert System Based on a Domain Ontology

YOSHINOBU KITAMURA, MITSURU IKEDA, AND RIICHIRO MIZOGUCHI

7 Intelligent System Control: A Unified Approach and Applications

HUI-MIN HUANG, HARRY SCOTT, ELENA MESSINA, MARIS JUBERTS, AND RICHARD QUINTERO

8 Real-Time Fault-Tolerant Control Systems

WEI LIU

CONTENTS OF VOLUME 2

9 Model of Reasoning with Conflicting Information Sources in Knowledge-Based Systems

JINXIN LIN

14 Intelligent Tools and Their Applications in Geographic Information Systems

ERH-CHUN YEH, ZARKO SUMIĆ, AND S. S. VENKATA

15 Microprocessor Systems

S. M. YUEN AND K. P. LAM

16 Scheduling Systems for Shipbuilding

JAE KYU LEE, JUNG SEUNG LEE, KYOUNG JUN LEE, AND JUNE SEOK HONG

CONTENTS OF VOLUME 3

23 CAD-Based Vision Systems in Pattern Matching Process

YVES LUCAS, TANNEGUY REDARCE, AND ALAIN JUTARD

24 Cellular Automata Architectures for Pattern Recognition

P. TZIONAS AND I. ANDREADIS

25 Machine Intelligent System Techniques for Automatic Harvest Systems

SEIICHI INOUE, TAKAHIRO KOBAYASHI, TAKEO OJIKA, AND RYUGO KIJIMA

26 Integrating Machine Learning with Knowledge Acquisition

GEOFFREY I. WEBB

27 Modeling Human Reasoning Processes under Uncertain Conditions

SUMIT SARKAR

CONTENTS OF VOLUME 4

28 Devising an Expert System for Pediatric Syndrome Diagnosis

ØIVIND BRAATEN

29 Automatic Knowledge Discovery in Larger Scale Knowledge–Data Bases

NING ZHONG AND SETSUO OHSUGA

30 Efficient Legacy Data Utilization

DAVID J. RUSSOMANNO

31 Investment Decision Making

SANJA VRANEŠ, MLADEN STANOJEVIĆ, AND VIOLETA STEVANOVIĆ

32 Intelligent Systems Control in Manufacturing Cells

YU-LIANG SUN AND YUEHWERN YIH

33 Knowledge-Based Approach for Automating Web Publishing from Databases

ZHANGXI LIN, MATTI HÄMÄLÄINEN, AND ANDREW B. WHINSTON

34 Neural Networks for Economic Forecasting Problems

KAZUHIRO KOHARA

35 Determination of Principal Components in Data

FERDINAND PEPER, HIDEKI NODA, AND MAHDAD N. SHIRAZI

36 Time-Series Prediction

HISASHI SHIMODAIRA

CONTENTS OF VOLUME 5

37 Hybrid Expert Systems: An Approach to Combining Neural Computation and Rule-Based Reasoning

ERNESTO BURATTINI, MASSIMO DE GREGORIO, AND GUGLIELMO TAMBURRINI

38 POPFNNS: Fuzzy Neural Techniques for Rule-Based Identification in Expert Systems

C. QUEK AND R. W. ZHOU

39 Preventive Quality Management

GERHARD PETER, ANITA KRÄMER, CHRISTIAN RUPPRECHT, AND BERND BERTHOLD

40 Distributed Logic Processors in Process Identification

E. IKONEN, U. KORTELA, AND K. NAJIM

41 Knowledge Representation By Means of Multilayer Perceptrons

ELENA PÉREZ MIÑANA

42 A Guide to Research in Assumption-Based Truth Maintenance System Constraint Satisfaction

J. TAY, C. QUEK, AND S. HUANG

43 Method for Utilization of Previous Experience in Design Expert Systems

TAKASHI ISHIKAWA AND TAKAO TERANO

44 Model-Based Process Fault Diagnosis

HISASHI SHIMODAIRA

CONTENTS OF VOLUME 6

45 Automation of Concept Development

RYUJI KUDO AND TAKAO TERANO

46 Methodology for Building Case-Based Reasoning Systems in Ill-Structured Optimization Domains

KAZUO MIYASHITA

47 The Trainer System: Applying QR Techniques to Intelligent Tutoring Systems

C. QUEK, W. C. SIM, AND C. K. LOOI

48 Structuring Expert Control Using the Integrated Process Supervision Architecture

C. QUEK, M. PASQUIER, AND P. W. NG

49 Tap: An Inquiry Teaching Shell Using Both Rule-Based and State-Space Approaches

C. QUEK, L. H. WONG, AND C. K. LOOI

50 Self Teaching and Exploratory Task-Learning Methods in Unknown Environments and Applications in Robotic Skills

RUI ARAÚJO, URBANO NUNES, J. LUÍS CRUZ, AND ANÍBAL T. DE ALMEIDA

PREFACE

Artificial Intelligence (AI) has expert systems as one of the areas in its domain. AI almost defines itself as the replication, to some degree of human intelligence by the utilization of computers, sensor systems, and other technologies, in the performance of useful or interesting tasks. While application of AI to areas such as natural language translation, original composition of music or prose, vision, and other diverse tasks which are more in keeping with human facilities is problematic, restriction of AI to some of its generally regarded subset areas may provide useful solutions. In particular, delimiting artificial intelligence to the area of expert systems has proven to offer many significant capabilities and applications. As in other cases, there are no doubt many possible definitions of expert systems. One such effective definition of expert systems is that an expert system is a knowledge-based computer system which emulates the decision making ability of a human expert.

It seems the primary role of expert systems is to perform their functions, where it is appropriate to do so, under the supervision or monitoring of the human that is being supported. That is, the primary role of expert systems would appear to be supporting the human or humans who are using them. A classic example of where this relationship failed and resulted in near catastrophic economic consequences, was computerized stock trading (a flawed expert system at the time). On Monday, October 19, 1987, a malfunctioning expert system resulted in the worst stock market crash in history. Indeed, it was noted at the time that stock traders watched in helpless shock as the "bottom dropped out of the stock market" because proper monitoring measures were not put in place, to say nothing of the fact that the system itself had design flaws. Of course, these flaws have since been corrected, and research continues to produce improvements so that this catastrophe will not be repeated. Incidentally, stock trading is an example of "forward chaining" expert systems, i.e., a cause (various economic indicators) produces a certain effect (stock trading).

The "flip side" of the 1987 collapse of the stock market due to computerized trading is the Chernobyl disaster which occurred April 26, 1986. In this instance, it has been observed that this disaster which occurred at 1:15 AM was probably, if not indeed, due to operator fatigue. These operators were not supported by an expert system, which very likely would have avoided this disaster. This would be an example of a "backward chaining" expert system, i.e., effects (reactor performance indications) resulting in correction of causes by making proper control changes.

In the case of the stock market collapse, the situation was an expert system which was neither properly designed nor had adequate provision for human intervention. In the case of the Chernobyl disaster, the system operators did not have the support of an expert system, which very likely could have averted this major disaster. In both cases, the wrong thing was done at times which just aggravated the respective situations. At the bottom, it is most important to be aware of this still relatively new and growing technology of expert systems, which can permeate virtually every area of human endeavor, so that it can be appropriately and necessarily utilized. Indeed, one more noteworthy example involves the two chess matches that world class champion Garry Kasparov played against IBM's expert system known as "Big Blue." The first match was a tie and Kasparov lost the second match! In any event, this is a particularly appropriate time to treat the issue of expert systems techniques and applications.

This set consists of six well-integrated volumes on the broad subject of expert systems techniques and applications. It is appropriate to mention that each of the six volumes can be utilized individually. The great potential pervasiveness of this broad field of major significance certainly suggests the clear requirement for an adequately comprehensive treatment. All of the contributors to this work are to be highly commended for their splendid contributions that will provide a significant and unique reference for students, research workers, practitioners, computer scientists, and others on the international scene for years to come.

Cornelius T. Leondes

CONTRIBUTORS

Numbers in parentheses indicate the pages on which the authors' contributions begin.

Yasuhiro Akiba (53) ATR Spoken Language Translation Laboratories, 2-2-2 Hikaridai, Seika-cho, Souraku-gun, Kyoto, 619-0288, Japan

Hussein Almuallim (53) Information and Computer Science Department, King Fahd University of Petroleum & Minerals, Dhahran, 31261, Saudi Arabia

Tom Andersen (411) Department of Civil Engineering, Technical University of Denmark, DK-2800 Denmark

I. Andreadis (771, 875) Department of Electrical and Computer Engineering, Democritus University of Thrace, Xanthi, 67100, Greece

Rui Araújo (1897) Electrical Engineering Department, Institute for Systems and Robotics (ISR), University of Coimbra, Polo II, Pinhal de Marrocos, Coimbra, 3030, Portugal

Meir Barzohar (741) Computer Vision Group, RAFAEL, Haifa, Israel

Bernd Berthold (1413) Daimler-Chrysler AG, Ulm, 89013, Germany

Charles A. Bouman (661) Computer and Electrical Engineering Department, Purdue University, West Lafayette, Indiana 47907

Øivind Braaten (979) Department of Medical Genetics, Ullevål University Hospital, Blindern, Oslo, 0315, Norway

Ernesto Burattini (1315) Instituto di Cibernetica, CNR, Via Toiano, 6, Arco Felice (NA), I-80072, Italy

M. Cabassud (443) Laboratoire de Genie Chimique, Ecole Nationale Superieure d'Ingenieurs de Genie Chimique, UMR CNRS 5503, 31078, Toulouse Cedex, France

G. Casamatta (443) Laboratoire de Genie Chimique, Ecole Nationale Superieure d'Ingenieurs de Genie Chimique, UMR CNRS 5503, 31078, Toulouse Cedex, France

David B. Cooper (741) Division of Engineering, Brown University, Providence, Rhode Island 02912

J. Luís Cruz (1897) Electrical Engineering Department, Institute for Systems and Robotics (ISR), University of Coimbra, Polo II, Pinhal de Marrocos, Coimbra, 3030, Portugal

Aníbal T. De Almeida (1897) Electrical Engineering Department, Institute for Systems and Robotics (ISR), University of Coimbra, Polo II, Pinhal de Marrocos, Coimbra, 3030, Portugal

Massimo De Gregorio (1315) Instituto di Cibernetica, CNR, Via Toiano, 6, Arco Felice (NA), I-80072, Italy

Anastasios N. Delopoulos (701) Electrical Engineering Department, Computer Science Division, National Technical University of Athens, Zografou, 15773, Greece

J. L. Dirion (443) Centre Energetique—Environnement Ecole des Mines d'Albi-Carmaux, Campus Jarlard, Route de Teillet, Albi Cedex 09, 81013, France

John Durkin (1, 23) Dept. of Electrical Engineering, College of Engineering, University of Akron, Akron, Ohio, 44325-3904

Mahmut Gülesin (327) Mechanical Education Department, Gazi University Technical Education Faculty, Beşevler, Ankara 06500, Turkey

Matti Hämäläinen (1155) The Center for Research in Electronic Commerce, Graduate School of Business, The University of Texas at Austin, Austin, Texas 78712-1175

June Seok Hong (617) Department of Business Administration, Inje University, Korea

Hui-Min Huang (197) Intelligent Systems Division, National Institute of Standards and Technology, Gaithersburg, Maryland, 20899

S. Huang (1525) Intelligent Systems Laboratory, School of Applied Science, Nanyang Technological University, 639798, Singapore

Mitsuru Ikeda (171) The Institute of Scientific and Industrial Research, Osaka University, Osaka, 567-0047, Japan

E. Ikonen (1457) Department of Process and Environmental Engineering, Systems Engineering Laboratory, University of Oulu, Oulu, FIN-90014, Finland

Seiichi Inoue (909) Fukui National College of Technology, Geshi, Sabae, Fukui, 916-8507, Japan

Takashi Ishikawa (1559) Kisarazu College of Science and Technology, Department of Information and Computer Engineering, 2-11-1 Kiyomidai Higashi, Kisarazu, Chiba, 292, Japan

Maris Juberts (197) Intelligent Systems Division, National Institute of Standards and Technology, Gaithersburg, Maryland, 20899

Alain Jutard (833) Laboratoire d'Automatique Industrielle, Institut National de Sciences Appliquées, Villeurbanne Cedex, 69621, France

Shigeo Kaneda (53) Graduate School of Policy and Management, Doshisha University, Imadegawa-Karasuma-Higashiiru, Kamigyou-ku, Kyoto, 602-8580, Japan

Khalid W. Khawaja (661) Structural Dynamics Research Corporation, Milford, Ohio 45150

Ryugo Kijima (909) Faculty of Engineering, Gifu University, Yanagido, Gifu, 501-1112, Japan

Yoshinobu Kitamura (171) The Institute of Scientific and Industrial Research, Osaka University, Osaka, 567-0047, Japan

Takahiro Kobayashi (909) International Academy of Media Arts and Sciences, Ryoke, Ogaki, Gifu, 503-0014, Japan

Kazuhiro Kohara (1175) NTT Cyber Solutions Laboratories, 3-9-11 Midori-cho, Musashino-shi, Tokyo, 180-8585, Japan

Yuichi Koike (801) C&C Media Research Laboratories, NEC Corporation, 4-1-1 Miyazaki, Miyamae-ku, Kawasaki, 216-8555, Japan

Stefanos D. Kollias (701) Electrical Engineering Department, Computer Science Division, National Technical University of Athens, Zografou, 15773, Greece

U. Kortela (1457) Infotech Oulu and Department of Process Engineering, Systems Engineering Laboratory, University of Oulu, Oulu, FIN-90014, Finland

Yoshiyuki Koseki (801) C&C Media Research Laboratories, NEC Corporation, 4-1-1 Miyazaki, Miyamae-ku, Kawasaki, 216-8555, Japan

Anita Krämer (1413) Research Institute for Applied Knowledge Processing (FAW), University of Ulm, Ulm, 89019, Germany

Ryuji Kudo (1641) Interdisciplinary Course on Advanced Science and Technology, Graduate School of Engineering, University of Tokyo, 4-6-1 Komaba, Meguro-ku, Tokyo, 153-8904, Japan

K. P. Lam (553) Department of Systems Engineering and Engineering Management, The Chinese University of Hong Kong, Hong Kong, China

M. V. Le Lann (443) Laboratoire d'Analyse et d'Architecture des Systemes, Institut National des Sciences Appliquées de Toulouse, 31077 Toulouse Cedex 4, France

Jae Kyu Lee (617) Graduate School of Management, Korea Advanced Institute of Science and Technology, Seoul, 130-012, Korea

Kyoung Jun Lee (617) School of Business, Korea University, Seoul, 136-701, Korea

Jung Seung Lee (617) Graduate School of Management, Korea Advanced Institute of Science and Technology, Seoul, 130-012, Korea

Jinxin Lin (305) Softouch Intelligence, Toronto, Ontario, M4Y 1R5, Canada

Grier C. I. Lin (381) Centre for Advanced Manufacturing Research, University of South Australia, Mawson Lakes, South Australia 5095, Australia

Zhangxi Lin (1155) The Center for Research in Electronic Commerce, Graduate School of Business, University of Texas at Austin, Austin, Texas 78712-1175

Wei Liu (267) Department of Automation Engineering, Hebei Institute of Technology, 1831 Tangsham, Hebei 063009, People's Republic of China

C. K. Looi (1831) Intelligent Systems Laboratory, Nanyang Technological University, 637989, Singapore

Tien-Fu Lu (381) Department of Mechanical Engineering, University of Adelaide, South Australia 5005, Australia

Yves Lucas (833) Laboratorie Vision & Robotique, Institut Universitaire de Technologie, Bourges Cedex, 18020, France

Anthony A. Maciejewski (661) Computer and Electrical Engineering Department, Purdue University, West Lafayette, Indiana 47907

Tay Kiang Meng (199) Systems Technology Division, Gintic Institute of Manufacturing Technology, Singapore 638075, Republic of Singapore

Elena Messina (197) Intelligent Systems Division, National Institute of Standards and Technology, Gaithersburg, Maryland, 20899

Kazuo Miyashita (1667) National Institute of Advanced Industrial Science and Technology, 1-1-4 Umezono, Tsukuba, Ibaraki, 305-8568, Japan

Riichiro Mizoguchi (171) The Institute of Scientific and Industrial Research, Osaka University, Osaka, 567-0047, Japan

K. Najim (1457) Process Control Laboratory, Ecole Nationale Superieure d'Ingenieurs de Genie Chimique, Toulouse Cedex, 31078, France

P. W. Ng (1773) Intelligent Systems Laboratory, Nanyang Technological University, 637989, Singapore

Hideki Noda (1199) Department of Electrical, Electronic, and Computer Engineering, Kyushu Institute of Technology, 1-1 Sensio-cho, Tobata-ku, Kita-Kyushu, 804-8550, Japan

Urbano Nunes (1897) Electrical Engineering Department, Institute for Systems and Robotics (ISR), University of Coimbra, Polo II, Pinhal de Marrocos, Coimbra, 3030, Portugal

Setsuo Ohsuga (1015) Department of Information and Computer Science, School of Science and Engineering, Waseda University, 3-4-1 Okubo, Shinjuku-Ku, Tokyo, 169, Japan

Takeo Ojika (909) Faculty of Engineering, Gifu University, Yanagido, Gifu, 501-1112, Japan

Simon Parsons (79) Department of Computer Science, University of Liverpool, Liverpool, LE9 7ZF, United Kingdom

M. Pasquier (1773) Intelligent Systems Laboratory, Nanyang Technological University, 637989, Singapore

Ferdinand Peper (1199) Communications Research Laboratory, Kansai Advanced Research Center, 588-2 Iwaoka, Iwaoka-cho, Nishi-ku, Kobe, 651-2492, Japan

Elena Pérez Miñana (1497) Philips Research Laboratories, Cross Oak Lane, Redhill, Surrey, RH1 5HA, England

Gerhard Peter (1413) Research Institute for Applied Knowledge Processing (FAW), University of Ulm, Ulm 89019, Germany

C. Quek (1355, 1699, 1773, 1831) Intelligent Systems Laboratory, School of Applied Science, Nanyang Technological University, 639798, Singapore

Richard Quintero (197) Intelligent Systems Division, National Institute of Standards and Technology, Gaithersburg, Maryland, 20899

Tanneguy Redarce (833) Laboratoire d'Automatique Industrielle, Institut National de Sciences Appliquées, Villeurbanne Cedex, 69621, France

Christian Rupprecht (1413) Research Institute for Applied Knowledge Processing (FAW), University of Ulm, Ulm, 89019, Germany

David J. Russomanno (1071) Department of Electrical Engineering, University of Memphis, Memphis, Tennessee, 38152

Sumit Sarkar (961) School of Management, University of Texas at Dallas, Management Science and Information Systems, Richard, Texas, 75080

Harry Scott (197) Intelligent Systems Division, National Institute of Standards and Technology, Gaithersburg, Maryland, 20899

Hisashi Shimodaira (1259, 1577) Faculty of Information and Communication, Bunkyo University, 2-2-16 Katsuradai, Aoba-Ku, Yokoha-city, Kanagawa 227-0034, Japan

Mahdad N. Shirazi (1199) Communications Research Laboratory, Kansai Advanced Research Center, 2-2-2 Hikaridai Seika-cho, Kyoto 619-0289, Japan

W. C. Sim (1699) Intelligent Systems Laboratory, Nanyang Technological University, 637989, Singapore

Milan Sonka (639) Department of Electrical and Computer Engineering, University of Iowa, Iowa City, Iowa 52242

Mladen Stanojević (1107) Computer Systems Department, Mihailo Pupin Institute, Volgina 15, Belgrade, 11060, Yugoslavia

Violeta Stevanović (1107) Computer Systems Department, Mihailo Pupin Institute, Volgina 15, Belgrade, 11060, Yugoslavia

Zarko Sumić (489) Connex T, 1301 5th Avenue, Ste. 1900, Seattle, Washington, 98101

Yu-Liang Sun (1135) iz Technologies, Inc., Dallas, Texas 75234

Guglielmo Tamburrini (1315) Instituto di Cibernetica, CNR, Via Toiano, 6, Arco Felice (NA), I-80072, Italy

Midori Tanaka (801) C&C Media Research Laboratories, NEC Corporation, 4-1-1 Miyazaki, Miyamae-ku, Kawasaki, 216-8555, Japan

J. Tay (1525) Intelligent Systems Laboratory, School of Applied Science, Nanyang Technological University, 639798, Singapore

Takao Terano (1559, 1641) Graduate School of Systems Management, University of Tsukuba, 3-29-1 Otsuka, Bunkyo-ku, Tokyo, 112-0012, Japan

Daniel Tretter (661) Hewlett-Packard Co., Palo Alto, California, 94304-1126

P. Tzionas (875) Department of Automation, Technological Educational Institute of Thessaloniki, Thessaloniki, 54101, Greece

S. S. Venkata (489) Department of ECE, Iowa State University, 2001 Coover Hall, Ames, Iowa, 50011-3060

Sanja Vraneš (1107) Computer Systems Department, Mihailo Pupin Institute, Volgina 15, Belgrade, 11060, Yugoslavia

Geoffrey I. Webb (937) School of Computing and Mathematics, Deakin University, Geelong, Victoria 3217, Australia

Andrew B. Whinston (1155) The Center for Research in Electronic Commerce, Graduate School of Business, University of Texas at Austin, Austin, Texas 78712-1175

L. H. Wong (1831) Intelligent Systems Laboratory, Nanyang Technological University, 637989, Singapore

Erh-Chun Yeh (489) Cegelec ESCA, 11120 NE 33rd Place, Bellevue, Washington 98006

Yuehwern Yih (1135) School of Industrial Engineering, Purdue University, West Lafayette, Indiana 47907-1287

S. M. Yuen (553) Department of Systems Engineering and Engineering Management, The Chinese University of Hong Kong, Hong Kong, China

Ning Zhong (1015) Department of Information Engineering, Maebashi Institute of Technology, 460-1 Kamisadori-cho, Maebashi City 371-8616, Japan

R. W. Zhou (1355) Intelligent Systems Laboratory, Nanyang Technological University, 637989, Singapore

1 HISTORY AND APPLICATIONS

JOHN DURKIN

Department of Electrical Engineering, College of Engineering, University of Akron, Akron, Ohio 44325-3904

I. INTRODUCTION

The wealth of a nation once arose from the physical labors of its people. For centuries, this wealth was limited by the size and stamina of the work force. With the dawn of the industrial revolution came a new opportunity to increase national wealth. Machines fueled by steam and oil were developed to assist labor-intensive tasks, providing dramatic increases in productivity. Today, national wealth is measured in intellectual capital. Nations that possess skillful people in such diverse areas as science, medicine, business, and engineering produce innovations that drive the nation toward a higher quality of life. To better use these valuable resources, new machines were sought that could capture the expertise of these talented people. This quest placed us in search of machines powered not by steam, but by *knowledge*, and into the *knowledge revolution* era.

Success in this endeavor could provide an enormous benefit to humankind. Nations that lack expertise could use these machines to improve their medical care, advance their engineering technology, or increase their manufacturing productivity. Companies could use them to assist decision making or to proliferate throughout

Expert Systems, Edited by Cornelius T. Leondes, Volume 1

ISBN: 0-12-443881-4 / $35.00

their organization the skills of a scarce number of experts. Researchers could also use them to better understand how humans reason. They could serve us today by meeting our mental challenges and provide a vehicle for discovering tomorrow's technology.

The quest for the holy grail of an intelligent machine is not new. For over 2000 years the search has been on, motivated, in part, by the practical benefits offered by success and, in part, by the sheer fascination of the effort. Philosophers, mathematicians, and technicians have contributed to the quest. In most cases, new discoveries rely on the previous labors of others, so that, although these other achievements may be small, they are seminal. This chapter reviews these important contributions and shows how they shaped our present day intelligent machine.

II. PHILOSOPHY (470–322 BC)

It can be argued that the foundation of artificial intelligence (AI) was first laid through the work of Socrates, Plato, and Aristotle, each of whom helped to define the philosophies that shaped western culture. Socrates (470–399 BC) held a strong belief in the doctrine that "mind" is the source of all cosmic order. He was a man composed of deep ethical beliefs, extraordinary insightful rational thought, and, at times, a touch of arrogance; he believed himself charged by God with the mission to make his fellow men aware of their ignorance. It is in his attempts to obtain an understanding of reasoning that we find his genius and his heritage to AI.

Socrates's vision of the *universal definition* (what the Phaedo calls a form), for example, is an attempt to formulate the meaning of a significant predicate. Plato reported a dialogue in which Socrates says to Euthyphro, "I want to know what is characteristic of piety which makes all actions pious . . . that I may have it to turn to, and to use as a standard whereby to judge your actions and those of other men." Socrates's concept of an universal definition (or form) contains a pattern of a particular category of things in the world, such as man, woman, and stone, or even intangible things, such as beauty and piety. Using a piety form as sort of a template, for example, he could judge a man's moral character or, more likely, point out his imperfections. Socrates's universal definition is the basis of a *class* in modern-day object-oriented programs and frame-based expert systems.

In another example, we can find his contribution to today's *rule-based* expert systems. Socrates was intrigued by logical thinking, particularly concerning what *deductions* one could make from available facts. His method was to start with some reasonable hypothesis given the available information and then consider the consequences that naturally follow from it. If these consequents can be reasonably expected, he argued that the hypothesis might be regarded as provisionally confirmed. Aristotle later refined this concept with his introduction of a syllogism.

Socrates was the first of the great Greek philosophers to study human intelligence and to set forth concepts to explain human reasoning. Unfortunately, he was not a writer. He conveyed his ideas verbally to his students, who expanded them and, fortunately for the rest of us, put them in print. His most notable pupil was Plato.

Building on the life and thought of Socrates, Plato (428–348 BC) developed a profound and very broad study of philosophy that was based on the proposition that reason must be followed wherever its leads. We can see his brilliance in his writings across a wide range of subjects, which include mathematics, physics, astronomy, politics, and philosophy. Carrying forward Socrates's work on universal definitions (forms) is one of his major contributions.

Socrates was convinced that knowing rests in the identification of objects or ideas that can be described in unrefutable terms. Plato discovered that such predicate items exist, for example, a circle. To say, "This is a circle," is to attribute a certain property to the specific object, such as its radius. Plato distinguished between a specific circle that can be drawn by knowing its radius and the common property of the predicate object. Plato called the predicate object a *form* and the specific object a *particular*. Today, we simply have renamed these *class* and *instance*, respectively. To the extent that humans have knowledge, Plato believed that they attained it through reasoning that leads to the discovery of forms. His theory of intelligence is thus composed of two parts: the *description of knowledge* contained in forms and the quest for knowledge by way of *reasoning*. These two parts represent the basic architecture of today's expert system, where we find a *knowledge base* and an *inference engine*.

Plato claimed that the search for definitions, and thereby the nature of forms, is a search for knowledge. He wrote that Socrates attempted to find a definition that would be immune to counterexamples. A definition is proposed and if any counterexample can be found, then it is rejected; otherwise, it is accepted. Aristotle credits Socrates with an another method based on "inductive arguments," which attempts to derive a definition through consideration of concrete illustrations. For example, the consider "shoemakers and carpenters," which the fashionable speakers regarded as "vulgar laborers." Here, *induction* is viewed as a function that puts the meaning of a proposed definition before the mind. Today, we build *induction-based* expert systems by using somewhat the same approach. Plato continued the work begun by the sophists and by Socrates. This effort was raised to a high art by Plato's pupil Aristotle.

Aristotle (384–322 BC) inherited from Plato a deep appreciation for theories that might explain the human intellectual process and a vast body of problems to test these theories. Fortunately, Aristotle possessed a highly analytical mind and sought to develop logical methods to support his studies. This rare combination of an understanding of both philosophy and logic enabled him to expand on the intellectual tradition bequeathed him.

Aristotle believed that the study of logical thought was the path to an understanding of human intelligence. In his *Logic*, he viewed knowledge in terms of necessary propositions that express causal relationships that take the form of categorical *syllogisms*. A syllogism is a form of an argument that proposes that a given proposition can be said to be true because it is related to another proposition that is known to be true. According to Aristotle, a syllogism contains three categorical propositions (two premises and a conclusion). The form of an "universally affirmative" syllogism is "If every β is an α and every γ is a β, then every γ is an α," where α, β, and γ are variables. Any argument that fits this pattern is a valid syllogism. For example, if we know that "every person is mortal" and that "every Greek is a person," then we can conclude that "every Greek is mortal." Aristotle was the first logician to use variables, and his use of them in syllogisms later became a standard way to process knowledge in *predicate calculus*.

Aristotle argued for the application of his logical theory to obtain a fundamental understanding of the sciences. In his *Posterior Analytics*, he wrote that each science must depend on a set of first principles, or axioms, that are necessarily true, and that the theorems that compose a science are deduced from its axioms. He also believed that all of these scientific deductions could be formed by way of syllogisms. Following this line of thought, he devoted much of the second book of the *Posterior Analytics* to Socrates's theory of the universal definition, because he felt that the most important axioms of any science are the definitions that constitute the field.

When we reflect on the contributions of philosophy to AI, our thoughts are naturally drawn to early Greece, where the study of *epistemology* was born. The name is derived from the Greek words *episteme* (knowledge) and *logos* (reason). It represents today one of the four main fields of philosophy. During the past 2000 years, through the Renaissance, the Age of Enlightment, the Industrial Revolution, and the Information Age, philosophers in the field have added to our understanding of the human intellect, but it will always be the three great Greek philosophers—Socrates, Plato, and Aristotle—to whom the field of AI is indebted. In our tour of the history of the intelligent machine, let us fast forward to the 1800s, where we find efforts to build such a machine.

III. MECHANICS (1800s)

During the early 1800s an enterprising group of individuals toured Europe and America demonstrating a device they called the chess automation. This was a large mechanical box that they advertised as being capable of playing chess on a par with humans. Like other mechanical devices of the day, it contained gears and levers that the spectators were told would move in accordance with deciding the next chess move. However, very much unlike the other devices, it also included one of the better chess players of the day. This famous hoax illustrates human's fascination with intelligent machines even in those early times.

In 1834, Charles Babbage conceived the design for the first mechanical computer, which he called the analytical engine [1], that foreshadowed many of the architectural plans of the modern computer. His design was the first mechanical rendition of Plato's notion of the separation of knowledge (the engine's memory which Babbage called the store) and reasoning (the engine's processor, which he called the mill). His design also introduced the concept of a programmable machine that could execute a series of operations encoded on punched cards. Babbage's friend and collaborator, Ada Lovelace, daughter of the poet Lord Byron, wrote programs for the analytical engine and went on to suggest that the machine might someday be able to play chess. We might consider Lovelace to be the world's first programmer.

Beyond the technological innovations offered by the analytical engine, we can find a value that is closer to the core objective of artificial intelligence. Babbage's work put forth the idea that an intellectual activity could be represented in a pattern of steps that could be encoded in a machine, which could then be studied to better understand the activity. On his effort to build the engine Babbage said, "If I should be successful . . . it will thus call into action a permanent cause of advancement toward the truth, continually leading to the more accurate determination of established fact, and to the discovery and measurements of new ones." Unfortunately, the analytical engine was never built for a reason that has become an all too often event within the history of the quest for the intelligent machine.

To obtain funding to build his machine, Babbage met with Prime Minister Lord Melbourne who was responsible for government sponsored research in England. To reach a decision, Melbourne sought the advice of Reverend Richard Sheepshanks, a secretary of the Royal Astronomical Society (and also Babbage's archenemy). Sheepshanks wrote of Babbage in his book *The Exposition of 1851*, "He was ill-judged enough to press the consideration of this new machine upon the members of Government." Melbourne's decision was then obvious. Failing to obtain the necessary funding, Babbage gave up all expectations of building the analytical engine and later wrote of his disillusionment, "Thus bad names are coined by worse men to destroy honest people." Skepticism, personal bias, and frustration are some of the human emotions that have marred the quest.

Logic has been called the grammar of reason. With its exact syntax and logical rules, logicians have long argued that logic offers a tool for creating a formal language for thought. There were two mathematicians during this era who agreed with this argument and went on to make major contributions to the field, and whose work later had a profound impact on AI.

The most important contributor to the field of logic during the early nineteenth century was the English mathematician George Boole, who established modern symbolic logic and the algebra of logic called Boolean algebra. Although the importance of the role of Boolean algebra in designing digital logic circuits is well known, Boole's real motivation for developing his system of symbolic logic appears to be well aligned with the goals of contemporary AI researchers. In his 1854 writing, *An Investigation of the Laws of Thought, on Which Are Founded the Mathematical Theories of Logic and Probabilities*, he states his goals as

> to investigate the fundamental laws of those operations of the mind by which reasoning is performed: to give expression to them in the symbolical language of a Calculus, and upon this foundation to establish the science of logic and instruct its method; . . . and finally to collect from the various elements of truth brought to view in the course of these inquiries some probable intimations concerning the nature and constitution of the human mind.

In 1847, Boole published another important work, *The Mathematical Analysis of Logic*, where he presented his general symbolic method of logical inference. Given a rule that contained premises and conclusions represented as symbolic propositions, Boole described how one can draw logical conclusions through the symbolic treatment of the premises. He went further and discussed his ambitious goal to symbolize, systematize, and generalize the concepts of logic invented by the early Greek philosophers. He wrote, "I propose to establish the Calculus of Logic." In so doing, he laid the groundwork for *propositional calculus* and the study of symbolic logic.

A proposition is a statement about the world that we consider as either true or false. For example, we might state, "Weather on weekends is lousy." In propositional calculus, symbols are associated with various propositions. By joining propositions together using *conjuncts* (ands), *disjuncts* (ors), and *implications* (if–thens), rules can be written to both capture and reason about knowledge. Propositional calculus was the first attempt to apply formal logic to the processing of symbols.

However, it was limited in its ability to offer a practical tool for managing complex problems, because each symbol could represent a proposition of some complexity and there was no way to access the components of the proposition—a requirement in most real intelligent machine applications. Fortunately, this situation changed in only a few years.

In 1879, the German mathematician and logician Gottlob Frege published the book *Begriffsschrift*. In it he wrote of the use of a *predicate* that describes a relationship between components of a proposition. For example, instead of assigning a symbol to the entire statement, "Weather on weekends is lousy," we can create a predicate *weather* and write "weather (weekends, lousy)." This idea alone was important because it offered the opportunity to describe a given proposition at the level of granularity that would be needed in intelligent systems. However, even better, Frege went much further. He was as much a philosopher as he was a logician. His primary goal was to create a formal mathematical language for logical deductive reasoning. In addition to introducing the use of a predicate to describe a proposition, he introduced quantifiers, functions, and variables into his symbolic algebra, which offered a language to describe mathematics and its philosophical foundations. His language, now called *predicate calculus*, later led to the popular AI programming language PROLOG in the twentieth century.

IV. COMPUTERS AND FIRST GLIMPSE AT ARTIFICIAL INTELLIGENCE (1940s)

Prior to the twentieth century, much of the scientific and mathematic intellectual prerequisites needed to create an intelligent machine were in place. Next the proper vehicle was needed. Mechanical machines, with all the gears and levers in the world, were not the answer. The search for an intelligent machine was waiting for technology to catch up to it; it was waiting for the electronic computer.

The earliest rendition of the modern digital computer was developed independently by engineers in three countries embattled in World War II. In 1940, Alan Turing and his team of researchers in England built the first operational computer called the Heath Robinson for the exclusive purpose of deciphering German coded messages. The system was effective but slow, because its design relied heavily on the use of electromechanical relays. As the German codes became more sophisticated, making the Robinson obsolete, a new computer called the Colossus was built in 1943 using vacuum tubes, which provided the necessary speed to decode the messages.

The first general-purpose *programmable* computer, called the Z-3, was developed in Germany in 1941. It was built by Konrad Zuse, who also invented floating-point numbers for the computer. Later in 1945, Zuse went on to invent the first high-level programming language called *Plankalkul*. The Z-3 project was partially funded by the Third Reich to assist in aircraft design. Beyond this application, however, the German military hierarchy did not place as much importance on computer technology as did their counterpart in England.

The credit for the first *electronic* computer should go to John Atanasoff and his graduate student, Clifford Berry, at Iowa State University. In 1939, they built a prototype computer, using 300 vacuum tubes and capacitors for memory, that stored data in binary form. They called their invention the Atanasoff–Berry Computer

(ABC). The prototype was built in a couple of months and worked continued for three years to build the complete system. However, with the onset of World War II, the project was abandoned when Atanasoff moved to Washington to work on a military research project.

Two other computer-related efforts in the United States were conducted during this period in support of military research. At Harvard University, Howard Aiken began work in 1939 on a machine that could perform the operations of addition, subtraction, multiplication, division, and reference to previous results. His machine, which he called the Mark I, was completed in 1944. The computer was used by the Navy for work in gunnery, ballistics, and design. At the University of Pennsylvania, John Mauchly and John Eckert were asked to devise ways to accelerate the recomputation of artillery firing tables for the U.S. Army. Their work led to the construction of a general-purpose digital computer called ENIAC, which contained more than 18,000 vacuum tubes and incorporated many of the features first introduced by Atanasoff in the ABC computer. Recognizing the potential commercial value of the technology, Mauchly later went on to develop UNIVAC I, which was specifically designed to handle business data.

The introduction of digital computers made AI a viable scientific discipline, because they provided the necessary memory and processing power to develop intelligent programs. Researchers were quick to seize the opportunity.

Most historic accounts of AI usually point to 1956 and the conference held at Dartmouth College as marking the birth of artificial intelligence. In the next section, we will take a look at this conference and its impact on the field. It can be argued, however, that the first work that is now generally recognized as AI (though it did not come with the AI label) was done by McCulloch and Pitts [2]. Their work was biologically inspired where they drew upon knowledge of the basic physiology and function of neurons in the brain to propose the creation of a network of artificial neurons that could model human reasoning. They showed how propositions of logic and any computable function could be computed by some network of connected neurons. They also felt that future physiological studies of human reasoning could be aided by the design of various sorts of simple neural networks. This novel idea of modeling the structure and function of the brain offered new hope for the quest of an intelligent machine.

The work of McCulloch and Pitts sparked a great amount of interest in neural computing. During the next 20 years, several developments occurred that seemed to indicate that researchers were on the right track using neural networks to replicate human reasoning in a machine. In 1949, Hebb [3] published *The Organization of Behavior* that proposed that the connectivity of neurons in the brain are continually changing as an organism learns differing functional tasks. He also proposed a learning law that showed, for the first time, that a network of neurons could exhibit learning behavior. In 1958, Rosenblatt [4] introduced the *perceptron* and the *perceptron convergence theorem*. Following this revolutionary work, Rosenblatt built the first neurocomputer called the *Mark I Perceptron*. In 1960, Bernie Widrow, working with his graduate student Ted Hoff (Hoff later went on to invent the microprocessor) introduced the *least means-square algorithm* and used it to formulate the Adaline [5]. The Adaline was used for a variety of applications such as speech recognition, character recognition, weather prediction, and adaptive control. The success of the Adaline gave rise to the belief that artificial brains were right around the corner. This illusion was soon dispelled with publication of the book *Perceptrons* by Minsky and Papert [6]. This book was mainly an attack on the perceptron. It showed the fundamental limits of a one-layer perceptron network in solving simple problems, such as the exclusive-or gate function. The book also cast a shadow over the neural network field because it implied that essentially all neural networks suffer from the same flaw as the perceptron, and it went on to conclude that the technology would never make a major contribution to the AI field. Discouraged researchers left the field, funding dried up, and the study of neural networks lapsed into obscurity for nearly two decades. The damage was done. Rather than focusing on the data processing techniques of neural networks, efforts in the field centered on the symbolic processing methods favored by the attendees of the 1956 Dartmouth College conference.

V. BIRTH AND RISE OF ARTIFICIAL INTELLIGENCE (1950s and 1960s)

Most people in the field point to 1956 as marking the birth of artificial intelligence. During the summer of that year, 10 of the leading computer scientists of the time attended a summer workshop at Dartmouth College sponsored by IBM. The main discussion was on their current research efforts in such areas as automatic theorem proving, neural networks, and new programming languages. They also discussed ways that their work might be directed to develop a computer that could simulate human reasoning. Two of the attendees, Allen Newell and Herbert Simon, both from Carnegie Tech (now Carnegie Mellon), had already developed a reasoning program for automatic theorem proving called the Logic Theorist, of which Simon claimed, "We have invented a computer program capable of thinking non-numerically." This statement served to convince the attendees that developing an intelligent machine was not only possible, it was probable. No new breakthroughs came from this workshop, but it did put into motion the wheels that drove the research needed to create an intelligent computer. It also left us with one legacy that has both helped and haunted the field. The group of attendees decided to adopt John McCarthy's name for the field: **artificial intelligence**.

Artificial intelligence is an intimidating term. It brings forth images as threatening to us as the cotton gin was to farm laborers during the Industrial Revolution. The fear of displacement by automated machines with superior brute force was now replaced by anxiety caused by the perceived risk of the loss to machines of our basic human trait: our intelligence. However, when we look beyond the alarming label to see what this field is about, a far less ominous picture is painted.

Most of the early work in AI was academic in nature, where programs were developed for playing games. A good example is the checkers-playing program developed by Samuel [7]. The program could beat most humans at the game and could improve its playing ability through automatic learning. Shannon's [8] chess-playing program is another good example. Many people outside the field were not impressed with these efforts; they considered the results only as interesting toys. Insiders, on the other hand, knew that ventures like these were exploratory in nature and were looking for ways to build intelligence into a computer.

Capturing the public's interest in a technology has always been important. Carl Sagan knew this. He recognized that communicating to the public the major events within the space program would draw the interest needed to further the program. His efforts had a profound effect on our imagination and NASA's projects. The AI field also has had its moments in the public spotlight. Samuel's checkers-playing program was successfully demonstrated on television in February 1956, creating in the public's mind a vision of an intelligent machine. During the 1970s, the expert system PROSPECTOR generated enormous publicity by recommending exploratory drilling at a geological site that proved to contain a $100-million molybdenum deposit. More recently, the grand chess master Gary Kasparov succumbed in a very well publicized chess match to Deep Blue. A lesson for AI researchers from these events is that beyond their technical achievements, they should recognize the importance of communicating their successes to the public to capture the public's imagination.

In 1958, John McCarthy at MIT was looking for a high-level programming language that would enable him to perform symbolic processing. He thought that the ability to easily process symbols in a computer was needed to build an intelligent program. His search led him to develop the language LISP, which was first reported in MIT AI Lab Memo 1. LISP soon became the language of choice among AI researchers. It also played an important role in the expert systems field, where we can find many systems built using the language. LISP remains popular today and is the second oldest programming language, just one year younger than Fortran, which also was developed at MIT.

One of the more ambitious projects of this era involved the development of the general problem solver (GPS) [9]. GPS was a general-purpose problem-solving technique, developed to solve a variety of problems ranging from games to symbolic integration. It also was designed to solve these problems using a humanlike style of problem solving by dissecting a given goal into subgoals and applying appropriate "operators" (such as legal chess moves) to accomplish them. In fact, having GPS solve a given problem in the same way that a human might was a major concern of Newell and Simon. This theme is the basis of the interdisciplinary field of *cognitive science*, which brings together computer models from AI and experimental techniques from psychology to develop theories about the workings of the human mind. Also worthy of note is that GPS was the first attempt to separate the problem-solving methods from the knowledge of the problem—a key characteristic of expert systems. Though GPS demonstrated interesting results, it was soon recognized that its general-purpose problem-solving strategy was too weak for complex problems.

By 1970, the early euphoria surrounding AI had burned off and was replaced with the sobering realization that building intelligent programs to solve real-world problems was not as easy as first believed. To make matters worse, it was clear that the technology had not lived up to some rather bold predictions. For instance, in 1957, Herbert Simon said

> It is not my aim to surprise or shock you, but the simplest way I can summarize is to say that there are now in the world machines that think, that learn and that create. Moreover, their ability to do these things is going to increase rapidly until—in a visible future—the range of the problems they can handle will be coextensive with the range to which human mind has been applied.

Without losing steam, Simon later predicted (in 1958) that within 10 years a computer would be a chess champion. Similar optimistic predictions were being made by others in the field. Though it is important to spread the word about the potential of a new technology, it can be a dangerous practice. If more is promised than can be delivered, skepticism will rise and won-over converts may be lost. Worse, a general disinterest might set in, making it difficult to attract talented people and needed funding to the field—a scenario that can doom the field, as almost happened to AI following the Lighthill [10] report.

VI. FALL AND REBIRTH OF ARTIFICIAL INTELLIGENCE (1970s)

In 1971, the Science Research Council of Britain commissioned Sir James Lighthill of Cambridge University to review the state of affairs in the AI field. The council was concerned. They had heard the many promises made and had provided considerable funding to support researchers in the field. They also had not seen much in return for their money and wanted to know if continuing to fund the effort was advisable. Lighthill reported, "In no part of the field have the discoveries made so far produced the major impact that was promised." He also noted that researchers at the time were predicting that ". . . possibilities in the 1980s include an all-purpose intelligence on a human-scale knowledge-base; that awe-inspiring possibilities suggest themselves based on machine intelligence exceeding human intelligence by the year 2000." Lighthill recognized that this was the same type of prediction researchers were making in the mid-1950s. In conclusion, he saw no need for a separate AI field and felt that if an intelligent computer were ever to be built, it would be a natural offspring of the combined efforts from the fields of automation and computer science.

The immediate impact of the Lighthill report was highly damaging to AI efforts in England and abroad. Funding started to evaporate and researchers began to look for greener pastures. Fortunately, mainly due to the efforts of a few researchers who remained and continued to labor within the shadow of this damning report, the field experienced a rebirth with a new direction.

On hindsight, the findings of the Lighthill report are highly debatable. We generally overestimate what a technology can do for us in a few years and underestimate what it can do in a few decades. When the report was written, AI was still a relatively new and emerging field with very few practical systems to show for the effort. Work to date was exploratory in nature. Most of the programs developed focused on games, such as checkers, chess, and robot control in a blocks world. To Lighthill, they probably appeared to be toys with no real value for addressing practical problems. Researchers in the field, on the other hand, saw their programs as testbeds for studying the theories of intelligent machine design. Lighthill was right on one important point, however. No program had yet been written that could manage a real-world problem. Though his report was damaging, ironically, it led to events that would mark the rebirth of the field.

Following the report, researchers performed a critical assessment of their previous work, looking for reasons that might help explain why the technology was not living up to expectations. One point that became immediately clear was that most of the prior research efforts emphasized search techniques. The common thinking at the time was that intelligent human behavior was primarily based on smart reasoning techniques, and to model this in a computer required clever search algorithms. However, whereas earlier programs failed to produce meaningful results, researchers realized that search techniques alone were probably not enough to produce an intelligent program.

In 1965, there was an effort going on at Stanford University that caught the attention of the AI community. NASA was planning to send an unmanned spacecraft to Mars and wanted a computer program that could perform chemical analysis of the Martian soil. Given mass spectral data of the soil, NASA wanted the program to determine its molecular structure. In a chemistry laboratory, the traditional method of solving this problem is through a generate-and-test technique. Possible structures that could account for the mass spectrogram data are first generated and then each is tested to see if it matches the data. The basic difficulty with this technique is that there are millions of possible structures that might be generated. NASA turned to researchers at Stanford University to see if a program could be developed that could solve this problem. The Stanford team found in practice that there were knowledgeable chemists who first used *rules of thumb* (heuristics) to weed out structures that were unlikely to account for the data. They then decided to capture these heuristics within their program to constrain the number of structures generated. The result was a computer program called DENDRAL [11] that operated as well as an expert chemist in recognizing molecular structures of unknown compounds. More important, it was the first program whose success was attributed to what it knew about the problem, rather than relying on complex search techniques. The success of DENDRAL with its emphasis on knowledge led Ed Feigenbaum at Stanford to claim, "In the knowledge lies the power." It also led to the concept of a **knowledge-based system** or **expert system**—the expert system era had begun.

Revitalized by the new direction the field had taken, researchers quickly began to look for better ways to represent and search knowledge in a computer program. Because DENDRAL was successful with its knowledge encoded in rule form, this seemed to be the way to go. In short order, programs were being built with a very simple architecture that contained the problem's knowledge in a set of rules that were placed in a module called the *knowledge base*, a processor of these rules by a second module called the *inference engine*, and another module called the *working memory*, which contained the problem-specific facts and conclusions derived by the inference engine. Collectively, these three modules form what is commonly referred to as a *rule-based expert system*. Armed with this architecture, expert system developers during the 1970s knew it was now time to develop systems and learn from the experience. They also knew that it was time to produce systems that provided real benefits.

No other system contributed more to our understanding of building rule-based expert systems than MYCIN [12]. The objective of MYCIN was to diagnose infectious blood diseases. With about 500 rules, MYCIN was able to perform as well as some experts and considerably better than junior doctors. However, through the eyes of the expert system developer, the real success story of MYCIN rests in the insight it provided into rule-based expert system design.

The first successful commercial expert system was developed during the 1970s and was called XCON. XCON, originally called R1, was built at Carnegie Mellon and was designed to aid Digital Equipment Company (DEC) in the configuration of their VAX computer systems [13]. XCON was developed using OPS, a rule-based programming language that remains today a popular language among expert system designers. XCON proved to be a valuable tool for DEC. By 1986, it was saving the company an estimated $20 million per year. The success of XCON led DEC to create a separate group within the company dedicated to AI efforts that by 1988 had developed over 40 other expert systems.

Another highly successful expert system developed during this decade was PROSPECTOR. It was developed at the Stanford Research Institute to aid geologists in the exploration of ore deposits [14]. The system generated enormous publicity by recommending exploratory drilling at a site near Mount Tolman, located in eastern Washington, that proved to contain a large molybdenum deposit worth approximately $100 million.

In 1979, a group of individuals who were intimately involved with the development of earlier expert systems met at a workshop chaired by Don Waterman and Frederick Hayes-Roth to exchange ideas about the field. Viewing the developments of the last decade, and with an understanding of the capability and potential of the technology, they predicted

> Over time, the knowledge engineering field will have an impact on all areas of human activity where knowledge provides the power for solving important problems.

This was another rather bold prediction. A skeptic might suggest it would be nothing more than another in a long line of predictions that failed. Things were different now, however. By the close of the 1970s, the field of expert systems was an established technology. The successes of systems such as MYCIN, XCON, and PROSPECTOR rekindled interest in the field and also provided a road map for others to follow for designing an expert system. The time was now ripe to build expert systems in large number across many application areas.

VII. PROLIFERATION OF EXPERT SYSTEMS (1980s)

With expert systems now recognized as a practical tool for solving real-world problems, the 1980s marked the technology's coming out party, and many attended. Most universities rapidly developed and offered expert system courses. Companies initiated expert system projects and often formed internal AI groups. DuPont, for instance, had their own group of AI specialists, who by 1988 had built 100 expert systems that were saving the company an estimated $10 million per year, and had another 500 systems under development. Over two thirds of the Fortune 1000 companies became involved in applying the technology in daily business activities. Government agencies responded by dramatically increasing available funding for expert system research and development. There also was a surge of international interest in the technology. In 1981, the Japanese announced the Fifth Generation Project, a 10-year plan to build intelligent machines. In response to this plan in the United States, the Microelectronics and Computer Technology Corporation (MCC) was formed as a research consortium dedicated to furthering expert system development. In Britain, though still shaken from the Lighthill report, the government used the more upbeat Alvey report on the technology to reinstate funding in the area.

In the early 1980s, medical expert system applications dominated the scene, primarily due to the diagnostic nature of these applications and the relative ease of developing such systems. However, as we moved toward the mid-1980s and the low-hanging fruit was picked, it was time to reach for more difficult problems. It was also time to begin developing systems that produced benefits for the commercial sectors. Unfortunately, initial attempts frequently met with limited success. In hindsight, three primary reasons help to explain this result. First, early applications of expert systems in industry often overchallenged the technology, leading to poor results. Fascinated by the notion of machines that could think, many designers attempted to build systems to solve problems that were beyond the reach of even the best experts. The thinking was, "Well, we can't solve this problem so let's try throwing AI at it." Second, other designers often took on a project whose scope was so broad that completing it within a reasonable time frame was impossible. Third, some designers developed remarkably intelligent systems; however, the effort was often divorced from an understanding of the client's need to integrate the system into existing hardware and software resources. The result was a powerful finished product that was left to collect dust on a shelf.

With the few successes being produced during this period, coupled with earlier glowing promises of the technology, critics crept out of the woodwork and quickly pounced on the situation. Journal and conference papers, newsletters, and the national media were swift to point to the shortcomings. Consider, for example, a report in *Forbes* magazine [15], where the question was asked, "What happened to those expert systems that were supposed to transform the world of business forever?" Expert system designers began to realize that finding a place for the technology could be as tedious as matching the glass slipper to Cinderella's foot.

The turning point came in the mid-1980s when designers began to focus on very narrow, well defined, and even sometimes mundane tasks. They also took the time to look at where the technology would be embedded. Although the systems developed following this theme may have seemed unimpressive to the AI researcher viewing the scene from an ivory tower, they were well received by managers in industry because they produced commercially worthwhile results.

Given this new direction, the number of deployed systems began to accelerate rapidly. From only a handful of systems developed during the 1970s, the number rose into the thousands by the end of the 1980s. It is also interesting to view the widespread use of the technology. Systems have been built for applications ranging from aiding miners a mile below the earth's surface to helping astronauts aboard the space station. A survey of the literature conducted in 1992 in search of developed expert systems uncovered applications that naturally fell into 1 of 23 areas as shown in Table 1 [16]. The breadth of the applications is remarkable. It is difficult now to find an area that has not been touch by the technology. In fact, we sometimes can find it in some strange places. Want assistance with your pig farm? Then get a copy of TEP (The Electronic Pig), an expert system that assists with diagnosing the causes of problems with pig litter size. Having trouble with your love life? Then fire up SEXPERT, which assesses and treats sexual dysfunction. Need help in getting rid of a problem employee? Then check out CLARIFYING DISMISSAL, which assists employers in the dismissal of employees.

Up to the mid-1980s, the field was dominated by rule-based systems. However, during the later part of the decade, there was a shift toward object-oriented systems.

TABLE 1 Major Application Areas of Expert Systems

Agriculture	Law
Business	Manufacturing
Chemistry	Mathematics
Communications	Medicine
Computer systems	Meteorology
Education	Military
Electronics	Mining
Engineering	Power systems
Environment	Science
Geology	Space technology
Image processing	Transportation
Information management	

In the world of expert systems, it was the frame-based system that began to take center stage. The word *frame* was coined by Minsky [17], but its concept dates to Socrates's idea of the universal definition. Due to their ability to represent both descriptive and behavioral object information easily, and the powerful set of utilities they bring to the table, frame-based systems can address applications of greater complexity than can be managed by rule-based systems. The areas where they are being applied are widespread and growing. Many of the early frame-based expert systems tackled simulation problems. This was a good choice, because a simulation task inherently involves interacting objects. Today, we see frame-based systems built for problems that traditionally have been managed using a rule-based approach, such as diagnosis and design.

During the 1980s neural networks resurfaced after being buried in 1969 by Minsky and Papert's book *Perceptrons*. Two major events occurred during the decade that led to the rebirth of interest in the technology. In 1982, John Hopfield wrote a paper that described a neural system called the *Hopfield model*, which represents neuron activity as a threshold operation and memory as information stored in the interconnections between neurons [18]. This model established, for the first time, the principle of storing information in a dynamically stable network. The next important event, particularly from an engineering viewpoint, was the development of the *backpropagation algorithm* for training multilayer perceptron networks [19]. Backpropagation has emerged as the most popular learning algorithm for the training of neural networks. It has been applied in a wide range of neural network applications, making the technology an effective tool for solving practical data classification problems.

In 1965, Zadeh [20] introduced a new field called fuzzy logic, which provided, for the first time, the ability to perform common sense reasoning in a computer. Mamdani and Assilian during the 1970s established the framework of a fuzzy controller and used it to develop the first real-world fuzzy expert system to control a steam engine. The use of fuzzy logic as an effective expert system tool was set in the 1970s, but unfortunately, few took note of its potential value. In the United States, the birthplace of the technology, progress in the field proceeded very slowly during the 1980s, mainly because very few individuals were working in the field. The Japanese, fortunately, saw the potential commercial value of the technology and began to develop numerous systems. The success in Japan caught the attention of the expert system community. In the United States, the number of fuzzy projects in both commercial and government sectors increased dramatically during the 1990s. Activity in Europe, South Korea, and Canada, also has been on the rise recently.

VIII. STATE OF THE FIELD (1990s)

During the early 1990s, the expert systems field continued to build on the momentum established in the 1980s. The number of deployed systems continued to increase rapidly. Many organizations not involved earlier initiated expert system projects and some began entire programs. New magazines, new special interest groups within professional organizations, and many more conferences dedicated to the technology emerged. To obtain a sense of the health of the field during this decade, we will consider a survey reported in the book *Expert Systems: Catalog of Applications* [16] and another survey conducted in 1996 in preparation for a new edition of the book.

A. Application Areas

Recall the earlier prediction from the 1979 workshop chaired by Waterman and Hayes-Roth, ". . . field will have an impact on all areas of human activity." The results from the surveys show that this prediction was right on the mark. Figure 1 shows the number of systems developed in the different areas shown in Table 1. We should not be surprised by the range of applications. An expert system is inherently a tool to assist human decision making. We apply it to knowledge-intensive tasks that require expertise to accomplish. Therefore, wherever we find humans in such activities as diagnosing a system, designing a structure, or tutoring a student, we also have found a home for the technology.

Figure 1 also provides insight into the direction that the technology has taken. During the 1970s, AI was a cult activity—almost a religion. Researchers centered on producing intelligent general-purpose reasoning machines. The fascination with achieving this academic challenge drove their efforts. By the 1980s, when fuel for advancement of the technology came from sectors that demanded a return on their investment, researchers began to realize that AI is not a religious experience, but an economic one. A 1986 survey conducted by Waterman [21] showed that the majority (30%) of applications were in the field of medicine. Figure 1 shows that this field remains attractive to expert system developers (10%), but percentagewise, activity in this area has decreased considerably. Even more revealing is the activity in business and industrial areas over recent years. According to Waterman's survey, about 10% of applications were in these areas in 1986. By 1996, these areas accounted for approximately 60% of the applications. In fact, it was found in the 1996 survey that one out of every five expert systems built to date has been applied in the area of business. A 1995 survey conducted in the United Kingdom alone found that 24% of the deployed expert systems were in the financial services sector [22]. This is clearly a sign that expert systems are merging with the mainstream of information processing that was previously dominated by conventional

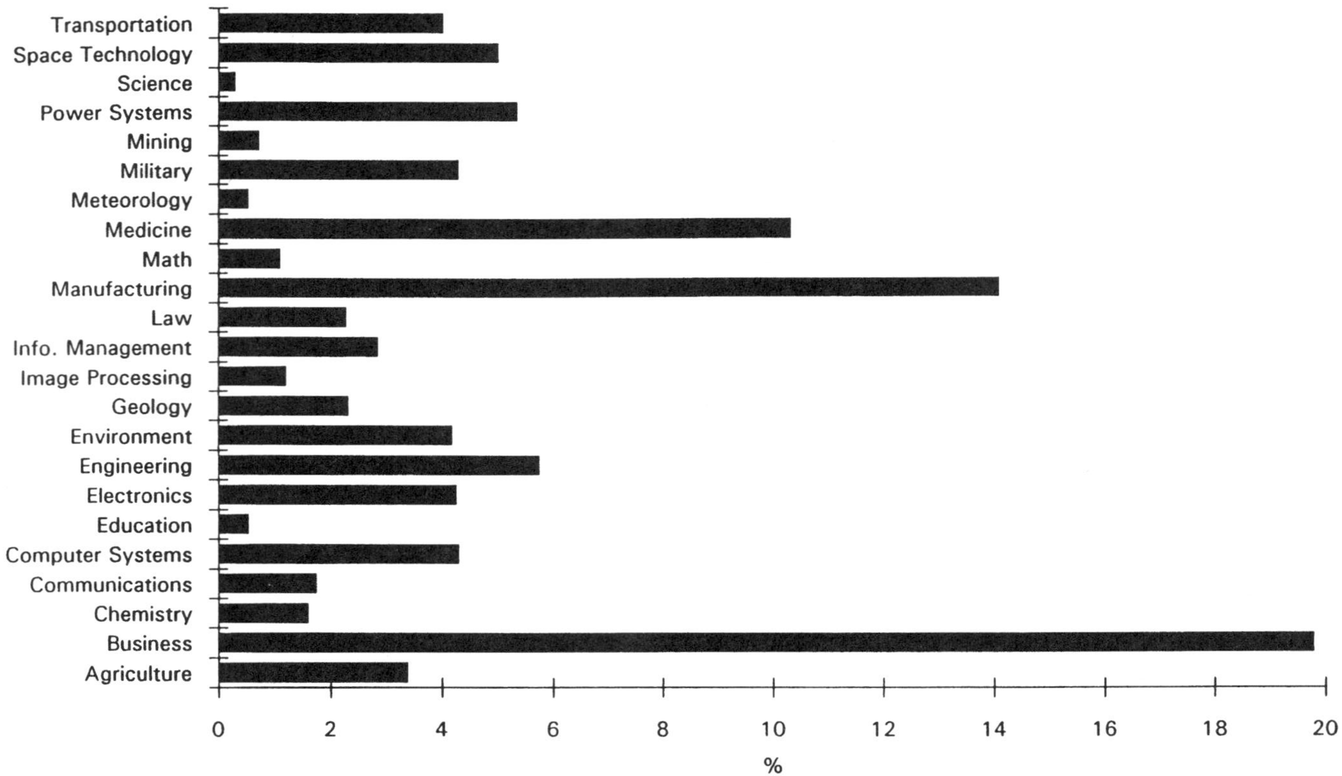

FIGURE 1 Percentage of developed expert systems in various applications areas.

data processors. It also shows that the field has matured considerably over recent years, where we now find the technology well received by the commercial sectors.

B. Application Activity

Another way that we can sort expert system applications is by *problem-solving type*. Regardless of the application area, given the type of problem, experts collect and reason with information similarly. Likewise, expert systems are designed to accomplish generic tasks on the basis of the problem type (see Table 2).

Figure 2 shows the percentage of applications for each problem type in Table 2. Be aware that many applications employ more than one activity. For example, a diagnostic system might first interpret the available data and later prescribe a remedy for the recognized fault.

As Figure 2 illustrates, the predominant role of expert systems has been diagnosis. The survey showed that one out of every four expert systems built has employed a diagnostic activity. One reason for this result is that this is the role most experts play. Fields such as medicine, engineering, and manufacturing have many individuals who help diagnose problems. Another reason for the large percentage of diagnostic systems is due to their relative ease of development. Most diagnostic problems have a finite list of possible solutions and a limited amount of information needed to reach a solution. These bounds provide an environment that is conducive to effective system design.

Another explanation for the large percentage of diagnostic expert systems can be traced to the practical considerations of introducing a new technology into an organization. Most organizations prefer to take a low-risk position when considering a new technology. As such, they prefer projects that require minimum resources and have maximum likelihood of success. Because these systems are relatively easy to build, they are attractive to firms venturing into the field.

The drop-off from the large number of diagnostic applications to that of some other problem types is dramatic. Two reasons help explain this result. First, tasks such as design and planning are difficult to implement in an expert system because their steps vary greatly between application areas and it is often hard to define these steps precisely. Second, tasks such as instruction, control, and simulation, although they are excellent areas for expert system applications, are relatively new ventures.

TABLE 2 Types of Problems Solved by Expert Systems

Problem-solving type	Description
Control	Governing system behavior to meet specifications
Design	Configuring objects under constraint
Diagnosis	Inferring system malfunctions from observables
Instruction	Diagnosing, debugging, and repairing student behavior
Interpretation	Inferring situation description from data
Monitoring	Comparing observations to expectations
Planning	Designing actions
Prediction	Inferring likely consequences of given situations
Prescription	Recommending solution to system malfunction
Selection	Identifying best choice from a list of possibilities
Simulation	Modeling the interaction between system components

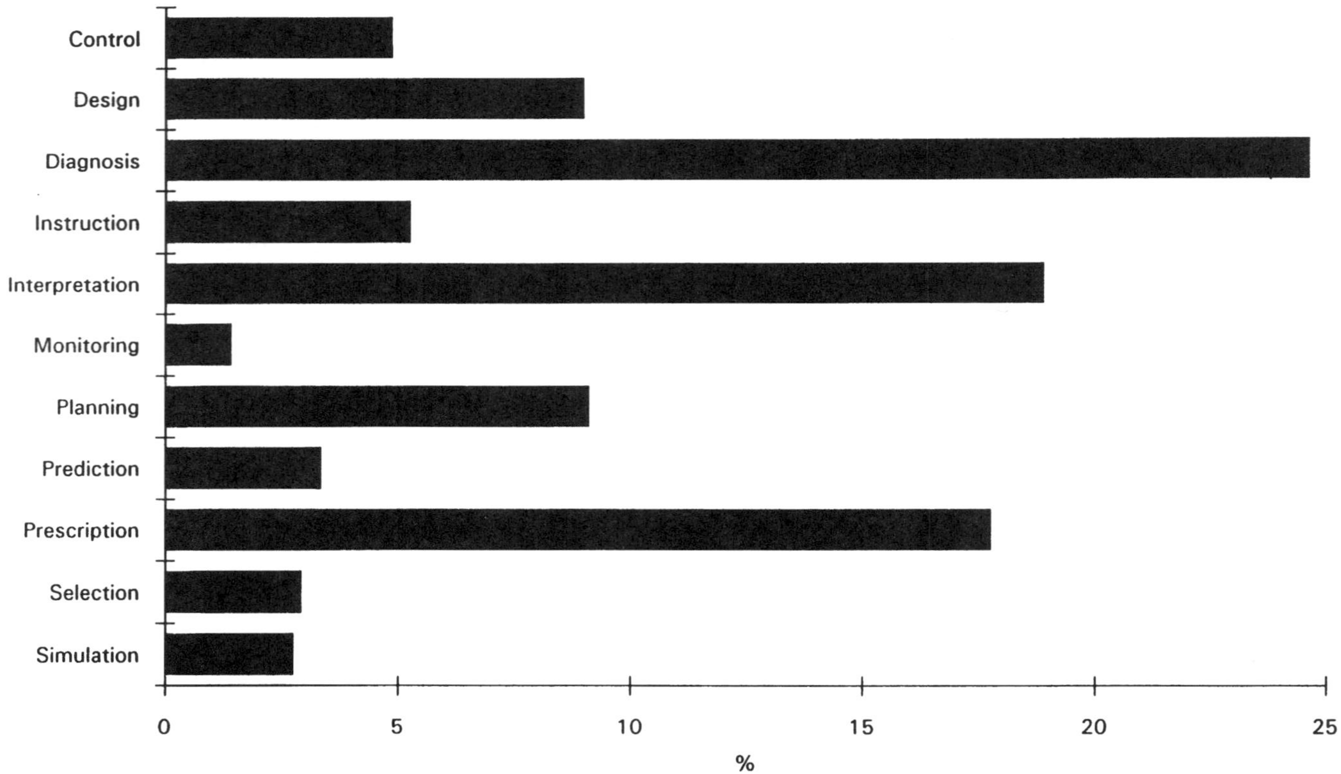

FIGURE 2 Percentage of expert system applications by problem type.

C. Rate of Development

One of the better ways to measure the success of a new technology is to look at its rate of application. If we see an upward trend, we obviously interpret it as a positive sign. Conversely, if the trend is downward or stagnant, we should be concerned. Consider the expert systems field.

During the 1970s, when researchers were feeling their way with the new technology, only a handful of expert systems were developed. Work during this period was focused mainly on looking for ways to better represent and process knowledge in a computer. Most systems developed were therefore more of an academic exercise, where the researchers worked in relative isolation from the realities of business-oriented needs. During the 1980s, with a better understanding of how to build an expert system, the situation changed dramatically.

To illustrate, consider a report by Paul Harmon. In 1990, Harmon and Sawyer [23] published *Creating Expert Systems for Business and Industry*. The book included estimates of the cumulative number of expert systems developed over the years 1985 and 1988 (Chap. 1). Figure 3 shows these estimates along with results from the 1992 and 1996 surveys. The impressive growth rate of expert systems is an indicator of the acceptance of the technology by industry and a testament to the labors of earlier researchers.

D. Software and Platforms

Another event that is attributed to the large growth rate in developed systems was the introduction during the 1980s of new hardware and software technologies that provided support for expert system designers. The rise in popularity of the technology during this decade led to the emergence of a new cottage industry that provided easy-to-use expert system development software called shells. These shells were built to run on platforms ranging from personal computers (PCs) to mainframes. Most expert systems during the 1970s were developed on powerful workstations, using languages such as LISP, PROLOG, and OPS. This left the challenge of developing systems in the hands of the select few who could afford the platforms and had the patience to learn the complexities of the available languages. During the 1980s, we witnessed the proliferation of PCs. With these widely available platforms coupled with the shells, the opportunity to develop an expert system was now in the hands of many individuals from all disciplines.

The 1996 survey found that most expert systems were built on a PC using a shell. It showed that approximately 60% of the systems were developed on a PC and 20% on a workstation; the minicomputer and mainframe accounted for 10% each. Approximately 45% of the systems were built using a shell and 25% using LISP; PROLOG and OPS accounted for 10% each, and the balance used the languages C, Pascal, LOOPS, Fortran, Smalltalk, and Basic.

IX. EPILOGUE

Leaning over the table, Garry Kasparov studied the chess pieces on the board in front of him. He realized there was no hope, he must resign. In so doing, the

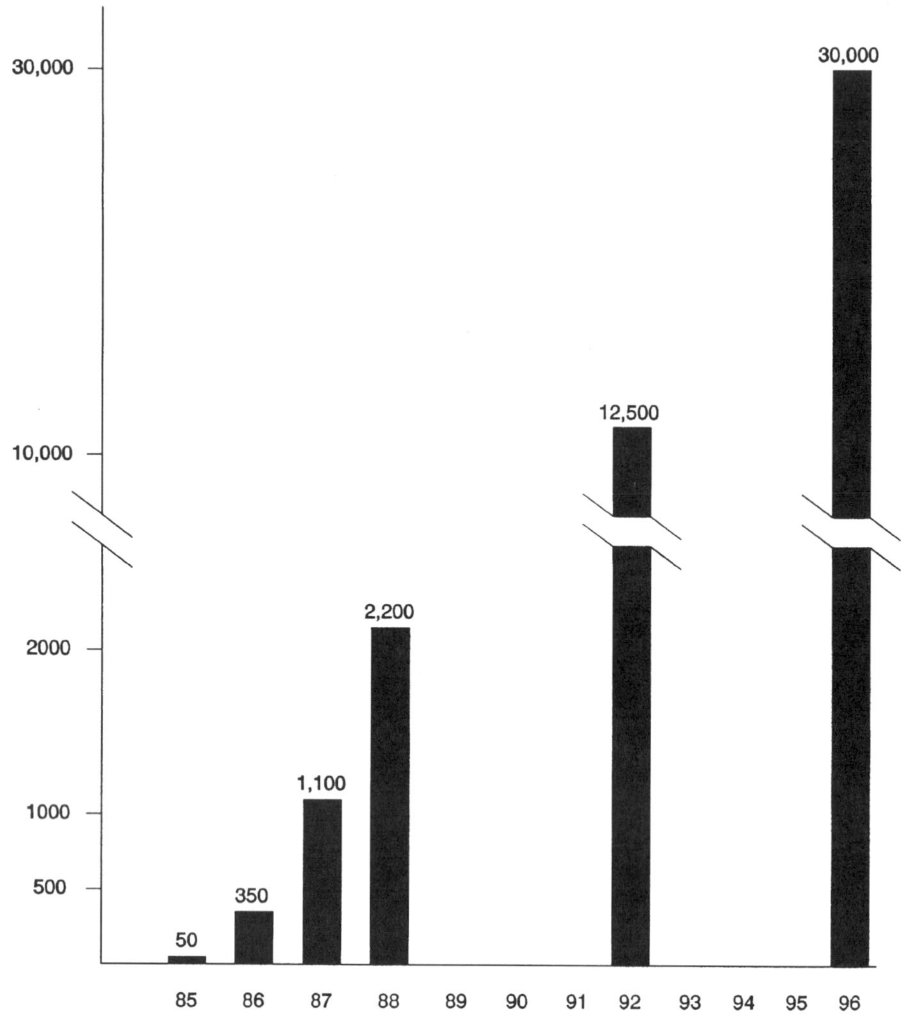

FIGURE 3 Total number of expert systems developed by each year.

man who is considered by many to be the greatest chess player ever had lost his first match. Without a congratulatory word, Kasparov quickly left the room in frustration. His opponent is likewise quiet and sits there dispassionately waiting for new instructions. Deep Blue had won.

Moments like this naturally stir the emotions. Perhaps it stems from the notion that although we can easily accept being surpassed by machines in mechanical tasks, we consider the kind of creativity required by chess to be the province of humanity. In the aftermath of the match, many individuals were quick to voice their opinions and concerns about the consequences of the event. "New technology is threatening," said John C. Norcross, a psychology professor at the University of Scranton. He also remarked, "There's a hunk of emotional work in accepting that the world is moving and evolving. We fear change, particularly change that we did not initiate." Others were captured by the fascination of the moment. "Eventually, they may become more capable than we are and will no longer need us to build even better machines," says Edward Cornish, president of the World Future Society, in Bethesda, MD. Even the vanquished Kasparov was profoundly effected: "I think this moment could mark a revolution in computer science." The Kasparov versus Deep Blue match was an event that brought forth the human emotions of fear, fascination, and hope—the backdrop of the history of the quest for the intelligent machine.

At the core of our concern is a simple question: If a machine can think, then where does that put us? We have always felt comfortable with theories that put us apart from and above the rest of our natural world. By tying our sense of self-importance to such theories, however, we feel less special when they turn out to be wrong. For instance, when Darwin put forth his version of our family tree, we felt somewhat diminished. To refortify our position, we argued to ourselves that it is our ability to reason that separates us from the beasts. Today, we feel threatened not by the beast, but by our own creation—the intelligent machine.

We have come to accept computers as a part of our lives. They help us to do calculations, balance our checkbooks, and take us on a virtual tour of the world over the Internet. Without them, planes would be grounded, cars would stall, phones would go dead, stock markets would stop, and man's footprint would never have appeared on the moon. We did not always embrace the technology, however. The introduction of the computer was met with open hostility by many individuals, who believed it was their birthright alone to partake in intellectual activities. After a while we became comfortable with the technology. Instead of seeing our silicon friend as a threat today, we view it as a collaborator.

Along the way we were provided with a glimpse of tomorrow's machine. For most of us, this first came from the storytelling of our science fiction writers. For instance, consider Hal. One of our most impressionable images of an intelligent machine was the computer Hal 9000 in Arthur C. Clarke's 1960s science fiction classic *2001: A Space Odyssey*. Hal conversed with crew members of a spaceship, understood their emotions, and seemed to be a conscious entity. Hal even played chess, but unlike Deep Blue, Hal was programmed to lose half its games to keep things interesting for the humans aboard. Viewers saw a computer that could assist and entertain humans, and, by the way, saw one that raised a small degree of concern because Hal also killed four astronauts. We were fascinated by the film. We also were fascinated by our own computers of the day when they did anything even remotely clever, but we also wondered how we might react if, or when, fiction became reality.

Since that film, we have watched our computers get smarter—and smarter faster than us. Instead of just processing information, a role that took us some time to become comfortable with, we watched as our computers acquired the ability to reason about the information. Expert systems stood out in this new role. They diagnosed patients, made investment recommendations, and fixed our cars. Many applauded the new technology. Many others saw it as a threat to humans' rightful monopoly of rational thought. A few decades ago, the idea of a computer beating a human at chess seemed ridiculous. Today we take it for granted. We are even starting to accept that a computer can beat our best. We get used to things.

It is unlikely that computers will suddenly become as intelligent as people in every way. The state of the art, the expert system, is nothing more than an idiot savant. It is smart only about a very narrow area. Given an IQ test, it would score less than a first grader. For now, we continue to hold the intellectual high ground. Machine intelligence will emerge gradually, improving decade by decade, giving us time to get accustomed to it. Will we continue to fear intelligent machines? Of course. It is part of our nature to fear things that we do not completely understand. It is also our nature to seek innovations that improve our quality of life. The early computer clearly did this. With our help, the technology will continue to evolve. In return, tomorrow's intelligent machines will help us with our intellectual endeavors. Computers and people are in this together, and this is a game where we can all claim victory. Checkmate.

REFERENCES

1. McCorduck, P. History of artificial intelligence. In *Proceedings of IJCAI-77*, 1977, pp. 951–954.
2. McCulloch, W. S. and Pitts, W. A logical calculus of the ideas imminent in nervous activity. *Bull. Math. Bio.* 5:115–133, 1943.
3. Hebb, D. *The Organization of Behavior: A Neuropsychological Theory*. Wiley, New York, 1949.
4. Rosenblatt, F. The perceptron: A probabilistic model for information storage and organization in the brain. *Psychol. Rev.* 65:386–408, 1958.
5. Widrow, B. and Hoff, M. E. Adaptive switching circuits. In *IRE WESCON Convention Record*, Part 4, pp. 96–104. IRE, New York, 1960.
6. Minsky, M. and Papert, S. A. *Perceptrons*. MIT Press, Cambridge, MA, 1969.
7. Samuel, A. L. Some studies in machine learning using the game of checkers. In *Computers and Thought* (E. A. Feigenbaum and J. Feldman, Eds.). McGraw-Hill, New York, 1963.
8. Shannon, C. E. A chess playing machine. In *The World of Mathematics*, Vol. 4 (J. R. Newman, Ed.). Simon and Schuster, New York, 1955.
9. Newell, A. and Simon, H. A. *Human Problem Solving*. Prentice–Hall, Englewood Cliffs, NJ, 1972.
10. Lighthill, J. Artificial intelligence: A general survey. Report 72-72, Scientific Research Council of Britain, 1972.
11. Buchanan, B. and Feigenbaum, E. DENDRAL and Meta-DENDRAL: Their applications dimension. *Artif. Intel.* 11, 5–24, 1978.
12. Shortliffe, E. H. *Computer-Based Medical Consultation, MYCIN*. Elsevier, New York, 1976.
13. McDermott, J. R1: An expert system in the computer systems domain. In *Proceedings of AAAI-80*, 1980.
14. Duda, R., Hart, P. E., Nilsson, N. J., Reboh, R., Slocum, J., and Sutherland, G. Development of a computer based consultant for mineral exploration. Report, Stanford Research Institute, Menlo Park, CA, 1977.
15. Simon, R. The morning after. *Forbes* 140(8):164–168, Oct. 19, 1987.
16. Durkin, J. *Expert Systems: Catalog of Applications*. Intelligent Computer Systems, Inc., Akron, OH, 1993.
17. Minsky, M. L. Frame system theory. In *Thinking: Readings in Cognitive Science* (P. N. Johnson-Laird and P. C. Watson, Eds.). Cambridge Univ. Press, Cambridge, UK, 1975.
18. Hopfield, J. J. Neurons with graded response have collected computational properties like those of two-state neurons. *Proc. Nat. Acad. Sci. U.S.A.* 81:3088–3092, 1982.
19. Rumelhart, D. E. and McClelland, J. L., Eds. *Parallel Distributed Processing Explorations in the Microstructure of Cognition*, Vol. 1. MIT Press, Cambridge, MA, 1986.
20. Zadeh, L. A. Fuzzy sets. *Inform. Control* 8, 338–353, 1965.
21. Waterman, D. A. *A Guide to Expert Systems*. Addison-Wesley, Reading, MA, 1986.
22. Coakes, E. and Merchant, K. Expert systems: A survey of their use in UK business. *Inform. Management* 30:223–230, 1996.
23. Harmon, P. and Sawyer, B. *Creating Expert Systems For Business and Industry*. Wiley, New York, 1990.

2 TOOLS AND APPLICATIONS

JOHN DURKIN

Department of Electrical Engineering, College of Engineering, University of Akron, Akron, Ohio 44325-3904

I. INTRODUCTION

An experienced expert system designer is a craftsman. We respectfully label this individual a knowledge engineer. A knowledge engineer knows the tools of the trade and, maybe more importantly, knows when to use a particular tool given the nature of the job. Consider skilled carpenters. They know how to use a saw, a hammer, and a plane, to name a few, and they also know when a given tool is needed. Through the proper choice and use of tools, a piece of furniture is made, a room is built, a house is created: A craftsman.

During the course of a career, knowledge engineers are exposed to a variety of tools for developing an expert system. Initially, they must learn how to use a given tool. This is often accomplished in an academic setting, where they hear about the theory of the tool, maybe see a few demonstrations of its use, and maybe even get the opportunity to build a small expert system using the tool. Though a valuable experience, it falls short of providing the understanding necessary for them to become proficient in the use of the tool. Proficiency can be accomplished only through the experience of applying the tool in several projects, where they learn both the science and art necessary to create an effective expert system. There is an old but wise proverb that captures this point:

I hear and I forget
I see and I remember
I do and I understand

After spending time with a given tool, getting their hands dirty using it in a variety of applications, the engineers should become proficient enough in its use to add it

Expert Systems, Edited by Cornelius T. Leondes, Volume 1

ISBN: 0-12-443881-4 / $35.00

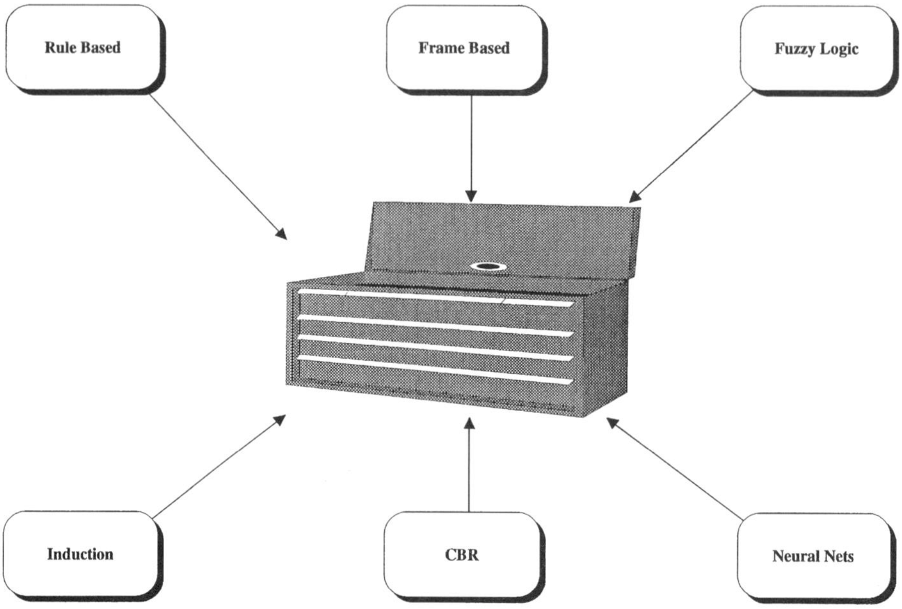

FIGURE 1 Expert system development tools.

to their toolboxes. It is then time to move on to other tools and repeat the process. After awhile, they should have a variety of tools in the box that they are is well versed in, and an understanding of their use and place: A craftsman.

This chapter explores the most popular expert system development tools. Figure 1 shows those that are used most often. This chapter includes sections that review each tool shown in the figure. In each section, we look briefly at the history of the development of each tool. This is important because it shows how the artificial intelligence (AI) community responded to problems beyond the reach of existing methods. We also consider how the tool works, not in great detail, but enough to provide the reader a general sense of its operation. We also consider the tool's appropriateness by considering its strengths and weaknesses, and by looking at applications where it is typically used. Finally, each section provides valuable references that allow the interested reader to probe further the tool's theory, applications, and use to design an effective expert system. This chapter will not create an expert system craftsman out of the reader, but it may help to point the way.

II. RULE-BASED TOOLS

Most of the expert systems developed during the 1960s and 70s, including classics such as MYCIN, Dendral, and R1 (later called XCON), were rule-based. The choice of a rule-based approach at the time was natural. The early thinking in the field was that experts used *rules of thumb* to solve problems. Expert system developers saw that experts, when armed with these rules, would try to prove some hypothesis or infer further information from problem-specific data. These rules and

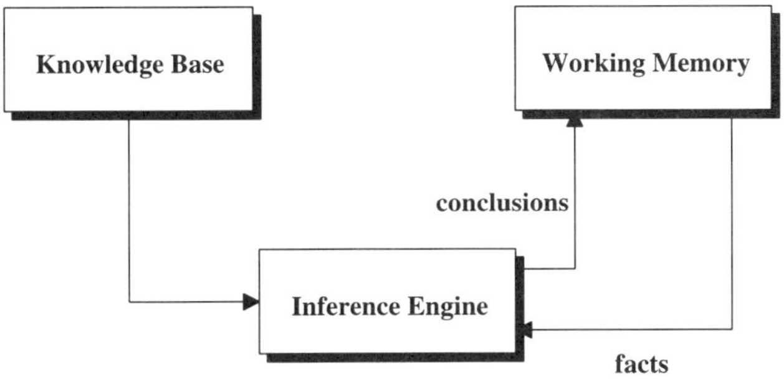

FIGURE 2 Rule-based model.

inference techniques used by the experts formed the early model of rule-based systems and led to widespread interest in expert system technology.

During the 1980s, many universities and companies turned their attention to expert systems. Most universities rapidly developed and offered expert system courses. Companies initiated expert system projects and often formed internal AI groups. Over two thirds of the Fortune 1000 companies became involved in applying the technology in daily business activities. Government agencies responded by dramatically increasing available funding for expert system research and development. The rise in popularity of the technology during this decade also led to the emergence of a new cottage industry that provided easy-to-use expert system development software called *shells*. These shells were built to run on platforms ranging from Personal Computer (PC) to mainframes. The widespread interest in the technology coupled with the availability of easy to use shells led to a dramatic increase in the number of deployed expert systems during the 1980s. Systems were built for applications ranging from aiding miners a mile below the earth's surface to helping astronauts aboard the space station.

The majority of expert systems developed to date have been rule-based. A survey of systems built since the 1970s shows that approximately 80% are rule-based [1]. Several reasons can be offered to explain this. First, many of the present designers share the same belief held by earlier ones that human expertise is best captured in a set of rules. Second, success breeds success. That is, because the field has an abundance of success stories of rule-based applications, it is only natural that designers would turn first to this design style. Third, of the expert system shells that have been marketed since the early 1980s, most have been rule-based development tools.

Figure 2 shows a block diagram of a rule-based expert system. The knowledge base contains the domain-specific knowledge in the form of rules. The working memory contains the problem-specific facts and conclusions derived by the inference engine. The inference engine uses the information in the working memory along with the rules in the knowledge base to derive the conclusions. There are two basic ways a rule-based system operates: backward and forward chaining.

Backward chaining starts with the system given some goal(s) to prove. The system attempts to prove the goal by using the rules along with information provided by the user. Along the way, it derives intermediate conclusions that help to support the quest for the goal. Backward chaining is well suited for problems that naturally start with some hypothesis to prove, such as attempting to prove whether or not a patient has some particular disease. Diagnostic and prescription type problems can be managed well with a backward chaining system. Consider MYCIN, a prototypical backward chaining system.

MYCIN [2] was developed at Stanford University to aid physicians in diagnosing and treating patients with infectious blood diseases caused by bacteremia (bacteria in the blood) and meningitis (bacterial disease that causes inflammation of the membrane surrounding the brain and spinal cord). These diseases can be fatal if not recognized and treated quickly. The system was developed during the mid-1970s and took approximately 20 person-years to complete. MYCIN is a backward chaining rule-based expert system that incorporates approximately 500 rules. During evaluation studies, MYCIN was found to do as well or better than human experts on infectious blood diseases.

Forward chaining, unlike backward chaining, has no goal to prove. Rather, it attempts to derive as much information as possible from available problem-specific facts. These facts, which are placed in the working memory, act as a catalyst for the system by causing the firing of rules that add further information to the working memory. This new information in turn causes the firing of more rules, and the process continues until no rules can fire given the information in the working memory. At this point, the working memory contains both the initial facts and all of the information inferred by the system.

Forward chaining is good for problems where it is desirable to learn as much as possible from the available problem information. For example, given a patient's symptoms, a forward chaining system can derive possible diseases that the patient might be suffering from. Forward chaining is also a good approach for design and planning tasks because the final product of these tasks is usually unknown a priori (a condition that is needed for a backward chaining approach) and is a result of combining problem specifications with domain-specific knowledge to formulate the product.

A good example of a forward chaining rule-based system in a design application is R1, later called XCON. R1 is an expert system developed for Digital Equipment Corp. (DEC) to aid in the configuration of VAX computer systems [3]. DEC offers a large number of components that can be configured in a number of ways to produce a computer system. DEC personnel work with a client to configure the system to meet all of the client's needs. Configuring a computer system is a complicated and time-consuming task, and DEC was looking for a better solution. Using several thousand rules processed through forward chaining, R1 was able to quickly and effectively configure VAX computer systems, bringing a savings to DEC of approximately 20 million dollars per year.

A trademark of expert systems is their ability to perform inexact reasoning. They can work on applications characterized by information that is uncertain, ambiguous, or even unavailable, and by domain knowledge that is inherently inexact. Most rule-based systems manage inexact reasoning by using *certainty factors* (CF), following the *certainty theory* work first proposed during the MYCIN project [4]. A certainty factor is a number between -1 and 1 that represents the degree of disbelief or belief in a piece of information or a rule. Using certainty factors enables an expert system to derive a "best guess" solution. To learn more about inexact reasoning in a rule-based expert system, see [5–8]. Consider the following rule-based systems that used certainty factors to successfully manage an application that required inexact reasoning.

The EEG analysis system applies fast Fourier transforms (FFT) to data received directly from electroencephalograms (EEG) connected to renal patients to determine whether the EEG data appear to be normal or abnormal [9]. The system studies spectral features of the FFT data to derive its decision. Using rules with associated certainty factors, the system is able to determine the degree of normalcy of the patient's EEG data.

An expert system was developed by Syntelligence, Inc., to assist in the underwriting of insurance policies at American International Group, Inc., New York, NY [10]. The system underwrites policies for a product called DIC, which covers major perils such as earthquakes and floods. It determines the risk and cost associated with an application, and provides a degree of belief through the use of certainty factors on whether or not to underwrite the application.

A rule-based expert system that employs certainty factors was developed at the Georgia Institute of Technology to aid in diagnosing coronary artery disease by nuclear medicine imaging [11]. The system combines user-provided symbolic descriptions of the image with other clinical patient-specific information to formulate diagnostic recommendations regarding the degree of presence (or absence) of disease. During evaluations, the system yielded over 90% agreement with human experts.

Some complex problems might require several experts to solve. Consider, for example, the business task of forming a new-product marketing strategy, which might be accomplished through the collective thought of company specialists. Each specialist brings to the table expertise on one aspect of marketing. Working together, this committee could then form an effective marketing plan. Rule-based expert systems are well suited to manage these types of problems. Separate systems can be built that contain specialized knowledge in appropriate areas, and the systems can communicate with each other over a *blackboard structure* to solve the problem. To learn more about building a community of expert systems in one application, see the book *Blackboard Systems* [12].

One of the first expert systems built using this approach to solve a complex problem was the HEARSAY-II speech understanding system [13]. The system interprets continuous speech drawn from a 1000-word vocabulary. To accomplish this goal, HEARSAY uses 12 expert system modules, each with its own separate expertise about the speech recognition problem. These modules work collectively by exchanging information with each other through a blackboard structure.

Another expert system that successfully uses this approach is DUSTPRO, which provides advice to coal mine operators for the control of the mine's ventilation system to minimize miners' exposure to respirable dust [14]. Respirable dust is the primary cause of black lung disease. The system uses information about the available ventilation equipment and control procedures, coupled with mine ventilation regulations, to provide recommendations for mine ventilation control to reduce dust levels within the mine to a safe level. The system uses 30 separate expert systems designed for specialized activities that communicate their results over a blackboard structure.

Rule-based tools should continue to be a popular choice of expert system developers. They offer a natural way to capture the knowledge of an expert who relies on rules of thumb to solve problems. We see this most often in activities such as diagnosis, planning, and design. Rule-based systems can be developed relatively quickly, which is important for a project that calls for a prototype to be developed and assessed before a total commitment is made to the effort. Rule-based shells are usually much cheaper than other shell types, which could be a major project consideration. There are several good books that provide details on rule-based programming [8, 15–17].

III. FRAME-BASED TOOLS

Although rule-based systems have dominated the scene, a review of deployed expert systems during the later 1980s and early 1990s clearly shows a swing toward frame-based systems. This new direction is mainly a product of the rich set of programming techniques offered by frame-based tools that go well beyond the capability of rule-based tools. It also can be argued that designers have turned toward frame-based tools because of the natural style of system design. Developing a frame-based system is not simply a different programming technique: it is a completely different style of programming by which we view a problem as a collection of related objects that naturally describe the problem.

The current work in frame-based expert systems has its roots in earlier human problem-solving studies by cognitive psychologists, who developed theories on how humans form mental models that they can draw upon to aid them when solving problems. One study by Bartlett [18] demonstrated that humans rely upon discrete knowledge structures formed from past experience that can be used to deal with a similar current situation. Bartlett used the term **schema** to refer to one of these knowledge structures that contains stereotypical information about some given concept. When faced with a given problem, a human relies on some relevant schema as sort of a template that contains a list of generic information needed to solve the problem.

Following the idea of Bartlett's schema, Minsky [19] proposed a data structure for encoding in a computer typical information on some concept and coined the term **frame** to describe this structure. A frame has a name, slots with labels that describe the concept's major properties, and possible values for each property. In addition, a frame may have attached procedures that capture procedural information about the concept. When a specific instance of the concept is encountered, then its property values are entered into the frame's slots. Consider, for example, the following two frames that represent the concept of a *human* and an instance of it called *jack*:

Concept frame	⟶	*Instance frame*
<u>*humans*</u>		<u>*jack*</u>
Age: unknown	⟶	Age: 30
# Legs: 2	⟶	# Legs: 2
Dressing: *Procedure1*	⟶	Dressing: *Procedure1*

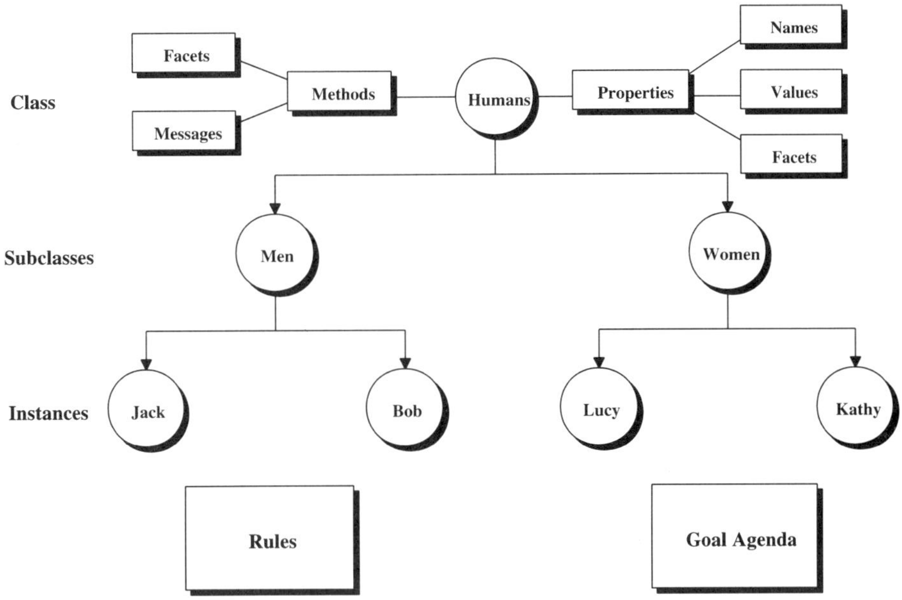

FIGURE 3 Frame world of humans.

The *humans* frame lists several properties common to all humans. Some properties, such as "age," have unknown values at the concept level. Other properties, such as "# legs," are assigned a default value if we expect most instances to have this value. For example, we would expect most humans to have two legs. We also can assign procedures (called **methods**) to a frame that describes typical actions. For instance, we might expect most humans to follow some set script when dressing (e.g., *Procedure1*). The *jack* frame represents an instance of the *human* frame. It inherits from the *human* frame its properties and default values. However, it could also contain property values specific to itself, such as its age value.

Frame-based expert systems expand on the ideas of the prior example and usually include a number of inter related frames and other utilities that enhance the power of these systems. To illustrate, consider the world of humans as shown in Fig. 3. The frames in the figure are organized in a hierarchical structure, moving from abstract issues at higher levels toward more specific ones at lower levels. This type of structure forms a "kind of" relationship between connected frames, which is typical in most applications. The frames also can be connected in other ways, such as a graph or network. The frame at the top level in the figure represents the abstract concept of humans. This frame is often called a *class*, because it provides a general description of objects common to some group or class. This class frame contains a list of properties common to objects from this class. All lower level frames attached to this class would inherit all of these properties. Each property has a name, a value, and possibly a set of *facets* that provide further information on the property. A facet can be used to define constraints on the property value or to define what methods are to be executed to obtain the property value or what to do if the value changes. Methods also can support *message passing*, a technique borrowed from object-oriented programming, that enables frames to communicate with one another.

In the middle level of Fig. 3 there are two other frames that represent the somewhat less abstract concepts of men and women. Notice also that these two frames are naturally attached to their parent frame of humans. These frames are also class frames, but because they are attached to an upper-level class frame, this type of frame is often called a *subclass*. At the bottom level we find specific objects attached to the middle-level frames. These lowest level object frames are usually called *instances*. That is, they are specific instances of their parent frame.

Some frame-based expert systems employ a goal agenda and a set of rules. The agenda provides a lists of tasks to perform. The rule set includes powerful *pattern matching* rules that are capable of drawing inferences from the entire frame world by scanning all of the frames to look for supporting information. To learn more about combining rules and frames, see Aikens [20].

Due to their ability to represent both descriptive and behavioral object information easily and the powerful set of utilities they bring to the table, frame-based tools permit the development of applications of greater complexity and flexibility than can be created using rule-based tools. The areas where they are being applied is widespread and growing.

Many of the early frame-based expert systems addressed simulation problems. This was a good choice, because a simulation problem inherently involves interacting objects. An interested reader may want to look at the book *Artificial Intelligence Simulation and Modeling* [21]. A good example of a frame-based simulation program is STEAMER, developed by Bolt Beranek, and Newman, which is an educational expert system that simulates and explains the operation of the Navy's 1078-class frigate steam propulsion plant to aspiring naval engineers [22]. The system simulates various plant components, such as valves and switches, that the user can adjust to observe the impact on the plant's overall operation of changes in such items as pressures and temperatures.

The application of frame-based systems in the area of control has been very active recently, particularly with the introduction by Gensym of G2, a powerful shell for creating frame-based control applications. One highly successful system built using G2 is EPAK, developed at Skogn Newsprint Mill in Norway [23]. EPAK is an on-line real-time expert system that improves the quality of paper during production. The system assesses paper quality, recommends control actions, and uses results from a simulation to predict the effects of the recommended actions. EPAK provides the quality engineer with constantly updated advice that takes into account the customer's requirements plus the current process and quality data.

Today, we also see frame-based systems being developed to attack problems that traditionally have been addressed using a rule-based approach. During the 1970s and for most of the 1980s, for example, when confronted with tasks such as diagnosis, design, and scheduling, expert system designers turned to rule-based tools. Designers now realize that these tasks can often be managed better using a frame-based tool. Consider the following successful applications.

CELLOS diagnoses problems in the manufacture of cellophane film [24]. It assists the operator in determining the causes of quality defects found in and related to viscose casting, and it can determine 22 basic quality defects and related problems. The system is rule and frame based and employs a backward chaining strategy. CELLOS was implemented using the shell NEXPERT OBJECT on an IBM PC. It also includes access to three databases that contain standard parameters of the different cellophane films produced. The system was developed by ITESM, Monterrey, Mexico, for Masterpak, a company of CYDSA Corporation.

BEADS, the building envelope analysis and design system, assists architects with budget and design issues that complicate the early conceptual phases of architectural design for both residential and commercial projects [25]. Design issues include selection of the skeletal components of a building, such as the walls and the roof, and design requirements that can vary with the climate at the site, geography, occupancy demands, and relevant building codes. After all these factors are considered and the best possible early design is agreed upon, matters such as material availability and cost effectiveness inevitably cloud the issue. As a result, architects and other conceptual-design participants rely heavily on judgment, expertise, and the heuristic lessons of past successful designs. BEADS contains knowledge about materials compatibility, construction data, suitability of certain envelope assemblies for different contexts, and other heuristics. The system interfaces to a database that contains information on building codes, material properties, and weather data. It produces a list of design alternatives ranked by performance attributes. BEADS was implemented using Knowledge Craft for the Macintosh and GoldWorks II for the IBM PC. The system was developed at Siricon Inc., Montreal, Canada.

Callisto assists in the scheduling tasks of a manufacturing process [26]. The system schedules the activities to accomplish the task, monitors the status of related activities to determine both plan and schedule changes required to meet goals, and manages changes in orders. As the design engineer is considering a design based on the availability of parts or components, the system can advise the engineer on parts, enabling the designer to reconsider a design based on an updated inventory. Callisto uses both frames and rules, and was developed at DEC.

For more information on frame-based expert systems, see [8, 16, 26].

IV. FUZZY LOGIC TOOLS

Many everyday problems are solved using good old *common sense*. We might hear, for instance, a person say, "When the motor is running *really hot* I decrease the speed *a little*." We are accustomed to hearing a problem described using vague terms like "really hot" and "a little," and usually have little difficulty in understanding the statement. However, how can we represent and reason with vague terms in a computer? The answer rests in **fuzzy logic**.

The form of fuzzy logic we are familiar with today first began to take shape during the 1920s through the work of Lukasiewicz (the inventor of reverse Polish notation) [27]. Lukasiewicz studied the mathematical representation of "fuzzy" terms such as *tall, old*, and *hot*. He recognized that these types of terms defined a truth representation in two-valued [0, 1] Aristotlian logic: true or false. Therefore, he developed a system of logic that extended the range of truth values to all real numbers in the range of 0 to 1 that represent the *possibility* that a given statement is true or false. This research led to a formal inexact reasoning technique aptly named **possibility theory**.

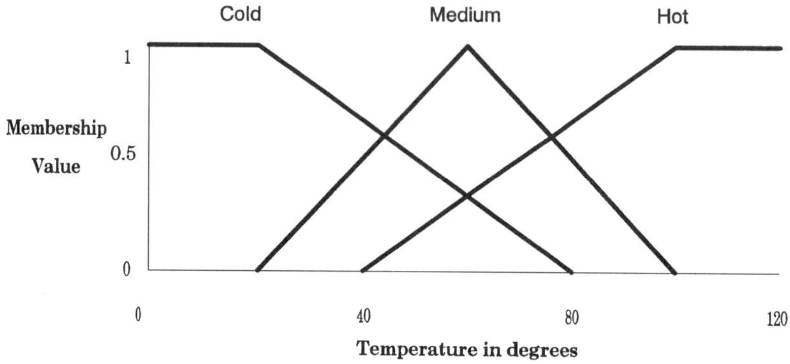

FIGURE 4 Fuzzy sets on temperature.

In 1965, Zadeh [28], who is considered the father of modern-day fuzzy logic, extended the work on possibility theory into a formal system of mathematical logic. Possibly more importantly, Zadeh brought to the attention of scientists and engineers a collection of valuable concepts for working with *fuzzy* natural language terms that were almost exclusively in the hands of academic philosophers for the past 40 years.

During the 1970s we saw the first real-world fuzzy expert system application. It was applied in the area of control, a place that was later found to be well suited for the technology. Mamdani and Assilian [29] established the framework of a fuzzy controller and used it to develop a system to control a steam engine. Later in the decade, Holmblad and Ostergaard [30] built a fuzzy controller for a cement kiln controller. In general, the foundation of fuzzy logic as an effective expert system tool was set in the 1970s, but, unfortunately, few took note of its potential value.

Progress in the field was very slow during the 1980s in the United States, the birthplace of the technology, mainly because very few individuals were working in the field. Fortunately, the Japanese, with their entrepreneurial instinct, saw the potential commercial value of the technology and began to develop numerous systems. Japan continues to be dominant in fuzzy logic applications today; only recently have others joined the parade.

In fuzzy logic we represent an ambiguous term using a **fuzzy set**, which assigns a membership value between 0 and 1 to reflect a member's association with the set. Consider, for example, Fig. 4, which shows three different sets for the fuzzy terms *cold, medium*, and *hot* temperature. Given a temperature value, we can use Fig. 4 to determine a level of belief that it belongs to one or more of these sets. For instance, a temperature of 60° is a member of *medium* temperature with a membership value of 1, and at the same time a member of *cold* and *hot* with a value of 0.25. Information to build fuzzy sets for a given application might come from an expert or from statistical procedures.

Fuzzy sets are used with fuzzy rules. For example, the fuzzy rule, "If the temperature is cold, then set the velocity to low," contains the fuzzy set *cold* defined on temperature (called the *universe of discourse*) and the set *low* on the universe of velocity. In operation, we would first take the present temperature and then determine its membership value to the set *cold*. Using "fuzzy inference," we could

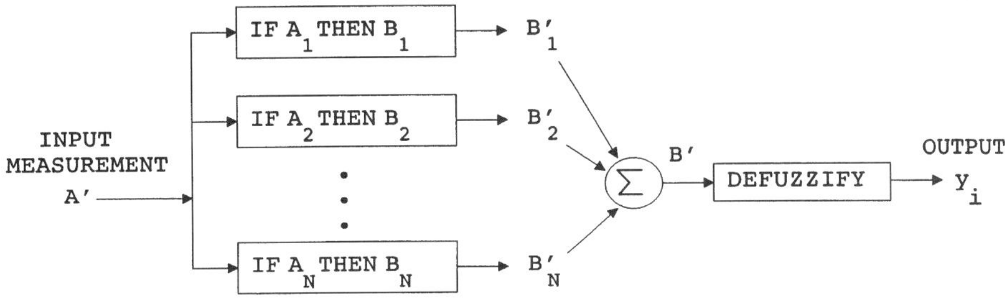

FIGURE 5 Fuzzy rule system architecture.

then obtain its expected membership value to the set *low* of the linguistic variable velocity.

Most fuzzy expert systems use several fuzzy rules that conclude the same event. Assume, for example, that we want a fuzzy system to tell us what velocity to set on some process control application, where all we have is information on the process temperature. We could write a set of fuzzy rules that relate temperature to velocity, such as

IF Temperature is cold A_1

THEN Set velocity to high B_1

IF Temperature is medium A_2

THEN Set velocity to medium B_2

IF Temperature is hot A_3

THEN Set velocity to low B_3

Fuzzy sets for velocity would need to be generated, in much the same way as the sets for temperature were formed (Fig. 4). In most fuzzy applications, the rules come from an expert on the problem. However, in some cases neural network techniques can be used to learn the rules from training data—a plus if no expert exists. For more information on these neural techniques, see Kosko [31].

To illustrate how a fuzzy system processes these rules, refer to Fig. 5. A given input temperature measurement (A') is applied in parallel to the if part fuzzy sets that provides a degree of belief in the temperature being cold, medium, and hot. Each rule then produces a belief in what velocity to set (B'_i). That is, the first rule forms a belief for setting the velocity to high, the second one for setting it to medium, and the third to low. These beliefs are actually in a form of an induced fuzzy set, where the then part fuzzy sets are scaled (max-product inference) or clipped (max–min inference), depending on the fuzzy inference technique used. These induced sets are then combined through a union operation to produce a combined fuzzy set (B'). To obtain the needed velocity value (y_i), a *defuzzification* process is next performed, which is usually done by taking the centroid of B'. In effect, this entire process takes a single temperature measurement and provides a single velocity setting. For a more detailed description of how this inference process works, see Kosko [32].

As this example illustrates, a fuzzy logic system is remarkably simple and relatively easy to build. Equally remarkable is how well it can perform with only a few commonsense rules. Developing the fuzzy sets and rules usually can be done quickly. The hard and time-consuming part is tuning the system, which is usually done by editing, adding, or deleting the fuzzy sets or rules. For example, consider the fuzzy controller built by Canon to provide autofocusing for their H800 camera [33]. It took only one week to develop the initial fuzzy rules and sets, but took several more months of system tuning to achieve satisfactory performance.

One key to developing an effective fuzzy system is to use just a few rules. If the membership functions have been constructed properly, then only a few rules are needed. For instance, Canon used only 13 rules in its autofocusing camera. Another good example of a small rule base was demonstrated at the Ford Motor Co., Dearborn, MI, where a fuzzy system with only three rules successfully backed a simulated tractor–trailer into a parking space. Most applications also use only a few inputs and outputs. Whereas fuzzy systems are highly nonlinear and model-free, most control applications require extensive simulation tests to study their sensitivity and stability.

Another important development issue is how the membership functions and rules are obtained. One of the better and more straightforward ways is to ask an expert. For an application that qualifies for a fuzzy logic approach, the expert typically will describe the problem using ambiguous terms that can be captured in fuzzy sets and fuzzy rules. A good example of a fuzzy control system that was built using this approach was the development of the electronic continuously variable transmission used in the Subaru Justy automobile. The system continuously adjusts the position of a belt that changes the transmission pulley ratio, which impacts the car's acceleration and performance. Designers questioned test drivers about their response to different pulley ratios to define how belt positions on the pulleys corresponded to the car's performance. Answers were then used to define the fuzzy sets and rules. Some fuzzy logic projects have no experts. In these situations, as previously mentioned, the designer must turn to statistical or neural schemes to formulate the fuzzy sets and rules.

Most fuzzy expert systems have been applied in the area of control for applications that are difficult or impossible to address using classical control techniques. To date, Japan has been the leader in developing fuzzy logic control systems for such diverse applications as washing machines, video camcorders, and railway systems [33, 34]. Over 1000 patents on fuzzy designs exist in Japan alone. Total world sales of fuzzy controllers is projected to rise to around $13 billion by the year 2000 from $1.5 billion in 1990 [35].

It comes as a surprise to many people how well a fuzzy control system works. With only a few commonsense rules, systems have been built that outperform conventional control techniques and even human operators in some cases. A good example is the fuzzy subway train control system in Sendai, Japan, developed by the Hitachi Corporation [36]. The system contains a set of rules to control the trains' speed and another set for braking. The system considers four performance criteria: safety, riding comfort, target speed, and accuracy of stopping gap. Before the system was put into operation, the Japanese government required extensive testing. In response, Hitachi performed over 300,000 simulations and ran over 3000 runs on real but empty trains. Following successful testing, the system was put into operation, where it provides nonhuman train control even during peak hours when the train is full of passengers. Results show that the system provides a smoother ride than did human controllers outperforms standard proportional-integrative-differential (PID) controllers in smoothness of acceleration and braking, and consumer less power than the PID. The system also provides more accurate stopping than a human train operator or the PID.

Fuzzy logic systems also are finding their place in the consumer market. Assume you want a smart washing machine. You do not want to think about how much detergent to add, how much water is needed, or how long to run the machine. You just want to dump the clothes in, push one button, and let the machine go about its business. Well, you are in luck. Several firms in Japan and Korea manufacture fuzzy washing machines that fill the bill. They tailor the wash to each set of clothes and change the wash strategy as the clothes are being cleaned. The fuzzy controller used in these machines uses data supplied by sensors as input. An optical sensor sends a beam of light through the water and measures how much light reaches the other side; this measurement provides information on the water's clarity and thus how dirty the load is. The optical sensor also can be used to tell whether the clothes are dirty from mud or from oil stains. Mud and dirt break down quickly in water, whereas oil stains break down slowly, so by monitoring the rate of change in the water clarity, the system knows something about the nature of the dirt it has to wash out. Some of these machines also use a load sensor. Using data from these sensors, the fuzzy controller can decide on such items as the needed agitation rate, water temperature, amount of detergent, and the wash time. The system makes these decisions when the wash begins and can make new ones (adaptive control) as the wash proceeds. These fuzzy washing machines have been found to produce a cleaner wash, while using less detergent and less power.

Mitsubishi Heavy Industries, Ltd. of Japan, in cooperation with Togai InfraLogic Inc. of Irvine, CA, developed a fuzzy logic expert system to control commercial air conditioners [37]. The system monitors the room temperature and temperature setting, and adjusts air flow to minimize cooling times to maintain a comfortable setting. The system can adapt smoothly to different room sizes and temperature variations, and can compensate for mass in the room. The system increases the air conditioner efficiency and cuts power consumption by 20%.

Another area that has seen considerable fuzzy expert system activity recently is information processing. Yamaichi Securities uses a system to manage a stock fund and Hitachi has one to assist in trading Japanese bonds and bond futures. Omron uses a system to manage information in a medical database to help in medical diagnosis and to generate a personal health plan. We should see a large increase in fuzzy logic information processing applications in the future as the business and industrial sectors begin to recognize the value of the technology for supporting intelligent decision making.

One of the more interesting recent trends in AI is an effort to combine tools to help build a better application. In fuzzy expert system design, there has been considerable activity using neural networks to aid development of the fuzzy system. Neural networks currently are used to define fuzzy sets and also to discover fuzzy rules. They also are used to help tune the fuzzy rules and sets. To return the favor, fuzzy systems can help design neural networks. The combination of the two tools has begat a new field called *neurocomputing*.

Fujitsu Laboratories Ltd. developed a neurofuzzy system to rate the investment quality of bonds. Inputs to the system include the ordinary profit, owned capital, interest coverage ratio, long-term loan ratio, and owned capital ratio. The system output is the bond rating with fuzzy sets of low, medium, and high, which further leads to determination of the bond's rating of AAA, AA, A, BBB, BB, and B. Each fuzzy rule was assigned an initial weight as provided by an expert in the area. Rules with small weights contribute less to the fuzzy inference process than rules with large weights. A neural network was used to adjust the weight for each rule. Some weights were raised, some lowered, and some were even set to zero, which in effect eliminated the rules. During evaluation, Fujitsu tested three different systems: the fuzzy system with initial rule weights, the system with the rule weights adjusted by the neural network, and a neural network built from past data on bond rating. Each system was tested on the bonds of 76 firms in the electrical equipment and machinery industries that previously had been rated by a human expert. The results showed that the neural network's bond rating recommendation agreed with the expert's in 80% of the test cases, the fuzzy system with initial rule weights agreed in 84% of the cases, and the fuzzy system that had its rule weights adjusted by the neural network agreed in 96% of the cases. Clearly, the use of the two tools was productive.

For control applications where neural networks have been used to learn fuzzy rules, the most popular approach is the differential competitive learning (DCL) method developed by Bart Kosko at the University of Southern California [31]. This technique uses a neural network to uncover control rules in an existing controller. Data from the existing controller are compiled into a series of input/output vectors and fed to the neural network. Predefined membership functions are assigned to the inputs and outputs of the network, and the network is studied to find clusters of data that indicate the presence of a rule.

In fuzzy applications where a neural network is used to support rule tuning, a neural network takes an initial set of fuzzy rules and tunes them to improve system performance. The net tunes a rule by slightly varying the size or shape of one fuzzy set used in the rule, and then sees how well the system performs with that change. The network keeps those changes that improve performance and ignores those that do not. It may run hundreds of thousands of test cases in its attempt to tune the rules. Sanyo in Japan, for instance, uses neural learning to tune the rules in its fuzzy microwave oven controller. The fuzzy system measures infrared light patterns, temperature, humidity, and changes in food shape. The fuzzy rules, which include fuzzy sets for these measurables, determine the cooking times and power control.

The success the Japanese have had with this technology has only recently caught the attention of others. In the United States, the number of fuzzy projects in both commercial and government sectors increased dramatically during the 1990s. Activity in Europe, South Korea, and Canada also has been on the rise. Several very good books are available, particularly from an engineering perspective, on the operation and design of fuzzy logic expert systems: Jamshidi et al. [38], Ross [39], Kosko [32], and Wang [40].

V. INDUCTION TOOLS

Most expert system projects involve a human expert who has specialized knowledge to solve problems in a focused area. Collaborating with the knowledge engineer, the expert provides the knowledge necessary to design the expert system. In some areas, however, no real experts exist. In this event, the knowledge engineer must find alternative ways to obtain the problem-solving knowledge.

One approach favored by expert system designers when confronted with this situation is to see if past examples exist from which the necessary knowledge can be extracted. An example consists of a set of conditions along with some found outcome. For instance, in the area of weather forecasting, conditions that might be considered are the temperature, wind direction, and barometric pressure, and the outcome might be whether it rained or not. Armed with a set of examples of this sort, the knowledge engineer could develop a weather forecasting expert system using an **induction** tool.

Induction is the process of reasoning from a given set of facts to conclude general principles or rules. For example, if we knew that Judy liked football, baseball, and basketball, we might reasonably conclude through induction that Judy likes sports. Induction looks for patterns in available information to infer reasonable conclusions.

Inductive learning is an important topic in AI research and in expert system development. Winston [41] applied inductive learning to derive conceptual descriptions to classify block world structures. The Meta-DENDRAL project used an induction technique to discover a set of rules to infer chemical structures from mass spectrometry data [42]. Michalski and Chilausky [43] showed that a combination of learning from examples and from being told could be used to form a body of knowledge for diagnosing soybean diseases in the PLANT expert system.

An induction tool uses an induction algorithm, several of which have been developed. The most popular one used in the creation of an expert system is ID3, which is a general-purpose rule induction algorithm developed by Quinlan [44] and is used today in most induction-based expert system shells. ID3 takes a set of problem examples and induces a decision tree. An example is a combination of decision factors, decision factor values, and actions specific to that example. For instance, an example set for weather prediction might look like that shown in Table 1. This example set would have come from a past history of weather patterns. Given this set, ID3 can now produce a decision tree that captures the knowledge for predicting the weather. To generate the decision tree, this algorithm uses a heuristic approach, which places the attributes in the nodes of the tree in a manner that can minimize the search effort to locate a solution. The algorithm also can determine if some attribute is irrelevant for predicting the final result. Applying ID3 to the example set of Table 1 produces the decision tree shown in Fig. 6.

Inductive learning can be viewed as a search through a problem space for a solution to a problem. The problem space is composed of the problem's major concepts, linked together by an inductive process that uses examples of the problem. Consider the decision tree in Fig. 6. We can search through the tree using given decision factor values of our current weather conditions to determine the expected forecast.

TABLE 1 Decision Table for Weather Prediction[a]

Decision factors				Result
Temperature	**Wind**	**Sky**	**Barometer**	**(Prediction)**
Above freezing	West	Cloudy	Falling	Rain
Below freezing	*	Cloudy	Steady	Snow
Above freezing	East	Cloudy	Rising	Shine
Above freezing	*	Partly clear	Steady	Shine
Above freezing	South	Clear	Falling	Rain
Freezing	North	Partly	Steady	Snow

[a] The asterisk (*) indicates "don't care."

Some induction algorithms produce rules that reflect the search through a problem space. This ability is important if the induction tool is acting in a support role during the development of a rule-based expert system. For instance, considering Fig. 6 again, we could obtain the rule

IF The barometric pressure is steady
AND The sky is clear
THEN The weather prediction is for clear

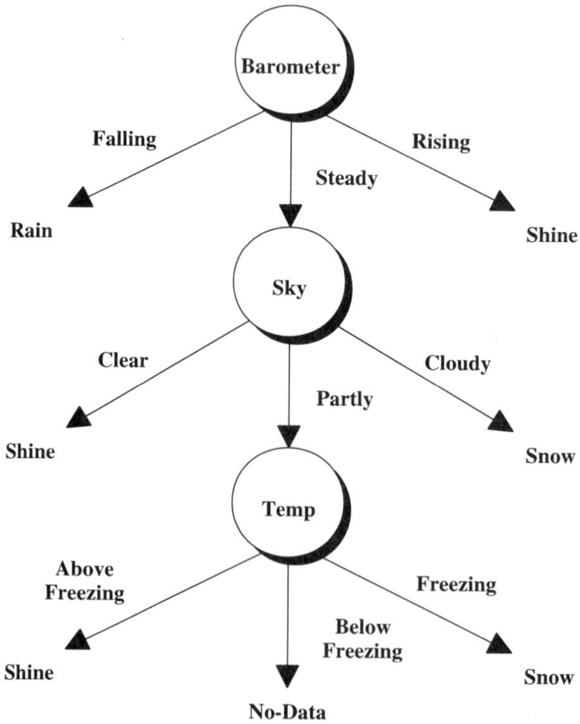

FIGURE 6 Decision tree for weather prediction.

The biggest advantage of an induction tool is that it offers a technique whereby the system's knowledge can be acquired directly through past examples, an important point if the problem domain has no available expert. Even if an expert is available, working directly with the set of examples rather than the expert avoids the often difficult and time-consuming knowledge acquisition task. Another plus is the ability to discover new knowledge. By processing the examples through an algorithm such as ID3, domain-specific rules can be uncovered that may not even be known to an expert in the field. Let us look at some induction applications.

AQ11 incorporates knowledge of plant environment and disease symptoms to provide advice on the diagnosis of soybean disease [43]. The system considers issues such as the month of year, temperature, plant height, and condition of the plants. Rules generated from an induction technique represent the knowledge by directly displaying the diagnostic expertise provided to the system. The system was developed at the University of Illinois.

One of the more popular application areas of induction expert systems has been in support of help-desk personnel. Many companies offer their customers a phone number they can call when they experience a problem with the company's product. The help-desk personnel who manage these phones usually will step the caller through a series of questions to identify the nature of the problem and to provide a remedy. In most cases, the current customer's problem is similar to past problems known to the company, making the job of helping the customer ideally suited for an induction approach.

An induction-based expert system was developed to assist service representatives of Wendy's International in responding to questions from staff at nearly 1200 company owned restaurants [1]. Prior to the system, employees had to rely on 2–3 months of training and on cumbersome service manuals to diagnose problems and provide solutions. Typical problems that the system provides assistance on are point-of-sale terminals, time clocks, and wireless headsets. It was developed using the induction shell 1STCLASS. The system runs on an IBM Personal System 2 model 30 and was developed by members of Wendy's Professional Computing Center and selected Field Operations Support Center staff.

MASK is an induction expert system developed to aid Norcom (Juneau, Alaska) help-desk operators manage customer questions on a product called Screenio [8]. Screenio is a screen management product for the popular Realia Cobol on the IBM PC. Norcom's customers use Screenio to design IBM PC screens for their Cobol programs—many of them adapted from the large base of existing corporate-frame Cobol programs. Norcom has over 500 customers for this product who often will contact Norcom for product support. To help alleviate the workload associated with their customer support, Norcom developed MASK to aid their support personnel. Norcom had 9 months of data on typical customer problems and associated solutions. They then decided to generate an expert system using the past cases as an example set. The example set contained nine decision factors and was developed in one day using the induction tool 1STCLASS.

READY REFERENCE ADVISOR is an induction expert system developed for the National Agricultural Library (Beltsville, MD) that assists users in finding answers to fairly simple, straightforward questions often asked at reference desks in libraries [1]. The system is linked to on-line bibliographic databases and also to a compact disk read-only memory database (CD-ROM). It system was built using 1STCLASS.

Another activity where induction expert systems have been applied successfully is prediction. Handicapping a horse race or picking the winner in a football game are typical examples, as is predicting stock market behavior. Common to these tasks is a list of factors that are generally known to be important to predicting the outcome. Also available is historical information that relates specific factor values to specific outcomes, that is, examples. An induction approach offers an opportunity to work with these examples to predict the expected outcome. One major advantage of an induction approach in a prediction application is that a system can be built to discover knowledge that is unknown even to an expert in the field.

An expert system was developed using an induction technique to improve the reliability of stock market prediction [45]. The problem chosen focused on predicting intermediate fluctuations in the movement of the market for nonconservative investors. Information for the system was obtained from the *Wall Street Journal* and from interpretations of trend-charting techniques. Three different results were used to categorize the prediction: bullish (forecasting an upward trend), bearish (forecasting a downward trend), and neutral (indicating that either call was too risky). The system was developed using the ID3 algorithm. In tests, the system correctly predicted the actual market movements 64.4% of time, whereas an expert analyst was correct 60.2%.

Another stock market expert system was designed to uncover knowledge from market activities that could assist in putting together a stock portfolio [46]. The system assists analysts in discovering regularities and patterns in stock trading that lead to profitable investment opportunities. The system has been found to produce portfolios that outperform the New York Stock Exchange Composite index and the Standard & Poor's 500.

Predicting the weather through induction also has been tried. Severe thunderstorms in the United States annually cause loss of lives and millions of dollars in property damage. Forecasting thunderstorms is done by expert meteorologists with the National Severe Storms Forecast Center (NSSFC). This task is time consuming and involves continuous analysis of vast amounts of data. An induction expert system called WILLARD was built to aid this task [47]. WILLARD was developed using 140 examples of thunderstorm weather data. The system queries the user about pertinent weather conditions for the area and then produces a complete forecast with supporting justification. It characterizes the certainty of a severe thunderstorm occurrence as none, approaching, slight, moderate, or high, and each prediction is given with a numerical probability range. WILLARD was developed using RULEMASTER, an inductive tool for generating decision rules. The system was tested over a 1-week period in late spring of 1984, in a region including west and central Texas, Oklahoma, and Colorado. During this period, five severe thunderstorms passed through this region. WILLARD's forecasts were found to compare favorably with those made by an expert meteorologist from NSSFC.

Induction systems were very popular during the 1970s and 1980s, but have fallen somewhat out of favor lately. When expert system developers need a learning tool, they most often today first turn to case-based reasoning or neural networks (subjects of the next sections). However, due to its relative ease of use and its ability to create rules from examples, an induction tool should continue to play an important role in the knowledge engineer's toolbox. To learn more about designing an induction expert system, see [48–50].

VI. CASE-BASED REASONING TOOLS

Most individuals prefer older doctors. Even though a doctor fresh out of schools has the latest book knowledge on diagnosing and treating medical problems, we tend to select one who has been around awhile. The major reason we typically feel more comfortable with experienced doctors is that we expect that they have treated others in the past with illnesses similar to our own and, therefore, quickly can arrive at an effective treatment. In effect, we value them more on the number of cases that they have worked on than on their medical diagnostic skills.

Case-based reasoning (CBR) is a technology that uses past experiences (cases) to solve current problems. Much in the same way as our older doctor treats a patient, a CBR system takes information on some current problem and looks for the most similar past case. If a reasonable match is found, the system suggests the same solution used in the past. When a search fails to locate a similar case, the search itself becomes the basis for a new case. In effect, a CBR system can learn from new experiences. A CBR system derives its power from its ability to retrieve relevant cases quickly and accurately from its case library, and its ability to learn. The basic operation of CBR system follows a four-step process: (1) input information about a current problem, (2) find a similar past case, (3) adapt this case to fit the current problem, (4) provide a suggested solution. Figure 7 shows this process in more detail.

In its simplest form, a case is a list of feature values that lead to a particular outcome, for example, a set of patient symptoms along with the corresponding diagnosis. Determining the appropriate features is one of the most important tasks when designing a CBR system.

In operation, a CBR system tries to find from its library of cases the one that best matches the conditions of a current problem. This step is called *case retrieval.*

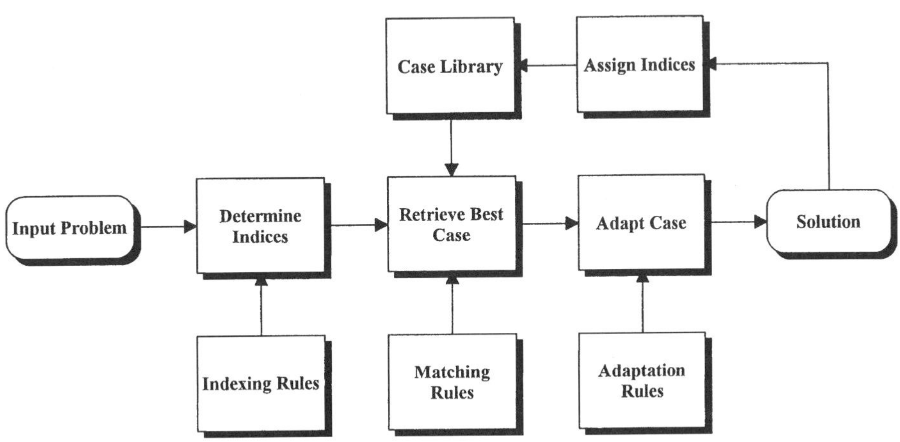

FIGURE 7 CBR flow chart.

First, the system determines, usually using a set of rules, the features of the current problem that are relevant to finding similar cases. These features are often called *indexes*, which the system uses to retrieve a set of potentially relevant cases from the case library. The purpose of this step is to winnow down the number of cases to few that should get us in the ballpark of the desired solution. The system then matches the current problem with this set to determine the most similar ones. The similarity of cases is based on how well they match on the relevant features and the relative importance of these features.

The most common matching technique uses a nearest-neighbor approach. The system takes a relevant case from the library and compares its feature values with those of the problem case. A numerical score is obtained for each feature that represents the degree of match between the library case and the problem case on the basis of that one feature. How well overall the library case matches the problem case is determined by adding all of the feature matching scores. Often, weighting factors are used to assign the importance of each feature to the matching process, and the overall case match is obtained from a weighted sum. These feature weighting factors can be fixed or, more interestingly, set by the system through the use of a set of rules that take into account the problem's context. This matching process is done for all the relevant library cases, resulting in a score for each one that represents how well it matches the current problem. The most similar case is the one with the highest matching score.

The next step in the CBR process is called *case adaptation*. Here, the system adapts the most similar case to fit the current problem, creating a new case that is then added to the library. This is accomplished by first determining what is different between the input and retrieved case and then modifying the retrieved case by taking into account the differences. A set of adaptation rules are typically used to accomplish this. The extent of the adaptation is based on the differences found. In some instances, no adaption is needed—what was done in the past is perfectly fine for the current problem. The chance of hitting this bull's-eye obviously will depend on the number of cases in the library. on other occasions, the degree of adaptation is simple, such as a change to a single feature value. Sometimes, the needed alterations are extensive, such as structural modification. For instance, a situation might arise where one component of the solution of the past case is deleted from the proposed solution. Kolodner [51] discussed 10 different adaptation techniques commonly used. Finally, there may be times when the differences are so great that the system cannot make the needed changes. when this happens, a human typically intervenes and solves the problem. Even with this worst case scenario, the system can provide the human with a good starting point. After presenting the final solution, the adapted case is indexed and added to the case library, which, in effect, makes the system smarter and better prepared to manage future problems.

Most people consider the work Schank [52] at Yale University, which was published in *Dynamic Memory*, to be the first effort that described a memory-based approach to reasoning. Schank proposed structures called memory organization packets (MOPs) that serve as both repositories of generalized knowledge and organizers of cases. MOPs contain knowledge that describes types of experiences in context frames and also index cases according to ways that they differ from the norm. Schank's ideas were expanded by his students, most notably by Kolodner [53], whose CYRUS system, built in 1983, was the first computer implementation of Schank's work. CYRUS (computerized Yale retrieval and update system) stores and retrieves events in the life of Cyrus Vance when he was secretary of state under President Carter. It can answer questions such as, "Did Vance's wife ever meet Mrs. Begin?" CYRUS was used to explore the basic ideas of CBR and to develop techniques that led to real-world applications. Fortunately, these aplications were quick in coming.

With an understanding of the potential of CBR techniques, researchers began looking for areas where individuals solve problems by relying on a comparison of the current problem with past experiences. The search did not take long. Examples were found in such varied domains as medicine, law, and manufacturing. Consider the area of help-desk automation—an arena well suited for the technology.

A help-desk is an information facility set up by an organization to manage problems that users of their products are having. Help-desk personnel manage a telephone where they take a description of the customer's problem and compare it with problems reported previously by other customers. This effort usually results in quick fix if the help-desk individual contacted is adept at making a good comparison. An example of a successful CBR help-desk application is CASCADE, a system developed at DEC to assist in recovering from VMS device driver failures [54]. Information provided by a caller about a current problem is entered into an on-line form by a help-desk technician and then CASCADE retrieves relevant cases that suggest solution. The system provides quick and effective solutions, increases customer satisfaction, and avoids the need to pass along problems to design engineers.

Another area that provides fertile ground for CBR technology is the legal profession, which thrives on judicial precedents established in landmark cases. The similarties, as well as the differences, between the current and the landmark case are considered to guide legal decision making. HYPO is a good example where CBR has helped to provide this guidance. HYPO supports legal reasoning in the area of patent law [55]. Provided a case description involving a given patent claim violation, the system uses a library of precedent cases and looks for those that are most similar to the given case that were decided in favor of the defense. HYPO then generates a plausible argument for the prosecution or defense. It can take the plaintiffs or defendant's side in a dispute and is equally good at creating arguments for each.

Another interesting CBR system in the area of law is JUDGE, which assists a judge during the sentencing phase of trail. JUDGE models a judge who is responsible for establishing a sentence for an individual convicted of a crime [56]. The system uses as input the charge, events that occurred, and legal statutes concerning related crimes. The system's case library contains previous crimes and the sentences imposed for each. After locating the most similar past case, JUDGE adapts the case to fit the current crime by making the sentence longer or shorter.

During the 1990s, the manufacturing sector also deployed CBR systems. Consider CLAVIER, which configures the layout of composite airplane parts for curing in an autoclave [57]. Given a list of parts that need curing and a time priority associated with each part, the system designs layouts for several loads of the autoclave that will cure all of the parts in a timely manner. Its case library consists of part layouts in the autoclave, including cases that worked well in the past and those that did not. In a little over a year of use at Lockheed, its library grew from 20 to over 150 cases. This growth was accomplished through the cooperation of several shop floor personnel who were responsible for the operation of the autoclave, where each would enter new experiences into the case library. In a sense, CLAVIER learns on the job.

As organizations begin to discover the potential value of CBR technology, we should see many more CBR systems. CBR technology offers many of the same advantages of induction methods, and more. For more details on the operation and design of a CBR system, see [51, 58].

VII. NEURAL NETWORK TOOLS

Although it is not technically a part of the symbolic processing world of expert systems, nevertheless, due to the power of a neural network to manage real-world pattern recognition problems, it has not surprisingly found its way into the expert system designer's toolbox. Neural networks have been one of the most rapidly expanding AI technologies during the past decade. Although excitement is high today, it has been awhile in coming.

The beginning of neurocomputing usually is attributed to the 1943 paper by McCulloch and Pitts [59]. Even though this paper never mentioned any practical uses for the technology, it showed that even simple neural networks could compute any arithmetic or logical function. In 1949, Hebb [60] published the book *The Organization of Behavior* that proposed that the connectivity of neurons in the brain are continually changing as an organism learns differing functional tasks. He also proposed a learning law that became the starting point for neural network training algorithms. He showed, for the first time, that a network of neurons could exhibit learning behavior. This book influenced the work of psychologists, but unfortunately, was ignored by the engineering community of the day.

The next major development in neural networks came in 1958 with Rosenblatt's [61] work on the *perceptron*, and his *perceptron convergence theorem*. Following this revolutionary effort, Rosenblatt built the first successful neural computer called the *Mark I Perceptron*. The perceptron is a pattern classification system that can identify both abstract and geometric patterns. It was primarily aimed at optical pattern recognition. Development of the perceptron sparked a great amount of interest in neural computing. In 1960, Bernie Widrow, working with his graduate student Ted Hoff (Hoff later went on to invent the microprocessor), introduced the *least means-square algorithm* and used it to formulate the *Adaline* [62]. The Adaline was used for a variety of applications such as speech recognition, character recognition, weather prediction, and adaptive control. Widrow used the Adaline to develop filters that eliminate echoes in phone lines—the first neural network applied to a real-world problem. The major difference between the perceptron and the Adaline lies in the training procedure. The Adaline uses a linear transfer function, whereas the perceptron uses hard limiting. Both also are limited to solving linearly separable problems. The success of the perceptron and the Adaline acted as a magnet to researchers and, equally importantly, it attracted much needed research funding into the field.

Enthusiasm for the technology was at an all time high. It seemed that neural networks had the potential to do anything and it was felt that artificial brains were right around the corner. This illusion was soon dispelled with publication of the book *Perceptrons* by Minsky and Papert [63]. This book was an attack on the perceptron, in particular, and the neural network field, in general. Minsky and Papert showed the fundamental limits of a one-layer perceptron network in solving simple problems, such as the exclusive-or gate function. The book also implied that essentially all neural networks suffer from the same flaw as the perceptron and that the technology would never make a major contribution to the AI field. Discouraged researchers left the field, funding dried up, and the study of neural networks lapsed into obscurity for nearly two decades. The damage was done.

The rebirth of interest in the technology is commonly attributed to John Hopfield, an established physicist, who had a worldwide reputation. In 1982, Hopfield [64] presented a paper to the National Academy of Science that was the first paper on neural networks presented to this distinguished body since the 1960s. The paper described Hopfield's neural system, called the *Hopfield model*, which represents neuron activity as a thresholding operation and memory as information stored in the interconnections between neurons. This model established, for the first time, the principle of storing information in a dynamically stable network. This well-received paper revitalized interest in neurocomputing, drawing new researchers and fresh funding into the field. Neural networks were soon developed that not only solved the trivial problems that Minsky and Papert used to downplay the field, but also ones that offered real, practical value. The game was back on.

The next important advancement, particularly from an engineering viewpoint, was the development of the *backpropagation algorithm* for training multilayer perceptron networks, which was discovered independently by several different researchers. The most influential publication of the algorithm was the two-volume book by Rumelhart and McClelland [65]. Backpropagation has emerged as the most popular learning algorithm for training neural networks. We will look at this algorithm in more detail later in this section.

A neural network is composed of a number of interconnected processing elements that process information dynamically in response to external data. A processing element typically has many inputs. Each one is assigned a weight, w, which serves to increase or decrease the effect of the corresponding input. The processing element combines, usually through summation, the weighted-input values. This weighted sum is then modified by a transfer function, such as a threshold function, which passes information only if the sum exceeds a certain level. In itself, a processing element is not very exciting. However, when we interconnect the processing elements to create a network structure, things get interesting.

Processing elements (also called nodes or neurons) usually are organized into groups called layers. There is an input layer that connects external input data (I_i) to the network, an output layer that provides the network's output data (O_i), and one or more layers between the input and output layers that are called *hidden* layers. They are called "hidden" because they do not communicate with the environment. Interconnection between processing elements of different groups can be full or partial. Figure 8 shows a typical neural network that is fully connected. Each connection between the input and hidden elements has an associated weight ($W_{I,H}$); likewise for connections between the hidden and output elements ($W_{I,H}$).

Before a neural network can be put to work on a given application, it must be trained using data obtained from the application along with a learning algorithm.

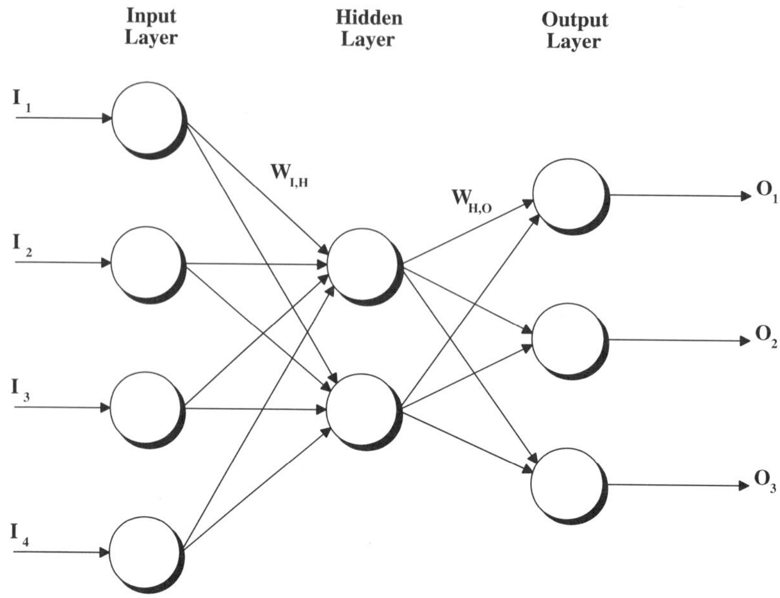

FIGURE 8 A multilayer neural network.

There are three training methods typically used. In one approach, called *supervised learning*, the network is provided a set of input data and the desired outputs (targets). As the input data are applied to the network, the network's outputs are compared to the targets. The learning algorithm then adjusts the weights of the network to move the network outputs closer to the targets. Supervised learning is the most common training method used when developing a neural network, and the backpropagation algorithm is the most popular supervised learning algorithm.

Another training method is called *unsupervised learning*. Here the neurons find a way to organize themselves without any external help. The weights are modified in response to network inputs alone. There are no output targets. Most unsupervised learning algorithms perform some kind of clustering operation, where they learn to categorize the input patterns into a small number of classes. This type of learning is applicable to problems where we want to *discover* significant patterns or features in the input data.

A third kind of learning, which falls between supervised and unsupervised learning, is called *reinforcement learning*. Instead of being provided the correct output for each input, as in the case of supervised learning, the algorithm is given only a grade that indicates whether the response to an input is good or bad. The advantage of this type of learning is that it is not necessary to know the correct answer for each input; only the degree of correctness is needed.

Since supervised learning has surfaced as the most practical and valuable training method, let us further explore backpropagation, the predominate learning algorithm used with this training method. The typical architecture of a backpropagation network has an input layer, an output layer, and usually only one or two hidden layers like the one shown in Fig. 8. The number of neurons in the input and output layers is equal to the number of input and output data, respectively. Each layer is fully connected to the succeeding layer. The interconnections between neurons contain a weight that is adjusted during training. The objective of training is to set the weight values such that the network can effectively predict the target output values for a set of input data.

To train the network, we need a set of data that contain both input and output (target) information about the application. These data look very much like records in a database, where several fields are used for the input information and the balance are used for the output information. In practice, most, but not all, of these records are used for training (called the training set), whereas the balance are used later for testing (called the test set).

Training the network is a two-step process. First, the input data are applied to the network and the resulting activity is allowed to spread through the network to the output layer. The resulting output is then compared to the target data, using some error function. This step results in an error for each neuron in the output layer. Next, this error is used to make adjustments to the various weights.

The basic idea behind backpropagation is to make a large change to a given weight if the change leads to a large reduction in the error calculated at the output of the network. On the other hand, if the weight change has little impact on the output error, little is done to the weight. In backpropagation, weight adjustments are done in a backward fashion. That is, weight adjustments in the output layer are computed first ($W_{H,O}$), then those in the hidden layer ($W_{I,H}$) are computed.

This two-step process is repeated for all of the records in the training set, usually many times. If things go well, then the network's global error (usually a mean-square-error measure) becomes small and the training task is done. At this point, the weights are set and contain the problem's knowledge for classifying data. The data records set aside earlier for later testing now can be used to see how well the network performs. A good description of the backpropagation process can be found in Chapter 8 of *Parallel Distributed Processing Explorations in the Microstructure of Cognition* [65] and Chapter 22 of *Artificial Intelligence* [66].

The characteristics of a neural network make it an attractive tool in many areas. Classifying data is one of the most popular applications of the technology. For example, it has been used successfully in several target marketing projects, where the network helps to decide how to direct promotional materials. Another productive area is forecasting. Examples include predicting interest rates, inventory levels, and stock index movements. Let us look at some typical applications.

Autonomous vehicle navigation and intelligent robot control have been hot areas of AI research for the past two decades. Over the past 10 years or so, neural network designers have tried their hand in these areas with considerable success. One of the better applications that demonstrates the simplicity and power of neural networks applied to autonomous vehicle navigation is ALVINN (autonomous land vehicle in neural networks), which was developed at Carnegie Mellon University (CMU) [67]. ALVINN was designed to navigate the CMU *Navlab* vehicle over a highway open to normal traffic. Navlab was equipped with video cameras and laser sensors. ALVINN's architecture consisted of 960 input nodes (input from the imaging sensors), a single hidden layer with 4 nodes, and 30 output nodes, each representing a steering decision. ALVINN was trained using the backpropagation algorithm by observing a person driving. Training pairs consisted of input image data and the driver's response. That is, the system learned how the driver steered the vehicle according to what he or she saw. Under the control of ALVINN, Navlab successfully navigated a highway for 21.2 miles at an average speed of 55 mph.

A pattern recognition problem is a natural for neural networks. In fact, Bishop [68] dedicated an entire book to the subject. In pattern recognition, an attempt is made to classify available data in a way that enables the identification of some object of interest. The area of signal processing has been one pattern recognition activity popular among neural network designers. Radar data processing, image processing, and machine vibration data processing are a few examples where neural networks have shown value. However, speech processing, in particular for the purposes of speech recognition, probably has been the most active area. Many different approaches to tackling the speech recognition problem using neural networks have been reported. For an extensive list of references, see Wu and Chan [69]. Let us look at one successful project that typifies neural network efforts in speech recognition.

Kohonen [70] developed a phonetic typewriter that takes speech and converts it to printed text using a neural network. The network is a speaker-dependent speech recognition system for continuous speech with unlimited vocabulary. It also can be applied for isolated word recognition. The network was trained in an unsupervised fashion to recognize phonemes. During training, the speaker spoke 100 words for 10 minutes. The spectral power of 15 different frequency bands obtained from a fast Fourier transform analysis was provided to the network. The network then formed as output clusters of phonemes through a self-organizing training process. During testing, the system provided 92–97% accuracy for continuous speech recognition and 98% for isolated word recognition.

Neural network activity in the finance sector has been very active lately. A number of publications have discussed applications of neural-based fraud detection, trading, portfolio management, and bond ratings. In 1993, the newsletter *New Science* [71] reported that over two thirds of the companies in this sector have had at least a few people investigating neural technology over the past five years, and one in five has developed a neural network. This area lends itself well to the strengths of neural networks, given their ability to work with multiple inputs, complex interactions, and past historical data, and their capability to adapt to new and changing conditions.

A good example of a neural network application in this area is the TOPIX forecasting system. Nikko Securities of Tokyo has a number of mathematical models for predicting the future value of the Tokyo Stock Exchange prices indices (TOPIX) stock market indicator. The TOPIX is a weighted average of market prices of all the stocks listed in the first section of the Tokyo Stock Exchange. It is weighted by the number of stocks issued to each company. Being able to predict the future value of this stock index offers an important investment opportunity. Nikko wanted to explore the potential of applying a neural network to predict the future value of this index. Nikko asked Fujitsu Laboratories to develop a neural network to forecast the future index value one month in advance and to use this value to produce a present buy or sell signal. Fujitsu used several technical indicators and market conditions as input to the network. The technical indicators included such items as stock turnover rates. The market conditions included information on foreign exchange rates, the Dow-Jones industrial average, and interest rates. The network's output is a single number between 0 and 1, where 0 represents a strong sell signal and 1 represents a strong buy signal. In simulated tests using data from January 1987 to July 1989, the network produced an annualized rate of return of 31.7%, far exceeding the performance of existing investment models at Nikko Securities.

Neural networks have particular value in applications where it is difficult or impossible to uncover relationships in parameters using traditional statistical means. In addition, in situations where data are noisy or incomplete, a neural network still can produce reasonable results. Some problems also can be solved much quicker through neural techniques than through other programming methods. For example, in an application to convert written text into speech, the neural network NETalk developed by Sejnowski and Rosenberg [72] took a only few weeks to build, whereas the rule-based program DECtalk developed by the Digital Equipment Corporation, which addresses the same problem, took several years to complete. To probe further on neural network theory, applications, and design, see [31, 73–77].

VIII. SUMMARY

Over the past 20 years, the knowledge engineer's toolbox has continued to grow to the point where today it contains a powerful set of tools for building expert systems to manage real-world problems across a wide range of application areas. Each tool offers unique features that make it well suited for certain types of problems. An experienced knowledge engineer knows not only how to use a given tool, but when the tool is appropriate: A craftsman. Though valuable today, tomorrow's toolbox should be much more powerful as we learn ways to improve our existing tools and add new ones to handle problems beyond our present reach.

We are the forgers of our tools. We shape them for our own purposes, but in many ways, they also shape us. As we use them, they tend to shape our conception of our world and show us ways that we might improve it. This interaction is an essential aspect of the evolution of human knowledge. We first develop a tool to assist us in some job. As we use it, the tool itself seems to suggest new ideas, leading to new questions and, ultimately, to the development of new tools. We learn from this experience how to change and improve; that is, *I do and I understand.*

Edward Feigenbaum of Stanford University shared this view when discussing AI tools. He has often said that he learns the most when he throws AI techniques against the wall of hard problems to see where they break. Many of the early AI tools worked well on toy applications such as Arthur Samuel's checkers-playing program and Claude Shannon's chess-playing program. However, these early tools did not scale up well enough to handle hard problems in science, engineering, and medicine. These early failures led to critical questions and eventually to the development of more robust methods.

In the near future, our existing tools should continue to serve us well. We should see a large increase in deployed expert systems built using them. We should also see the application of tools outside of their common habitats. For example, fuzzy logic has found a home in control applications, but we should see more use of the technology for information processing. The marriage of tools will be a part of our future. We already have seen applications where our tools work in concert, adding terms like neurofuzzy and neurogenetic to our vocabulary. This trend will no doubt continue where designers will blend the advantages of various tools, creating an effective synergy.

One of the most exciting parts of the more distant future will be to watch the birth of new AI tools. Researchers in AI are doing the heavy lifting in the quest for an intelligent machine. The expert systems community is the benefactor of this research, by inheriting effective intelligent programming methods. Future researchers, many who have not been born yet, will see things that we have not seen and will use their vision to create new tools to enable the development of more intelligent machines. Our toolbox will then grow and so will we.

REFERENCES

1. Durkin, J. *Expert Systems: Catalog of Applications.* Intelligent Computer Systems, Inc., Akron, OH, 1993.
2. Shortliffe, E. H. *Computer-Based Medical Consultation, MYCIN.* Elsevier, New York, 1976.
3. McDermott, J. R1: An expert system in the computer systems domain. In *Proceedings of AAAI-80,* 1980.
4. Shortliffe, E. H. and Buchanan, B. G. A model of inexact reasoning in medicine. *Math. Biosci.* 23:351–379, 1975.
5. Bonissone, P. Editorial: Reasoning with uncertainty in expert systems. *Int. J. Man-Mach. Stud.* 22:241–250, 1985.
6. Giarratano, J. and Riley, G. *Expert Systems: Principles and Programming.* PWS–Kent, Boston, 1989.
7. Neapolitan, R. E. Models for reasoning under uncertainty, *Appl. Artif. Intel.* 1(4):337–366, 1987.
8. Durkin, J. *Expert Systems: Design and Development.* Prentice-Hall, Englewood Cliffs, NJ, 1994.
9. Baas, L. and Bourne, J. R. A rule-based microcomputer system for electroencephalogram evaluation. *IEEE Trans. Biomed. Eng.* BME-31(10), 1984.
10. Turban, E. *Decision Support and Expert Systems.* Macmillan, New York, 1990.
11. Ezquerra, N. F., Shapiro, S., Garcia, E. V., DePuey, E. G., and Hise, H. L. A knowledge-based system for interpreting cardiovascular nuclear medicine images. In *Proceedings of Computers in Cardiology*, IEEE Computer Society, Boston, MA, 1986, pp. 3–8.
12. Engelmore, R. and Morgan, T. *Blackboard Systems.* Addison–Wesley, Reading, MA, 1988.
13. Erman, L. D. The HEARSAY-II speech understanding system: Integrating knowledge to resolve uncertainties. *Comput. Surveys* 12(2):213–253, 1980.
14. Durkin, J. DUSTPRO: A distributed expert system for coal mine dust control, In *ESD/SMI Second Annual Expert Systems Conference*, Detroit, MI, 1988, pp. 377–385.
15. Pedersen, K. *Expert System Programming: Practical Techniques for Rule-Based Systems.* Wiley, New York, 1989.
16. Harmon, P. and Sawyer, B. *Creating Expert Systems for Business and Industry.* Wiley, New York, 1990.
17. Giarratano, J. and Riley, G. *Expert Systems: Principles and Programming.* PWS–Kent, Boston, 1994.
18. Bartlett, F. C. *Remembering: A Study in Experimental and Social Psychology*, Cambridge Univ. Press, 1932.
19. Minsky, M. L. Frame system theory. In *Thinking: Readings in Cognitive Science* (P. N. Johnson-Laird and P. C. Watson, Eds.). Cambridge Univ. Press, Cambridge, UK, 1975.
20. Aikens, J. S. A representation scheme using both frames and rules. In *Rule-Based Expert Systems* (B. G. Buchanan and E. H. Shortliffe, Eds.), pp. 424–440, Addison–Wesley, Reading, MA, 1984.
21. Widman, L. E., Loparo, K. A., and Nielson, N. R., Eds. *Artificial Intelligence Simulation and Modeling.* Wiley, New York, 1989.
22. Williams, M. D., Hollan, J. D., and Stevens, A. L. Human reasoning about a simple physical system. In *Mental Models* (D. Genter and A. Stevens, Eds.), pp. 131–153. Erlbaum, Hillsdale, NJ, 1983.
23. Yeager, R. Norske Skog calls in the experts, *Pulp Pap. Int.* 32(12):55–57, 1989.

24. Aguirre-Cervantes, J. and Sahagun, R. CELLOS: An expert system for diagnosis of quality defects in cellophane film production. In *Operational Expert System Applications in Mexico* (F. J. Cantu-Ortiz, Ed.). Pergamon Press, Elmsford, NY, 1991.
25. Kestelyn, J. Application watch. *AI Expert* 5(11):71, 1990.
26. Rauch-Hindin, W. B. *A Guide to Commercial Artificial Intelligence: Fundamentals and Real-World Applications*. Prentice–Hall, Englewood Cliffs, NJ, 1988.
27. Rescher, N. *Many-Valued Logic*. McGraw-Hill, New York, 1969.
28. Zadeh, L. A. Fuzzy sets. *Inform. Control* 8, 338–353, 1965.
29. Mamdani, E. H. and Assilian, S. An experiment in linguistic synthesis with a fuzzy controller. *Int. J. Man-Mach. Stud.* 7(1):1–13, 1975.
30. Holmblad, L. P. and Ostergaard, J. J. Control of a cement kiln by fuzzy logic. In *Fuzzy Information and Decision Processes* (M. M. Gupta and E. Sanchez, Eds.), pp. 398–409. North-Holland, Amsterdam, 1982.
31. Kosko, B. *Neural Networks and Fuzzy Systems*. Prentice–Hall, Englewood Cliffs, NJ, 1992.
32. Kosko, B. *Fuzzy Engineering*. Prentice–Hall, Englewood Cliffs, NJ, 1997.
33. Self, K. Designing with fuzzy logic. *IEEE Spectrum* 27:42–44, 1990.
34. Waller, L. Fuzzy logic: It's comprehensible, it's practical, and it's commercial, *Electronics* 102–103, 1989.
35. Kaplan, G. Industrial electronics. *IEEE Spectrum* 47, 1992.
36. Yasunobu, S., Miyamoto, S., and Ihara, H. Fuzzy control for automatic train operation system. In *Proceedings of the 4th IFAC/FIP/FORS International Conference on Control in Transportation Systems*. Baden-Baden Germany, 1983, pp. 33–39.
37. Caudill, M. Using neural nets: Fuzzy decisions. *AI Expert* 5(4):59–64, 1990.
38. Jamshidi, M., Vadiee, N., and Ross, T. *Fuzzy Logic and Control*. Prentice–Hall, Englewood Cliffs, NJ, 1993.
39. Ross, T. *Fuzzy Logic with Engineering Applications*. McGraw-Hill, New York, 1995.
40. Wang, L. *A Course in Fuzzy Systems and Control*. Prentice–Hall, Englewood Cliffs, NJ, 1997.
41. Winston, P. Learning structural descriptions from examples. In *The Psychology of Computer Vision*. McGraw-Hill, New York, 1975.
42. Buchanan, B. and Mitchell, T. Model-directed learning of production rules, In *Pattern-Directed Inference Systems* (D. Waterman and F. Hayes-Roth, Eds.). Academic Press, New York, 1978.
43. Michalski, R. and Chilausky, R. Learning by being told and learning from examples: An experimental comparison of the two methods of knowledge acquisition in the context of developing an expert system for soybean disease diagnosis. *Policy Anal. Inform. Syst.* 4(2):125–260, 1980.
44. Quinlan, J. R. Discovering rules from large collections of examples: A case study. In *Expert Systems in the Micro-Electronic Age* (D. Michie, Ed.). Edinburgh Univ. Press, Edinburgh, 1979.
45. Braun, H. and Chandler, J. S. Predicting stock market behavior through rule induction: An application of the learning-from-example approach. *Decision Sciences* 8(3):415–429, 1987.
46. Tam, K. Inducing stock screening rules for portfolio construction. *J. Oper. Res. Soc.* 42(9):747–757, 1991.
47. Michie, D., Muggleton, S., Riese, C., and Zubrick, S. RULEMASTER: A second-generation knowledge-engineering facility. In *Proceedings of the First Conference on Artificial Intelligence Applications*, IEEE Computer Society, 1984.
48. Quinlan, J. R. *Machine Learning: An Artificial Intelligence Approach* (R. Michalski, J. Carbonell, and T. Mitchell, Eds.). Morgan Kaufmann, Los Altos, CA, 1986.
49. Shapiro, A. D. *Structured Induction in Expert Systems*. Addison-Wesley, Reading, MA, 1987.
50. Durkin, J. Designing an induction expert system. *AI Expert* 6(12):29–35, 1991.
51. Kolodner, J. *Case-Based Reasoning*. Morgan Kaufmann, San Mateo, CA, 1993.
52. Schank, R. *Dynamic Memory: A Theory of Learning in Computers and People*. Cambridge Univ. Press, New York, 1982.
53. Kolodner, J. Maintaining organization in a dynamic long-term memory. *Cognitive Sci.* 7(4), 1983.
54. Simoudis, E. Knowledge acquisition in validated retrieval. *Int. J. Expert Syst.* 4(3), 299–315, 1991.
55. Rissland, E. L. and Ashley, K. D. Hypotheticals as heuristic device. In *Proceedings of AAAI-89*, pp. 289–297. Morgan Kaufmann, San Mateo, CA, 1986.
56. Bain, W. M., Case-based reasoning: A computer model of subjective assessment. Ph.D. Thesis, Yale University, 1986.

57. Hennessy, D. H. and Hinkle, D. Applying case-based reasoning to autoclave loading. *IEEE Expert* 7(5):21–26, 1992.
58. Riesbeck C. H. and Schank, R. C. *Inside Case-Based Reasoning*. Erlbaum, Hillsdale, NJ, 1989.
59. McCulloch, W. S. and Pitts, W. A logical calculus of the ideas imminent in nervous activity. *Bull. Math. Biol.* 5:115–133, 1943.
60. Hebb, D. *The Organization of Behavior: A Neuropsychological Theory*. Wiley, New York, 1949.
61. Rosenblatt, F. The perceptron: A probabilistic model for information storage and organization in the brain. *Psychol. Rev.* 65:386–408, 1958.
62. Widrow, B. and Hoff, M. E. Adaptive switching circuits. In *IRE WESCON Convention Record,* Part 4, pp. 96–104, IRE, New York, 1960.
63. Minsky, M. and Papert, S. A. *Perceptrons*. MIT Press, Cambridge, MA, 1969.
64. Hopfield, J. J. Neurons with graded response have collected computational properties like those of two-state neurons. *Proc. Nat. Acad. Sci. U.S.A.* 81:3088–3092, 1982.
65. Rumelhart, D. E. and McClelland, J. L. Eds. *Parallel Distributed Processing Explorations in the Microstructure of Cognition,* Vol. 1. MIT Press, Cambridge, MA, 1986.
66. Winston, P. *Artificial Intelligence.* Addison–Wesley, Reading, MA, 1992.
67. Pomerleau, D. A. ALVINN: An autonomous land vehicle in a neural network. In *Advances in Neural Information Processing Systems I* (D. Touretzky, Ed.), Morgan Kaufmann, San Mateo, CA., 1989.
68. Bishop, C. M. *Neural Networks for Pattern Recognition*, Oxford Univ. Press, New York, 1995.
69. Wu, J. X. and Chan, C. Isolated word recognition by neural network models with cross-correlation coefficients for speech dynamics. *IEEE Trans. Pattern Anal. Mach. Intel.* 15:1174–1185, 1993.
70. Kohonen, T. The neural phonetic typewriter. *IEEE Comput.* 21:11–22, 1988.
71. New Science. *Applied Intelligent Systems Response Selections Management Summary*. New Science, Inc., Westport, CT, 1993.
72. Sejnowski, T. J. and Rosenberg, C. R. Parallel networks that learn to pronounce English text. *Complex Syst.* 1:145–168, 1987.
73. Wasserman, P. *Neural Computing: Theory and Practice.* Van Nostrand–Reinhold, New York, 1989.
74. Hecht-Nielsen, R. *Neurocomputing*. Addison–Wesley, Reading, MA, 1989.
75. Dayhoff, J. *Neural Network Architectures*, Van Nostrand–Reinhold, New York, 1990.
76. Hagan, M. T., Demuth, H. B., and Beale, M. *Neural Network Design*. PWS–Kent, Boston, 1996.
77. Bose, N. K. and Liang, P. *Neural Network Fundamentals with Graphs, Algorithms, and Applications*. McGraw-Hill, New York, 1996.

3

DEVELOPMENT AND APPLICATIONS OF DECISION TREES

HUSSEIN ALMUALLIM

Information and Computer Science Department, King Fahd University of Petroleum & Minerals, Dhahran 31261, Saudi Arabia

SHIGEO KANEDA

Graduate School of Policy and Management, Doshisha University, Imadegawa-Karasuma-Higashi-iru, Kamigyou-ku, Kyoto 602-8580, Japan

YASUHIRO AKIBA

ATR Spoken Language Translation Research Laboratories, Souraku-gun, Kyoto 619-0288, Japan

Expert Systems, Edited by Cornelius T. Leondes, Volume 1

ISBN: 0-12-443881-4 / $35.00

I. INTRODUCTION

A critical issue in artificial intelligence research is to overcome the so-called "knowledge-acquisition bottleneck" in the construction of knowledge-based systems. Experience in typical real-world domains has shown that the conventional approach of extracting knowledge directly from human experts is associated with many problems and shortcomings. Interviews with experts are usually slow, inefficient, and frustrating for experts and knowledge engineers alike [1]. This is particularly true in those application domains in which decisions made by experts are "intuitive" ones, guided by imprecise and imperfect knowledge. In such domains, different experts may make substantially different judgments, and even the same expert may not give the same solution when confronted with the same problem twice over a period of time. These problems become more acute when dealing with large knowledge-based systems in which upgrading the knowledge base, fixing previous erroneous knowledge, and maintaining integrity are extremely challenging tasks.

A promising approach to ease the knowledge-acquisition bottleneck is to employ some learning mechanism to extract the desired knowledge automatically or semiautomatically from actual cases or *examples* that have been previously handled by the domain experts. This *machine learning* approach enjoys several advantages: (i) In problems for which knowledge is expert-dependent, one can simply learn from examples handled by different experts, with the hope that this will *average* the differences among different experts. (ii) Being able to construct knowledge automatically makes the upgrading task easier because one can rerun the learning system as more examples accumulate. Some learning methods are indeed "incremental" in nature. (iii) Machine learning can be applied to problems for which no experts exist. This is the case in data mining and knowledge discovery in databases, for which machine learning techniques are employed to automatically discover *new* knowledge.

Considerable attention has been devoted by the machine learning research community to the task of acquiring "classification knowledge" for which, among a predeclared set of available classes, the objective is to choose the most appropriate class for a given case. The goal in such research is to develop methods that induce the desired classification knowledge from a given set of preclassified examples. Significant progress has been made in the last decade toward this goal, and various methods for automatically inducing *classifiers* from data are now available. In particular, constructing classifiers in the form of decision trees has been quite popular, and a number of successful real-world applications that employ decision tree construction methods has been reported.

For knowledge-based systems, decision trees have the advantage of being comprehensible by human experts and of being directly convertible into production rules. Moreover, when used to handle a given case, a decision tree not only provides the solution for that case, but also states the reasons behind its choice. These features are very important in typical application domains in which human experts seek tools to aid in conducting their job while remaining "in the driver's seat." Another advantage of using decision trees is the ease and efficiency of their construction compared to that of other classifiers such as neural networks.

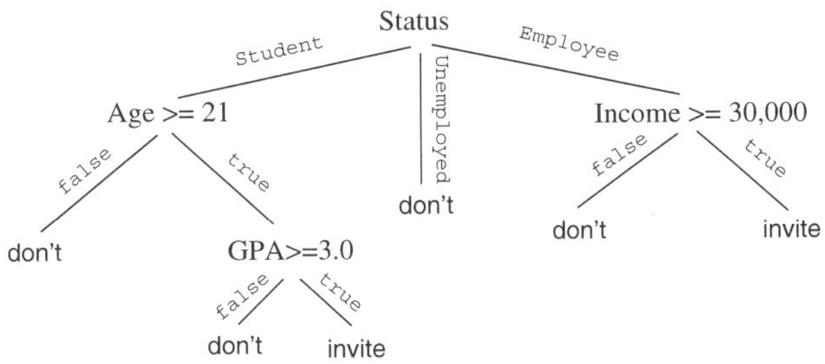

FIGURE 1 A decision tree that determines whether or not to offer a credit card invitation.

In this chapter, we first present a basic method for automatically constructing decision trees from examples and review various extensions of this basic procedure. We then give a sample of real-world applications for which the decision tree learning approach has been reported to be successful.

II. CONSTRUCTING DECISION TREES FROM EXAMPLES

A decision tree is used as a classifier for determining an appropriate action (among a predetermined set of actions) for a given case. Consider, for example, the task of targeting good candidates to be sent an invitation to apply for a credit card: given certain information about an individual, we need to determine whether or not he or she can be a candidate. In this example, information about an individual is given as a vector of *attributes* that may include sex (male or female), age, status (student, employee, or unemployed), college grade point average (GPA), annual income, social security number, etc. The allowed actions are viewed as *classes,* which are in this case to offer or not to offer an invitation. A decision tree that performs this task is sketched in Fig. 1. As the figure shows, each internal node in the tree is labeled with a "test" defined in terms of the attributes and has a branch for each possible outcome for that test, and each leaf in the tree is labeled with a class.

Attributes used for describing cases can be nominal (taking one of a prespecified set of values) or continuous. In the above example, *Sex* and *Status* are nominal attributes, whereas *Age* and *GPA* are continuous ones. Typically, a test defined on a nominal attribute has one outcome for each value of the attribute, whereas a test defined on a continuous attribute is based on a fixed threshold and has two outcomes, one for each interval as imposed by this threshold.[1] The decision tree in Fig. 1 illustrates these tests.

To find the appropriate class for a given case (individual), we start with the test at the root of the tree and keep following the branches as determined by the values of the attributes of the case at hand, until a leaf is reached. For example, suppose the attribute values for a given case are as follows:

$$\textit{Name} = \text{Andrew};\ \textit{Social Security No.} = 199199;\ \textit{Age} = 22;\ \textit{Sex} = \text{Male};$$

$$\textit{Status} = \text{Student};\ \textit{Annual Income} = 2,000;\ \textit{College GPA} = 3.39.$$

[1] Other kinds of attributes and tests also exist as will be explained later.

To classify this case, we start at the root of the tree of Fig. 1, which is labeled *Status*, and follow the branch labeled *Student* from there. Then at the test node $Age \geq 21$, we follow the *true* branch, and at the test node $GPA \geq 3.0$, we again follow the "true" branch. This leads finally to a leaf labeled "invite", indicating that this person is to be invited according to this decision tree.

Decision tree *learning* is the task of constructing a decision tree classifier, such as the one in Fig. 1, from a collection of *historical cases*. These are individuals who are already marked by experts as being good candidates or not. Each historical case is called a *training example*, or simply an *example*, and the collection of such examples from which a decision tree is to be constructed is called a *training sample*. A training example is assumed to be represented as a pair $\langle X, c\rangle$, where X is a vector of attribute values describing some case, and c is the appropriate class for that case. A collection of examples for the credit card task is shown in Fig. 2. The following subsections describe how a decision tree can be constructed from such a collection of training examples.

A. A Basic Tree Construction Procedure

Let $S = \{\langle X_1, c_1\rangle, \langle X_2, c_2\rangle, \ldots, \langle X_k, c_k\rangle\}$ be a training sample. Constructing a decision tree form S can be done in a divide-and-conquer fashion as follows:

Step 1: If all the examples in S are labeled with the same class, return a leaf labeled with that class.

Step 2: Choose some test t (according to some criterion) that has two or more mutually exclusive outcomes $\{o_1, o_2, \ldots, o_r\}$.

Step 3: Partition S into disjoint subsets $S_1, S_2, \ldots, S_r$, such that S_i consists of those examples having outcome o_i for the test t, for $i = 1, 2, \ldots, r$.

Step 4: Call this tree-construction procedure recursively on each of the subsets $S_1, S_2, \ldots, S_r$, and let the decision trees returned by these recursive calls be $T_1, T_2, \ldots, T_r$.

Step 5: Return a decision tree T with a node labeled t as the root and the trees $T_1, T_2, \ldots, T_r$ as subtrees below that node.

For illustration, let us apply the above procedure on the set of examples of Fig. 2. We will use the Case IDs 1–15 (listed in the first column) to refer to each of these examples.

- $S = \{1, 2, 3, \ldots, 15\}$ has a mixture of classes, so we proceed to Step 2.
- Suppose we use the attribute *Status* for our test. This test has three outcomes, "*Student*", "Unemployed", and "Employee". It partitions S into the subsets $S_1 = \{1, 4, 6, 7, 9, 10, 11\}$, $S_2 = \{5, 8, 12, 13\}$, and $S_3 = \{2, 3, 14, 15\}$, respectively, for these outcomes.
- Note that S_1 has a mixture of classes. Suppose we choose the test $Age \geq 21$?. This test partitions S_1 into $S_{11} = \{6, 10\}$ for the *false* outcome and $S_{12} = \{1, 4, 7, 9, 11\}$ for the *true* outcome.
- $S_{11} = \{6, 10\}$ has just one class "don't", so a leaf labeled with this class is returned for the call on S_{11}.
- For the set S_{12}, which has a mixture of classes, if we choose $GPA \geq 3.0$?, then the set will be partitioned into $S_{121} = \{7, 9\}$ and $S_{122} = \{1, 4, 11\}$.

Case ID	*Name*	*Social Security No.*	*Age*	*Sex*	*Status*	*Income*	*GPA*	Class
1	John	123321	22	Male	Student	3,000	3.22	Invite
2	Mary	343422	38	Female	Employee	32,000	2.00	Invite
3	Ali	876345	46	Male	Employee	69,000	2.90	Invite
4	Lee	673245	23	Male	Student	3,500	3.1	Invite
5	Ted	451087	45	Male	Unemployed	5,000	3.1	Don't
6	Nick	239847	19	Male	Student	1,300	3.8	Don't
7	Liz	229951	23	Female	Student	12,000	2.8	Don't
8	Debby	234819	33	Female	Unemployed	5,000	0.00	Don't
9	Pat	258199	32	Male	Student	1,000	2.1	Don't
10	Peter	813672	20	Male	Student	32,000	3.9	Don't
11	Dona	501184	23	Female	Student	6,600	3.3	Invite
12	Jim	619458	40	Male	Unemployed	35,000	3.3	Don't
13	Kim	654397	31	Female	Unemployed	14,000	3.0	Don't
14	Pan	350932	59	Male	Employee	29,000	2.8	Don't
15	Mike	357922	33	Male	Employee	19,000	2.6	Don't

FIGURE 2 Examples for the credit card task.

- The calls on the sets S_{121} and S_{122} will return leaves labeled "don't" and "invite", respectively, and thus, the call on the set S_{12} will return the subtree of Fig. 3a.
- Now that we are done with the recursive calls on S_{11} and S_{12}, the call on the set S_1 will return the subtree of Fig. 3b.
- The call on the set S_2 will return a leaf labeled "don't".
- For S_3, which contains a mixture of classes, suppose we choose the test *Income* $\geq 30,000$?. This will partition S_3 into $S_{31} = \{14, 15\}$ for the *false* outcome and $S_{32} = \{2, 3\}$ for the *true* outcome.
- The recursive calls on S_{31} and S_{32} will return leaves labeled "don't" and "invite", respectively, and thus, the call on S_3 will return the subtree of Fig. 3c.
- Finally, the call on the entire training sample S will return the tree of Fig. 1.

Obviously, the quality of the tree produced by the above top-down construction procedure of decision trees depends mainly on how tests are chosen in Step 2.

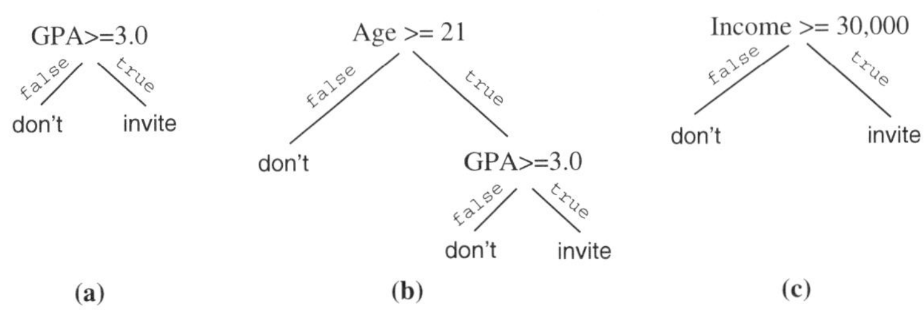

FIGURE 3 Subtrees returned by recursive calls on subsets of the training examples for credit card invitations.

Moreover, the stopping criterion of Step 1 (which requires that the passed set of training examples have a single class) may not be the best strategy to quit recursion and stop growing the tree. We will elaborate on these points in the following subsection and in Section IV.

B. Which Test to Select?

Regardless of the test selection criterion adopted in Step 2 of the above tree-construction procedure, the procedure would eventually lead to a decision tree that is *consistent* with the training examples. That is, for any training example $\langle X, c\rangle \in S$, the learned tree gives c as the class for X. Nevertheless, the tree-building process is not intended to merely do well for the training examples themselves. Rather, the goal is to build (among many possible consistent trees) a tree that reveals the underlying structure of the domain, so that it can be used to "predict" the class of new examples not included in the training sample and can also be used by human experts to gain useful insight about the application domain. Therefore, some careful criterion should be employed for test selection in Step 2 so that important tests (such as *Income* and *Status* in our credit card example) are preferred and irrelevant ones (such as *Name* and *Sex*) are ignored. Ideally, one would like the final tree to be as compact as possible, because this is an indication that attention has been focused on the most relevant tests.

Unfortunately, finding the most compact decision tree is an intractable problem (as shown in [2]), so one has to resort to heuristics that help in finding a "reasonably small" one. The basic idea is to measure the importance of a test by estimating how much influence it has on the classification of the examples. In this way, correct classification is obtained using a small number of tests, meaning that all paths in the tree will be short and the tree as a whole will be small.

Note that, at any stage, the absolutely best test would be a test that partitions the passed training sample S into subsets $S_1, S_2, \ldots, S_r$ such that each subset S_i contains examples that are all of the same class (such subsets are called "pure"). Choosing such a test would immediately lead us to stop further recursive partitioning. The goodness of a test can thus be estimated on the basis of how close it is to this "perfect" behavior. In other words, the higher the purity of the subsets $S_1, S_2, \ldots, S_r$ resulting from a test t, the better that test is.

A popular practice in applying this idea is to measure the expected amount of information provided by the test based on information theory. Given a sample S, the average amount of information needed to find the class of a case in S is estimated by the function

$$\text{info}(S) = -\sum_{i=1}^{k} \frac{|S^i|}{|S|} \times \log_2 \frac{|S^i|}{|S|} \text{ bits},$$

where $S^i \subseteq S$ is the set of examples S of class i and k is the number of classes. For example, when $k = 2$ and when S has equal numbers of examples of each class, the above quantity evaluates to 1, indicating that knowing the class of a case in S is "worth" one bit. On the other hand, if all the examples is S are of the same class, then the quantity evaluates to 0, because knowing the class of a case in S provides no information. In general, the above non-negative quantity (known as the *entropy* of the set S) is maximized when all the classes are of the same frequency and is equal to 0 when S is pure, that is, when all the examples is S are of the same class.

Suppose that t is a test that partitions S into $S_1, S_2, \ldots, S_r$; then the *weighted average entropy* over these subsets is computed by

$$\sum_{i=1}^{r} \frac{|S_i|}{|S|} \times \text{info}(S_i).$$

Evaluation of the test t can then be based on the quantity

$$\text{gain}(t) = \text{info}(S) - \sum_{i=1}^{r} \frac{|S_i|}{|S|} \times \text{info}(S_i)$$

which measures the reduction in entropy obtained if test t is applied. This quantity, called the *information gain* of t, is widely used as the basis for test selection during the construction of a decision tree.

For illustration, let us compute the gain of the test on the nominal attribute *Status* in the set of training examples of Fig. 2. In this set of examples, there are 5 and 10 examples of the classes "invite" and "don't", respectively. Therefore, the entropy of the set is computed as

$$-\frac{5}{15}\log_2\frac{5}{15} - \frac{10}{15}\log_2\frac{10}{15} = 0.918 \text{ bits.}$$

The test on *Status* partitions the set into three subsets, $S_1 = \{1, 4, 6, 7, 9, 10, 11\}$, $S_2 = \{5, 8, 12, 13\}$, and $S_3 = \{2, 3, 14, 15\}$. In S_1 there are 3 and 4 examples of the classes "invite" and "don't", respectively. Therefore, the entropy of S_1 is computed as

$$-\frac{3}{7}\log_2\frac{3}{7} - \frac{4}{7}\log_2\frac{4}{7} = 0.985 \text{ bits.}$$

All the examples of S_2 are of one class "don't", and thus the entropy of this set is 0. Finally in S_3, there are 2 examples of each of the classes "invite" and "don't". Therefore, the entropy of S_3 is

$$-\frac{2}{4}\log_2\frac{2}{4} - \frac{2}{4}\log_2\frac{2}{4} = 1 \text{ bit.}$$

Thus, the weighted average entropy after applying the test "status" becomes

$$\frac{7}{15} \times 0.985 + \frac{4}{15} \times 0 + \frac{4}{15} \times 1 = 0.726 \text{ bits,}$$

and the gain of this test is

$$0.918 - 0.726 = 0.192 \text{ bits.}$$

To select the most informative test, the above computation is repeated for all the available tests and the test with the maximum information gain is then selected.

Although the information gain test selection criterion has been experimentally shown to lead to good decision trees in many cases, it was found to be biased in favor of tests that induce finer partitions [3]. As an extreme example, consider the (meaningless) tests defined on attributes *Name* and *Social Security Number* in our

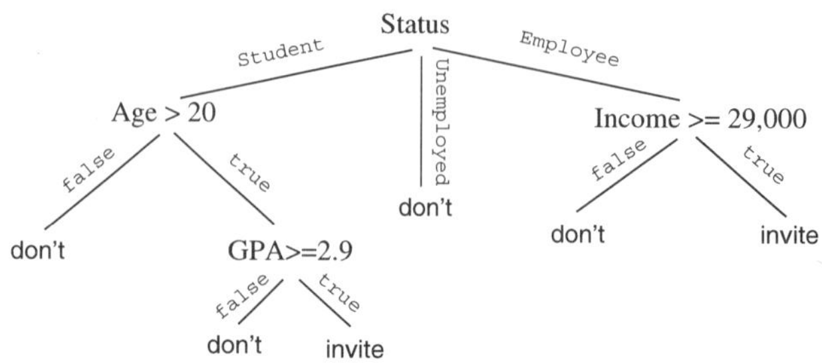

FIGURE 4 Decision tree learned from the credit card training examples using information gain as the test selection criterion.

credit card application. These tests would partition the training sample into a large number of subsets, each containing just one example. Because these subsets do not have a mixture of examples, their entropy is just 0, and so the information gain of using these trivial tests is maximal.

This bias in the gain criterion can be rectified by dividing the information gain of a test by the entropy of the test outcomes themselves, which measures the extent of splitting done by the test [3]

$$\text{split}(t) = -\sum_{i=1}^{r} \frac{|S_i|}{|S|} \log \frac{|S_i|}{|S|},$$

giving the *gain-ratio* measure

$$\text{gain-ratio}(t) = \frac{\text{gain}(t)}{\text{split}(t)}.$$

Note that split(t) is higher for tests that partition the examples into a large number of small subsets. Therefore, although the tests on the *Name* and *Social Security Number* attributes have high gain, dividing by split(t) in the above manner inflicts a high "penalty" on their scores, not allowing them to be selected.

Applying the basic tree-construction procedure to the set of examples of Fig. 2, using the gain-ratio as the criterion for test selection, leads to the decision tree given in Fig. 4.[2]

III. EVALUATION OF A LEARNED DECISION TREE

In evaluating a decision tree, it is necessary to distinguish between the *training error* of a decision tree, which is the percentage of *training* examples that are misclassified by the tree, and the *generalization error*, which is the probability that a randomly selected *new* case is misclassified by that tree. This latter quantity measures the tree's prediction power, and thus, it is a reasonable measure of how well the learning process was able to capture the underlying regularities of the application domain.

[2] Although the gain-ratio test selection criterion is the most widely used in decision tree learning, many other criteria are found in the literature. For experimental comparisons of various criteria see [4–6].

The generalization error is usually estimated by *cross-validation* where the available set of preclassified examples is randomly divided into *training* and *test* sets. Only the training set is used during tree construction. For each example in the test set, the class *predicted* by the learned tree is compared to the *actual* class as given in the test set. The percentage of misclassified examples is then used as an approximation of the generalization error.

Note that in the above procedure, different partitions of the examples into training and test sets may lead to different error estimates. A common practice to avoid this sensitivity to partitioning is to perform *m-fold* cross-validation. Here, the data are partitioned into m disjoint subsets of sizes that are as equal as possible. Then, one of these subsets is kept aside as a test set, and the remaining examples are used as a training set. This is repeated m times, each time using a different subset as a test set, so that each of the m subsets is used exactly once as a test set. The resulting errors are then averaged over the m runs to get the final approximation of the generalization error.

Usually, m is chosen to be about 10. A special case of m-fold cross-validation is when m is equal to the number of examples, in which case, the test set each time will have exactly one example. This is usually called the *leave-one-out* method.

IV. OVERFITTING AVOIDANCE

A major concern in decision tree construction is the risk of "overfitting" the training data. In most practical applications, the training cases are usually expected to have some level of *noise*, that is, some incorrect attribute measurements and/or class labels. In such situations, taking the training examples "too seriously" by attempting to completely eliminate the training error eventually leads to a decision tree that deviates from the actual underlying regularities of the application domain by modeling the noise present in the training examples. Consequently, this overfitting of the training examples would hurt the generalization performance as well as the intelligibility of the learned tree.

By assuming no conflicts in the training examples (no two identical training cases are labeled with different classes), Step 1 of the tree construction procedure ensures that the tree classifies all the training cases correctly; that is, zero training error is guaranteed. However, splitting of the training examples eventually makes the number of examples available at lower nodes too small to evaluate the available test reasonably. If we insist on growing the tree all the way until pure leaves are reached, this will result in an overly complex decision tree that (although it fits the training examples well) is expected to have a high generalization error.

Experience in decision tree learning has shown that it is often the case that smaller trees that are less consistent with the training examples can outperform (in terms of generalization error) more complex trees that fit the training examples perfectly. Simplifying decision trees to avoid overfitting of the data is usually achieved by the process of *pruning*, which is the removal of those lower parts of the tree where tests are chosen based on an inadequately small number of examples. Pruning can take place during the construction of the tree or by modifying an already constructed complex tree. These approaches are sometimes called *prepruning* and *postpruning*, respectively.

In the prepruning approach, splitting of the sample is stopped as soon as we reach a conclusion that further growing of the tree is not useful. This is done by changing Step 1 of the tree-construction procedure to be as follows:

Step 1: If one of the *stopping conditions* is satisfied, return a leaf labeled with the *most frequent class* in S.

For example, early stopping of the recursive splitting process may be forced in the following situations:

- When the information gain score for all the available tests falls below a certain threshold, and so, further error reduction is not expected using these tests.
- When all the available tests are statistically found to be irrelevant. Based on the χ^2 test, the procedure neglects any test whose irrelevance cannot be rejected with high confidence.

In practice, however, it is usually hard to design good stopping rules with perfect thresholds so that splitting is terminated at just the right time. This fact makes the other approach, postpruning, more popular. In this approach, the tree-construction procedure is allowed initially to keep growing the tree, leading eventually to an overly complex decision tree. This tree is then simplified by explicitly substituting some of its subtrees by leaves.

When plenty of training examples are available, one can divide these into two sets: one used as a training sample for the actual construction of the tree and the other used as a test sample for assessing the performance of the tree, that is, its generalization error on unseen cases. Replacement of subtrees by leaves can then be carried out such that this estimated generalization error is minimized. This can be done using the OPT-2 algorithm introduced in [7], which for any given error level finds the smallest tree whose error is within that level.

Constructing the decision tree based only on a subset of the available training examples, however, is not an attractive approach when the number of available examples is not large (which is usually the case in practice). There are two well-known approaches to get around this problem.

- **Cost-complexity pruning with cross-validation** [8]: Under this approach, a score for a given decision tree is computed as a weighted sum of its complexity (number of leaves) and its training error. Note that for any fixed weighting, lower complexity means higher training error and vice versa. The goal of this approach is to strike a good balance between the tree size and its training error, that is, to minimize the weighted sum of these quantities for some appropriate weighting. Such weighting is determined through cross-validation over the set of the training examples: the training examples are randomly divided into, say, m equally sized subsets (usually $m = 10$). The examples of $m - 1$ subsets of these are used to construct a decision tree, and the mth subset is used to estimate the generalization error of various pruned trees generated from the learned decision tree. This is repeated m times, using each of the m subsets exactly once for the evaluation of the pruned trees. The appropriate weighting is then taken as the weighting that minimizes the average error over the m runs. Then, once this appropriate weighting is determined, a decision tree is learned from the entire training sample (all the m subsets), and by using that appropriate weighting, the pruned tree that minimizes the weighted sum of the complexity and training error is returned.

- **Reduced-error pruning** [3]: Quinlan introduced the idea of computing at each leaf an amount U such that the probability that the generalization error rate at the leaf exceeds U is very small (with respect to some preset confidence factor). The amount U is then used as an estimate of the generalization error at that leaf, and pruning is based on this estimate. That is, a subtree is replaced by a leaf if the estimated error is reduced by such an action.

V. EXTENSIONS TO THE BASIC PROCEDURE

A. Handling Various Attribute Types

In Section II.B we explained how scores are computed for the available tests in Step 2 of the tree-construction procedure to choose the most significant test for the current node in the decision tree. The actual computation of a test score depends on the type of the attribute used in that test. The computation is straightforward for a test defined on a nominal attribute having a reasonably small number of values. All that is needed is to partition the training sample according to this attribute, to compute the class frequency in each of the resulting subsets, and then to apply the gain-ratio formula directly. Score computation for other attribute types, however, may be more involved as discussed below.

1. Continuous Attributes

At a first glance, it may seem that continuous attributes are difficult to handle because arbitrary thresholds lead to an infinite number of tests to be considered. This is not true, however. For a given attribute x, suppose that we sort the training examples according to the values of x in each example. For two consecutive examples e_1 and e_2, using any threshold θ that lies between the values of x in e_1 and e_2 would obviously lead to the same partitioning of the training examples. All these thresholds are, thus, equivalent as far as the training examples are concerned because they lead to exactly the same tree. Therefore, one has to consider only one "representative" threshold from each interval (usually, the midpoint) between each two consecutive examples, and so the number of thresholds to be considered is not more than the number of training examples themselves.

In fact, the process can be made even more efficient based on results of Fayyad and Irani [9], in which they show that the threshold that gives the best gain-ratio score must be in some interval lying between two consecutive training examples labeled with different classes. This means that one can safely ignore any interval between two examples of the same class.

Another approach for handling continuous attributes is to *discretize* them. Based on the training examples, a sequence of "break points" is determined, and the continuous attribute is treated as a nominal one with each interval between the break points considered as one value for this attribute. Techniques for discretization of continuous attributes can be found in [9, 10].

2. Set-Valued Attributes

Unlike a nominal attribute, a *set-valued* attribute is one whose value is a *set* of strings (rather than a single string). For example:

The *Hobby* attribute for a person who likes soccer, volleyball, and skiing would have the value {*Soccer, Volleyball, Skiing*}.
The value of the *Color* attribute for a "white and black" dog is {*White, Black*}.

The sets of elements (hobbies and colors in the above examples) are not assumed to be taken from some small, predetermined set, because otherwise one could simply use a boolean attribute for each possible element (for example, an attribute *Soccer*, which indicates whether or not a person likes soccer) to replace the original set-valued attribute.

Tests for this kind of attribute take the form $s \in x$? where x is a set-valued attribute and s is a string. The outcome of this test is *true* for objects in which the string s appears in their set-value of x and *false* otherwise. For instance, in the above hobby example, a possible test is *Soccer* ∈ *Hobby*?, which is true if and only if *Soccer* is included in the set of hobbies of a person.

A procedure for finding the best test defined on a set-valued attribute x is given in [11]. The procedure computes the class frequency in the subsets that results from partitioning the training sample using a test of the form $s \in x$ for every string s that appears in the training examples within the set-values for the attribute x. These class frequencies are then used to evaluate the possible tests and return the best one.

3. Tree-Structured Attributes

In some domains, discrete attributes may be associated with *hierarchical* structures such as the *Shape* and *Color* hierarchies shown in Fig. 5. Such attributes are called *tree-structured* attributes. Only the values at the leaves of the hierarchy are observed in the training examples. That is, only values such as *Triangle, Square*, and *Star*, would appear in the training examples as values for *Shape*. These low-level values, however, may be too specific to concisely describe the underlying regularities in the domain. Consider, for example, a situation in which "colored polygons" constitute one class, and all other objects constitute another class. Suppose our goal is to construct from a given training sample a decision tree that discriminates between these two classes. If we are to use only those low-level values of the hierarchies shown in Fig. 5, that is, the values observable in the training examples, then the resulting tree would be overly complex and not at all comprehensible. Allowing tests in the tree that are defined using higher level categories from the given hierarchies (such as *Chromatic* and *Polygon* in this case) would greatly simplify the tree.

In general, tests defined using categories from hierarchies could be binary tests or have multiple outcomes. A binary test checks whether an object is an instance of a specific category. For example, the test *Shape* = *Polygon?* is a binary test that gives *true* for objects of shape *Triangle*, *Hexagon*, or *Square* and *false* otherwise. An algorithm for finding the best binary test for a given tree-structured attribute can be found in [12].

A multiple-split test corresponds to a *cut* or a *partition* in the hierarchy. For example, for the attribute *Shape* we may have a test with three outcomes {*Polygon*,

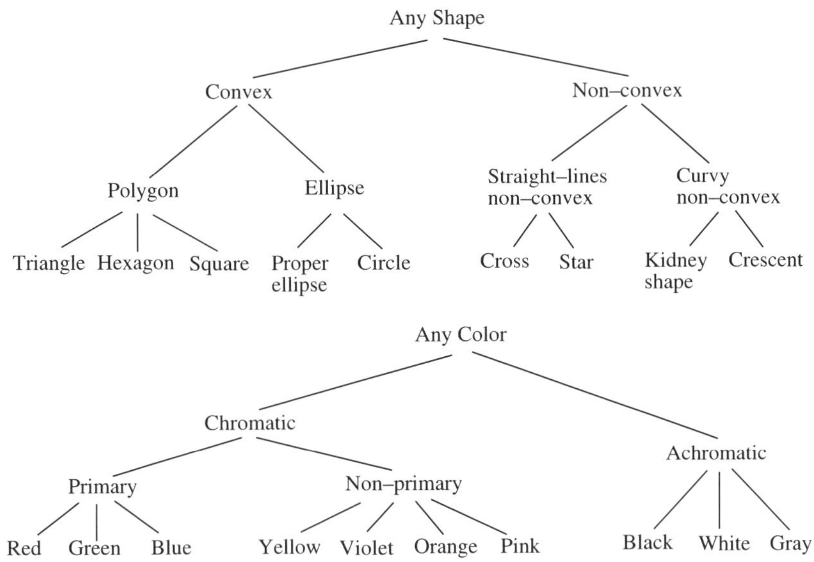

FIGURE 5 Hierarchies for *Shape* and *Color*.

Ellipse, *Nonconvex*}. In this case, objects that are *Triangle*, *Hexagon*, or *Square* give the first outcome, those that are *Proper Ellipse* or *Circle* give the second outcome, and all other objects give the third one. Note that the set of categories constituting a cut should be chosen such that any object would give exactly one outcome for the resulting test.

Finding the cut that gives the test with the best gain-ratio score for a given tree-structured attribute is a rather complicated task because the number of all possible cuts grows exponentially in the number of leaves of the associated hierarchy. An algorithm that solves this optimization problem is given in [13].

B. Incorporating More Complex Tests

In our discussion so far, we have mentioned only simple tests that are defined on a single attribute. Although the restriction to such simple tests may be justified for computational efficiency reasons, more complex tests are sometimes needed to construct decision trees with improved performance. Examples of such more complex tests are discussed here.

1. Linear Combination Tests

In some domains, the underlying regularities of the domain are best described using some linear combination of numerical attributes. A linear combination test is a test of the form

$$w_1x_1 + w_2x_2 + \cdots + w_nx_n > \theta?,$$

where x_1 through x_n are numerical attributes and $w_1, w_2, \ldots, w_n\theta$ are real-valued constants. This is a binary test which may be viewed as a hyperplane that partitions the space of objects into two halves. Under this view, a test on a single numerical attribute is an "axis-parallel" hyperplane. In domains that involve oblique (non-axis-parallel) hyperplanes, the standard tree-construction procedure would generate large trees that perform poorly, because the procedure attempts to approximate the needed oblique hyperplanes using axis-parallel ones.

Abandoning the restriction to axis-parallel hyperplanes makes the task of finding the best test considerably harder. In [14], it is shown that this task is nondeterministic polynomial-hard; that is, it probably has no polynomial time algorithm. A heuristic is introduced in [8] in which attributes are considered one at a time. For each attribute x_i, the current hyperplane is perturbed to find w_i and θ (with all other coefficients fixed) that give the best result. This is a hill-climbing heuristic, and as such, it may get trapped at local maxima. Randomized approaches are proposed in [14] and [15] to avoid this problem.

2. Boolean Combination Tests

Boolean combination tests are binary tests defined by applying logic operators, such as *and*, *or*, and *not*, on simpler binary tests. Boolean combination tests are important in domains in which one has to check several attributes simultaneously to proceed to the final decision. For example, in medical diagnosis, a useful test may look like "Is either symptom *A* or *B* present and is the result of test *C* negative?"

In such domains, the basic tree-construction procedure can still generate a tree using only single-attribute tests that simulate tests of the above form. However, the cost will be too many splits that eventually lead to an overly complex tree in which the lower level subtrees may be based on inadequately small numbers of examples.

Given the fact that the number of all Boolean combinations is extremely large, Breiman *et al.* [8] restrict their attention to only those "conjunctive" combinations; that is, tests that look like

$$\text{test}_1 \text{ and } \text{test}_2 \text{ and } \cdots \text{ test}_d$$

where each test_i is a binary test on a single attribute (for example, *Status* = *Student*? or *Age* > 23?). Note that *and* is the only operator used.

Even with such a restriction to conjunctive combinations, finding the best possible test remains computationally hard. An iterative heuristic is given by Breiman *et al.* [8], in which the combined test is constructed by adding one single-attribute test to the current conjunct each time. Starting with the single-attribute test that gives the best possible score, they add each time the single-attribute test that leads to the best improvement in the score, and so on, stopping when the improvement in the score falls below a certain threshold.

A different approach is followed in the FRINGE family of algorithms [16, 17]. In this approach, a decision tree is initially constructed as usual using only single-attribute tests. Then, by examining this tree, new attributes are defined by combining tests that appear at the *fringe* of the tree. These combined attributes are then added to the description of the training examples.

For example, let us consider again the decision tree of Fig. 4 which was constructed from the examples of Fig. 2. Among the new combined attributes that would be defined from this tree by the FRINGE family of algorithms is the attribute "*Age* > 20 and *GPA* > 2.9". The set of training examples of Fig. 2 is then modified by adding a new column for each newly defined attribute. The column of the attribute "$Age > 20$ and $GPA > 2.9$" would have the value *true* for the examples $\{1, 4, 5, 6, 10, 11, 12, 13\}$ and *false* for the rest of the examples.

A new decision tree is then constructed from the training examples with the new combined attributes included. This new tree may include tests defined on these combined attributes if such attributes score well during the tree-construction process. A new set of attributes is then defined again from this new tree, and a new tree is constructed after adding these attributes to the training examples. This process is iterated several times until the tree becomes stable or until a maximum number of iterations is reached.

Note that because new attributes may be defined in terms of previously introduced combined attributes and so on, arbitrary Boolean combinations of attributes can be generated in this approach. Unlike the work of Breiman *et al.* [8] which restricts attention to pure conjuctive tests, the FRINGE approach allows the introduction of candidate arbitrarily combined attributes, which are then filtered by the test selection criterion based on the training examples.

3. Grouping Attribute Values

In this discussion so far, we have assumed that a test defined on a nominal attribute has one branch for each value of that attribute. In some applications, however, it may be advantageous to group some of the values together in one branch. For example, consider an attribute *Day* with the 7 days of the week as its values. Imagine that, for the task at hand, the only concern is whether the day is a weekend day or not. Thus, the same conclusion is reached whether *Day* = *Saturday* or *Day* = *Sunday*, and similarly, the conclusion for all working days is the same. In this case, having seven branches for the test on the attribute *Day* is not desirable since it imposes unnecessary fragmentation of the training examples over these many branches. The generalization performance and the intelligibility of the decision tree would improve if the tree construction procedure introduces only two branches for the attribute *Day*, one for *Saturday* and *Sunday*, and the other for the rest of the days.

Of course, if we know in advance that such grouping of the values is more suitable for the application at hand, preprocessing can be done so that the attribute *Day* is turned into a binary attribute. The discussion here, however, is meant for situations in which "background knowledge" about which values should be grouped together is not available, and the goal is to let the tree-construction procedure "discover" the most appropriate grouping that improves the final tree.

Considering *all* possible groupings of values is computationally infeasible. In [3], a hill-climbing heuristic is introduced that iteratively merges values together in the best way that improves the gain-ratio measure. The initial value groups are just the individual values of the attribute under consideration and, at each cycle, the procedure evaluates the consequences of merging every pair of groups. This is repeated in a hill-climbing manner until no improvement in the gain-ratio score is observed. Alternatively, if so desired, this may be forced to continue until only two groups remain, leading eventually to a binary test (just like the *Day* example above).

In the GID3$*$ algorithm [18], an alternative approach is introduced which allows one branch per value for certain values, while grouping the rest of the values in one "default" branch. For example, for our *Day* attribute, it may be that *Monday* and *Friday* are of special interest (say, being the first and last working days of the week), whereas the rest of the days are all indistinguishable for the application at hand. In this case, the test on *Day* is to have three branches, one for *Monday*, another for *Friday*, and more for the remaining 5 days. For an attribute A with values $\{a_1, a_2, \ldots, a_r\}$, a decision has to be made for each value a_i whether to have a separate branch or to let the value be part of the default branch. To handle this task, Fayyad [18] introduced a measure called Tear(a_i). This quantity measures the degree to which the partition induced by the test $A = a_i$? avoids separating training examples of the same class (see [18] for details). Because it is preferred to have examples of the same class go to the same branch as much as possible, large values for Tear(a_i) make the attribute value a_i more "qualified" to have its own branch.

In GID3∗, the gain-ratio score is first computed for each binary test of the form $A = a_i$?, for $1 \leq i \leq r$, and the value, say a_j, that scores best will have its own branch. Then, Tear(a_i) for each value a_i other than a_j is compared to Tear(a_j), and any value a_i with Tear$(a_i) \geq$ Tear(a_j) will also have its own branch. The rest of the values constitute the default branch.

C. Attributes with Missing Values

In real-world applications, it is usually unrealistic to expect that all the attribute values are specified for each case seen. Quite often cases with incomplete descriptions are encountered in which one or more of the values are missing. This may occur, for example, because these values could not be measured or because they were believed to be irrelevant during the data collection stage. For example, in our previous credit card application example, the *GPA* attribute may be missing in some of the cases either because such information is not available or because *GPA* becomes not relevant once we know that the person is employed.

The problem of missing values has to be dealt with both when processing the training examples during the decision tree construction and when we wish to classify a new case using a learned tree. We describe here one solution to this problem that was introduced in [3].

1. Handling Missing Values During Tree Construction

To handle missing values in the training examples, the basic tree-construction procedure is modified as follows:

- A real-valued *weight* is assigned to each training example. This weight is initially set to 1.0 for every example and may decrease later during the construction of the tree. Counting the *number* of examples in a given set S (i.e., quantities of the form $|S|$ that appear in the gain-ratio computation) is then replaced by summing the weight of all the examples in S, that is, by $\Sigma_{e \in S}$ weight(e).
- To evaluate the gain-ratio for a given test t, we first exclude those training examples for which the outcome of t cannot be computed due to missing attribute values. We next initially compute the gain of t using the rest of the training examples and call this the *initial-gain*. The actual gain is then computed as

$$\text{gain}(t) = F \times \text{initial-gain}(t),$$

where F is the fraction of the excluded examples (those with missing values). For computing the *split* of t, we consider t as having one more outcome that covers those examples with missing values. So, if t has n outcomes, its split information will be computed as if it divides the cases into $n+1$ subsets.

- The remaining issue now is how to partition the training sample into subsets in Step 3 of the tree-construction procedure, after the best test t has been chosen. That is, suppose t has the outcomes $\{o_1, o_2, \ldots, o_r\}$ that will partition the training examples S into the corresponding subsets $S_1, S_2, \ldots, S_r$. The question is to which subset should we send a training example for which the outcome of t cannot by specified due to missing features?

  Let S' be the subset of S with known outcomes on the test t. We partition S' into the disjoint subsets $S_1, S_2, \ldots, S_r$, where, as usual, each S_i contains the examples in S' with outcome o_i. For each outcome o_i, we then estimate the probability of that outcome as

$$p_i = \frac{\text{The sum of the weights of the examples in } S_i}{\text{The sum of the weights of the examples in } S'}.$$

  Then, for each training example $e \in S - S'$, we create r copies $e_1, e_2, \ldots, e_r$ and set the weight for each copy to be

$$\text{weight}(e_i) = \text{weight}(e) \times p_i.$$

  Each copy e_i is then included in the subset S_i with the above weight.

  Note that under this approach, the sets $S_1, S_2, \ldots, S_r$ are no longer disjoint. However, for any example with weight w in S, if we sum up the weights of all the copies of that example in all these subsets, the result would obviously be w.
- Step 1 of the tree-construction procedure is modified so that each leaf stores the "class probability" information, which is estimated by counting the number of training examples of each class that reach that leaf. This information is stored for later use when a case with missing attribute value(s) is classified as explained below.

2. Classifying a New Case with Missing Values

As usual, a new case is classified by starting at the root of the decision tree and following the branches as determined by the attribute values for the case. However, when a test t is encountered for which the outcome cannot be determined because of missing values, all the outcomes of t are considered. The classification results for all these outcomes are then combined by considering the probability of each outcome. More precisely, to classify a case e using a decision tree T, we run the following recursive procedure ClassProb(e, T) which eventually returns a vector of class probabilities:

- If T is a leaf return the class probability vector associated with the leaf.
- Let t be the test at the root, where t has the outcomes $o_1, o_2, \ldots, 0_r$, leading to subtrees $T_1, T_2, \ldots, T_r$. If the outcome of t for e is o_i,

then return ClassProb(e, T_i). Otherwise, if the outcome of t cannot be determined due to missing value(s), then return

$$\sum_{i=1}^{r} P_j \times \text{ClassProb}(e, T_j),$$

where p_i is the estimated probability of outcome o_i as explained above.

Finally, the class probability vector returned by ClassProb(e, T) is scanned and the class with the highest probability is returned as the classification result for e.

VI. VOTING OVER MULTIPLE DECISION TREES

Significant reduction in the generalization error can be obtained by learning *multiple* trees from the training examples and then letting these trees *vote* when classifying a new case. Bagging (short for *b*ootstrap *agg*regat*ing*) [19] and boosting [20, 21] are two techniques that follow this approach, which has recently been shown to provide excellent improvement [22] in the final generalization performance. Note that this improvement is, however, bought by a significant increase in computation as well as by degradation of the intelligibility of the final classifier for human experts.

In the following, we will denote by T^k the decision tree generated in the kth iteration and by T the final composite classifier obtained by voting. For a case e, $T^k(e)$ and $T(e)$ are the classes returned by T^k and T, respectively.

A. Bagging

In this approach, in each iteration $k = 1, 2, \ldots, K$ (where K is a prespecified constant), a training set S^k is sampled (with replacement) from the original training examples S, such that $|S^k| = |S|$. From each S^k, a decision tree T^k is learned, and a final classifier T is formed by aggregating the trees $T^1, T^2, \ldots, T^K$. To classify a case e, a *vote* is given for the class $T^k(e)$, for $k = 1, 2, \ldots, K$, and $T(e)$ is then the class with the maximum number of votes.

B. Boosting

Boosting was experimentally found to be superior to bagging in terms of the generalization performance [22]. In boosting, each training example is assigned a real-valued *weight*, quantifying its influence during tree construction. A decision tree is learned from these weighted examples, and at each iteration, the weight of those examples that are misclassified in the previous iteration is increased. This means that such examples will have more influence when the next tree is constructed. Finally, after generation of several decision trees, *weighted* voting is conducted, for which the weight of each tree in the voting process is a function of its training error.

More precisely, let w_e^k denote the weight of case e at iteration k, where for every e, $w_e^1 = 1/|S|$. The following is repeated for $k = 1, 2, 3, \ldots$:

1. A tree T^k is constructed, taking into account the weights of the training example. That is, during the computation of gain-ratio, the size $|S|$ of a set S is replaced by the total weight of the examples in S; that is, $\sum_{e \in S} w_e^k$.

2. The training error ϵ^k of T^k is then measured as the sum of the weights of the training example that are misclassified by T^k.
3. Let $\beta^k = \epsilon^k/(1-\epsilon^k)$. Note that $\beta^k < 1$ because $\epsilon^k < 0.5$.
4. For each example e that is correctly classified by T^K, the weight of e is decreased to become $w_e^{k+1} = w_e^{k+1} \times \beta^k$.
5. Renormalize the weights of all the examples so that $\sum_{e\in S} w_e^{k+1} = 1$.

The preceding loop is terminated whenever one of the following cases holds:

- $k = K$.
- $\epsilon^k = 0$ (that is, T^k commits no errors on S). In this case K becomes the current value of k.
- $\epsilon^k \geq 0.5$ (that is, T^k is of a very bad quality). In this case T^k is discarded and K becomes $k-1$.

When classifying a new case e, we first find $T^k(e)$ for all the generated trees T^k. Voting is then conducted such that the vote of T^k is worth log $(1/\beta^k)$ units, where β^k is as defined previously. Thus, unlike the bagging approach, the contribution of each tree in the voting processing is dependent on its training error.

Note that the above vote weight of $\log(1/\beta^k)$ is fixed for each tree regardless of the case being classified. An alternative is proposed by Quinlan [22] in which the vote weight depends on the leaf of the tree that is used to classify the new case: Let ℓ_e be the leaf used by T^k to classify a new case e as belonging to class $j = T^k(e)$, and let $S(\ell_e)$ denote the set of training examples at that leaf. The subset of these examples that belongs to class $j = T^k(e)$ is denoted $S(\ell_e)^j$. In the work of Quinlan [22], the vote weight of tree T^k is then set to be

$$\frac{|S| \times \Sigma_{e\in S(\ell_e)^j} w_e^k + 1}{|S| \times \Sigma_{e\in S(\ell_e)} w_e^k + 2},$$

where S is the entire set of training examples. Using this quantity was experimentally reported to yield better generalization performance compared to the fixed vote weight of $\log(1/\beta^k)$ [22].

VII. INCREMENTAL TREE CONSTRUCTION

In our discussion so far, we have assumed that all the training examples are available prior to tree construction. This kind of "batch" learning, however, is not suitable in real-time applications in which new training examples keep arriving over time. Upon the availability of new data, one may consider discarding the current tree and learning a completely new decision tree by including the newly available data in the training sample. To reduce the computational costs, however, it is more attractive to attempt to modify the current decision tree in the light of the new examples, rather than to start from scratch each time an example arrives. The objective here is to produce a tree by incorporating the new data that is the same as the tree that would have been generated by batch learning using all the available examples. This "incremental" approach has been studied by Utgoff in his ID5R algorithm [23] and then more recently in his ITI algorithm [24].

In the ITI algorithm, to permit later modification, counts used for test evaluation are stored at the nodes of the tree, and the training examples are stored at the leaves. When a new example arrives, the branches of the tree are followed according to the values in the example until a leaf is reached. If the example has the same class as the leaf, the example is simply added to the set of examples saved at that leaf. Otherwise, if the example has a different class from the leaf, the algorithm attempts to replace the leaf by a subtree generated by running the tree-construction procedure on the examples of the leaf.

After the example has been incorporated into the tree, the tree is traversed from the root recursively, ensuring that the best test possible at each node (according to the test evaluation criterion) is the test actually conducted at that node. Otherwise, when a different test should replace the current one, tree revision operators (see [24] for details) are used to restructure the tree as necessary.

VIII. EXISTING IMPLEMENTATIONS

A number of packages are now available that can be used for decision tree generation. The most well-known and widely used package is Quinlan's C4.5 [3]. This package is capable of handling nominal as well as numerical attributes and is equipped with several features such as pruning, handling missing values, and grouping attribute values. It also includes routines for running cross-validation experiments and for converting learned decision trees to production rules that are more suitable for expert system development. The source code of the package (in C) is distributed with Quinlan's book, which makes it possible to experiment with variants of the original tree-construction procedures.

An alternative package is *MLC++* reported in [25]. This package implements in C++ a variety of learning algorithms including decision tree learning algorithms. It is meant to aid in the development and comparison of learning algorithms, but can also be utilized by end users. This package can be retrieved using the URL http://robotics.stanford.edu://users/ronnyk/mlc.html.

IX. PRACTICAL APPLICATIONS

In this section, we present some recent successes in applying decision tree learning to solve real-world problems. This sample is not comprehensive by any means but is only meant to demonstrate the usefulness of the decision tree learning approach in practical applications.

A. Predicting Library Book Use

In [26], decision trees are developed that predict the future use of books in a library. Forecasting book usage helps librarians to select low-usage titles and move them to relatively distant and less expensive off-site locations that use efficient compact storage techniques. For this task, it is important to adopt a book choice strategy that minimizes the expected frequency of requesting removed titles. For any choice policy, this frequency depends, of course, on the percentage of titles that have to be removed for off-site storage (as dictated by the capacity of the main library); the higher this percentage is, the higher this frequency is expected to be. Taking the random choice policy as the benchmark, the quality of a given choice policy is evaluated using a measure called the "expected advantage over random" (EAR). This evaluation measure for choice policy is calculated given no assumptions about how many titles to store off-site.

For the Harvard College Library, where the work of Silverstein and Shieber [26] was conducted, an ideal *clairvoyant* policy can achieve an EAR of 90.51% at best, whereas a choice policy that is based on books' checkout history alone achieves an EAR of 58.86%.

In simulation experiments, book usage records for 80,000 titles during the period July 1975 to June 1984 were used to prepare examples, where each example is described using six attributes (checkout history, last use, publication date, language, country, and alphabetic prefix of the Library of Congress classification). These examples are then labeled by classes, indicating how often they are checked out in the "future," where the future information is simulated using records of the period July 1984 to June 1993. It is shown that a choice policy based on a decision tree learned from these examples gives an EAR as high as 73.12%. This is a considerable achievement given that, in the same setting, a choice that is based on books' checkout history alone gives an EAR of 58.86% and a choice policy that is based on last use alone (which is what is recommended to be best by experts) gives an EAR of 60.02%.

Furthermore, Silverstein and Shieber [26] show that the improvement is particularly striking if the percentage of titles to be moved off-site is between 20 and 40%. For example, if the Harvard College Library had implemented the last-use choice policy to choose which 20% of its collection to move to the depository in 1985, they would have had to retrieve volumes from the depository about 34,000 times per year. If they had, instead, used the decision tree constructed from examples, there would have been less than one-fifth as many retrievals—only 6,200.

B. Exploring the Relationship Between the Research Octane Number and Molecular Substructures

Figuring out what molecule information one needs to predict the research octane number (RON) is a nontrivial problem of particular interest to chemists. In the work of Blurock [27], substructure presence–absence information is used for RON prediction, not only because this is believed to give good prediction results, but also because asking directly about the presence or absence of substructures in molecules is easily interpretable by chemists, and hence, valuable intuitive information can be gained by studying the substructure–RON relationship.

The 230 hydrocarbons for which RON is known in the literature were used in the study of Blurock [27]. The attributes used are predicates about whether a particular substructure (e.g., hexane) is a member of the molecule being analyzed. Given these attributes, the goal is to predict whether RON is less than a given threshold α. Thus, there are two classes in this task: RON $< \alpha$ and RON $\geq \alpha$. Different decision trees are learned for different values of α, and these are then used to predict a range in which RON falls, that is, α_1 and α_2 such that $\alpha_1 \leq$ RON $< \alpha_2$, in which case, the predicted RON is taken as $(\alpha_1 + \alpha_2)/2$.

Of the 230 hydrocarbons, 48 were used as a test set and the rest were used for generating decision trees. The overall RON range was between 40 and 105. For this wide range, the predicted RON was within 10, 5, and 3 RON units for 65, 58, and 44% of the test cases, respectively. The greatest accuracy was achieved for a RON range of 90 to 105 units, which is also the range with the greatest concentration of cases. For this range, the predicted RON was within 10, 5, and 3 RON units for 85, 93, and 98% of the test cases, respectively. These results show that decision tree learning achieves reasonable results in this application domain given enough data points of good quality.

In addition to demonstrating the predictive power of the learned decision trees, analyzing these trees was useful in providing insight about the significance of different substructures for RON prediction. It was reported that among a total of 230 substructures, only 31 were actually needed to make the prediction. Moreover, within this subset, conclusions were drawn based on the decision trees on which substructures are important to which RON range. These findings are viewed as a contribution to better understanding of the underlying principles that determine RON of molecules.

C. Characterization of Leiomyomatous Tumors

This application was reported in [28], in which the goal was to generate hypotheses about tumor diagnosis/prognosis problems when confronted with a large number of features. For a given tumor, it is desired to know to *which* group this tumor belongs and *why*.

Traditionally, tumor characterization is made on the basis of features (such as tumor differentiation, cellularity, mitotic count, age, location, and cell types) that are difficult for a pathologist to evaluate. The task is, thus, carried out subjectively, and the quality of the results is determined by the pathologist's experience with the group of tumors concerned. To achieve a higher level of objectivity, many more quantitative measurements (related to DNA content, morphonuclear characteristics, and immunohistochemical specificities) need to be considered. Furthermore, useful information can result from interactions between several of these features that cannot be detected using traditional univariate statistical analysis.

In the work of Decaestecker *et al.* [28], decision tree learning was applied to the difficult problem of leiomyomatous (or soft muscle) tumor diagnosis. In this application, there are 31 features and 2 classes (benign leiomyomas and malignant leiomyosarcomas). The C4.5 package was run on a collection of 23 cases, each of which was preclassified independently by three pathologists. Because of the limited number of available cases, the leave-one-method was used to estimate the generalization error.

In the reported experiments, the goal of the authors was first to determine the subset of features that are most relevant to the task. Using the leave-one-out method, inclusion and exclusion of features were conducted while the authors watched the estimated generalization error, and the subset of features that gave the best results was isolated. Only those features eventually selected were given to C4.5 as the actual attributes. Decaestecker *et al.* [28] reported that the decision tree learning approach was superior (in terms of the generalization accuracy) to other classifiers (logistic regression and neural networks) for the studied task. Furthermore, the authors note that the decision tree approach is more suitable for this task because it led to explicit logical rules that can be interpreted by human experts, which meet the exploratory nature of their job.

D. Star/Cosmic-Ray Classification in Hubble Space Telescope Images

Salzberg *et al.* [29] applied decision tree learning to the task of distinguishing between stars and cosmic rays in images collected by the Hubble Space Telescope. In addition to high accuracy, a classifier for this task must be fast due to the large number of classifications and to the need for online classification. In their experiments, a set of 2211 preclassified images was used as a training sample for decision tree construction, and a separate set of 2282 preclassified images was used to measure the generalization performance of the learned decision tree. Each of these images was described using 20 numerical features and labeled as either a star or a cosmic ray. The reported experiments show that quite compact decision trees (no more than 9 nodes) achieve generalization accuracy of over 95%. Moreover, the experiments suggest that this accuracy will get even higher when methods for eliminating background noise are employed.

X. FURTHER READINGS

Although we have attempted to summarize in this chapter the most central issues in learning decision trees from examples, many important details and extensions have not been discussed. For the interested reader, we give in this last section information on where some of the related literature can be found.

Extended explanations of the basic tree-construction procedure and many of the extensions presented in this chapter can be found in books by Breiman *et al.* [8] and Quinlan [3] devoted to decision tree learning.

Studies that compare the information gain and the gain-ratio criteria to other test selection criteria can be found in Mingers [4], Buntine and Niblett [5], and Liu and White [6]. An interesting experimental work on improving the gain-ratio criterion is presented by Dietterich *et al.* [30], which is based on the theoretical work of Kearns and Mansour [31].

Construction of *fuzzy* decision trees in domains with fuzzy attributes is studied in Umano *et al.* [32], Yuan and Shaw [33], and Ichihashi *et al.* [34].

A larger variety of applications of decision tree learning in real-world applications can be found in the literature, for example, for electrical power systems [35], air defense [36], and monitoring of manufacturing processes [37].

ACKNOWLEDGMENTS

The first author acknowledges partial support from NTT Communications Science Laboratory, Japan, through a research grant. He also thanks King Fahd University of Petroleum & Minerals for their support.

REFERENCES

1. Buchanan, B. G. and Wilkins, D. C. (Eds.). *Readings in Knowledge Acquisition and Learning.* Morgan Kauffman, San Mateo, CA, 1993.
2. Hyafil, L. and Rivest, R. L. Constructing optimal binary decision trees is NP-complete. *Inform. Process. Lett.* 5(1):15–17, 1976.
3. Quinlan, J. R. *C4.5: Programs for Machine Learning.* Morgan Kauffmann, San Mateo, CA, 1993.
4. Mingers, J. An empirical comparison of selection measures for decision tree induction. *Mach. Learn.* 3:319–342, 1989.
5. Buntine, W. and Niblett, T. A further comparison of splitting rules for decision-tree induction. *Mach. Learn.* 8:75–86, 1992.
6. Liu, W. Z. and White, A. P. The importance of attribute selection measures in decision tree induction. *Mach. Learn.* 15:25–41, 1994.
7. Almuallim, H. An efficient algorithm for optimal pruning of decision trees. *Artif. Intell.* 83:347–362, 1996.
8. Breiman, L., Friedman, J. H., Olshen, R. A., and Stone, C. J. *Classification and Regression Trees.* Wadsworth, Belmont, CA, 1984.
9. Fayyad, U. M. and Irani, K. B. Multi-interval discretization of continuous valued attributes for classification learning. In *Proceedings of the 13th International Joint Conference on Artificial Intelligence*, 1993, pp. 1022–1027.
10. Kohavi, R. and Sahami, M. Error-based and entropy-based discretization of continuous features. In *Proceedings of the 2nd International Conference on Knowledge Discovery and Data Mining,* 1996, pp. 114–119.
11. Cohen, W. Learning trees and rules with set-valued features. In *Proceedings of the 13th National Conference on Artificial Intelligence (AAAI96)*, 1996, pp. 709–716.
12. Almuallim, H., Akiba, Y., and Kaneda, S. On handling tree-structured attributes in decision tree learning. In *Proceedings of the 12th International Conference on Machine Learning,* 1995, pp. 12–20.
13. Almuallim, H., Akiba, Y., and Kaneda, S. An efficient algorithm for finding optimal gain-ratio multiple-split tests on hierarchical attributes in decision tree learning. In *Proceedings of the 13th National Conference on Artificial Intelligence (AAAI96)*, 1996, pp. 703–708.
14. Heath, D., Kasif, S., and Salzberg, S. Induction of oblique decision trees. In *Proceedings of the 13th International Joint Conference on Artificial Intelligence,* 1993, pp. 1002–1007.
15. Murthy, S., Kasif, S., Salzberg, S., and Beigel, R. OC1: Randomized induction of oblique decision trees. In *Proceedings of the 11th National Conference on Artificial Intelligence,* 1993, pp. 322–327.
16. Pagallo, G. and Haussler, D. Boolean feature discovery in empirical learning. *Mach. Learn.* 5:71–99, 1990.
17. Yang, D., Rendell, L., and Blix, G. A scheme for feature construction and a comparison of empirical methods. In *Proceedings of the 12th International Joint Conference on Artificial Intelligence,* 1991, pp. 699–704.
18. Fayyad, U. M. Branching on attribute values in decision tree generation. In *Proceedings of the 12th National Conference on Artificial Intelligence (AAAI94),* 1994, pp. 601–606.
19. Breiman, L. Bagging predictors. *Mach. Learn.* 24:123–140, 1996.
20. Fruend, Y. and Schapire, R. E. A decision theoretic generalization of online learning and an application to boosting. *Journal of Computers and System Sciences,* 55(1):119–139, 1997.
21. Fruend, Y. and Schapire, R. E. Experiments with a new boosting algorithm. In *Proceedings of the 13th International Conference on Machine Learning,* 1996, pp. 148–156.
22. Quinlan, J. R. Bagging, boosting and C4.5. In *Proceedings of the 13th National Conference on Artificial Intelligence (AAAI96),* 1996, pp. 725–730.
23. Utgoff, P. E. Incremental induction of decision trees. *Mach. Learn.* 4:161–186, 1989.
24. Utgoff, P. E. An improved algorithm for incremental induction of decision trees. In *Proceedings of the 11th International Conference on Machine Learning,* 1994, pp. 318–325.
25. Kohavi, R., Sommerfield, D., and Dougherty J. *MLC++*: A machine learning library in C++. In *Proceedings of the 8th International Conference on Tools with Artificial Intelligence,* 1996, pp. 234–245.
26. Silverstein, C. and Shieber, S. M. Predicting individual book use for off-site storage using decision trees. *Lib. Q.* 66(3):266–293, 1996.

27. Blurock, E. S. Automatic learning of chemical concepts: Research octane number and molecular substructures. *Comput. Chem.* 19(2):91–99, 1995.
28. Decaestecker, C., Remmelink, M., Salmon, I., Camby, I., Goldschmidt, D., Petein, M., Van Ham, P., and Pasteels, J. Methodological aspects of using decision trees to characterize leiomyomatous tumors. *Cytometry* 24:83–92, 1995.
29. Salzberg, S., Chandar, R., Ford, H., Murthy, S. K., and White, R. Decision trees for automated identification of cosmic-ray hits in Hubble Space Telescope images. *Publ. Astron. Soc. Pacific* 107:279–288, 1995.
30. Dietterich, T. G., Kearns, M., and Mansour, Y. Applying the weak learning framework to understand and improve C4.5. In *Proceedings of the 13th International Conference on Machine Learning,* 1996, pp. 96–104.
31. Kearns, M. and Mansour, Y. On the boosting ability of top-down decision tree learning algorithms. In *Proceedings of the 28th ACM Symposium on the Theory of Computing,* 1996.
32. Umano, M., Okamoto, H., Hatono, I., Tamura, H., Kawachi, F., Umedzu, S., and Kinoshita, J. Fuzzy decision trees by Fuzzy ID3 algorithm and its application to diagnosis systems. In *Proceedings of the IEEE International Conference on Fuzzy Systems,* 1994, pp. 2113–2118.
33. Yuan, Y. and Shaw, M. J. Induction of fuzzy decision trees. *Fuzzy Sets Syst.* 69:125–139, 1995.
34. Ichihashi, H., Shirai, T., Nagasaka, K., and Miyoshi, T. Neuro-fuzzy ID3: A method of inducing fuzzy decision trees with linear programming for maximizing entropy and an algebraic method for incremental learning. *Fuzzy Sets Syst.* 81:157–167, 1996.
35. Hatziargyriou, N. D., Papathanassiou, S. A., and Papadopoulos, M. P. Decision trees for fast security assessment of autonomous power systems with a large penetration from renewables. *IEEE Trans. Energy Conversion* 10(2):315–325, 1995.
36. Lee, Y. and Lo, C. Optimizing an air defense evaluation model using inductive learning. *Appl. Artif. Intell.* 8:645–661, 1994.
37. Du, R., Elbestawi, M. A., and Wu, S. M. Automated monitoring of manufacturing processes. Part 1. Monitoring methods. *J. Eng. Ind.* 117:121–132, 1995.

4

REASONING WITH IMPERFECT INFORMATION

SIMON PARSONS

Department of Computer Science, University of Liverpool, Liverpool, L69 7ZF United Kingdom

Handling imperfect information is an important problem for any intelligent system that has to deal with the real world. As a result, there have been many proposals for how this problem may be solved. This chapter surveys some of the most important of these proposals, discusses their advantages, limitations, and interrelationships, and provides some examples of their use in building intelligent systems.

Expert Systems, Edited by Cornelius T. Leondes, Volume 1

ISBN: 0-12-443881-4 / $35.00

I. INTRODUCTION

Much of the data that are available about the real world are imperfect. As I sit here writing, I am also planning a trip to the dentist this afternoon. To make this trip I have to walk to the station, catch a train, and then walk to the dentist's surgery. My appointment is at 5:15. If I am late, I will have to come back another time and if I am early, I will have to sit and wait, wasting time I could be spending writing this text. Much of the information I have with which to make this plan is imperfect. I do not know how long it will take to walk to the station or from the station to the surgery. I do not know what time the trains run, although I do know that they run about every half an hour and take about half an hour to get to the station nearest my dentist. I do not know if it will rain—it is raining now, I think, because I noticed it was raining 5 minutes ago when I looked out of the window, but I have no information about the weather this afternoon—so I do not know if I should take my umbrella or whether a hat and coat will suffice. Despite all these imperfections in the data available to me, I do not have much difficulty in coming up with a workable plan, and not much more difficulty sifting through all the most workable plans to come up with the best plan of all. However, were I to try and formalize my reasoning using first order logic or production rules—the kinds of methods favored in the early days of artificial intelligence—I would quickly run into difficulties because I would be unable to represent the imperfect knowledge I have. Thus, if we are to build systems that demonstrate even the modest level of intelligence necessary to plan my trip to the dentist, we will need new methods for representing information and reasoning with it that take into account the imperfections that are bound to pervade it.

This point has been obvious for some time and, as a result, there have been a large number of proposals for handling imperfect information. To set things in context, it is helpful to consider the different types of imperfection that might arise. This can be done in a number of ways (for a discussion of some of these, see [93]), but whatever way the universe of imperfect information is sliced up, the same broad distinctions fall out. One major distinction is between information that is complete and information that is incomplete. Another major distinction is between information that is believed to be true (by whomever or whatever is using the information) and information that is uncertain to some degree. These distinctions give us two orthogonal axes to divide up the space of types of information. Information that is complete and certain is perfect and can be represented adequately using logic or production rules. However, it is scarce, especially when one moves out of the domain of mathematics. Information that is certain but incomplete is typified by a database of statements like

Canaries fly.
Penguins don't fly.

Each statement is true, but in any resource-bounded system, such a database will be incomplete (does a Squarx del Thargo fly?). Information that is complete but uncertain is information such as

The probability that it will rain tomorrow is 70%.

The necessary information is available, but it is subject to some degree of uncertainty.

It is techniques to handle information that is certain but incomplete or complete but uncertain that have been the focus of most of the research to date and, consequently, it is these techniques that will be the focus of this chapter. As it happens, the bulk of the techniques suggested to handle information that is certain but incomplete have been symbolic, often being variations of first order or propositional logic, which make assumptions to complete what is known. The bulk of the techniques for handling complete but uncertain information are basically numerical, being different systems for handling the 70% in the preceding statement about rain. Now, this chapter does not pretend to cover the full range of techniques that have been developed: there are far too many such techniques for one chapter to do them justice (the interested reader is referred to [63, 72, 93, 94] for more extensive surveys). Instead, this chapter focuses on the three main numerical methods and the three main symbolic methods, covering these in some detail in Sections II and III, respectively. Those sections also contain brief descriptions of some of the more interesting lesser models (in the sense that they are less established, less widely used, or less well studied). We suggest reasons for the introduction of the more novel techniques and sketch in the technical differences between the approaches. With this background well established, Section IV then considers work on bringing techniques together, both within their genres and, perhaps more interestingly, between them. Finally, Section V discusses applications of some of the techniques.

It should be noted that fuzzy sets and fuzzy logic are not covered in any detail herein (although we do discuss possibility theory, which is built on fuzzy set theory, at some length in the section on numerical methods). This disregard is for two main reasons: one philosophical and one practical. The philosophical reason is that, as stated before, the techniques discussed here deal with uncertain and incomplete information, whereas fuzzy approaches deal with vague information—such as modeling the statement "Simon is reasonably tall"—and have nothing to say about uncertainty, a point discussed at length by Dubois, Prade, and Smets [38]. The practical reason is that there has been so much work on fuzzy approaches that this chapter could not possibly do them justice. The interested reader is referred to [27, 36] for a comprehensive review of the field.

II. NUMERICAL APPROACHES

Over the last two decades, numerous formal and informal systems have been introduced for reasoning under conditions of ignorance and uncertainty. The first uncertainty management technique to be introduced was probability theory. This was not only developed many years before the first computer, but also was used in computer decision aids before the advent of artificial intelligence as a discipline. Dempster [19, 20] generalized Bayes's theorem in 1967, although his work remained confined to the field of statistics until Shafer [113] reformulated the theory and published it as *A Mathematical Theory of Evidence* in 1976. This body of work, often referred to as Dempster–Shafer theory, has several interpretations, including the transferable belief model [119, 121]. Another much studied approach is possibility theory [33, 135], which grew out of work on fuzzy sets [134]. There are numerous other numerical techniques for dealing with uncertainty, often developed from pragmatic considerations. These include certainty factors [118] and probabilistic logic [91], to name but two.

A. Overview

The methods that we consider in the following sections are the main formal theories introduced to handle uncertainty, probability theory, possibility theory, and evidence theory. For theories that traditionally have been seen as rivals, one might expect that they would appear radically different, but this is not so. Indeed, they are remarkably similar, differing largely in subtleties of meaning or application, although this is not entirely surprising because they are intended, essentially, to do the same thing.

The basic problem is how to weigh up the degree to which several uncertain events are believed to occur so that the most believed may be unambiguously identified. The basis on which the "belief"[1] is assigned is a contentious issue, although all the theories that we consider assume allocation by an assignment function that distributes belief to events under consideration. Belief may be distributed on the basis of statistical information [112], physical possibility [135], or purely subjective assessment [12] by an expert or otherwise. The belief assigned is a number between 0 and 1, with 0 being the belief assigned to a fact that is known to be false and 1 the belief assigned to a fact known to be definitely true. The infinite number of degrees of belief between the limits represent various shades of uncertainty. Now, some formalisms restrict the amount of belief that may be assigned. Both probability theory and evidence theory, which is after all derived from probability theory, limit the total belief that may be assigned by a particular distribution function by constraining the sum of all the beliefs to be 1. This may be interpreted to mean that one particular observer cannot believe in a set of uncertain events more than he or she would have believed in an event of total certainty. There is no such restriction on a possibility distribution, because several alternative events are conceivable that are perfectly possible and so have a possibility of 1. Probability theory, unlike the other theories, also introduces a restriction on the belief that may be applied to a hypothesis based on the belief assigned to its negation. If we have an event A, then

$$\Pr(A) = 1 - \Pr(\neg A).$$

Given the result of a belief distribution, we are interested in how the assigned beliefs can be manipulated. Given our belief in two events, what is our belief in either of them occurring (our belief in their union) and what is our belief that both will occur (our belief in their intersection)? More importantly perhaps, especially for artificial intelligence applications where we often wish to assess the combined belief that results from several different pieces of information, we are interested in combining the effects of two or more belief distributions over the same set of hypotheses. Each distribution will, in general, assign different beliefs to a given hypothesis, and we require some means to assess a final belief that takes into

[1] In this section we use the term "belief" to stand for any measure of belief, whether a probability, possibility, or the measure handled by evidence theory.

account all the different assignations. The way in which this is done is based on the interpretation that the theory gives to the belief it assigns, and thus it is not surprising that each theory should "pool the evidence" in a different way.

B. Probability Theory

Probability theory has existed in one form or another for several hundred years. During this time various alternative formulations have been introduced, and it is now difficult to say where the definitive account may be found. This is in contrast to the other methods described in this chapter, where the descriptions are drawn from the original articles on the subject. The introduction presented here is drawn from the discussion of probability theory in Lindley's excellent book *Making Decisions* [78]. Lindley asserts that probability theory is built on three axioms or laws that define the behavior of a probability measure, which may be used as an estimate of the degree to which an uncertain event is likely to occur. The measure may be assessed by reference to a standard, such as the likelihood of drawing a black ball out of an urn containing 5 black balls and 10 red balls. The first law of probability theory is the convexity law, which states that the probability measure for an event A given information H is such that

$$0 \leq \Pr(A \mid H) \leq 1.$$

The second law is the addition law, which relates the probabilities of two events to the probability of their union. For two exclusive events A and B, that is, two events that cannot both occur, we have

$$\Pr(A \cup B \mid H) = \Pr(A \mid H) + \Pr(B \mid H),$$

which is commonly written

$$\Pr(A \cup B) = \Pr(A) + \Pr(B)$$

without explicit reference to the information H, because the information is the same in all cases. If the events are not exclusive, we have, instead,

$$\Pr(A \cup B) = \Pr(A) + \Pr(B) - \Pr(A \cap B).$$

Furthermore, the sum of the probabilities of a set of mutually exclusive and exhaustive data ("exhaustive" meaning that they are the only possible events that may occur) is constrained to sum to 1 so that

$$\Pr(A) + \Pr(\neg A) = 1,$$

or, more generally for a set of n such events A_i,

$$\sum_{i=1,\ldots,n} \Pr(A_i).$$

The final law is the multiplication law, which gives us the probability of two events occurring together; the probability of the intersection of A and B is written

$$\Pr(A \cap B \mid H) = \Pr(A \mid H) \cdot \Pr(B \mid A \cap H).$$

Again this may be written as

$$\Pr(A \cap B) = \Pr(A) \cdot \Pr(B \mid A)$$

without explicit reference to H. Note that $\Pr(A \cap B)$ is often written as $\Pr(A, B)$. The probability measure $\Pr(B \mid A)$ is the *conditional* probability of B given A, the probability that B will occur, given that A is known to have occurred. There is a further rule concerning probability measures that is crucial from the point of view of artificial intelligence: Bayes's theorem, named after an eighteenth century nonconformist English clergyman. This is not a fundamental law in the sense of those already presented, but may be derived easily from them. Bayes's theorem states that

$$\Pr(A \mid B) = \frac{\Pr(B \mid A) \cdot \Pr(A)}{\Pr(B)}.$$

Another important relationship between probabilities is encoded in Jeffrey's rule:

$$\Pr(A) = \sum_{i=1,\ldots,n} \Pr(A \mid B_i)\Pr(B_i).$$

Several adaptations of probability theory have appeared within the literature of artificial intelligence, including the odds-likelihood formulation used by Prospector [39] and the cautious approach adopted by INFERNO [100]. Nilsson [91] provided an interesting variation with his probabilistic logic, an attempt to combine propositional calculus with a numerical uncertainty handling formalism by associating probability measures with logical sentences. Perhaps the most important feature of the formalism is that it handles incompletely specified probabilistic models by computing the allowed bounds on the derived consequents.

Much attention has been given to the problem of propagating probabilities through causal networks—directed graphs structures where an arc from node A to node B signifies that A and B are related. Perhaps the best way to get an understanding of causal probabilistic networks is by looking at an example such as that in Fig. 1. This is part of a probabilistic network for diagnosing faults in a car (this example is drawn from [57]). This captures the fact that the age of the battery (the node *battery old*) has an influence on whether or not the battery is good (*battery good*), and that whether or not the alternator is good (*alternator ok*) has an effect on whether or not the battery is charging (*battery charging*); together the quality of the battery and whether or not the battery is charging affect whether the battery is working (*battery ok*) and this has an effect on the radio (*radio ok*) and the lights (*lights ok*). All the random variables in this example are either true or false, so that the random variable *battery old* can be instantiated with the event *battery old* meaning that the battery is old or the event ¬*battery old* meaning that the battery is not old.

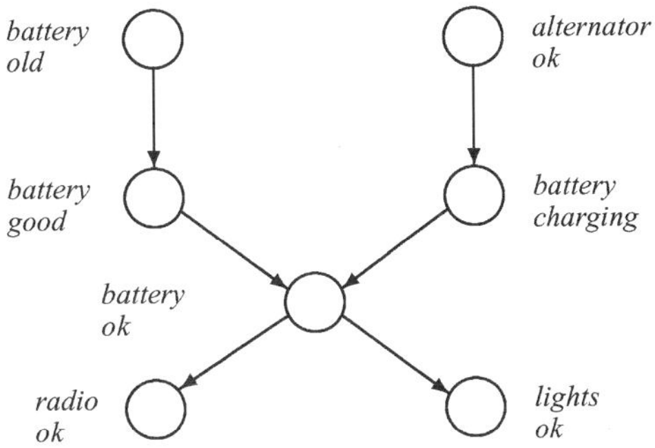

FIGURE 1 Part of a probabilistic network for diagnosing faults in a car.

Each of the links in the network is quantified by giving the relevant conditional probabilities, which in this case include

$$\Pr(\textit{battery good} \mid \textit{battery old}) = 0.1,$$
$$\Pr(\textit{battery good} \mid \neg\textit{battery old}) = 0.8,$$
$$\Pr(\textit{battery ok} \mid \textit{battery good, battery charging}) = 0.9,$$
$$\Pr(\textit{battery ok} \mid \textit{battery good}, \neg\textit{battery charging}) = 0.2,$$
$$\Pr(\textit{battery ok} \mid \neg\textit{battery good, battery charging}) = 0.6,$$
$$\Pr(\textit{battery ok} \mid \neg\textit{battery good}, \neg\textit{battery charging}) = 0.05.$$

Note that the conditional probabilities reflect the direction of the arrows. Both, broadly speaking, capture a notion of causality (which is why probabilistic networks are also known as causal networks): if the battery is old it causes the battery to be less likely to be good and it is, therefore, easier to assess Pr(*battery good* | *battery old*) than Pr(*battery old* | *battery good*), although the two probabilities each may be computed from the other using Bayes's theorem.

Now, given the network and the prior probabilities of the battery being old, Pr(*battery old*), and the alternator being ok, Pr(*alternator ok*), it is possible to compute the probability of each state of each random variable in the network (for instance Pr(*battery good*) = 0.58 if Pr(*battery old*) = 0.4) by simple application of Jeffrey's rule. It is also possible to take account of evidence that, for instance, the radio is not ok (which means that Pr(¬*radio ok*) = 1) and to use Bayes's theorem to revise the probabilities. Much attention has been given to the problem of efficiently propagating probabilities through probabilistic networks. Pearl [95] provided a comprehensive introduction to the use of probabilistic causal networks, along with an efficient scheme for the propagation of probabilities in singly connected networks[2] that is based on autonomous message passing. Another method that has received wide attention was presented by Lauritzen and Spiegelhalter [75] and has been used as the basis of the expert system shell HUGIN [2].

[2] Singly connected networks are those in which, for every pair of nodes, there is at most one path along arcs that join them. When assessing connectedness, arcs may be traversed in both directions, but any arc may be traversed only once.

C. Evidence Theory

Evidence theory is the term commonly used to refer to the body of work carried out by Dempster [19, 20] and Shafer [113] to remedy some of what they saw as the limitations of probability theory, in particular [21] disposing of the "completeness" axiom of probability theory [59]. This theory deals with the so-called frame of discernment, the set of base elements $\Theta = \theta_1, \ldots, \theta_n$ in which we are interested, and its power set 2^Θ, which is the set of all subsets of the interesting elements. The distribution in evidence theory is given by a probability mass function $m(\cdot)$ that assigns zero mass to the empty set,

$$m(\emptyset) = 0,$$

and a value in [0,1] to each element of 2^Θ, the total mass distributed being 1 so that

$$\sum_{A \subseteq \Theta} m(A) = 1.$$

Since we deal with all possible subsets of the set of all base propositions, rather than the propositions themselves as in probability theory, we can apportion the probability mass exactly as we wish, ignoring assignments to those levels of detail that we know nothing about. This allows us to model ignorance, $m(\Theta)$ being the probability mass we are unable, through lack of knowledge, to assign to any particular subset of Θ. We can define our belief in a subset A of the set of all propositions as the sum of all the probability masses that support its constituents,

$$\mathrm{Bel}(A) = \sum_{B \subseteq A} m(B),$$

and the plausibility of A may be defined as the probability mass that does not support $\neg A$,

$$\mathrm{Pl}(A) = \sum_{B \cap A \neq \emptyset} m(B),$$

which also may be written as

$$\mathrm{Pl}(A) = 1 - \mathrm{Bel}(\neg A).$$

The interval [Bel(A), Pl(A)] can be considered to be a measure of our ignorance about A and can vary from zero when we have the same degree of belief in A as would be generated by probability theory to 1 when A is supported by the vacuous belief [0, 1].

Evidence is combined by Dempster's rule of combination. This computes the probability mass assigned to $C \subset \Theta$ from the probability mass assigned to A and B, where both A and B are also subsets of Θ. If the distribution function that assigns probability mass to A is $m_1(\cdot)$ and the function that distributes probability mass to B is $m_2(\cdot)$, then the mass assigned to C is defined by

$$m_{12}(C) = \frac{\sum_{A \cap B = C} m_1(A) m_2(B)}{1 - \sum_{A \cap B = \emptyset} m_1(A) m_2(B)},$$

where the division *normalizes* the new distribution by reassigning any probability mass that is assigned to the empty set $\emptyset$ by the combination. To clarify what is going on here, we consider a simple example of the use of Dempster's rule in combining evidence.

Consider a world with only four car manufacturers, Nissan, Toyota, GM, and Chrysler, all trying to break into a new car market [15]. We are interested in who will dominate the market. There are four singleton hypotheses that correspond to the assertions that each of the four manufacturers will dominate the market. Consider the case in which there are two mass functions m_1 and m_2. Now, m_1 assigns 0.4 to {*Nissan, Toyota*}, the hypothesis that Japanese manufacturers dominate, and the remaining 0.6 to the set {*Nissan, Toyota, GM, Chrysler*}, modeling ignorance about the behavior of American manufacturers. Similarly, m_2 assigns 0.8 to the set {*Toyota, GM, Chrysler*} and 0.2 to Θ, and Dempster's rule of combination assigns the product of the two belief masses to the intersection of the sets to which they are assigned. Table 1 explains the calculation. The masses after combination are

$$\begin{aligned} m_{12}(\{Toyota\}) &= 0.32, \\ m_{12}(\{Nissan, Toyota\}) &= 0.08, \\ m_{12}(\{Toyota, GM, Chrysler\}) &= 0.48, \\ m_{12}(\Theta) &= 0.12. \end{aligned}$$

The belief that the Japanese will dominate is computed from the sum of the belief masses of all the subsets of the hypothesis. Thus,

$$\begin{aligned} \mathrm{Bel}_{12}(\{Nissan, Toyota\}) &= m_{12}(\{Toyota\}) + m_{12}(\{Nissan, Toyota\}) \\ &\quad + m_{12}(\{Nissan\}) \\ &= 0.32 + 0.08 + 0 \\ &= 0.4. \end{aligned}$$

For this simple example, no normalization is required.

The problems of the computational complexity of Dempster's rule have been discussed by several authors. Barnett [5] showed that the apparent exponential time requirement of the theory can be reduced to simple polynomial time if the theory is applied to single hypotheses, rather than sets of hypotheses, and the evidence is combined in an orderly fashion. Gordon and Shortliffe [52] extended Barnett's approach to compute approximate beliefs in a space of hierarchically organized sets of hypotheses in linear time. This approach was then subsumed by that of Shafer and Logan [115], who provided an exact algorithm for hierarchically organized sets of hypotheses that is also linear in time while being slightly more general than that of Gordon and Shortliffe. More recently, Shenoy and Shafer [116] introduced a method for the efficient propagation of belief functions in networks by means of

TABLE 1 Applying Dempster's Rule

	{*Toyota, GM, Chrysler*}	Θ
	0.8	0.2
{*Nissan, Toyota*}	{*Toyota*}	{*Nissan, Toyota*}
0.4	0.32	0.08
Θ	{*Toyota, GM, Chrysler*}	Θ
0.6	0.48	0.12

local computations, and Wilson [128] proposed a method in which the explicit use of Dempster's rule of combination is avoided. This permits an exact calculation of belief to be performed in worse than polynomial but better than exponential time and an approximate calculation, based on a Monte Carlo simulation and giving results that are arbitrarily close to the exact solution, to be performed in linear time even when the hypotheses are not hierarchically structured. More recent advances are explored in [88, 130].

D. Possibility Theory

A formal theory of possibilities, based on the notion of a fuzzy set [134], was first introduced by Zadeh [135]. However, the concept of using the notion of possibilities as an alternative to probabilities was mooted much earlier. The economist Shackle [112], unhappy with the use of subjective probability for handling uncertainty, proposed an alternative formalism. This formalism was the calculus of potential surprise, where uncertainty about an event is characterized by a subjective measure of the degree to which the observer in question would be surprised by its occurrence. Potential surprise is clearly linked to the intuitive notion of possibility. If an event is entirely possible, then there is no surprise attached to its occurrence. If an event is wholly impossible or is believed to be so, then if it occurs it will be accompanied by the maximum degree of surprise. In this section we present a simple overview of Zadeh's theory, demonstrating its similarity to and differences from probability theory, and briefly discuss possibilistic logic [30] that is derived from it.

First we need the concept of a fuzzy set [134]. A fuzzy set is a set whose membership is not absolute, but a matter of degree, such as the set of tall people. A fuzzy set F is characterized by a membership function μ_F which specifies the degree to which each object in the universe U is a member of F. One way to consider F is as a fuzzy restriction on X, a variable that which takes values in U, in that it acts as an elastic constraint on the values that may be assigned to X. The assignment of a value u to X has the form

$$X = \mu : \mu_F(\mu),$$

where $\mu_F(u)$ is the degree to which the constraint F is satisfied when u is assigned to X. To denote the fact that F is a fuzzy restriction on X, we write

$$R(X) = F.$$

Now, the proposition "X is F," which translates into "$R(X) = F$," associates a possibility distribution Π_X with X and this distribution is taken to be equal to $R(X)$:

$$\Pi_X = R(X).$$

Along with this we have a possibility distribution function π_X, which is defined to be equal to the membership function of F:

$$\pi_x = \mu_F.$$

Thus $\pi_x(u)$, the possibility that $X = u$, is taken to be equal to $\mu_F(u)$. As an example, let U be the set of positive integers and let F be the fuzzy set of small integers. This set is described by the following set of pairs, each of the form $(u, \mu_F(u))$:

$$F = \{(1, 1), (2, 1), (3, 0.8), (4, 0.6), (5, 0.4), (6, 0.2)\}.$$

Given this, the proposition "X is a small integer" associates the possibility distribution Π_X with X, where Π_X is written as a set of pairs $(u, \pi_X(u))$:

$$\Pi_X = \{(1, 1), (2, 1), (3, 0.8), (4, 0.6), (5, 0.4), (6, 0.2)\}.$$

Thus, the possibility that X takes the value 3, given that X is a small integer, is 0.8. We can use possibility distributions to define possibility measures. If A is fuzzy subset of U, then the possibility measure $\Pi(A)$ of A is defined by

$$\begin{aligned}\mathrm{Poss}(X \text{ is } A) &= \Pi(A)\\ &= \sup_{u\in U} \mu_a(u) \wedge \Pi_X(u).\end{aligned}$$

Possibility measures clarify the comparison between possibility and probability theory. We can establish that

$$\Pi(A \cup B) = \max(\Pi(A), \Pi(B)), \tag{1}$$

$$\Pi(A \cap B) = \min(\Pi(A), \Pi(B)), \tag{2}$$

which contrast with the corresponding results for probability theory.[3] Zadeh stressed the fact that possibility and probability are essentially different concepts by using the example of Hans's breakfast. Consider the statement, "Hans ate X eggs for breakfast" with $X \in \{1, \ldots, 8\}$. We can associate both a possibility distribution, based on the ease with which Hans can eat eggs, and a probability distribution with X, giving something of the form

u	1	2	3	4	5	6	7	8
$\Pi_x(u)$	1	1	1	1	0.8	0.6	0.4	0.2
$\mathrm{Pr}_x(u)$	0.1	0.8	0.1	0	0	0	0	0

So although it is perfectly possible that Hans can eat three eggs for breakfast, he is unlikely to do so. There is a heuristic connection between possibility and probability, because if something is impossible, it is likely to be improbable, but a high degree of possibility does not imply a high degree of probability nor does a low degree of probability reflect a low degree of possibility. Dubois and Prade [32] pointed out that a weak theoretical connection exists because for all A,

$$N(A) < \mathrm{Pr}(A) < \Pi(A),$$

where $N(A)$ is the necessity of A, defined by

$$N(A) = 1 - \Pi(A).$$

[3] The use of maximum and minimum is not compulsory. For further discussion of this point, see [33].

It is possible to extend these ideas to possibility distributions that depend on more than one attribute and marginal possibility distributions. Explanations of these concepts will be omitted in interest of saving space (but see [135]).

Possibility theory was extended by Dubois and Prade [30] to create as numerically quantified logic called possibilistic logic. In this formalism, either a possibility or a necessity measure is attached to every formula of classical first order logic with nonvague predicates, and classical inference patterns, such as modus ponens and the resolution principle, are extended for such weighted clauses. As a result, possibilistic logic provides a basis for theorem proving under uncertainty [23] which, thanks to the combination rules for possibility measures, does not suffer from some of the problems of probabilistic logic. In particular, possibility theory allows the possibility of the implication $p \supset q$ to be interpreted as a conditional possibility. In addition it has been proved that a linear resolution strategy generates a solution with the greatest possible lower bound on necessity, giving a simple means of determining the most certain conclusion that may be inferred from a set of uncertain clauses. Further work [24, 29, 35] has extended the system in a number of ways. Perhaps the most important extension is that of the resolution principle so that a clause weighted with a possibility measure can be combined with one weighted with a necessity value. In addition, a scheme for including vague predicates has been introduced, and possibilistic logic has been shown to be complete in the sense that any logical inconsistency in a set of clauses will be detected by repeated applications of the resolution principle. This compares well with probabilistic logic, which can be shown to be incomplete. There are also soundness and completeness results for possibilistic logic [27].

There are other developments in possibilistic logic that are worth mentioning. Just as in classical logic, one can discover whether a clause is satisfiable either by syntactic or semantic means, so one can consider semantic ways of performing inference in possibilistic logic to go with the resolution method already mentioned. This was demonstrated by Lang [73], who gave a method for finding the best interpretation, in the sense that it has the largest necessity measure, of a set of clauses of possibilistic logic.

E. Other Approaches

There are a number of other numerical techniques that, although we do not have space to consider them in any detail, are worth mentioning for their particular historical or theoretical interest. Certainly factors [118], perhaps because of their simplicity and intuitive appeal, have been widely used to handle uncertainty. The certainty factor approach assigns a numerical weight, the certainty factor, to the consequent of every

$$\text{If}\langle \textit{evidence} \rangle \text{ then } \langle \textit{hypothesis} \rangle$$

rule in a rule-based system. The value of the certainty factor, which lies in the interval $[-1, 1]$, is assessed by the domain expert from the degree, between 0 and 1, to which a given piece of evidence causes belief and disbelief in the hypothesis to be increased. The certainty factors rules fired during inference are then combined to give an overall certainty for the support given to a particular hypothesis by the known evidence. Several people have challenged the validity of the certainty factor model. For instance, Heckerman [54] showed that the original definition of the model is flawed, because the belief in a hypothesis given two pieces of evidence will depend on the order in which the effect of the pieces of evidence is computed.

Smets adapted evidence theory as introduced by Dempster and Shafer in two important ways. The first [119] was to relax the assumption that all hypotheses have been identified before the evidence is considered. Instead, Smets makes an *open-world* assumption that the frame of discernment does not necessarily contain an exhaustive set of hypotheses. Under this assumption there is no normalization in Dempster's rule of combination, because the mass pertaining to the empty set $\emptyset$ is taken to indicate belief in a hypothesis outside the frame of discernment. The open-world assumption requires a modification of the definitions given earlier for the calculation of belief and plausibility from probability mass distributions (which are just called mass functions by Smets). Belief is defined as

$$\mathrm{Bel}(A) = \sum_{B \subseteq A,\, B \neq \emptyset} m(B),$$

whereas plausibility is defined as

$$\begin{aligned}\mathrm{Pl}(A) &= \textstyle\sum_{B \cap A \neq \emptyset} m(B) \\ &= 1 - (m(\emptyset) + \mathrm{Bel}(\neg A)).\end{aligned}$$

Dempster's rule of combination becomes

$$m_{12}(C) = \sum_{A \cap B = C} m_1(A) m_2(B).$$

Smet's other innovation was to introduce an alternative interpretation of the theory of evidence called the transferable belief model. The transferable belief model rejects any suggestion that the numbers manipulated by the theory are probabilities. Instead, they are taken to be pure expressions of belief suitable for reasoning at an abstract *credal* level and are transformed into probabilities at the *pignistic* level when decisions are necessary. In the model, the basic belief mass $m(A)$ in any subset A of a frame of dicsernment Θ is the amount of belief that supports A, that, due to ignorance, does not support any strict subset of A. If we have new evidence that excludes some of our original hypotheses and so points to the truth being in $\Theta' \subset \Theta$, then the basic belief mass $m(A)$ now supports $A \subset \Theta'$. Thus the belief originally attributed to A is transfered to that part of A not eliminated by the new evidence, giving the system its name.

F. Limitations of Numerical Techniques

As one might expect, none of the systems mentioned in preceding section is perfect, and there are a number of problems common to all numerical formalisms. The first is perhaps the simplest. When Cohen [15] criticized possibility theory, saying

> relatively little has been made of the idea of fuzzy sets and possibility theory...(this) may be because the idea does not improve on any of the difficult methodological problems that beset probability theory, such as the assessment of prior probabilities.

he is restating an argument that has been made time and again. Obtaining the "numbers," be they probabilities, possibilities, or mass distributions, does seem to be a major problem. Clearly, without good numerical assessments the sophisticated computational mechanisms are of little value. A refinement of this argument that applies only to probability theory is that there are domains in which it is not possible to obtain the kind of strong statistical data necessary to apply probability theory in its "frequentist" interpretation.[4] This has been used by many (see, for example, [41]) people to argue against the use of probability theory to deal with uncertainty. However, the *personalist* and *necessarian* [114] school of probabilists argues that probabilities always may be obtained, either from rational human reasoning or because they exist as a measure of the degree to which sets of propositions confirm one another. It seems, then, as though there is no clear cut winner in this argument: the moral appears to be

> if you can obtain the numbers to your satisfaction, then use them.

As a final word, it is worth mentioning that it also has been convincingly argued in several places (see for example [11, 98]) that even if the numbers are available, they make little difference to the business of weighing up the evidence. This, however, is a different argument altogether and we will say no more about it.

A second problem stems from the use of numbers: the interpretation of the results of applying a numerical formalism given the notorious irrationality that human beings exhibit when dealing with numbers [125]. All the techniques generate results as numerical values. These values, however, have been generated in different ways and thus measure different things, although they are just numbers and may be compared and contrasted by the uninitiated as though they were identical. Indeed, to interpret them correctly, it is perhaps necessary to label them with the type of belief that they measure to prevent a probability of 0.5 being compared unfavorably with a possibility of 0.8. In addition, there is the problem of ranking different solutions. A common argument for including numbers is that they allow one to choose the best of several courses of action that must be differentiated by using uncertain knowledge, and of course numerical results can be used to do this. However, using the ordinal value of the results alone to do this can obscure important information concealed in the ratio of the results, namely, how close the second largest value is to the largest. If the values are close, but separated by a wide margin from the third, then rather than choosing the first, it might be profitable to review the criteria upon which the assessment was made in the hope that some telling difference between the alternatives might be found.

Finally, there are problems associated with computational expense. The massive amount of time needed to apply the full formal methods to realistically large problems was one of the main reasons that such ad hoc methods as certainty factors were introduced. Although, as outlined in earlier sections, there have been

[4] In which the probability of an event is the value to which the ratio of occurrences to trials converges after a large number of trials.

several attempts to find computationally efficient methods of calculating the results of applying probability and evidence theories in particular situations, the general problem of computational expense remains.

III. SYMBOLIC APPROACHES

Most of the symbolic approaches for handling imperfect information that we consider here were introduced to allow programs to deal with incompleteness by exhibiting "commonsense" reasoning, thus avoiding the need to state every possible exception to a general rule. In other words, they were introduced to deal with incomplete information. The initial papers introduced three methods: Reiter's default logic [102], McCarthy's circumscription [82], and the modal approach of McDermott and Doyle's nonmonotonic logic I [85] and nonmonotonic logic II [84]. The first two methods have been widely accepted, studied, and revised, whereas the third has been less successful. For various reasons, neither nonmonotonic logic I or II took off, and it was not until several years later that the modal approach was finally vindicated by Moore [87], who solved several of the problems inherent in the earlier logics.

In this section, we discuss these three main nonmonotonic logics in some detail, before briefly mentioning some of the other more interesting proposals for nonnumerical reasoning and debating the failings of symbolic approaches in general. First, however, we discuss the motivation for and common features of symbolic approaches.

A. Overview

The common motivation behind all of the systems of nonmonotonic logic that we discuss subsequently is the attempt to devise sound formal mechanisms for reasoning that overcome the limitations of first order logic. At first sight, first order logic seems to be a panacea for all the problems of knowledge representation and deduction for AI systems. This is unfortunately a naive impression, and there are many problems that beset the use of classical logic, especially when attempting to model the kind of "commonsense" reasoning at which human beings excel. Israel [66] credits Minsky with being the first to consider the matter, pointing out that there are two particular properties of first order logic that are at odds with commonsense human behavior. The first results in the so-called qualification problem. Say, to take the classic example, we are interested in building a system that reasons about animals and their athletic abilities. One of the facts that we want to encode is the fact that generally birds can fly. Unfortunately, there is no "generally" quantifier in first order logic, so we must approximate this by asserting that all birds fly:

$$\forall x, \qquad bird(x) \supset flies(x). \tag{3}$$

This seems fine until we recall that penguins do not fly, and so we have to augment the rule. This may be done in several ways: we choose to write

$$\forall x \qquad bird(x) \wedge \neg penguin(x) \supset flies(x). \tag{4}$$

However, this formulation becomes problematic when we want to reason about ostriches, kiwis, and birds whose feet have been set in concrete. For any general rule of this kind, we can think up an arbitrarily large number of exceptions, and it is the provision of a compact means of handling all of these exceptions that is the qualification problem. The second troublesome property is that of monotonicity. In first order logic, there is no mechanism for retracting inferences once they have been made or facts once they have been added to the database. If a sentence ψ is a logical consequence of a theory A, then it is still a consequence of any theory that includes A, such as the theory $A \cup \phi$. This is true even if we have $\phi \equiv \neg\psi$, although in this latter case, adding ϕ leads to inconsistency (because we can derive both ψ and its negation). Monotonicity is particularly troublesome when, in attempting to solve the qualification problem, we allow systems to make "guesses" about the state of the world that are used in the absence of more detailed information. For instance, consider a particular bird, Joe. It is natural to assume that Joe flies, because nothing is known to the contrary. In a monotonic system, when it is learnt that Joe has been nailed to his perch, there is no means to retract the inference that Joe can fly. To solve such problems, researchers turned to nonmonotonic logical systems that allow plausible inferences to be made to defeat the qualification problem and permit failed inferences to be withdrawn when their falsity becomes apparent.

There are three main ways in which a solution to these problems has been attempted: closed-world reasoning, prototypical reasoning, and reasoning about beliefs. These methods can be summarized as follows. Closed-world reasoning makes the assumption that all relevant positive knowledge has been explicitly stated. Working on this assumption, systems are permitted to deduce any negative facts that they desire so that they may reason about the state of the world. Thus a system reasoning about connecting flights that has no knowledge of a flight between London and Ankara is allowed to deduce that there is no such flight and is allowed only to postulate the existence of a flight joining London and Paris if such a flight is explicitly recorded in its database. Prototypical, or default, reasoning proceeds from rules that relate to typical individuals of some class to make plausible assumptions about particular individuals. If and when specific information about the individual that contravenes the plausible deduction comes to light, the assumption is retracted. Our example about flying is of this kind. We know that birds fly in general, so that when we hear of a bird Opus, we assume that it can fly. Later we learn that Opus is a penguin and knowing that penguins do not fly allows us to retract our assumption that Opus is capable of flying. Finally, reasoning about beliefs allows a system to make sound deductions based on what it believes to be true. Assuming rationality, the system is allowed to logically deduce facts from what it knows, what it believes to be true, and what it believes to be false, which is everything that it does not believe to be true. Thus a system reasoning about its siblings can deduce that it is an only child, because were it not, it would know about a brother or sister.

B. Circumscription

Circumscription [82, 83] is an attempt to formalize closed-world reasoning in a way that defeats some of the problems of simple techniques such as the closed-world assumption [101] and negation as failure [14], where the failure to derive particular facts allows their negation to be assumed. Unlike other techniques, circumscription applies a set of rules of conjecture that are based on syntactic manipulation rather than appeals to undecidable provability or consistency. We will deal with predicate circumscription [82], the first variant to be introduced and, consequently, the most studied of the differing varieties of circumscription. Predicate circumscription allows explicit assumptions of completeness to be made as required, providing a way to apply a closed-world assumption to a particular predicate at a given moment. A schema for a set of first order sentences is generated and then instantiated, replacing predicate variables with particular predicates; the choice determines the composition of the extension of the circumscribed predicate. This has the effect of asserting that the only positive instances of that predicate that exist are those known to exist at that time within the circumscribed domain. Any instances that are not known to be positive are assumed to be negative.

McCarthy provided a second order axiom schema that had the effect of circumscribing a single predicate and that can be generalized to allow a set of one or more predicates to be circumscribed jointly. If we have P as a n-ary relationship and $A(\Phi)$ is the result of replacing all occurrences of P in A by the predicate expression Φ, basically a predicate symbol, then the circumscription of P in A is

$$\begin{aligned}\text{Circum}(A, P) = A(\Phi) \wedge (\forall x_1, \ldots, x_n)(\Phi(x_1, \ldots, x_n) \supset P(x_1, \ldots, x_n))\\ \supset ((\forall x_1, \ldots, x_n)(P(x_1, \ldots, x_n) \supset \Phi(x_1, \ldots, x_n)).\end{aligned}$$

This says that if Φ satisfies the conditions satisfied by P and that every $x_1, \ldots, x_n$ that satisfies Φ satisfies P, then every $x_1, \ldots, x_n$ that satisfies P also satisfies Φ. Given this definition of Circum(A, P), it is possible to define circumscriptive inference $\vdash_c$,

$$A \vdash_c B \quad \text{iff} \quad A \wedge \text{Circum}(A, P) \vdash B,$$

where $\vdash$ is the consequence relationship for classical logic. So, if we have

$$A = \text{Block}(a) \vee \text{Block}(b),$$

then we can circumscribe Block in A to get

$$(\Phi(a) \vee \Phi(b)) \wedge (\forall x)(\Phi(x) \supset (\text{Block}(x)) \supset (\forall x)(\text{Block}(x) \supset \Phi(x)),$$

and, substituting in $x = a$ and $x = b$, we get

$$(\forall x)(\text{Block}(x) \supset x = a) \wedge (\forall x)(\text{Block}(x) \supset x = b),$$

so circumscription closes the world, assumes that there is only one block, and deduces that it is either a or b.

The underlying meaning of the circumscription is that closed-world reasoning about one or more predicates of a theory is equivalent to truth in all models of the theory that are minimal in those predicates. In other words, any predicate P is satisfied only by those $x_1, \ldots, x_n$ that must satisfy it. Minimality is defined as follows. If we have two models M and M' of a sentence A, we have $M \sqsubseteq M'$ iff M and M' have the same domain and agree on the interpretation of variables, functions, and relationships other than P, and the extension of P in M is a subset of that in M'. We say that a model M of A is minimal in P iff $M' \sqsubseteq M$ only when

$M' = M$, and A minimally entails B with respect to P, that is, $A \vdash_c B$, iff B is true in all models of A that are minimal in P. McCarthy then goes on to prove that any instance of the circumscription of P in A is true in all models of A that are minimally entailed by A in P.

Predicate circumscription has been amended and refined to handle various technical difficulties that have been discovered in the years since the formalism was introduced. These refinements include formula circumscription [83], which permits arbitrary predicate expressions to be circumscribed and which forms the basis of a simple means of implementing commonsense reasoning, commonly known as abnormality theory. In this approach, the usual "birds fly" example is formalized by writing the first order sentences

$$\forall x, \qquad bird(x) \wedge \neg \text{abnormal}(aspect_1, x) \supset flies(x)$$

$$\forall x, \qquad penguin(x) \wedge \neg \text{abnormal}(aspect_2, x) \supset \text{abnormal}(aspect_1, x)$$

$$bird(tweety)$$

$$penguin(opus).$$

This says that all birds that are not abnormal in some way fly, all penguins that are not abnormal in some other way are abnormal in the first way, Tweety is a bird, and Opus is a penguin. If the abnormality predicate abnormal is then circumscribed, the number of occurrences of abnormal things will be minimized and, roughly speaking, we will get the following. Because there is nothing that says that Tweety is abnormal in any way, the first implication applies and we deduce that Tweety flies. Because there is nothing saying that Opus is abnormal with regard to $aspect_2$, we deduce that he is abnormal with respect to $aspect_1$ and thus we cannot deduce that he flies. Clearly we could add additional sentences to ensure that we can deduce that Opus does not fly.

Another variant of circumscription is pointwise circumscription [76] in which the circumscription, instead of being carried out everywhere simultaneously, is performed by minimizing one point at a time. This fixes circumscription so that it gives the correct results when reasoning about time. There is also domain circumscription [40], which provides a formalization of the so-called domain closure assumption—the assumption that the only individuals that a system must deal with are those explicitly named.

C. Default Logic

Default logic [102] models prototypical reasoning by allowing special inference rules, known as default rules, to be added to a standard first order logic. These rules differ from first order rules of the form

$$\forall x, \qquad A(x) \supset B(x)$$

in that they include an explicit consistency check that prevents the rule from being applied in inappropriate situations and allows the expression of rules such as

$$\frac{Bird(x):M\,Flies(x)}{Flies(x)},$$

which is read "if x is a bird and it is consistent to believe that x flies, then conclude that x flies".[5] Default rules can be considered as meta rules that tell us how to complete first order theories that are incompletely specified. Now, a default theory (W, D) is a set of first order axioms W and a set of default rules D of the form

$$\frac{\alpha(\tilde{x}):\beta_1(\tilde{x})\cdots\beta_m(\tilde{x})}{\gamma(\tilde{x})},$$

where $\alpha(\tilde{x})$, $\beta_i(\tilde{x})$, and $\gamma(\tilde{x})$ are all formulas whose free variables are among those in $\tilde{x} = x_1, \ldots, x_n$. $\alpha(\tilde{x})$ is termed the precondition or prerequisite, the $\beta_i(\tilde{x})$ are the gating facts or justifications, and $\gamma(\tilde{x})$ is the consequent. Given a set of default rules D and a first order theory W, it is possible to define an extension of the default theory as the closure of W plus a maximal consistent set of consequences of D. It is possible to distinguish several classes of such default rules, some of which have attractive properties such as always having extensions. Chief among these are those with a single justification $\beta(\tilde{x})$ that divides into normal defaults, the set of defaults such that $\beta(\tilde{x}) = \gamma(\tilde{x})$, and seminormal defaults, where $\beta(\tilde{x}) = \gamma(\tilde{x}) \wedge \omega(\tilde{x})$ for some $\omega(\tilde{x})$.

An extension, E, of a default theory is a minimal set of beliefs that contain W, are deductively closed, and are maximally consistent with the rules in D. Thus E is an extension for (W, D) if

$$\Gamma(E) = E,$$

where for any set of sentences S, $\Gamma(S)$ is a minimal set such that[6]

$$W \subseteq \Gamma(S),$$
$$\mathrm{Th}(\Gamma(S)) = \Gamma(S)$$

and if D contains

$$\frac{\alpha(\tilde{x}):\beta_1(\tilde{x})\cdots\beta_m(\tilde{x})}{\gamma(\tilde{x})}$$

and both $\alpha(\tilde{x}) \in \Gamma(S)$ and $\neg\beta_i(\tilde{x}) \notin \Gamma(S)$ for all i, then it is the case that $\gamma(x) \in \Gamma(S)$.

Reiter proved some interesting results for normal default theories that include no free variables. First, every closed normal default theory has an extension, so something always can be conjectured about such a theory. Second, if a closed normal default has two extensions, then the union of these is inconsistent, so that multiple extensions are generated only if the default rules have inconsistent consequents. Finally, Reiter showed that closed normal default theories are semimonotonic. If we have two default theories where the sets of default rules of one are a subset of the default rules of the other, then an extension of the theory with the smaller set of defaults will be a subset of an extension of the other. Thus, adding default rules to a theory does not cause its extensions to need revision: new default inferences are simply added to the existing extensions (they may, of course, cause

[5] Recent work on default logic tends to drop the operator M for simplicity. We use it here for comparison with other systems, but leave it out later.

[6] $\mathrm{Th}(T)$ is the deductive closure of T.

new extensions to arise). There are also some more general results, applicable to all closed default theories, the most important of which are that if such a theory (D, W) has an inconsistent extension, then it is its only extension and it is inconsistent because W is inconsistent—default rules alone do not generate inconsistent extensions.

Łukaszewicz [79] proposed translations between defaults, replacing

$$\frac{\alpha(\tilde{x}):\beta(\tilde{x})}{\gamma(\tilde{x})}$$

by

$$\frac{\alpha(\tilde{x}):\beta(\tilde{x}) \wedge \gamma(\tilde{x})}{\gamma(\tilde{x})},$$

making a general default into a seminormal default, and replacing

$$\frac{\alpha(\tilde{x}):\beta(\tilde{x}) \wedge \gamma(\tilde{x})}{\gamma(\tilde{x})}$$

by

$$\frac{\alpha(\tilde{x}):\beta(\tilde{x}) \wedge \gamma(\tilde{x})}{\beta(\tilde{x}) \wedge \gamma(\tilde{x})},$$

converting a seminormal default into a normal default. The first is noncontroversial, but the second, despite being applicable for a large range of practically occurring defaults, has some rather alarming exceptions [40]. By using both translations sequentially, we can replace the eminently sensible

$$\frac{has\_motive(x):guilty(x)}{suspect(x)}$$

by the rather unreasonable

$$\frac{has\_motive(x):suspect(x) \wedge guilty(x)}{suspect(x) \wedge guilty(x)}.$$

In a further paper, Łukaszewicz [80] generalized default logic, providing an alternative formalization of an extension and proving that seminormal default theories are guaranteed such extensions. He also showed that seminormal default theories are semimonotonic, that is, monotonic with respect to default rules.

D. Autoepistemic Logic

Moore [87] distinguished between default reasoning of the prototypical type discussed in the previous section and what he calls autoepistemic reasoning. The latter is defined as the kind of reasoning employed by an ideally rational agent reasoning about his or her own beliefs. Moore claims that autoepistemic reasoning is the kind of reasoning intuitively employed in many situations, giving the example of how he determines whether or not he has an elder brother. He argues that he knows that he has no elder brother, not because he has been told explicitly that no such person exists or because he has carefully sifted through all the available evidence, but simply because he knows that if he had an elder brother, he would know about him. This does seem very appealing and, despite some sharp criticism [117], autoepistemic reasoning has become well established within the nonmonotonic logic community.

Having identified the differences between prototypical and autoepistemic reasoning, Moore distinguishes between the types of nonmonotonicity that they support. Default reasoning makes plausible inferences based on plausible grounds, which later may be shown to be untenable, at which point the beliefs will have to be retracted. Autoepistemic reasoning, on the other hand, makes only valid inferences, although these inferences are dependent on the knowledge available. When the knowledge is updated, the valid inferences may change, hence introducing nonmonotonicity. Moore formalized this style of reasoning by introducing autoepistemic logic, defining the stable expansions of a consistent set of premises A that may be maintained by an ideally rational agent as being those sets of beliefs T such that

$$T = \mathrm{Th}(A \cup \{L\varphi\colon \varphi \in T\} \cup \{\neg L\varphi\colon \varphi \notin T\}),$$

where $L\varphi$ means that φ is believed. A stable expansion includes the premises and states what is and is not believed, including no beliefs that are not supported by the premises.

Moore demonstrated that stable expansions contain all and only those formulas that are true in every interpretation that satisfies all the premises, and makes $L\varphi$ true for every formula φ in the expansion. Now, if the premises are true and the set of beliefs are the beliefs in a particular expansion, then the formulas in that expansion are the only formulas that can be true—in other words, the expansion accurately characterizes those things that may be deduced from those facts known to be true and those facts currently believed to be true. The dependency on the current set of beliefs corresponds to the intuitive notion that what may be deduced is determined by what is believed.

In its original form [87], autoepistemic logic is a purely propositional modal logic, with no means of incorporating quantifiers or individual variables. Konolige [68] extended Moore's approach to a first order system that does not allow "quantifying in" to the scope of a modality; thus statements of the form

$$\forall x, \qquad \psi(x) \supset L\varphi(x),$$

where modal operators occur within the scope of quantifiers, are not allowed. In a later paper [69], a scheme for tackling this problem was introduced. $L\varphi$ is interpreted as an inquiry as to whether φ is in the set of beliefs, and so $L\varphi(x)$ is interpreted by querying whether $\varphi(x)$ is believed, and $\varphi(x)$ is believed if x has a name t and $\varphi(t)$ is believed.

E. Other Approaches

There are, as mentioned previously, several other symbolic techniques of note. The first two of these are important from a historical point of view. Among the first nonmonotonic logics to be introduced was McDermott and Doyle's nonmonotonic logic I [85], which was based on the use of a consistency operator M. $\vdash \mathsf{M}\varphi$

is roughly equivalent to $\nvdash \neg\varphi$. An extension of the logic is essentially equivalent to the logical closure of the original theory along with the intersection of all the maximal allowable sets of assertions of the form $\vdash \mathsf{M}\varphi$. Comparing this with default logic, which has an extension for every maximal set of consistent assertions, nonmonotonic logic I can be seen to be the more cautious. Unfortunately, as McDermott and Doyle point out, the logic does not ensure that $\vdash \mathsf{M}\varphi$ and $\neg\varphi$ are necessarily inconsistent, a fact which allows for many anomalies. This, among other things, led McDermott to define nonmonotonic versions of the modal logics T, S4, and S5 [62]. These are identified under the title nonmonotonic logic II. Unfortunately nonmonotonic S5, whose axioms intuitively suggest it captures the ideas about belief that McDermott wants for his logic, collapses to monotonicity, leaving only the less desirable nonmonotonic T and S4. Moore [87] identified the problem with nonmonotonic logic II as being the acceptance of the characteristic axiom of the T system,

$$L\varphi \supset \varphi,$$

which may be read as "whatever is believed is true," and, after rejecting it as only being appropriate for dealing with infallible agents, went on to define autoepistemic logic.

Another interesting approach is subimplication [9], which extends the idea of closed-world reasoning, as formulated by Reiter [101], to make it consistent and closed under deduction. Subimplication deals with classical logic, and is thus compatible with methods applicable to classical logic. Subimplication is also closely related to circumscription. However, there are some problems with the formalism. Most importantly, the language over which subimplication applies is a rather restrictive subset of classical logic, so that it is not possible to express the nonmonotonic reasoning example that "with a few exceptions, birds fly."

Not all logical formalisms for dealing with incomplete data are nonmonotonic. Poole [97] proposed a novel means of handling prototypical reasoning without resorting to a nonmonotonicity. Indeed, reasoning in his system is carried out using the mechanism of ordinary first order logic. The crucial point is that reasoning is not considered as deduction, but as a form of theory formation. The idea is formalized in terms of whether or not propositions are explainable, which they are if it is possible to deduce them from a consistent set of formulas that consist of a set of facts, and a set of possible hypotheses that roughly correspond to the prototypical facts from which we make our default inferences. Poole proved that his system can represent default knowledge that corresponds to a restricted case of Reiter's normal defaults and may be generalized to cover other classes of defaults with, he claims, more attractive properties than the nearest equivalents in Reiter's formalization.

Another interesting symbolic formalism is Cohen's [15] theory of endorsements. Cohen's aim was to replace the handling of uncertainty by attaching numerical valuations to uncertain facts by heuristic reasoning about the nature of the uncertainty. Facts and rules in Solomon, the implementation of the model, have labels known as endorsements attached to them that specify the degree to which uncertainty is inherent in them. Thus rules may be labeled "maybe too general" and data are tagged with their source to allow their reliability to be assessed.

Knowledge about the different forms of uncertainty associated with each continuing inference and the reason that the particular inference is being propagated are then used to control the spread of uncertainty in pursuit of a particular deduction. Cohen argued that dealing with the reasons for the existence of the uncertainty that pervades real life problems and the control strategy that endorsements enable give a far deeper and more accurate means of handling uncertainty than using a flat numerical measure.

In fact, despite their apparent differences, both Poole's work and Cohen's endorsements can be seen as early efforts in the growing field of argumentation. This work is predicated on the idea that the way people reach conclusions is often by constructing arguments for and against different options and then weighing up the arguments to decide which option is best. One thing argumentation does very neatly is to give an account of default reasoning. If I know that Tweety is a bird, then I can argue that Tweety will fly on the basis that most birds fly. However, if I learn that Tweety is a penguin, I also can argue that Tweety cannot fly. Because the second argument is stronger than the first, I conclude that Tweety the penguin does not fly. The idea that argumentation could be used to underpin nonmonotonic reasoning appears to have been first suggested by Lin and Shoham [77], and the most extensive piece of work on the subject is [8]. Other notable works on argumentation as a general approach to nonmonotonic reasoning are [96, 126]. This is not the only way in which argumentation can be useful. It also can form the basis of a general approach to handling uncertain (rather than incomplete) information [71].

F. Limitations of Symbolic Techniques

One major failing of all of the nonmonotonic reasoning systems discussed here is that, as originally presented, there was no mechanism for enumerating the extensions of a given theory. As a result, several researchers have presented theorem provers for deciding if particular formulas are true in the extensions of particular theories. For example, Besnard et al. [6] tackled a subset of default logic, Ginsberg [49] dealt with circumscription, and Brewka [10] considered nonmonotonic logic I. There also have been attempts to provide procedures to construct extensions. Etherington [40], for instance, gave a method applicable to arbitrary finite default theories based on constraint propagation. However, the specification of decidable procedures for establishing the extensions of nonmonotonic formalisms remains an area of active research.

A further problem is that of dealing with multiple extensions. The failure of default logic to provide a means of choosing between several extensions is often stated as a fatal flaw in the formalism. However, as Reiter and Criscuolo [103] rightly pointed out with reference to the "Nixon diamond,"[7] there are many situations in which it is inappropriate for the formalism to choose between extensions. This may be justified on the grounds that such choices, when they may be made intuitively, depend on information implicit in the premises that is not accessible

[7] The Nixon diamond is a classic problem in nonmonotonic reasoning. Dick is a Quaker and Dick is a Republican. Most Quakers are pacifists; most Republicans are not pacifists. Is Dick a pacifist or not? The intuitive answer is that there is not enough information to say either way. The name arises from the fact that if you draw the information in the problem using arrows to join the propositions *Dick, Quaker, Republican*, and *Pacifist*, you get a diamond shape.

to the syntactic mechanism of the logic. If it is not necessary to make choices between extensions, then a reasoner may use default logic alone. If choices are necessary, some suitable mechanism must be appended to the basic default logic, a common one being to choose the extension that uses the most specific information. Alternatively, it is possible to pick an extension and use it until one of the deduced facts is found to be contrary to the state of the world, at which point an alternative extension that excludes the relevant fact is adopted as a basis for reasoning. This is an approach closely related to the behavior of justification-based truth maintenance systems (see Section V).

This latter approach ties up with some remarks made by McDermott in his second paper on nonmonotonic reasoning [84], were, conjecturing about robots reasoning using nonmonotonic logics, he distinguishes between those *brave* robots that use default logic and thus believe anything that may be true in one extension, and *cautious* robots that use circumscriptive type systems that believe only facts that may be deduced in every possible world view.[8] Clearly, one type of robot will be applicable to particular types of tasks and the other to different tasks. The fact that the selection criteria for brave robots is likely to be task specific is an argument for the correctness of default logic in providing no mechanism for choosing between extensions. Such a mechanism is a feature that the designer of a reasoning system based on default logic can introduce if and when it is required.

The final limitation of nonmonotonic reasoning systems is their inability to distinguish between different degrees of belief. Once facts have been derived, either from true axioms or plausible assumptions, they are regarded as true in their own right. It is thus impossible to formalize statements such as

I believe that A is usually true, but not as often as B

in any way that approximates the meaning of the original. There have been attempts to classify nonmonotonic reasoning within the framework of multivalued logics [48] and to relate inference to the ease with which the fact may be removed from a knowledge base [45], which may help to remedy this problem. There is, however, a more obvious way to remedy this problem, namely incorporating some uncertainty handling mechanism, and we shall come back to this in later sections.

IV. UNIFYING APPROACHES

Recently a school of thought has emerged ([13, 41, 72, 94, 104], for example) that acknowledges that all formalisms are useful for the solution of different problems. A general realization of the strength of this *eclectic* position has motivated research both into ways in which different formalisms may be used in combination

[8] The terms "brave" and "cautious" are used to refer to the systems used by the robots and the inferences made by the systems rather than the robots themselves. Thus circumscription is a cautious system that makes cautious inferences. The terms "credulous" and "skeptical" are synonyms for "brave" and "cautious." The bias in terminology is interesting. Implicit in "brave" and "cautious" seems to be the idea that brave is best, whereas implicit in "skeptical" and "credulous" is the idea that "skeptical" is best. I am not aware of any survey that attempts to identify whether people who propose cautious systems prefer to call them "skeptical" and if people who propose credulous systems prefer to call them "brave." It might be illuminating to find out.

to solve interesting practical problems and into establishing the formal differences and similarities between different systems. In this section we examine work that supports this eclectic viewpoint.

A. Overview

The idea that various techniques are complementary is borne out by several comparative studies and some well known results. For instance, Dubois and Prade [31] pointed out that evidence theory subsumes probability theory and possibility theory [135]. However, possibility theory does not encompass probability theory and has its own unique advantages over evidence theory. Similar results have been obtained for wholly symbolic formalisms. Etherington [40] compares default logic and circumscription, and finds that neither wholly encompasses the other with, for example, circumscription unable to express more of default theory than seminormal defaults without preconditions. Similarly, Konolige [68] proved that default logic and autoepistemic logic are formally equivalent, although autoepistemic logic has the intuitive advantages of dealing directly with an agent's beliefs.

The combination of several formalisms within one framework is not straightforward. As discussed in [31], the numerical techniques that we are interested in combining have been developed independently, and to a large degree rely on different modeling assumptions and use different inference techniques. These differences complicate the combination of formalisms. Some formalisms deal with vague knowledge, where the boundaries of the situations addressed by a statement are not clear. Other formalisms are concerned with precisely stated situations about which possibly incorrect facts are known. A third group of formalisms deals with both incorrectness and vagueness, differing both from the ways with which the problems are dealt by the dedicated calculi and from the ways that other members of the group deal with them. Some formalisms make use of deductive inference in which classical inference techniques such as modus ponens and modus tollens are extended to propagate numerical values as a consequence of the mathematical axioms of the underlying uncertainty theory [31]. This is the case in possibilistic logic where we have the analog of modus ponens:

$$\begin{array}{rl} N(p \rightarrow q) & = \alpha \\ N(p) & = \beta \\ \hline \alpha \geq N(q) & \geq \min(\alpha, \beta) \end{array}$$

In contrast, inductive reasoning, typified by the pattern

$$\begin{array}{l} \text{If } A\text{, then } B \\ B \text{ is observed} \\ \hline A \text{ becomes more plausible} \end{array}$$

is the inference technique of methods based on Bayes's rule, and the conclusion is the posterior likelihood of A given the observation. The inference has a direction, from B to A, that is not found in deductive reasoning.

Similar problems exist when considering the alternative formalisms developed for dealing with incompleteness. The most obvious of these is the distinction between brave systems such as default logic and cautious systems such as circumscription. Brave systems assume that results consistent with any subset of their knowledge may be true and so assume that any sentence in any extension may be taken to describe the state of the world accurately. Cautious systems, in contrast, assume that only results consistent with all their knowledge are accurate and so take only those sentences that appear in all extensions as true. Clearly, this is an important difference between methods and is likely to form one of the criteria for choosing between them. It is also possible to distinguish between those symbolic techniques that explicitly deal with belief or knowledge as well as truth and those that ignore the distinction. Autoepistemic logic and its predecessors nonmonotonic logics I and II define what is known by modal [62] operators L and M. These operators are related to each other and the usual connectives of first order logic by a set of axioms that are supposed to summarize the connection between knowledge or belief and truth.

A third important difference between nonmonotonic formalisms is the way in which the notion of provability is defined. Autoepistemic logic, for instance, by tying the notion of provability to that of knowledge, which is defined by the modal operator L, keeps the idea of a proof within the propositional language that it describes. In contrast, Reiter's default rules are defined using a meta-level operator M, which tests for the consistency of the gating fact in the default. This reliance on operators external to the first order language that the logic deals with can be seen as the reason for the difficulties that exist in constructing the extensions of default theories. Another difference is between those formalisms described in terms of proof theory, such as default logic, and those described in terms of model theory, such as circumscription. Although proof theoretic descriptions lead naturally to theorem proving techniques for that formalism [102], they can lead to difficult technical problems when attempting to cast the formalism in model theoretic terms [117], frustrating attempts to align them with a common view of nonmonotonic systems.

B. Combining Numerical Formalisms

There are also a number of papers in the literature that discuss the formal relationships between different numerical methods for handling imperfect information. Here we concentrate on work that involves the three main formalisms discussed previously.

Dubois and Prade [34] discussed the relationship between belief functions and possibility theory. Their paper presents an interpretation of the theory of evidence that aligns it with a general view of reasoning under uncertainty. Dubois and Prade were able to relate possibility theory to probability theory by interpreting possibility measures as special cases of plausibility measures in which the underlying belief functions are consonant (meaning that mass assignments are to concentric sets). Similarly, necessity measures are special cases of belief measures for which the beliefs functions are consonant. After effecting a similar comparison for evidence theory, they are able to claim that neither belief functions nor possibility theory are related to probability theory in an ad hoc or unprincipled way. In addition, they show that blind use of combination rules can lead to incorrect results where important information about the sources of the evidence is not taken into account, and it is suggested that some scheme, such as that proposed by Cohen [15], may be necessary to record the reasons for the numerical uncertainties that are being combined. This work was later extended [37] in a paper that identifies a number of different rules proposed in various places as ways to update for probability, possibility, and evidence theories, and relates them to one another, showing which generalize which, and which have similar ways of behaving.

Another relevant body of work is that of Gebhardt and Kruse [46, 47]. Their approach, termed the context model, provides an general framework in which different formalisms may be captured. In particular, the framework can encompass probability theory, evidence theory [46], and possibility theory [47]. What the context model provides is a way to identify differences between the different formalisms, giving an objective basis for comparing their different features and thus giving some basis on which to select the best model for given data. However, the down side is that to place the various models into the framework, they need to be reinterpreted in the terms of the context model and this seems to suggest that the versions of the formalisms being compared in the context model differ, at least semantically, from the versions espoused by other researchers. So, although the context model gives a fine basis for comparison if one is happy with the context model interpretation, it is not the only means to compare the formalisms in question.

Of course, this kind of theoretical approach is only one way to relate formalisms—it is also possible to perform experimental comparisons. An early piece of work in this vein was carried out by Wise and Henrion [131], who looked at the performance of certainty factors and an early form of Bayesian networks (as well as a method based on fuzzy sets) on a diagnosis problem relating to nuclear reactor accidents and found that the Bayesian network approach performed best. A more recent effort is that of [106].

C. Combining Symbolic Formalisms

There has been considerable interest, as demonstrated by the number of relevant papers in the literature, in making formal comparisons of symbolic reasoning techniques. For example, Konolige investigated the relationships between autoepistemic logic and default logic [68] and circumscription [69]. In the course of this research, he has considerably adapted and extended autoepistemic logic, solving several of the problems stated by Moore in his original work on the formalism. Konolige started by equating Reiter's consistency operator M to the dual of the provability operator L. This allows defaults to be expressed within the base language of the formalism, disposing of the metatheoretic nature of the consistency check, but complicates the interpretation of the theories generated by the formalism. However, interpreting consistency in this way allows the formal equivalence of autoepistemic and default logic to be established. Konolige proved that both default logic and autoepistemic logic sanction the same inferences if given the same initial theories, and neither is more expressive than the other. Furthermore, he gives an effective translation of default logic into autoepistemic logic and of autoepistemic logic into default logic. However, to establish the equivalence of the inferences sanctioned by autoepistemic and default logic, Konolige had to alter the notion of what could be inferred from an autoepistemic theory. In its original form, autoepistemic logic allowed more facts to be derived from a theory than would be permitted from the corresponding theory in default logic. Thus Konolige's amendment takes the form of restricting the inferences possible from an autoepistemic to those possible from the corresponding default theory.

Marek and Truszczyński [81] took the opposite view and modified default logic by relaxing the constraints on what may be derived from a default theory. This had the effect of permitting the extensions of a given default theory to contain all the formulas derivable from the corresponding autoepistemic theory. Marek and Truszczyński showed that if default extensions are allowed to contain all the formulas weakly provable from the original theory, where a weak proof relaxes the conditions on the prerequisites of the default rules, then default logic and autoepistemic logic are equivalent. Marek and Truszczyński also analyzed Konolige's approach proof theoretically, defining a further set of translations. More recently, Gottlob [53] showed that altering either autoepistemic logic or default logic is not necessary by providing a translation from default logic into standard autoepistemic logic (although he also showed that a modular translation between the two is impossible), and Schwarz [111] improved upon this translation.

Konolige [69] also gave attention to the relationship between autoepistemic logic and circumscription. He showed that a particular class of autoepistemic theories, what he terms the MIN$^=$ theories, allows all the first order consequences of predicate circumscription to be simply expressed in autoepistemic logic. This work requires the extension of autoepistemic logic to the full first order case (see Section III.D), and the definition of MIN theories as all those theories of the form

$$W \bigcup_i \{\forall x_i \neg LP_i x \supset \neg P_i x\}.$$

Such theories minimize the extension of the P_i so that every individual not known to have the property P_i does not. Augmenting such theories with a fixed equality predicate forms the class of MIN$^=$ theories that correspond to the minimal models of W.

There also has been work on relating circumscription and default logic. Imielinski [65] was concerned with "modular translations" between the two formalisms, where the introduction of new facts does not require the complete recomputation of the translation. He showed that it is possible to find modular translations for seminormal defaults without prerequisites, but proves that it is impossible to capture normal defaults with prerequisites in any system, such as the abnormality theory formalization of circumscription [83], which is based on the application of a preorder over the models of its theories. Etherington [40] demonstrated that default logic is capable of making conjectures that are not possible in circumscription, and used this to assert that default logic subsumes circumscription in certain cases. He also showed that there are situations where default logic and circumscription do not correspond, and proved that the existence of fixed predicates precludes translations from circumscription into default logic.

On a different note, Konolige and Myers [70] investigated the representation of defaults, implications that typically but not always hold, that cannot be easily expressed in Reiter's default logic. It turns out that such troublesome defaults may be represented using the epistemic concept of self-belief. Defaults of the form

As are typically *B*s

are represented using rules of the form

If x is believed to be an A

and x is not known to be an exception,

then x is a B.

This scheme is very similar to McCarthy's abnormality theory [83]. Once the defaults have been established in this autoepistemic form, they may be translated into default logic using the translation defined in [68].

Finally, it should be pointed out that the work by, for example, Lin and Shoham [77] and Bondarenko et al. [8] on argumentation-based approaches to nonmonotonic reasoning also could be viewed as attempts to combine different approaches within one framework.

D. Combining Numerical and Symbolic Formalisms

In some ways, the real challenge in building systems that use more than one approximate reasoning technique is to combine numerical and symbolic methods. This has proved a popular area for research, and there are a number of systems that implement what may be termed as symbolic/numerical inference.

One approach to combining different inference techniques, which gets around the problems of having to fully integrate symbolic and numerical techniques, is to apply them to a given problem sequentially. This has particular advantages if one of the formalisms is computationally expensive, because it allows the more time consuming method to be applied to a group of hypotheses that already has been restricted to a most plausible set. Systems in which the first inference is by symbolic methods dominate the current attempts to combine reasoning techniques. These apply logical techniques to establish a set of possible hypotheses from a larger initial set of exhaustive hypotheses, and then use numerical techniques to rank the plausible set. Typical of such systems are those of Provan [99], Bigham [7], and Laskey and Lehner [74]. In all three of these systems, the semantic equivalence of the ATMS [17] (see Section V.B) and the Dempster–Shafer method, proved by Provan, is exploited, ensuring that no information is lost in the initial round of inference. Bigham's system is particularly interesting in that it also permits beliefs based on possibility theory to be propagated. A similar system is de Kleer and William's [18] GDE for fault diagnosis. In GDE all inference directed at discovering the fault is carried out by symbolic methods, with probabilities invoked, not to determine the most likely of several solutions in a static analysis, but to suggest the next measurement. Thus the numerical computation sparks another round of symbolic inference and the cycle continues until the fault is found. A similar combination of symbolic and numerical systems is provided by the possibilistic ATMS [26] in which both assumptions and justifications may be associated with a possibility weight and, because the propagation of the weights is carried out for every clause in the ATMS, there is no separation of the management of uncertainty from the usual functionality of an ATMS. Furthermore, the possibilistic ATMS allows inconsistent knowledge bases to be revised using the principles of epistemic entrenchment [45].

Clearly the best possible combination of numerical and symbolic formalisms is one in which the degree of belief and the symbolic formalism are closely bound together so that an inference step involves the propagation of both formalisms at the same time. To some extent this has been achieved by graded default logic [43], which combines default logic and possibility theory. Attaching a numerical weight to the logical sentences changes none of their basic properties, so normal techniques can be used to propagate inference alongside some piece of computational machinery that propagates the possibility measures. Thus when two clauses are combined or a default rule fired, the antecedents are combined logically to give a consequent that has a possibility measure that is the result of the correct combination of the measures associated with the antecedent. The fact that the two processes, although simultaneous, are independent, means that a theorem prover for graded default logic may be obtained by augmenting a standard theorem prover for the underlying logic with a means of propagating the numerical measure. Froidevaux and Mengin [44, 86] took this course, adapting saturation [9] in the style of Besnard *et al.* [6] and adding the correct style of measure propagation. Something rather similar is provided by Neufeld and Poole [89] in their system, which suggests computing the probabilities of extensions of default logic as a means of choosing between them.

A development that ties default logic even more closely to numerical methods is the discovery of relationships between default logic and evidence theory. Wilson [127] considered the similarities between belief functions and default logic, and showed that, despite their initial dissimilarities, they are, in fact, closely related. Indeed, when using Łukaszewicz's [80] modification of default logic, the extensions of general closed default theories correspond to the sets of formulas whose beliefs, calculated by the theory of evidence, tend to 1 when the reliability of the sources of evidence tends to 1. This work was extended in [129], where, by modifying the Dempster–Shafer framework, Wilson was able to capture the full expressiveness of default logic. The existence of a strong relationship between default logic and the theory of evidence is borne out by Smets and Hsia [120], who demonstrated how to represent normal defaults (both with and without prerequisites) using the transferable belief model.

V. APPLICATIONS

In this section we identify a number of systems that have employed methods for dealing with imperfect information. In doing so, we take a very catholic view of the term "application," taking it to cover not only systems that use methods for handling imperfect information to deal with real problems, but also environments that allow such systems to be built. The reason for this is that the development of such environments, shells if you will, is an important step toward building applications in the narrow sense of "systems that solve problems." We start by considering applications of numerical formalisms.

A. Applications of Numerical Formalisms

Possibly the most famous system that makes use of numerical techniques for handling imperfect information is the expert system MYCIN [118], which inspired the invention of certainty factors. The success of MYCIN led to the development of the expert system shell EMYCIN, which was used to construct a number of other expert systems. For details of an example of such a system, see [42]. Despite this, the most widely applied technique, certainly in recent years, is that of Bayesian networks. Some of the more notable applications are the MUNIN system for the interpretation of electromyographic findings [3, 92], the ARCO system for financial forecasting [1], and the Pathfinder system for diagnosing lymph-node diseases [55, 56]. There are many others, including the CONVINCE system for situation assessment [67], the VPROP system for reducing the complexity of information presented to human operators in complex domains (such as space shuttle mission control) [58], and a system for analyzing adverse drug reaction [16].

In addition to this growing list of applications, there are a growing number of implementations of the various schemes for propagating probabilities—shells that can be instantiated to build new applications.[9] One of the best known of these is the commercial system HUGIN [2], which is essentially the inference engine from MUNIN. Another system that is widely used is IDEAL [123, 124], a set of LISP macros that implement just about every propagation algorithm proposed for probabilistic networks. Also worthy of note is Microsoft Bayesian Networks, a recent offering from the Microsoft Decision Theory Group, and Knowledge Industries' DXpress.

In comparison with this honor roll, the applications of other numerical techniques are less impressive, although there are exceptions. The first technique to count as an exception is possibilistic logic. Possibilistic logic has been implemented in a number of interesting ways. POSLOG [25] is an automated theorem prover based on resolution refutation for first order clauses weighted with lower bounds on their possibility or necessity degree. The system is complete in that is has been proved that or finds optimal refutations—those refutations with maximal possibility or necessity degrees. In an extension of this work, Dubois, Lang, and Prade [28] laid the groundwork for a logic programming environment based on Prolog in which clauses may be quantified with possibility measures. Such a logic programming language looks to be useful for solving min–max computations as well as for reasoning with uncertain knowledge. The possibilistic ATMS [26] also could be considered an implementation. The second exception is evidence theory when the local computation work of Shenoy and Shafer [116] is used as a means to compute values, because there are three systems that implement this scheme: Delief [136, 137], its successor MacEvidence [60, 61], and TresBel [132, 133]. All of these are shells in the sense that they provide the necessary mechanisms for solving problems using evidence theory, rather than being solutions to problems. Finally, it should be noted that techniques other than probability theory are beginning to be applied more widely, as the systems described in [64] demonstrate.

B. Applications of Symbolic Formalisms

In general, symbolic techniques have been applied much less widely than numerical ones. However, there are a number of notable developments. The first is the construction of theorem provers for the various logics. Some of these have been

[9] The most comprehensive list is that maintained by Russell Almond on his Belief Networks World-Wide Web page: http://bayes.stat.washington.edu/almond/belief.html.

mentioned already and this continues to be an active area of research, Nicolas and Schaub's XRay system [90] being a recent addition to the canon. The second development is in the area of truth maintenance systems, which can be considered as practical systems that implement a form of default reasoning.

Truth maintenance systems[10] provide the computational machinery to keep track of the relationships between sentences in logical representations of the world. The original variety of truth maintenance system was the justification-based truth maintenance system [22] (JTMS). A JTMS keeps track of the grounds on which facts are deduced and the relationship between those grounds, and checks for consistency across these grounds and the things that are deduced. When an inconsistency is detected, the fact that the relationship between the grounds are known means that the JTMS can identify which grounds are responsible for the inconsistency, thus helping to decide how the inconsistency can be rectified. The assumption-based truth maintenance system [17] (ATMS) can be considered to be a parallel JTMS that maintains all the possible sets of consistent grounds. Thus, in default logic terms, a JTMS maintains a single extension, whereas an ATMS maintains all the possible extensions. It is the ability of truth maintenance systems to cope with inconsistency, either by identifying how it might be rectified or by keeping track of all possible consistent views of the world, that makes it possible to consider them systems for default reasoning—they make it possible to solve the monotonicity problem.

Finally, there have been a number of papers that reported the use of approaches to default reasoning for tasks such as requirements engineering, control systems, and legal decision support. Antoniou [4] provided a summary of the state of the art.

C. Applications That Combine Formalisms

There are a few noteworthy attempts to build systems that make it possible to use several formalisms together. The first of these is Saffiotti's [105] hybrid belief system, which arose out of the author's conviction that in the pursuit of suitable methods for handling uncertainty, the use of knowledge representation techniques has been unjustly abandoned. To rectify this oversight, Saffiotti proposed a unifying formal framework for representing uncertain knowledge composed of categorical knowledge to which data about its uncertainty are attached, thus treating uncertainty as metaknowledge. The system handles the categorical knowledge (the knowledge component) as separate from the uncertainty component, treating the uncertainty component as information about the validity of the knowledge. This is a rather limited view of uncertainty, and whether it is possible to generalize this view is an open problem. The system provides an abstract knowledge base built around operations "Empty," which initializes the knowledge base, "Tell," which updates it, and "Ask," which queries it.

Any knowledge representation scheme and uncertainty handling formalism may be built into the hybrid belief system by supplying the appropriate functions. In general, Ask is a function of an item of knowledge and a belief that returns some "validity token" such as *true* or *false*, which identifies the degree to which the item is believed, and Tell is a function of an item of knowledge, its current

[10] Which are often, possibly more correctly, known as reason maintenance systems.

validity token, and the whole set of beliefs, which returns a new set of beliefs. To separate the knowledge and uncertainty components of a particular piece of datum, Saffiotti distinguishes between the intention of a sentence, which is its meaning and thus the knowledge component, and the extension, which is the object it denotes, here the truth value that corresponds to the uncertainty component. This structure maps onto a system that communicates with a user via Ask, Tell, and Empty, and may be decomposed into two modules, one to handle knowledge and one to handle uncertainty, each dealing with a different part of the sentences that make up the uncertain information passed to the system. The whole system turns on the use of the sentences and the fact that both the knowledge representation and the uncertainty handling systems deal with complementary part of them.

The second system, Enamora [50, 51], is an environment in which different approaches to handling uncertainty may be studied as a basis for developing a deeper theoretical understanding of their capabilities by means of comparative testing. Identifying the need to vary control knowledge between methodologies, the authors proposed handling this problem by holding the necessary information, including the interpretation of operators and inference rules, as metaknowledge. This allows Enamora to be constructed from a general database of knowledge that does not change between the uncertainty handling formalism and the representation and domain. If we consider domain-independent information, we can see that the general information will correspond to Saffiotti's [105] set of sentences that link uncertainty representation to knowledge representation. This, in turn, suggests that the hybrid belief system and Enamora are essentially two different ways to look at the same functional system, and that the most important features in both are the set of facts that release the uncertainty and the knowledge components, and the mapping between them.

The third system is Pulcinella [107, 108]. Pulcinella is an implementation of Shenoy and Shafer's [116] local computation scheme, but one that makes use of its generality to make it possible to propagate probabilities, possibilities, and belief functions (as well as logical *true* and *false*). Although one can only use a single formalism at a time, the system has considerable potential. As in [106, 110], the Pulcinella can be used to investigate the performance of different formalisms on the same problem (because the same representation is used regardless of what formalisms are adopted). Furthermore, because the system is written as a set of Lisp functions (the interaction with the user being very similar to that used by the hybrid belief system), it is quite possible to use Pulcinella to construct systems that build upon its basic functionality. An example of such an extended system is Mummu [93], which uses the computational machinery provided by Pulcinella to propagate interval values. It would be quite straightforward to adapt Pulcinella to use a number of different formalisms simultaneously. Recent work on the Pulcinella approach has resulted in a system that takes as input a set of clauses in first order logic and uses them to build the dependency network that is needed by the local computation scheme that underlies Pulcinella [109].

VI. SUMMARY

This chapter has provided a wide-ranging survey of the state of the art in reasoning with imperfect information. It began by dividing imperfect information into three classes based upon whether it is complete or incomplete and certain or uncertain (certain and complete information is, of course, perfect), and pointing out that certain but incomplete information is handled mainly by symbolic techniques whereas uncertain but complete information is handled mainly by numerical models. The chapter then surveyed the three main numerical and symbolic models. On the numerical side, probability theory, possibility theory, and evidence theory were discussed in some detail, and a number of other models were mentioned more briefly. On the symbolic side, default logic, circumscription, and autoepistemic logic were considered in detail, and a number of other models were mentioned more briefly. This material was then followed by a survey of work that attempted to combine or relate different approaches, and a section that discussed applications of various models.

ACKNOWLEDGMENTS

This research was supported by ESPRIT Basic Research Actions 3085 DRUMS and 6156 DRUMS II, and EPSRC Grant GR/L84117.

REFERENCES

1. Abramson, B. ARCO1: An application of belief networks to the oil market. In *Proceedings of the 7th Conference on Uncertainty in Artificial Intelligence*, pp. 1–8. Morgan Kaufmann, San Mateo, CA, 1991.
2. Andersen, S. K., Jensen, F. V., Olesen, K. G., and Jensen, F. HUGIN—A shell for building Bayesian belief universes for expert systems. In *Proceedings of the 11th International Joint Conference on Artificial Intelligence*, pp. 783–791. Morgan Kaufmann, San Mateo, CA, 1989.
3. Andreassen, S., Woldbye, M., Falck, B., and Andersen, S. K. MUNIN—A causal probabilistic network for interpretation of electromyographic findings. In *Proceedings of the 10th International Joint Conference on Artificial Intelligence*, pp. 366–372. Morgan Kaufmann, San Mateo, CA, 1987.
4. Antoniou, G. A tutorial on default reasoning. *Knowledge Eng. Rev.* 13, 225–246, 1998.
5. Barnett, J. A. Computational methods for a mathematical theory of evidence. In *Proceedings of the 7th International Joint Conference on Artificial Intelligence*, pp. 868–875. Morgan Kaufmann, San Mateo, CA, 1981.
6. Besnard, Ph., Quinou, R., and Quinton, P. A theorem prover for a decidable subset of default logic. In *Proceedings of the 3rd National Conference on Artificial Intelligence*, pp. 27–30. Morgan Kaufmann, San Mateo, CA, 1983.
7. Bigham, J. Computing beliefs according to Dempster–Shafer and possibilistic logic. In *Proceedings of the 3rd International Conference on Information Processing and Management of Uncertainty*, Paris, 1990, pp. 59–61.
8. Bondarenko, A., Dung, P. M., Kowalski, R. A., and Toni, F. An abstract, argumentation-theoretic approach to default reasoning. *Artif. Intel.* 93:63–101, 1997.
9. Bossu, G. and Siegel, P. Saturation, nonmonotonic reasoning, and the closed world assumption. *Artif. Intel.* 25:13–64, 1985.
10. Brewka, G. Tweety—Still flying, some remarks on abnormal birds, applicable rules and a default prover. In *Proceedings of the 5th National Conference on Artificial Intelligence*, pp. 8–12. Morgan Kaufmann, San Mateo, CA, 1986.
11. Chard, T. Qualitative probability versus quantitative probability in clinical diagnosis: A study using a computer simulation. *Medical Decision Making* 11:38–41, 1991.
12. Cheeseman, P. An inquiry into computer understanding. *Computational Intel.* 4:58–142, 1988.
13. Clark, D. A. Numerical and symbolic approaches to uncertainty management in AI. *Artif. Intel. Rev.* 4:109–146, 1990.

14. Clark, K. L. Negation as failure. In *Logic and Databases* (H.Gallaire and J. Minker, Eds.), pp. 293–322. Plenum Press, New York, 1978.
15. Cohen, P. R. *Heuristic Reasoning about Uncertainty: An Artificial Intelligence Approach.* Pitman, London, 1985.
16. Cowell, R. G., Dawid, A. P., Hutchinson, T. A., and Spiegelhalter, D. J. A Bayesian expert system for the analysis of an adverse drug reaction. *Artif. Intel. in Medicine* 3:257–270, 1991.
17. de Kleer, J. An assumption-based TMS. *Artif. Intel.* 28: 127–162, 1986.
18. de Kleer, J. and Williams, B. C. Diagnosing multiple faults. *Artif. Intel.* 32:97–130, 1987.
19. Dempster, A. P. Upper and lower probabilities induced by a multi-valued mapping. *Ann. Math. Statist.* 38:325–339, 1967.
20. Dempster, A. P. A generalisation of Bayesian inference (with discussion). *J. Roy. Statist. Soc. Ser. B.* 30:205–232, 1968.
21. Dempster, A. P. Comments on "An inquiry into computer understanding" by Peter Cheeseman. *Computational Intel.* 4:72–73, 1988.
22. Doyle, J. A truth maintenance system. *Artif. Intel.* 12:231–272, 1979.
23. Dubois, D., Lang, J., and Prade, H. Theorem proving under uncertainty—A possibility-theory based approach. In *Proceedings of the 10th International Joint Conference on Artificial Intelligence*, pp. 984–986. Morgan Kaufmann, San Mateo, 1987.
24. Dubois, D., Lang, J., and Prade, H. Automated reasoning using possibilistic logic: Semantics, belief revision and variable certainty weights. In *Proceedings of the 5th Workshop on Uncertainty in Artificial Intelligence*, pp. 81–87. Association for Uncertainty in AI, Mountain View, CA, 1989.
25. Dubois, D., Lang, J., and Prade, H. POSLOG, an inference system based on possibilistic logic. In *Proceedings of the North American Fuzzy Information Processing Society Conference*, 1990, pp. 177–180.
26. Dubois, D., Lang, J., and Prade, H. A possibilistic assumption-based truth maintenance system with uncertain justifications, and its application to belief revision. In *Truth Maintenance Systems* (J. P. Martins and M. Reinfrank, Eds.), pp. 87–106, Springer-Verlag, Berlin, 1990.
27. Dubois, D., Lang, J., and Prade, H. Fuzzy sets in approximate reasoning, Part 2: Logical approaches. *Fuzzy Sets and Systems* 40:203–244, 1991.
28. Dubois, D., Lang, J., and Prade, H. Towards possibilistic logic programming. In *Proceedings of the 8th International Conference on Logic Programming*. MIT Press, Cambridge, MA, 1991.
29. Dubois, D., Lang, J., and Prade, H. Automated reasoning using possibilistic logic: Semantics, belief revision and variable certainty weights. *IEEE Trans Knowledge Data Eng.* 6:64–71, 1994.
30. Dubois, D. and Prade, H. Necessity measures and the resolution principle. *IEEE Trans. Sys., Man., Cybernet.* 17:474–478, 1987.
31. Dubois, D. and Prade, H. A tentative comparison of numerical approximate reasoning methodologies. *Int. J. Man-Mach. Stud.* 27:717–728, 1987.
32. Dubois, D. and Prade, H. Modelling uncertainty and inductive inference: A survey of recent nonadditive probability systems. *Acta Psychologica* 68:53–78, 1988.
33. Dubois, D. and Prade, H. *Possibility Theory: An Approach to Computerized Processing of Uncertainty.* Plenum Press, New York, 1988.
34. Dubois, D. and Prade, H. Representation and combination of uncertainty with belief functions and possibility measures. *Computational Intel.* 4:244–264, 1988.
35. Dubois, D. and Prade, H. Resolution principles in possibilistic logic. *Int. J. Approx. Reasoning* 4:1–21, 1990.
36. Dubois, D., and Prade, H. Fuzzy sets in approximate reasoning, Part 1: Inference with possibility distributions. *Fuzzy Sets and Systems* 40:143–202, 1991.
37. Dubois, D. and Prade, H. Updating with belief functions, ordinal conditional functions and possibility measures. In *Uncertainty in Artificial Intelligence 6* (P. P. Bonissone, M. Henrion, L. N. Kanal, and J. F. Lemmer, Eds.), pp. 311–329. Elsevier Science, Amsterdam, 1991.
38. Dubois, D., Prade, H., and Smets, Ph. Partial truth is not uncertainty. *IEEE Expert* 9(4):15–19, 1994.
39. Duda, R. O., Hart, P. E., and Nilsson, N. J. Subjective Bayesian methods for a rule-based inference system. In *Proceedings of the National Computer Conference*, 1976, pp. 1075–1082.
40. Etherington, D. W. *Reasoning with Incomplete Information.* Pitman, London, 1988.

41. Fox, J. Three arguments for extending the framework of probability. In *Uncertainty in Artificial Intelligence* (L. N. Kanal and J. F. Lemmer, Eds.), pp. 447–458. Elsevier Science, Amsterdam, 1986.
42. Fox, J., Myers, C. D., Greaves, M. F., and Pegram, S. Knowledge acquisition for expert systems: experience in leukaemia diagnosis. *Methods Inform. Medicine* 24:65–72, 1985.
43. Froidevaux, C. and Grossetête, C. Graded default theories for uncertainty. In *Proceedings of the 9th European Conference on Artificial Intelligence*, pp. 283–288. Pitman, London, 1990.
44. Froidevaux, C. and Mengin, J. A theorem prover for free graded default theories. In *Proceedings of the Workshop of Esprit Basic Research Action 3085, DRUMS*, 1990, pp.194–205.
45. Gärdenfors, P. *Knowledge in Flux: Modelling the Dynamics of Epistemic States*. MIT Press, Cambridge, MA, 1988.
46. Gebhardt, J. and Kruse, R. The context model: an integrating view of vagueness and uncertainty. *Int. J. Approximate Reasoning* 9:283–314, 1993.
47. Gebhardt, J. and Kruse, R. A new approach to semantic aspects of possibilistic reasoning. In *Symbolic and Quantitative Approaches to Reasoning and Uncertainty* (M. Clarke, R. Kruse, and S. Moral, Eds.), pp. 151–159. Springer-Verlag, Berlin, 1993.
48. Ginsberg, M. L. Multivalued logics: A uniform approach to reasoning in artificial intelligence. *Computational Intel.* 4:265–316, 1988.
49. Ginsberg, M. L. A circumscriptive theorem prover. *Artif. Intel.* 39:209–230, 1989.
50. González, J. C. Arquitectura para sistemas expertos con razonamiento approximado. Ph.D. Thesis, Universidad Politécnica de Madrid, 1989.
51. González, J. C. and Fernández, G. ENAMORA: A general framework for approximate reasoning methodologies. In *Proceedings of the North American Fuzzy Information Processing Society Conference*, 1990.
52. Gordon, J. and Shortliffe, E. H. A method for managing evidential reasoning in a hierarchical hypothesis space. *Artif. Intel.* 26:323–357, 1985.
53. Gottlob, G. The power of beliefs or translating default logic into standard autoepistemic logic. In *Proceedings of the 13th International Joint Conference on Artificial Intelligence*, pp. 563–569. Morgan Kaufmann, San Mateo, CA, 1993.
54. Heckerman, D. E. Probability interpretation for MYCIN's certainty factors. In *Uncertainty in Artificial Intelligence* (L. N. Kanal and J. F. Lemmer, Eds.), pp. 167–196. Elsevier Science, Amsterdam, 1986.
55. Heckerman, D. E., Horvitz, E. J., and Nathwani, B. N. Towards normative expert systems: Part I. The Pathfinder project. *Methods Inform. Medicine* 31:90–105, 1992.
56. Heckerman, D. E. and Nathwani, B. N. Towards normative expert systems: Part II. Probability-based representations for efficient knowledge acquisition and interface. *Methods Inform. Medicine* 31:106–116, 1992.
57. Henrion, M., Provan, G., Del Favero, B., and Sanders, G. An experimental comparison of numerical and qualitative probabilistic reasoning. In *Proceedings of the 10th Conference on Uncertainty in Artificial Intelligence*, pp. 319–326. Morgan Kaufmann, San Mateo, CA, 1994.
58. Horvitz, E., Ruokangas, C., Srinivas, S., and Barry, M. A decision-theoretic approach to the display of information for time-critical decisions: Project Vista. Technical Memorandum 96, Rockwell International Science Center, Palo Alto Laboratory, 1992.
59. Horvitz, E. J., Heckerman, D. E., and Langlotz, C. P. A framework for comparing alternative formalisms for plausible reasoning. In *Proceedings of the 5th National Conference on Artificial Intelligence*, pp. 210–214. Morgan Kaufmann, San Mateo, CA, 1986.
60. Hsia, Y-T. and Shenoy, P. P. An evidential language for expert systems. In *Methodologies for Intelligent Systems 4*, (Z. W. Ras, Ed.), pp. 9–16. Elsevier Science, Amsterdam, 1989.
61. Hsia, Y-T. and Shenoy, P. P. MacEvidence, a visual environment for constructing and evaluating evidential systems. Working Paper 211, School of Business, University of Kansas, Lawrence, 1989.
62. Hughes, G. E. and Cresswell, M. J. *An Introduction to Modal Logic*. Methuen, London, 1968.
63. Hunter, A. *Uncertainty in Information Systems*. McGraw-Hill, London, 1996.
64. Hunter, A. and Parsons, S., Eds. *Applications of Uncertainty Formalisms*. Springer-Verlag, Berlin, 1998.
65. Imielinski, T. Results on translating defaults to circumscription. *Artif. Intel.* 32:131–146, 1987.

66. Israel, D. J. Some remarks on the place of logic in knowledge representation. In *The Knowledge Frontier: Essays in the Representation of Knowledge* (N. Cercone and G. McCalla, Eds.), pp. 80–91: Springer-Verlag, New York, 1987.
67. Kim, J. H. and Pearl, J. CONVINCE: A conversational inference consolidation engine. *IEEE Trans. Syst., Man., Cybernet.* 17:120–132, 1987.
68. Konolige, K. On the relation between default and autoepistemic logic. *Artif. Intel.* 35:343–382, 1988.
69. Konolige, K. On the relation between autoepistemic logic and circumscription. In *Proceedings of the 11th International Joint Conference on Artificial Intelligence*, pp. 1213–1218. Morgan Kaufmann, San Mateo, CA, 1989.
70. Konolige, K. and Myers, K. Representing defaults with epistemic concepts. *Computational Intel.* 5:32–44, 1989.
71. Krause, P., Ambler, S., Elvang-Gøransson, M., and Fox, J. A logic of argumentation for reasoning under uncertainty. *Computational Intel.* 11:113–131, 1995.
72. Krause, P. J. and Clark, D. A., *Representing Uncertain Knowledge: An Artificial Intelligence Approach.* Intellect, Oxford, UK, 1993.
73. Lang, J. Semantic evaluation in possibilistic logic: Application to min–max discrete optimisation problems. In *Uncertainty in Knowledge Bases* (B. Bouchon-Meunier, R. R. Yager, and L. A. Zadeh, Eds.), pp. 260–268. Springer-Verlag, Berlin, 1990.
74. Laskey, K. B. and Lehner, P. E. Assumptions, beliefs and probabilities. *Artif. Intel.* 32:65–77, 1990.
75. Lauritzen, S. L. and Spiegelhalter, D. J. Local computations on graphical structures, and their application to expert systems. *J. Roy. Statist. Soc. Ser. B.* 50:157–224, 1988.
76. Lifschitz, V. Pointwise circumscription: preliminary report. In *Proceedings of the 5th National Conference on Artificial Intelligence*, pp. 406–410. Morgan Kaufmann, San Mateo, CA, 1986.
77. Lin, F. and Shoham, Y. Argument systems: A uniform basis for nonmonotonic reasoning. In *Proceedings of the 1st International Conference on Knowledge Representation and Reasoning*, pp. 245–255. Morgan Kaufmann, San Mateo, CA, 1989.
78. Lindley, D. V. *Making Decisions.* Wiley, Chichester, 1975.
79. Łukaszewicz, W. Two results on default logic. In *Proceedings of the 9th International Joint Conference on Artificial Intelligence*, pp. 459–461. Morgan Kaufmann, San Mateo, CA, 1985.
80. Łukaszewicz, W. Considerations on default logic: An alternative approach. *Computational Intel.* 4:1–16, 1988.
81. Marek, W. and Truszczyński, M. Relating autoepistemic and default logics. In *Proceedings of the 1st International Conference on Knowledge Representation and Reasoning*, pp. 276–288. Morgan Kaufmann, San Mateo, CA, 1989.
82. McCarthy, J. Circumscription—A form of non-monotonic reasoning. *Artif. Intel.* 13:27–39, 1980.
83. McCarthy, J. Applications of circumscription to formalising commonsense knowledge. *Artif. Intel.* 28:89–116, 1986.
84. McDermott, D. V. Nonmonotonic logic II: Nonmonotonic modal theories. *J. Assoc. Comput. Mach.* 29:37–57, 1982.
85. McDermott, D. V. and Doyle, J. Non-monotonic logic I. *Artif. Intel.* 13:41–72, 1980.
86. Mengin, J. Un démonstrateur de théorèmes pour la logique des défauts libres gradués. In *Actes du 8ème Congrès Reconnaissance des Formes et Intelligence Artificielle*, 1991, pp. 363–368.
87. Moore, R. C. Semantical considerations on nonmonotonic logic. *Artif. Intel.* 25:75–94, 1985.
88. Moral, S. and Wilson, N. Importance sampling Monte-Carlo algorithms for the calculation of Dempster–Shafer belief. In *Proceedings of the 6th International Conference on Information Processing and the Management of Uncertainty*, 1996, pp. 1337–1344.
89. Neufeld, E. and Poole, D. Towards solving the multiple extension problem: Combining defaults and probability. In *Uncertainty in Artificial Intelligence 3* (L. N. Kanal, T. S. Levitt, and J. F. Lemmer, Eds.), pp. 35–44. Elsevier Science, Amsterdam, 1989.
90. Nicolas, P. and Schaub, T. The xray system: An implementation platform for local query-answering in default logics. In *Applications of Uncertainty Formalisms* (A. Hunter and S. Parsons, Eds.) Springer-Verlag, Berlin, 1998.
91. Nilsson, N. J. Probabilistic logic. *Artif. Intel.* 28:71–87, 1986.

92. Olesen, K. G., Kjaerulff, U., Jensen, F., Jensen, F. V., Falck, B., Andreassen, S., and Andersen, S. K. A MUNIN network for the median nerve—A case study in loops. *Appl. Artif. Intel.* 3:385–404, 1989.
93. Parsons, S. *Qualitative Approaches to Reasoning Under Uncertainty.* MIT Press, Cambridge, MA, 1998.
94. Parsons, S. and Hunter, A. A review of uncertainty handling formalisms. In *Applications of Uncertainty Formalisms* (A. Hunter and S. Parsons, Eds.). Springer-Verlag, Berlin, 1998.
95. Pearl, J. *Probabilistic Reasoning in Intelligent Systems: Networks of Plausible Inference.* Morgan Kaufmann, San Mateo, CA, 1988.
96. Pollock, J. *Cognitive Carpentry.* MIT Press, Cambridge, MA, 1995.
97. Poole, D. A logical framework for default reasoning. *Artif. Intel.* 36:27–47, 1988.
98. Pradhan, M., Henrion, M., Provan, G., Del Favero, B., and Huang, K. The sensitivity of belief networks to imprecise probabilities: An experimental investigation. *Artif. Intel.* 85:363–397, 1996.
99. Provan, G. M. Solving diagnostic problems using extended assumption-based truth maintenance systems: Foundations. Technical Report 88-10, Department of Computer Science, University of British Columbia, 1988.
100. Quinlan, J. R. INFERNO: A cautious approach to uncertain inference. *Comput. J.* 26:255–269, 1983.
101. Reiter, R. On closed world databases. In *Logic and Databases* (H. Gallaire and J. Minker, Eds.), pp. 55–76. Plenum, New York, 1978.
102. Reiter, R. A logic for default reasoning. *Artif. Intel.* 13:81–132, 1980.
103. Reiter, R. and Criscuolo, G. On interacting defaults. In *Proceedings of the 7th International Joint Conference on Artificial Intelligence*, pp. 270–276. American Association for Artificial Intelligence, Menlo Park, CA, 1981.
104. Saffiotti, A. An AI view of the treatment of uncertainty. *Knowledge Eng. Rev.* 2:75–97, 1987.
105. Saffiotti, A. A hybrid framework for representing uncertain knowledge. In *Proceedings of the 9th National Conference on Artificial Intelligence*, pp. 653–658, AAAI Press/MIT Press, Menlo Park, CA, 1990.
106. Saffiotti, A., Parsons, S., and Umkehrer, E. A case study in comparing uncertainty management techniques. *Microcomput. Civil Eng.* 9:367–380, 1994.
107. Saffiotti, A. and Umkehrer, E. PULCINELLA: A general tool for propagating uncertainty in valuation networks. In *Proceedings of the 7th Conference on Uncertainty in Artificial Intelligence*, pp. 323–331. Morgan Kaufmann, San Mateo, CA, 1991.
108. Saffiotti, A. and Umkehrer, E. PULCINELLA user's manual. Technical Report 91-5, IRIDIA, Université Libre de Bruxelles, 1991.
109. Saffiotti, A. and Umkehrer, E. Inference driven construction of valuation systems from first-order clauses. *IEEE Trans. Syst., Man, Cybernet.* 24:1611–1624, 1994.
110. Saffiotti, A. and Umkehrer, U. Choosing between uncertainty management techniques. Technical Report 91-7, IRIDIA, Universié Libre de Bruxelles, 1991.
111. Schwarz, G. On embedding default logic into moore's autoepistemic logic. *Artif. Intel.* 80:349–359, 1996.
112. Shackle, G. L. S. *Decision, Order and Time in Human Affairs.* Cambridge Univ. Press, Cambridge, UK, 1961.
113. Shafer, G. *A Mathematical Theory of Evidence.* Pricneton Univ. Press, Princeton, NJ, 1976.
114. Shafer, G. Comments on "An inquiry into computer understanding" by Peter Cheeseman. *Computational Intel.* 4:121–124, 1988.
115. Shafer, G. and Logan, R. Implementing Dempster's rule for heirarchical evidence. *Artif. Intel.* 33:271–298, 1987.
116. Shenoy, P. P. and Shafer, G. Axioms for probability and belief function propagation. In *Uncertainty in Artificial Intelligence 4* (R. D. Shachter, T. S. Levitt, L. N. Kanal, and J. F. Lemmer, Eds.), pp. 169–198. North-Holland, Amsterdam, 1990.
117. Shoham, Y. Nonmonotonic logics: Meaning and utility. In *Proceedings of the 10th International Joint Conference on Artificial Intelligence*, pp. 388–393. Morgan Kaufmann, San Mateo, CA, 1987.
118. Shortliffe, E. H. *Computer-Based Medical Consultations: MYCIN.* Elsevier, New York, 1976.
119. Smets, Ph. Belief functions. In *Non-Standard Logics for Automated Reasoning* (Ph. Smets, E. H. Mamdani, D. Dubois, and H. Prade, Eds.), pp. 253–275. Academic Press, London, 1988.

120. Smets, Ph. and Hsia, Y-T. Default reasoning and the transferable belief model. In *Uncertainty in Artificial Intelligence 6* (P. P. Bonissone, M. Henrion, L. N. Kanal, and J. F. Lemmer, Eds.), pp. 495–504. Elsevier Science, Amsterdam, 1991.
121. Smets, Ph. and Kennes, R. The transferable belief model. *Artif. Intel.* 66:191–234, 1994.
122. Spiegelhalter, D. J., Dawid, A. P., Hutchinson, T. A., and Cowell, R. G. Probabilistic causality assessment after a suspected adverse drug reaction: A case study in Bayesian network modelling. Report 90–11, Biostatistics Unit, Medical Research Council, 1990.
123. Srinivas, S. and Breese, J. IDEAL: Influence diagram evaluation and analysis in LISP. Documentation and user guide. Technical Memorandum 23, Rockwell International Science Center, 1989.
124. Srinivas, S. and Breese, J. IDEAL: A software package for analysis of influence diagrams. In *Proceedings of the 6th Conference on Uncertainty in Artificial Intelligence*, pp. 212–219. Association for Uncertainty in AI, Mountain View, CA, 1990.
125. Tversky, A. and Kahneman, D. Judgement under uncertainty: Heuristics and biases. *Science* 185:1124–1131, 1974.
126. Vreeswijk, G. A. W. Abstract, argumentation systems. *Artif. Intel.* 90:225–279, 1997.
127. Wilson, N. Rules, belief functions, and default logic. In *Proceedings of the 6th Conference on Uncertainty in Artificial Intelligence*, pp. 443–449. Association for Uncertainty in AI, Mountain View, CA, 1990.
128. Wilson, N. *Some theoretical aspects of the Dempster–Shafer theory.* Ph. D. Thesis, Oxford Polytechnic, 1992.
129. Wilson, N. Default logic and Dempster–Shafer theory. In *Symbolic and Quantitative Approaches to Reasoning and Uncertainty* (M. Clarke, R. Kruse, and S. Moral, Eds.), pp. 372–379. Springer-Verlag, Berlin, 1993.
130. Wilson, N. and Moral, S. Fast Markov chain algorithms for calculating Dempster–Shafer belief. In *Proceedings of the 12th European Conference on Artificial Intelligence*, pp. 672–676. Wiley, Chichester, 1996.
131. Wise, B. P. and Henrion, M. A framework for comparing uncertain inference systems to probability. In *Uncertainty in Artificial Intelligence* (L. N. Kanal and J. F. Lemmer, Eds.), pp. 69–83. Elsevier Science, Amsterdam, 1986.
132. Xu, H. TRESBEL: User's manual. Technical Report 91-11, IRIDIA, Université Libre de Bruxelles, 1991.
133. Xu, H. An effciient tool for reasoning with belief functions. In *Proceedings of the 4th International Conference on Information Processing and Management of Uncertainty*, pp. 65–68. Universitat de les Illes Balears, Palma, Mallorca, 1992.
134. Zadeh, L. A. Fuzzy sets. *Inform. Control* 8:338–353, 1965.
135. Zadeh, L. A. Fuzzy sets as a basis for a theory of possibility. *Fuzzy Sets and Systems* 1:1–28, 1978.
136. Zarley, D. An evidential reasoning system. Working Paper 206, School of Business, University of Kansas, Lawrence, 1988.
137. Zarley, D., Hsia, Y-T., and Shafer, G. Evidential reasoning using Delief. In *Proceedings of the 7th National Conference on Artificial Intelligence*, pp. 205–209. Morgan Kaufmann, San Mateo, CA, 1988.

5 EXPERIMENTAL DESIGN AND DECISION SUPPORT

TAY KIANG MENG

Systems Technology Division, Gintic Institute of Manufacturing Technology, 638075, Singapore

Expert Systems, Edited by Cornelius T. Leondes, Volume 1

ISBN: 0-12-443881-4 / $35.00

I. INTRODUCTION

Although design of experimental methodologies is well established, several problems and controversies still remain in existing experimental design techniques.

First, much of our knowledge of the existing experimental design methods such as the classical techniques, Taguchi methods, and response surface methodology is limited to comparative studies of assumed discrete or linear systems, and is not adequate to model the representation of many underlying multiresponse manufacturing problems and is not adequate to provide decision support.

Second, many problems exist in statistical data analysis because of the difficulty to understand, to analyze (due to confounding effect), and due to the inherent complexity of the tools and methods. The general output used with the analysis of variance technique and the related hypothesis computations, proposed by Taguchi as well as others, is not easily understood by those with little training in statistical techniques. Thus, interpretation of significant effects, especially interactions, is therefore a difficult task. Furthermore, converting the information gained by the experiment into actions to be taken on the system can be very difficult and complicated for many engineers and researchers in industry. The data analysis (which include sensitivity analysis, hypothesis testing, predictive learning, and inverse modeling) techniques are problems which engineers face today in implementing the design of experiments.

Third, there is a lack of integration and understanding between the hard core statistical techniques and the experimental planning and management procedures among the existing design of experiment methods. This problem arose due to the implementation gaps between statisticians and experimenters.

In addition, there are controversies regarding Taguchi analysis such as signal-to-noise ratio, orthogonal arrays, etc. The universal use of the signal-to-noise ratio approach to optimization can confuse the experimenter because it is sometimes unnecessarily complicated and inefficient. A common criticism of Taguchi quality engineering is his mathematical and statistical methods because Taguchi orthogonal arrays ignore the interaction effects [8, 26, 39, 60, 65, 70, 75]. Some researchers regard the Taguchi techniques as rough cuts and they do not work at the refinement stage where all interactions must be known. Others believe that the Taguchi signal-to-noise ratio is not a good performance criterion and has been labeled by some as statistically inefficient. Gunter [26] wrote that the methods for analysis in Taguchi experiment design are nonstandard, and no scientific, that is, mathematical justification has yet been provided for their use. Box *et al.* [8] stated that the statistical procedures set forth by Taguchi are statistically inefficient, cumbersome, and sometimes naive, and the universal use of signal-to-noise ratios for the choice of criteria is unconvincing. He further argued that such inefficiencies in statistical procedures may lead to throwing away hard-won data and, consequently, overlooking important effects. These controversies created a "gray area" for experimental data analysis because the classical and Taguchi methods sometimes give conflicting conclusions. This puts the modern engineer in a dilemma when he comes to experimental data analysis. While leading statisticians and academicians waste time arguing over mathematical nuances in various design of experiments (DOE) theories, engineers facing the real problems need immediate answers, not arguments.

Moreover, although modern computing facilities have many canned programs which analyze data from most classical designs, the statistical models based on assumptions are not realistic, causing improper tests and possibly false conclusions. In general, existing computer-aided experimental design and analysis software cannot be modified to accept new models and restriction errors. In addition, the recommendations provided in the documentation or literature are not helpful for experimenters with little expertise in statistics.

More recently, neural networks have received increased attention. They have been used in a wide variety of applications, ranging from classification and pattern recognition to optimization and control [20, 46, 51, 71]. Neural networks also provide a generic technique for the realization of continuous mappings, providing several advantages compared to conventional statistical techniques. They are suitable for incremental learning, enabling the neural network models to be improved incrementally as new data become available. They are also suitable for fast computation on parallel architectures and have good generalization capabilities (universal approximators) and can approximate a variety of functions [14, 68, 77, 84].

Neural networks are typically constructed from parallel layers of simple computational nodes, with weighting elements between nodes that define the strength of connection between nodes, which are adapted during learning by some optimization procedure to yield the appropriate input–output mapping. Neural networks are specified by the network topology (structure), node characteristics, and the learning algorithm. There are many types of neural networking systems in terms of both their mode of operation and their method of development, each with its own characteristics and appropriate areas of application. The majority of these weight update rules are based on least mean square, recursive least mean square, stochastic gradient algorithms, etc. An important class of neural networks are feedforward networks, in which the input feeds forward through network layers to the output. They are frequently able to learn complex input–output functional mappings which are ideal for the purpose of modeling nonlinear experimental design and decision support.

Neural network topology and dynamics define a black-box approximator from input to output. Therefore, demystifying the black box for experimental design and decision support problems requires the definition and solutions to appropriate neural network architecture, operation modes (such as training, learning algorithm, stability, convergence, etc.) and network evaluation including interpretation of results and requirements for representation, etc. The neural network requires minimal statistical knowledge and can be used for cases where there are incomplete data, a large problem space, complex relations, multiple concepts, generalization, etc.

Although there is already a considerable amount of research in the application of neural network learning techniques, no studies have been reported as applications of fuzzy neural network learning techniques for experimental design and decision support. No existing methodology provides any framework to tackle the problems and issues identified for experimental design and decision support. There is no known published evidence in the literature that deals with nonlinear experimental design and analysis using adaptive fuzzy neural networks.

Research in design of experiments has mainly concentrated on the hard core statistical techniques on designing and developing formal models. In addition, no work has been done on blending the planning management and statistical techniques with fuzzy neural networks for design of experiment and decision support. Therefore, exploring fuzzy neural network techniques for experimental knowledge acquisition involves investigation ranging across neural networks, fuzzy logic, and experimental design concepts. Taking a joint perspective of industrially designed experiments and fuzzy neural network learning, this research explores, designs, develops, and implements fuzzy neural network models for organizing and learning experimental data and knowledge that can be useful in generating fuzzy neural experimental decision support systems for many domains.

II. NEW CONCEPT OF EXPERIMENTAL DESIGN AND DECISION SUPPORT

The main objective of experimental design is to construct an empirical model to approximate an unknown relationship (to understand complex phenomena) up to a given level of accuracy. These empirical models tend to be algorithmically nonexpressible, algebraically difficult to model and ill-structured. Such problems are not formulated with a high degree of mathematical structure and involve both discrete and continuous variables which are incomplete and noisy. Fundamentally, since such an unknown relationship can be denoted as functions on some appropriate input space and output spaces, such an objective can be translated into finding a mapping relation between the input space and the output space, which can approximate the desired function within a given accuracy. Experimental design and decision support problems can therefore be conceptualized by mapping the performance requirements of a product or process (as expressed by values of certain performance measures) onto suitable values of the decision input parameters. These are the parameters that describe the physical design or the manner of operation of the manufacturing system. This leads to a new concept for experimental design based on the function approximation concept as shown in Fig. 1.

A. Function Approximation Concept

This concept implies that learning and approximating functions from data given on a set of scattered points in an *n-dimensional* domain surface space is equivalent to

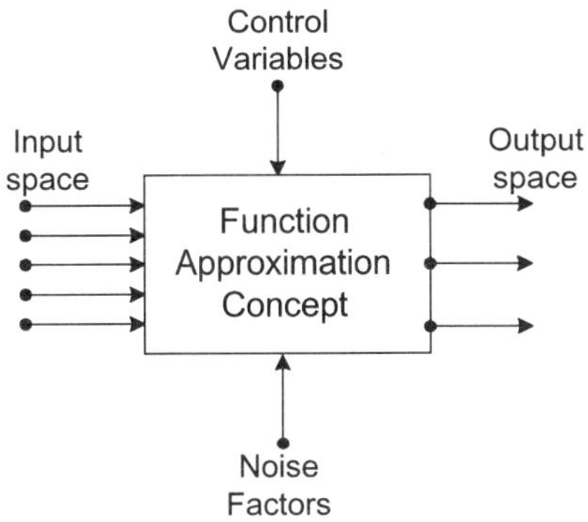

FIGURE 1 New concept for experimental design and decision support.

the problem of synthesizing a model that retrieves the appropriate output when presented with the input and generalizes when presented with new inputs. The concept of function approximation consists of representing an unknown function y, *where* $y = f(\cdot)$, by $f(\mathbf{W}, x)$, an approximating function that uses a set of parameters $\mathbf{W}$. The task consists of either finding a set $\mathbf{W}$ for a given function f or finding both f and $\mathbf{W}$ to perform the best possible approximation. Classical approximation theory provides well-established results for such a query [16, 59, 63]. The classical function approximation theory, which deals with the problem of approximating or interpolating a continuous function y by an approximating function $f(\mathbf{W}, x)$, can be described by

$$y = f(\cdot) = f(\mathbf{W}, x) + \text{ error},$$

where (x, y) is the data set such that $x \in R^n$, $y = f(\cdot) \in R$, and $\mathbf{W}$ are real weight vectors $\mathbf{W} = w_1, w_2, w_3, \ldots, w_m$. Therefore, to obtain an approximation to the unknown underlying function $y = f(\cdot)$, it is very important to choose an approximating function $f(\mathbf{W}, x)$ that is as compatible as possible with $f(\cdot)$. This includes the choice of a model architecture, desired accuracy of fit, and complexity of computations. The function approximation can then be expressed formally as a search for the set of parameters $\widetilde{\mathbf{W}}$ that satisfies

$$d[f(\widetilde{\mathbf{W}}, x), f(\cdot)] \le d[f(\mathbf{W}, x), f(\cdot)]$$

for all $\mathbf{W}$, where d is a suitable distance metric, and x is the multidimensional input. The solution $\widetilde{\mathbf{W}}$ satisfying the previous equation is referred to as the best approximation. The likelihood of finding the best approximation depends on both the class of functions to which $f(\mathbf{W}, x)$ belongs and the original function $y = f(\cdot)$. The process of searching for the "right" functional form and/or parameters is analogous to learning if the function is realized through a parallel distributed computational neural network based on samples of the input–output map.

The issue on function approximation for experimental design and decision support can be very complicated by the fact that the real-world problems are characterized by complex nonlinear interactions involving both discrete and continuous variables. For such problems, some linear and polynomial regression methods are commonly employed. However, conventional surface fitting techniques require the segmentation of the independent variable domain to successfully approximate the unknown underlying function. One line of thought to solve this function approximation problem for experimental design and decision support is to sample the unknown underlying function $f(\bullet)$ and then to reconstruct a nonlinear surface in a higher dimension with the samples as a full approximation of the function $f(\bullet)$ using specific architecture.

Pictorially, the concept of function approximation can be viewed as reconstructing a surface (the desired function) from sparse sample data points. A concept related to function approximation is interpolation, which can be stated as follows:

CONCEPT 1 (Interpolation). *For a given set of n different points, $x_i \in \Re^n / i = 1, 2, \ldots, n$, and n are real integer numbers, $y_i \in \Re / i = 1, 2, \ldots, n$; interpolation is to find a function $y = f(\bullet)$ from $\Re^n \rightarrow \Re$, such that $f(x_i) = y_i$, for $i = 1, 2, \ldots, n$.*

The objective is to learn y where $y = f(\bullet)$ from a set of training sample data characterized by a number of sets of corresponding input and output so as to give a complete description of the problem and further input and output data pairs will be correctly described by $f(\bullet)$.

B. Spatial Sampling Concept

In reconstructing the surface for the desired function (function approximation), a critical issue is the adequacy of the data used for re-construction (i.e., does the data contain enough information and density to describe the function). One line of thought is to regard the available input and output data as samples of the unknown functions $f(\bullet)$. Therefore, the issue on the adequacy of data can be regarded as to whether the given samples will allow the full re-construction of $f(\bullet)$ using a specific structure. This leads to the concept of sampling.

Using the sampling concept, for a given function $f(\bullet)$, there exists a critical sampling density (multidimensional equivalent of the sampling rate) so that the exact construction (approximation) of the underlying function is possible on a surface set S using its samples at this or at a higher sampling density. This kind of conventional sampling theory is based on the Fourier frequency analysis, which assumes that the unknown function $f(\bullet)$ has a limited bandwidth.

CONCEPT 2 (Sampling theorem). *For any chosen basis function structure and an approximation error, there always exists a sampling density at which the model approximates the unknown underlying function $y = f(\bullet)$ on surface set S with the required error bound.*

Although the theory is sound, the results cannot be applied practically for two reasons. First, the exact functions are not available for many real-world problems, for learning only the samples of $f(\bullet)$, not the function $f(\bullet)$ itself, are usually available. Thus, there is a need to ensure that all the function samples are dense enough to allow the re-engineering of the function. However, without knowing the function, its samples cannot be verified against the prescribed conditions required by the sampling theorems. Moreover, even if the function $f(\bullet)$ is given, the computation involved to determine such critical features as bandwidth is very demanding, and often impractical.

In addition, although most neural networks can successfully learn given a sufficiently flexible model structure or an appropriate learning algorithm, the question of whether the adequacy of the training set size or the structure will possess the ability to generalize correctly (or sufficiently accurately) is still unresolved. Presently, the size of the training samples is increased if the neural networks do not generalize well enough.

These difficult issues can be resolved in this present research by employing the idea of localized sampling and adaptive reconstruction as shown in Fig. 2.

Specifically, localized sampling involves arranging the function into samples, for example, a time series such that (x_t, y_t), *where* $t = 1, 2, \ldots,$ so that at any discrete time instance t, only one new sample (x_t, y_t) will be available. Next, adaptive reconstruction involves building a partial model that will only make use of this new sample at this particular instance. Accumulating this adaptive reconstruction over time, at any time t, a partial model is built to approximate the part of the real-world system that is revealed by the samples up to t. According to the sampling theorems that when the samples are dense enough in a region of operation surface S, the model will be able to approximate the given nonlinear real-world system at the required accuracy.

The advantage of localized sampling and adaptive reconstruction is that there is no need to ascertain if the samples are up to the required density. It even avoids the need to be concerned with the specificity of a sample series. As long as the samples are dense enough in surface S, the required approximation error will be reached. Moreover, for its nature, only the convergence for a particular sample series needs to be ascertained. The approximation over the entire surface S is covered by the sampling theorem. Along with the experimental design and decision support, this idea appears to be one of the two key ingredients in formulating and solving nonlinear experimental data analysis, hypothesis testing, prediction, and inverse modeling problems without assuming specific knowledge about the underlying system.

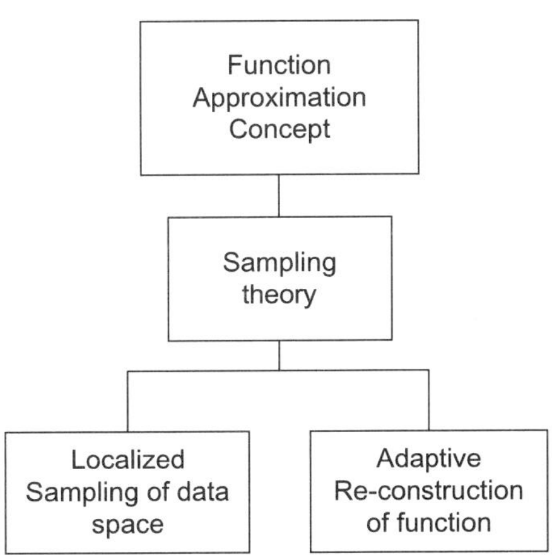

FIGURE 2 Localized sampling and adaptive re-construction.

C. Neural Networks Approach

In general, all function approximation problems can be depicted as feedforward neural networks possessing different basis functions. This is because feedforward neural networks provide a mapping between the input and output variables where the mapping can be represented by a family of nonlinear functions. Recent developments in neural networks theory [1, 11, 14, 21, 32, 48, 51, 53, 56, 67] have shown that the multilayer feedforward neural networks with one hidden layer of neurons can be used to approximate any measurable functions to any desired accuracy. The basic idea is that if the nonlinear laws can govern the system, even the dynamic behavior is chaotic, the future to some extent may be predicted by the behavior of the past values. The learning is carried out by iteratively adjusting the linking weights in the network so as to minimize the differences between the actual output vector of the network and the target vector.

The Kolmogorov's theorem is an important theorem which illuminates the capability of a parallel distributed computational multilayer neural network that was proven by Kolmogorov and is described in [63]. This theorem states that any continuous function can be represented in terms of nonlinear and continuously increasing functions of only one variable. Kolmogorov's mapping parallel distributed computational neural network existence theorem essentially states that any continuous function can be implemented exactly by a three-layer feedforward neural network [14, 32, 83]. The general results of Kolmogorov's theorem provide the key for the existence of multiple multilayer neural network structures to a function approximation.

The universal approximation theorem is important from a theoretical viewpoint because it provides the necessary mathematical tool for the viability of a feedforward neural network with a single hidden layer as a class of approximate solutions. The universal approximation theorem is an existence theorem in the sense that it provides the mathematical justification for the approximation of an arbitrary continuous function (approximation by finite Fourier series) as opposed to exact representation. In effect, the theorem states that a single hidden layer is sufficient for a multilayer perceptron to compute a uniform ε approximation to a given training set represented by the set of inputs and a desired output (where ε denotes the errors). However, the theorem is only an existence proof; it does not imply that a single hidden layer is optimum in the sense of learning time or ease of implementation.

D. Relation between Neural Networks and Fuzzy Logic

Experimental design problems are usually associated with system inputs and outputs. In fuzzy systems input–output mappings are made from one universe of discourse U to another Y through fuzzy algorithms based on collections of implication statements of rules of the form of the conditional statements,

$$R_i: \text{IF } A_i(\mu) \text{ THEN } B_i(y).$$

This links input set A_i with output set B_i. In general, the fuzzy logic provides an inference structure that enables approximate human reasoning capabilities [28, 38, 73, 88, 97, 104–108]. The theory of fuzzy logic is based upon the notion of relative graded membership and so are the functions of mention and cognitive processes.

Thus, the utility of fuzzy sets lies in their ability to model uncertain or ambiguous data which is often encountered in real life. Since the introduction of fuzzy set theory by Zadeh in 1965, there have been a number of applications based on this theory, especially in system identification. In most of these applications, the main objective is to construct a fuzzy system to approximate a desired control or a decision up to a given level of accuracy which can be formulated as a function approximation problem.

In recent years, many researchers have studied the relationship between parallel distributed computational neural networks and fuzzy systems. It is shown that under some minor restrictions, the functional behavior of a single layer feedforward neural network, that is, radial basis functions nets or a B-splines network, and fuzzy inference systems are actually equivalent [38, 42, 49, 50]. For example, in a parallel distributed computational feedforward (static) neural network, the neuron responds instantaneously to the fuzzy inputs because of the absence of a dynamic element (no feedback) in the structure.

The parallel distributed computational neural mathematical operations in a feedforward neural network can be performed either by fuzzy arithmetic or by fuzzy logic operations. Based on the analogy of the mathematical operation involved in a parallel distributed computational neuron, a fuzzy neural architecture can be achieved by fuzzy arithmetic operations such as fuzzy multiplication and summation operation by fuzzy addition, which can be modeled by

$$y_t = \varphi\left[\overset{n}{\underset{i=o}{(+)}}\, w_i(\cdot)x_i\right],$$

where $(+)$ and $(\cdot)$ are fuzzy addition and fuzzy multiplication operators, respectively, which is equivalent to a feedforward neural network with linear output units such as the radial basis function described by

$$y_t = \left[\sum_{j=1}^{n} w_{ij}\mathbf{z}_j(x)\right],$$

where w_{ij} is the weight and $\mathbf{z}_j$ is the basis function.

It is of interest to observe that two models stemming from different origins turn out to be functionally equivalent. This architecture is similar to several neural networks such as the radial basis function, in which the Euclidean distance between the input and a set of function centers are calculated, these distances are then passed through a nonlinear basis function to form an output through a normalized linear sum. The relation between parallel distributed computational neural networks and fuzzy systems can be described as shown in Fig. 3.

III. NEURAL NETWORK REPRESENTATION OF EXPERIMENTAL DESIGN AND DECISION SUPPORT

In view of the preceding discussion, experimental design and decision support can be represented by a parallel distributed computational approach using the concept of function approximation, sampling and universal approximation theorem, which can be viewed as re-constructing a surface of the desired function from the sparse

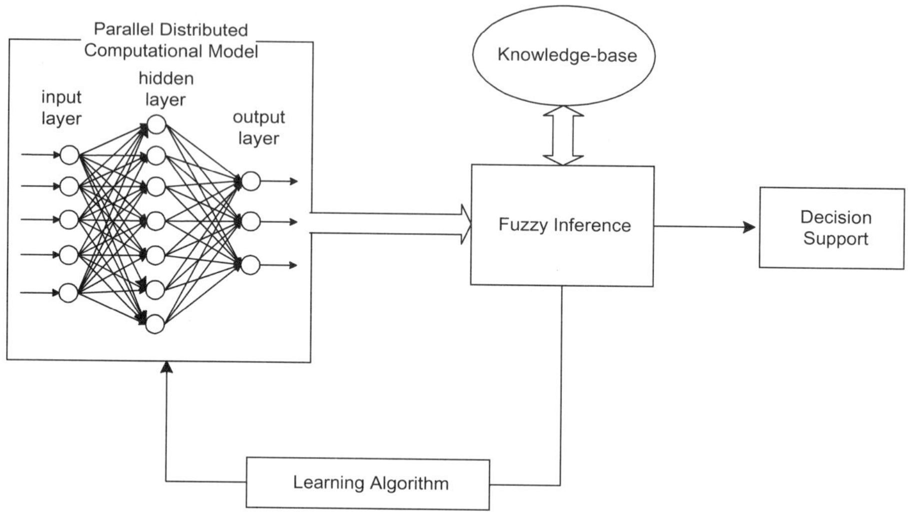

FIGURE 3 A parallel distributed computational fuzzy neural network model.

data points (the training set). The relation between experimental design and function approximation theory offers a link which connects two seemingly different research areas, that is, parallel distributed computational neural networks, experimental design, and decision support as shown in Fig. 4. This is the rationale for using function approximation theory for experimental design and decision support, which provides the linkage to parallel distributed computational neural network models. The function approximation process can be considered as a three step process:

(a) Select a set of basis functions $\{\mathbf{z}(x)\}$ such as the Gaussian radial basis function, that is defined in the region of interest of the independent variable space.
(b) Determine the structural parameters (e.g., center and width) in the basis functions of $f(\mathbf{W}, x) = \mathbf{W}\mathbf{z}(x)$ to obtain a good fit.
(c) Determine the weight initialization scheme, the activation-calculating formula, and the learning algorithm.

IV. FRAMEWORK FOR DESIGNING AND BUILDING PARALLEL DISTRIBUTED COMPUTATIONAL ADAPTIVE NEURAL NETWORKS

A parallel distributed computational neural network is typically constructed from dense layers of simple computational interconnecting neurons which are able to store information (as weighting elements between nodes that define the strength of connection between nodes) in a distributed manner as interconnecting weights between the neurons, which are adapted during learning by some optimization procedure to yield the appropriate input–output mapping. It is a technology that emulates the low-level operation of the central nervous system that is manifested in the brain, such as automatic learning, generalization, and error tolerance. All

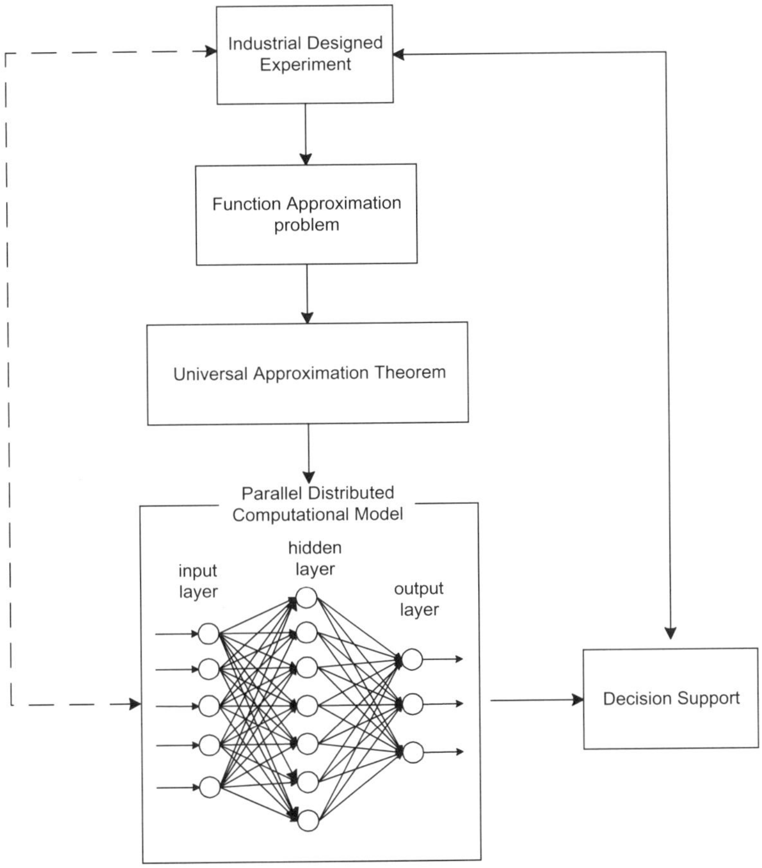

FIGURE 4 A neural network representation for experimental design and decision support.

neurons perform simple and similar processing tasks that collectively, within the network structure, perform some higher order functions.

Although a single neuron can perform certain simple pattern detection functions, the power of neural computation comes from the neurons connected in a network structure. Larger networks generally offer greater computational capabilities. Arranging neurons in layers or stages is supposed to mimic the layered structure of a certain portion of the brain. The parallel distributed computational model (comprises an input layer, an output layer, and one hidden layer of neurons) is shown in Fig. 5.

A framework for designing and building a parallel distributed computational adaptive neural network for experimental design and decision support is described as follows (Fig. 6):

(a) Select a suitable parallel distributed computational neural network model (supervised or unsupervised) based on the nature of the problem.
(b) Construct the parallel distributed computational neural network system according to the characteristics of the application domain and building

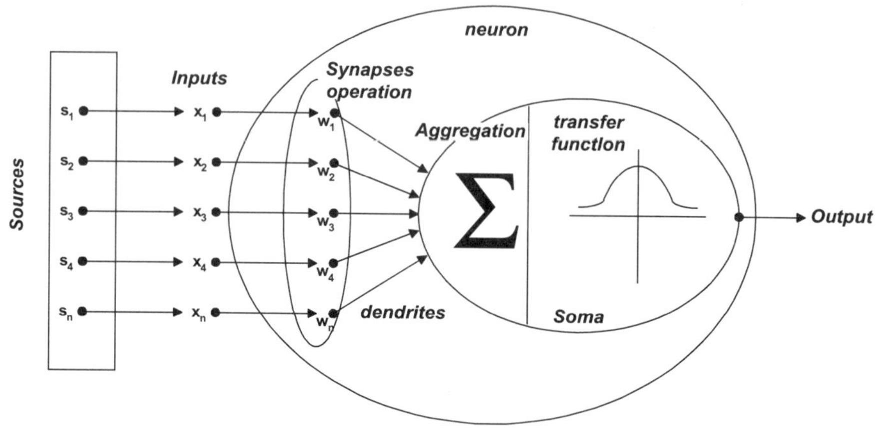

FIGURE 5 A parallel distributed computational model.

blocks of neural network by:

- Determine network properties—the network topology (connectivity), the types of connections, the order of connections, and the weight range and the state of activation.
- Determine neuron properties—the processing neurons, the activation range, and the activation (transfer) function, which determine the new level of activation based on the effective input and the current state.
- Determine the neurodynamics—the weight initialization scheme, the activation-calculating formula, and the learning rule including the propagation rule.

(c) Generate training patterns from historical, analytical, observational, and experimental data through the use of experimental design.

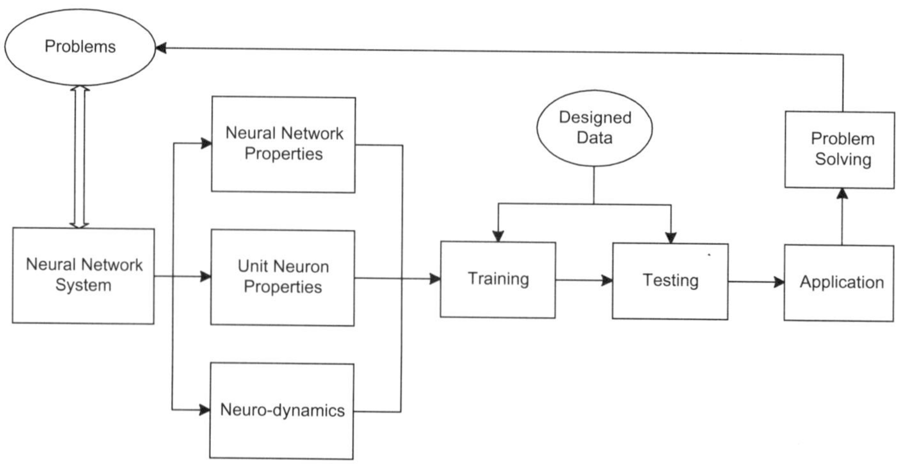

FIGURE 6 Designing and building a parallel distributed computational neural network.

(d) Train and test the parallel distributed computational neural network with the learning algorithm procedure of the selected model.
(e) Use the trained network for making inference or solving problems and decision making.

The parallel distributed computational neural network is able to learn by updating the weights between these units, after being exposed to a set of training data. Each unit receives information from units it is connected to, processes it, and sends out an output to other units. The trained network is able to generalize when a new set of input data is presented to it, that is, to produce a prediction of the actual output.

A critical fact about the parallel distributed computational neural network is that they are statistical associative models. The parallel distributed computational neural network has a set of input vectors and a set of output vectors. The role of the parallel distributed computational neural network is to perform a function that associates each input vector with an output vector. Then, a learning algorithm uses statistical properties of a set of input–output pair (called a training set) to generalize, that is, to generate outputs from novel (new) inputs.

Pursuing this analogy, generalization can be defined as estimating the height of the surface (the output value) at a point in space where no examples are available. If the surface is reconstructed faithfully, generalization ability will be good, and the system will have "learned" the mapping. Clearly, generalization is based on the assumption that there is redundant information in the data. If a mapping is totally random, generalization is not possible because there is no regularity that can be learned. If the parallel distributed computational neural network models do not have the ability to generalize, it would purely be a "look-up" table, which is of little interest.

A significant problem in the design and implementation of a parallel distributed computational representation for application in experimental design and decision support is to control the magnitude and the variance of errors when it is used in the field. From the preceding discussion, it can be concluded that it is only possible to approximate an unknown function (in the context of experimental design and decision support) to the desired accuracy if and only if:

(a) The learning algorithm is efficient and is able to find the global minimum for the performance function.
(b) The density of the training data in the input space is dense enough, that is, there are enough neurons in the hidden layers.
(c) The training data contain enough information to map out the unknown solution space with respect to both nonlinear and dynamic behavior.

The first and second points can be solved by the novel ideas of localized sampling and adaptive re-construction using an online structure adaptive parallel distributed computational neural network with local training. In practice, the second point can cause problems especially when using the feedforward neural network with an error backpropagation learning algorithm, but can be solved by using the Gaussian radial basis functions.

The major problem is the third point because it is often not possible to know and to generate the learning data which contain enough information and represent the entire working area. However, the third point can be solved by using the proper design of the experiment to investigate and to collect data samples for the entire work space. This is the rationale and application for a designed experiment approach (experimental design) to data collection as a tool for decision making. First, experimental design provides active manipulation of input parameters directly to create information-laden data. Second, the problem of variability, uncertainty, and noise reduction can be reduced by using experimental designs which use the principles of averaging; and third, the total sample size (total number of runs which can actually afford to perform—being pragmatically sensitive to both cost and time constraints) of an experiment is the most important factor which dictates the chosen experiment design plan. Finally, with a designed approach to data collection, more than one aspect of the system can be investigated simultaneously and unambiguously. This generates more information for return on investment. The next section describes the design, development, and implementation of an intelligent technique and application to experimental design and decision support.

V. FUTURE PREDICTIONS ON ADVANCED QUALITY ENGINEERING AND ITS METHODOLOGY

The advances in computer technology allow the development of useful neural networks in a wide variety of applications, ranging from classification and pattern recognition to optimization and control [20, 46, 51, 71]. Neural networks also provide a generic technique for the realization of continuous mappings, providing several advantages compared to conventional statistical techniques. They are suitable for incremental learning, enabling the neural network models to be improved incrementally as new data become available. They are also suitable for fast computation on parallel architectures and have good generalization capabilities (universal approximators) and can approximate a variety of functions [68, 77, 84].

Similarly, the advances in computer technology can be expected to totally transform quality aspects of both product development and manufacturing processes. With the increasing pressures on manufacturers to improve quality, computer integrated quality engineering is going to be an essential tool in achieving improvements in quality and productivity performance. The future will be one in which decisions are made using advanced computers, which possess more complex capabilities using artificial neural networks and fuzzy systems, machine learning, etc. The software will be dominated by decision strategies, which maintain complete control over the ongoing real-time process.

One way the technology of neural networks can impact the concept of experimental design and decision support system is by extending the conventional DOE system into an intelligent system which is capable of assisting engineers and managers in their decision processes with data information analysis capabilities such as sensitivity analysis, hypothesis testing, predictive learning, inverse modeling, etc. Here, artificial intelligence, neural networks, and other adaptive systems techniques can be applied to automate the generation of decisions or strategies for the design of industrial experiments.

Design of experiments is the most valuable advanced quality engineering tool which enables engineers to study the effects of multiple factors and their interactions upon a response or dependent variable to discover how these manipulations can affect the outcome of a certain system or process. Most of these techniques are well documented in Taguchi quality engineering or classical experimental designs literature. The use of full and fractional factorial, Taguchi orthogonal arrays, nested and blocked designs, etc; and traditional statistical tools such as *F tests* and *t-tests*, analysis of variance, and Taguchi signal-to-noise ratio, to analyze the results have been accepted practice for the last few years [9, 18, 19, 65, 91].

However, the historical use of one factor at a time experimentation and/or arbitrary selection of incomplete full factorial designs has resulted in very inefficient and ineffective attempts to understand and to optimize real-world multiple responses problems. In addition, to overcome the statistical analysis problems and controversies [8, 26, 39, 60, 65, 70, 75] regarding existing experimental design methodologies, a PC-based software is developed to integrate and to facilitate the combined use of Taguchi quality engineering with adaptive neural network analysis to model empirical investigation and decision support characterized by complex nonlinear interactions involving discrete and continuous variables. The software consists of two modules as follows:

(a) An experiment reference template (ERT)—as an aid for systematic experimentation planning, designs, data collection, and management procedures, so as to provide discussion of complex trade-offs between practical limitations and statistical preferences in an experiment.
(b) An intelligent adaptive neural network system—to provide a nonlinear, model-free, multivariate surface data fitting learning algorithm, which automatically determines and learns the underlying functional relationship between inputs and outputs directly from data without a hypothesized functional form.

This is schematically illustrated in Fig. 7. In the ERT, the real-world engineering problem is translated into a design of experiments problem, and the user specifies the objectives, the number of input parameters (including held constant and nuisance factors) and output responses, along with their relevant background, names, range, delta values, and levels. A decision is made using an effective orthogonal array on whether to use standard classical orthogonal arrays (fractional factorial) design or a custom Taguchi sparser orthogonal array design requiring fewer experiments. The key is to choose a design that uses the information gained in the analysis for the specific situation. The experiment reference template then helps to assist and recommends a table of experiments to be performed. The design includes experiments for both training and testing samples for the adaptive neural network.

The use of the experiment reference template provides a specific procedure for the execution of the experiment. It provides details and vital information of the experiment and enhances communication among the team members on how the experiment is to be conducted. The vital information includes the reasons for planning and designing the experiment, the way the experiment will be conducted, procedures for sampling and testing, etc. It presents the generic technical issues and experimental features found in an industrial experiment, to support the experimental design activities. The specific components that constitute the experiment reference template will be described in the next section.

After the completion of the experiment, the training samples are entered into the data table, either online or offline, of the adaptive neural network. The adaptive

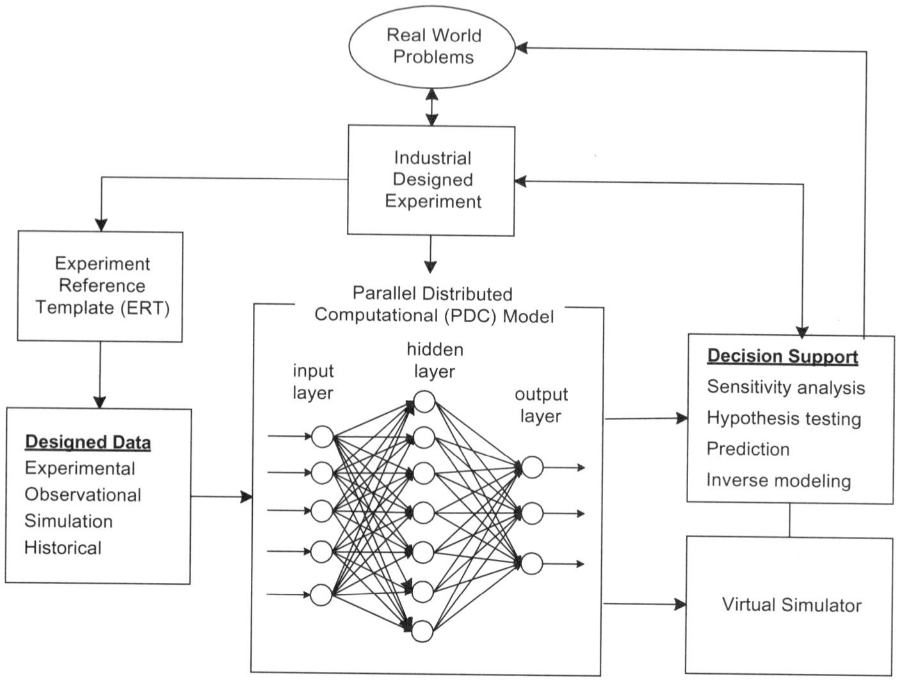

FIGURE 7 New method for experimental design and decision support.

neural analyzer uses a unified parallel distributed computational adaptive feedforward GaRBF neural network to provide a nonlinear, model-free, multivariate data fitting learning algorithm. After training, the neural network automatically determines the functional relationship between inputs and outputs directly from data without a hypothesized functional form.

VI. OVERVIEW OF THE PROTOTYPE

The prototype consists of core software and utilities for simulating the adaptive GaRBF neural network models. The software is written in Matlab (mathematical hypermedia) and has a Microsoft Visual C++ Window-based graphical interface. The prototype currently is implemented as a stand-alone executable software running on any IBM-compatible PC with a Pentium-133 processor and 32 Mb RAM. The prototype environment is divided into three stages as shown in Fig. 8. The first stage is called model design where users create an architecture, specifying network parameters, and designing model connectivity using Matlab software. In addition, users may customize the functional behavior of individual units through the use of Matlab functions. Matlab is a hypermedia programming environment for numeric computation and visualization. The next stage is the simulation construction stage, where an M file, describing the structure of the model is created. A Matlab simulator builder combines and builds the data structure with the users defined functions. The main advantage is that it is able to adapt to users needs and the visual information is easy to understand. The final stage is the user interface stage, where

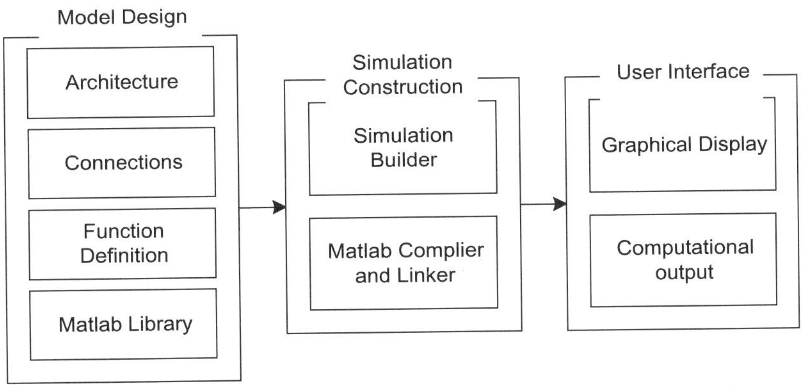

FIGURE 8 The three stages of the prototype simulation environment.

the user interacts with the model through the graphical display and computational output, by performing sensitivity analysis, prediction, and inverse modeling.

The prototype was designed with a number of novel features which decrease the turnaround time between design, simulation, and modification for the neural network model. These features are:

(a) A parallel distributed computational adaptive GaRBF neural network fast learning algorithm that creates a solution space of topographic neural map architecture which allows creation of large neural networks with a minimum of specification by exploiting redundancy and adaptivity between units and enforcing topographic constraints.
(b) Programmable generalized neural units which allows both architecture and functional behavior of the model to be defined and controlled by the users.
(c) Scaleable and modular simulation which allows progressive and modular model development.

VII. EXPERIMENT REFERENCE TEMPLATE

The ERT is used as an aid to encourage the discussion and resolution of generic technical issues by a multidisciplinary experimentation team. It will also help structure the problem, identify important issues and practical constraints, and indicate the effect of various compromises on the inferences that can be validly drawn for the experimental data. The proposed framework for the ERT is developed as shown in Fig. 9. Some sample printouts from the ERT are shown in Tables 2–4. The required input details of the ERT are described as follows:

(a) Formulation of problem and experiment objectives. The statement of the problem is discussed and stated with reference to the current and preferred level of performance. This leads to the identification of an improvement project which can be achieved from the design of experiments. The experiment objectives respond to how to fulfil its purpose which may be related to continuous improvement defined in quantifiable terms.

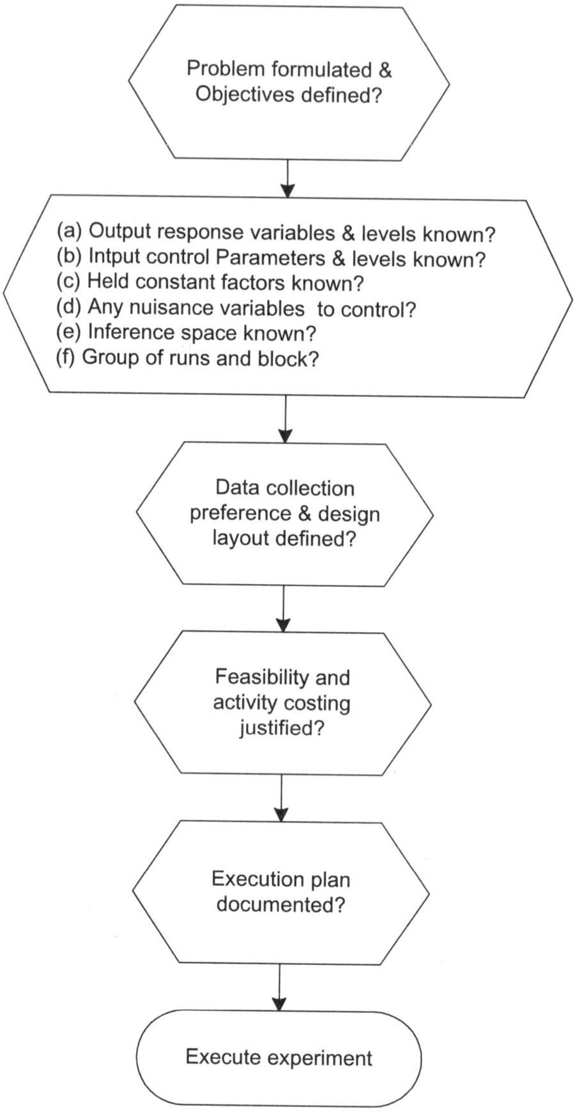

FIGURE 9 Flowchart for experiment reference template.

(b) Parameters and variables characterization. Specific information to be incorporated (as shown in Table 1) in the experiment description includes:
- Definition of performance characteristics and target value. The factors of interest must be identified by making a cause-and-effect or fishbone diagram of the process which will help to identify possible factors.
- Identification of output response, input parameters, held-constant factors, nuisance factors, and interactions.

(c) Define design preference model. The selection of which orthogonal arrays to use depends on the number of factors and interactions of

TABLE I Parameters and Variables Characterization

Input parameters	Measurement precision and how to obtain it (i.e., choice of measurement system or repeated measurements) is important, and poorly understood systems should be evaluated with a measurement capability study, a designed experiment of the measurement process.	Input parameters can be discrete or continuous. The knowledge of the allowed ranges and nominal values of input parameters under current use provides the experimenter a range large enough to produce an observable effect and to span a good proportion of the operating range. In addition, historical process data can be used to gain relevant knowledge.
Output response	One might be forced to resort to observational data and/or historical data and experience or weaken the experimental objective to obtain ranking, selection, or a binary response instead of quantification.	Output responses are the observed system outputs in an experimental design. There can be an unlimited number of responses for each experimental run.
Held constant factors	Measurement precision.	Held-constant factors are controllable factors whose effects are not of interest in this experiment.
Nuisance factors	Passive strategies such as randomization, blocking, analysis of covariance can reduce the impact of nuisance factors. These strategies may be constrained by limits on the number of observations, costs of changing control-variable settings, and logistic considerations.	Nuisance factors are not controlled and are not of primary interest in this experiment. They differ from held-constant factors in that they cannot be deliberately set to a constant level for all experimental units. Nuisance factor can inflate experimental error and bias results, making it more difficult to assess the significance of control variables.

interest, and on the number of levels for the factors of interest. These two items determine the total degrees of freedom required for the entire experiment (degree of freedom for each factor is the number of levels minus one), which is needed to determine the experiment run size. The minimum required degree of freedom in the experiment is the sum of all the factors and interaction degrees of freedom. A flowchart for the selection of orthogonal arrays (OA) is shown in Fig. 10.

(d) Experiment run sheet and data worksheet. The data worksheet is the logbook for recording pertinent information, specifically designed to record process variables readings, product dimensions, test data, and inspection findings, depending on the nature of the quality characteristic of interest.

VIII. SAMPLE OUTPUTS FROM THE EXPERIMENT REFERENCE TEMPLATE

TABLE 2 Sample Printout of the Input and Output Vectors

Input parameters	Range	Delta	Levels	Remarks
(A) Cutting speed (m/min) based on the percentage of nominal	50–300	50	6	This range includes the recommended cutting conditions as the average value. Six levels of cutting speeds were used to cover the entire cutting conditions. The coolant used is Castrol clearedge EP284.
(B) Feedrate (mm/rev) based on the percentage of nominal	0.15–0.35	0.1	3	The feedrate affects both surface roughness and tool life. The experiment range includes the recommended cutting conditions as the average value. The depth of cut is assumed to be 1.5 mm.
(C) Tool nose radius (mm)	0.4–1.2	0.4	3	The cutting inserts used in this experiment for outside diameter turning is the Sandvik CNMG 190616 MR Coated GC425 with a different tool nose radius. The insert geometries, mainly the insert corner and edge, are selected based on the workpiece design features, surface finish, chip form, machining process, operation, and state.
(Noise) workpiece material hardness (HB) The workpiece material used is of Grade 1040 medium carbon steel (hardness 180–240 HB)	180–250	35	2	The given workpiece material in terms of its hardness determine the insert material grade and feedrate. The workpieces used are based on a 750 mm diameter and 300 mm length connector ring pin. Each component has five hardnesses tested with a Brinell (10 mm ball, 3000 kgf) hardness test performed as per ASTM E10. Chemical composition (0.01%) by lab test.

Output parameters	Remarks
(1) Tool Life (min)	Tool life for roughness and finishing operations are different. The tool life is measured with a stop watch. In determining tool life, the criterion is 0.5 mm of major flank wear and 0.3 mm of nose wear. The crater wear is ignored and catastrophic failures should not be achieved. Although other wear phenomena such as notch wear and plastic deformation may occur in practice, they will eventually result in one of the preferred criteria being valid. The tool wear were measured using a 10× magnification microscope.
(1) Surface roughness RMS (μm)	The surface roughness is an important specification on a machined part and it depends on the insert geometries such as the nose radius and edge. A reading of an average surface roughness values (Ra) on the workpiece is taken at a right angle to the feed mark after every cut using Mitutyo portable surface roughness measuring equipment.

TABLE 3 Sample Printout of the Held Constant and Nuisance Factors

Held constant factors (units)	Desired experimental level and allowable range	Measurement precision	How to control (in experiment)	Anticipated effects
Type of cutting fluid	Standard type	Not sure but thought to be adequate	Use one type	None
Temperature of cutting fluid	Machine need to warm up	Estimated 1–2°	Do experiment run after machine has warmed up	None
Depth of cut	1.5 mm	Program	By machine tool	None
Operator	Several operators normally work in the process	Productivity performance measure	Use one "mid-level" operator	None

Nuisance factors (units)	Measurement precision	Strategy (e.g., randomization, blocking, etc.)	Anticipated effects
Viscosity of cutting fluid	Standard viscosity	Measure viscosity at start and end	None to slight
Ambient temperature	Estimated 1–2° by room thermometer	Make experiment run at room temperature	Slight, unless very hot weather
Vibration of machine during operation	?	Do not move heavy objects in the CNC machine shop	Severe vibration can introduce variation

TABLE 4 Sample Printout of the Experimental Data

Expt no:	A: Cutting speed (m/min)	B: Feedrate (mm/rev)	C: Tool nose radius (min)	Tool life data I (min)	Tool life data II (min)	Surface roughness data I (μm)	Surface roughness data II (μm)
1	50	0.15	0.4	51.5	50.2	7.22	7.21
2	50	0.25	0.8	49.5	48.8	6.78	6.75
3	50	0.35	1.2	41.2	40.2	11.12	11.15
4	100	0.15	1.2	40.8	40.5	5.85	5.88
5	100	0.25	0.4	30.2	30.5	9.99	10.21
6	100	0.35	0.9	32.8	32.5	12.35	12.38
7	150	0.15	1.2	29.2	28.6	1.33	1.35
8	150	0.25	0.4	27.3	27.8	9.05	9.07
9	150	0.35	0.8	20.2	21.2	13.25	13.88
10	200	0.15	0.4	21.3	21.3	8.58	8.55
11	200	0.25	0.8	19.5	20.1	6.12	6.15
12	200	0.35	1.2	17.2	18.2	11.89	11.85
13	250	0.15	0.8	17.5	17.2	2.58	2.59
14	250	0.25	1.2	15.2	15.8	4.45	4.48
15	250	0.35	0.4	13.3	13.2	14.58	14.81
16	300	0.15	0.8	13.5	13.4	3.66	3.65
17	300	0.25	1.2	10.5	11.2	15.45	15.48
18	300	0.35	0.4	8.9	9.1	16.88	16.85

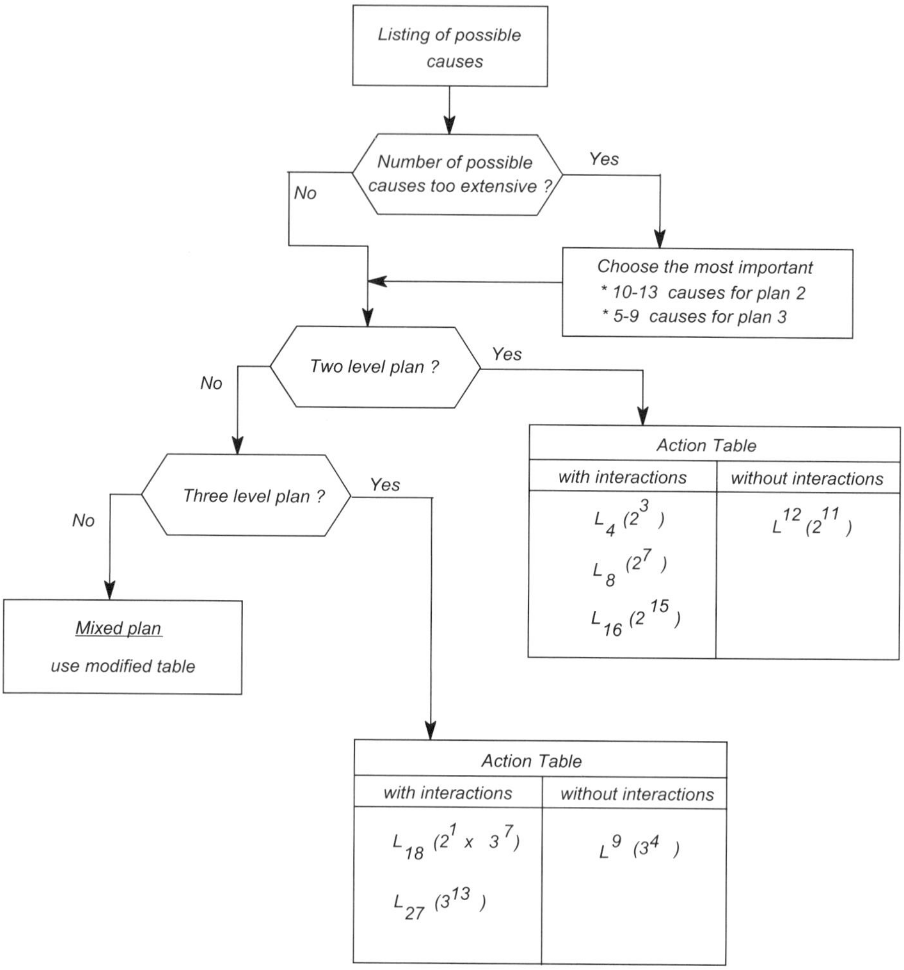

FIGURE 10 Flowchart for selection of orthogonal arrays.

IX. DATA ANALYSIS USING NEURAL NETWORK

After the experiment has been run and the data have been collected, the appropriate analyses of the results are carried out using an adaptive GaRBF neural network. While the experiment reference template is used for determining the measurements to adopt to extract maximum information within minimum experimental efforts, the parallel distributed computational neural network provides a nonlinear multivariate data fitting algorithm for analyzing the result of experimental design and for providing decision support.

A. Neural Network Architecture

An adaptive neural network is designed based on Tay [95] for experimental design. The proposed neural network system consists of a parallel distributed computa-

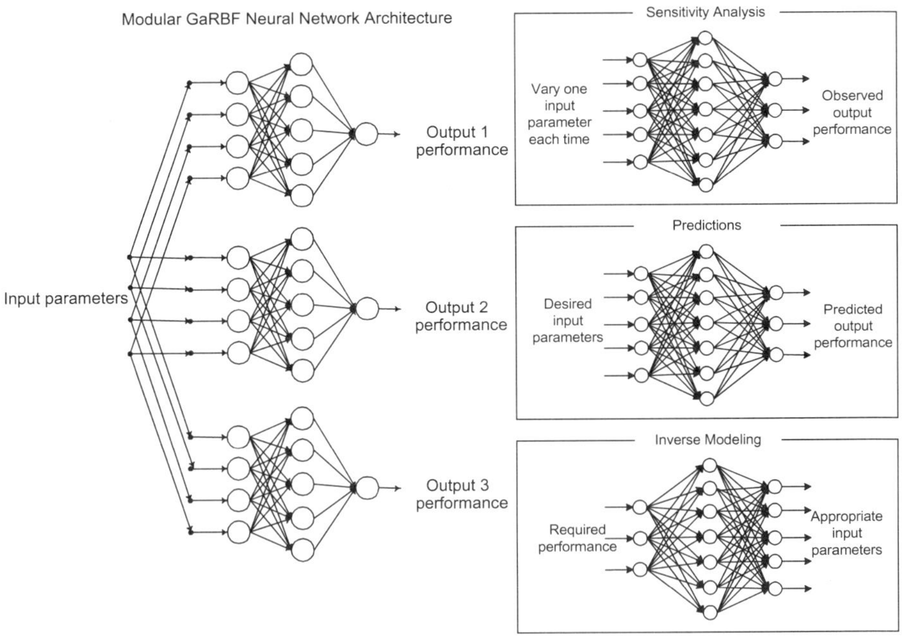

FIGURE 11 Modularized parallel distributed GaRBF neural network.

tional adaptive Gaussian radial basis function neural network for analyzing experimental data as shown in Fig. 11.

A modularized neural network architecture for multiple input and multiple output problems, overcoming the problem of the curse of dimensionality caused by GaRBF is proposed. The approach is to split the multiple input and multiple output (MIMO) problem into a collection of modules with each module as a single output neural network. The modules are trained and compute independently in parallel. Each module has many inputs but only computes one element of output vector and has one hidden layer. In the context of parallel distributed neural networks, the advantages are:

(a) It is easier to learn a set of simple functions separately than to learn a complex function which is a combination of the simple functions. In many cases, training nonparallel distributed neural networks is unsuccessful even when indefinitely long training periods are permitted, whereas parallel distributed neural networks converge quickly and successfully.
(b) In a nonparallel distributed neural network, conflicting signals from different output nodes retard learning. Parallel distributed learning is likely to be more efficient, since weight modification is guided only by one output node.
(c) Individual modules in a parallel distributed network are likely to be simpler than the corresponding nonparallel distributed neural network, and this is yet another reason to expect better generalization properties.
(d) Explaining the results of a parallel distributed neural network will be easier than for a nonparallel distributed neural network, since the relation

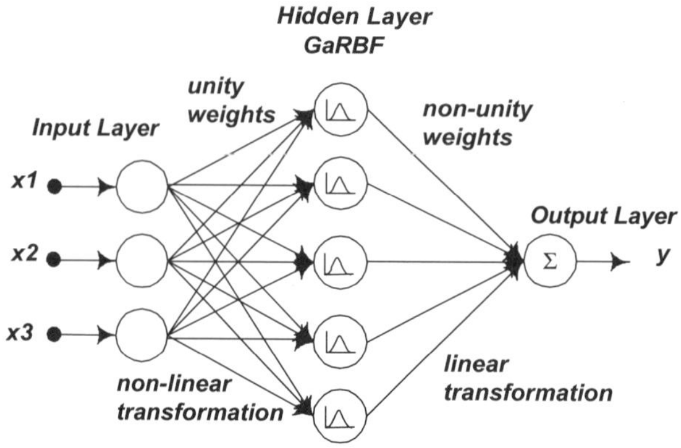

FIGURE 12 A GaRBF neural network.

between input nodes, various hidden nodes, and the output nodes is easier to establish (by examining the connection weights) in each module.

(e) The modules of a parallel distributed neural network can be trained independently, and in parallel. They can also be operated in parallel. Software simulations of the parallel distributed neural network can thus use massively parallel computing systems much more effectively than the nonparallel distributed network.

The adaptive Gaussian radial basis function neural network architecture consists of a three-layer feedforward network with the first layer of input factors (input layer), second layer of GaRBF neurons (hidden layer), and the third layer of linear neurons (output layer) as shown in Fig. 12.

The inputs are directly connected to the nonlinear Gaussian function neurons in the hidden layer with output related to the distance between the input vectors and the centroid of the basis function. The output layer forms a linear combiner which calculates the weighted sum of the outputs of the hidden units. Nonunity weights among the neurons only exist from neurons in the first layer to those in the second layer. The inputs are simply directly connected to the neurons in the first layer via unity weights. The means that the transformation from the input space to the hidden-unit space is nonlinear, whereas the transformation from the hidden-unit space to the output space is linear. A mathematical justification for this rationale may be traced back to an early paper on Cover's theorem [13] on the separability of patterns, which states that a complex pattern-classification problem cast in high-dimensional space nonlinearly is more likely to be linearly separable than in a low-dimensional space [11, 68, 77]. There are two parameters associated with every GaRBF node, namely, the "*center* ($\boldsymbol{\rho}$)" and the "*width* ($\boldsymbol{\sigma}$)" of the GaRBF neurons. Both of these quantities refer to properties of the Gaussian function.

B. Graphical Representation

The theory behind the architecture of the GaRBF neural network can best be visualized from a graphical representation and interpretation of the way it works. Figure 13 illustrates an example of a GaRBF neural network comprising two inputs

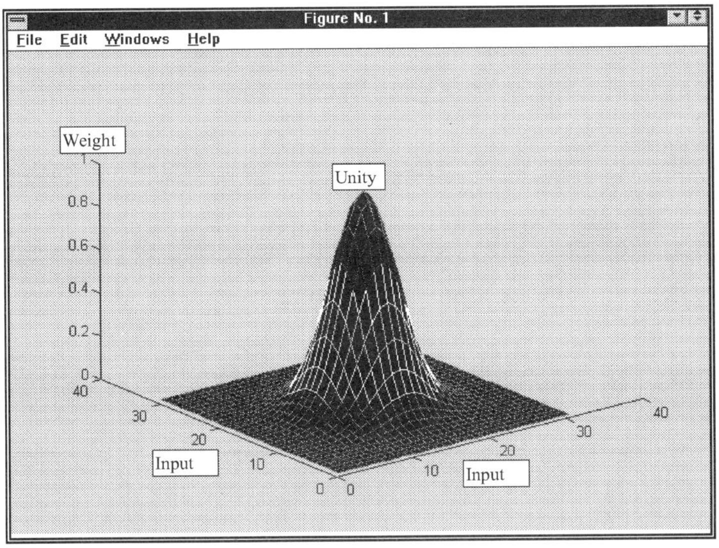

FIGURE 13 A Gaussian-shaped surface solution space of topographical neural map.

x_1 and x_2, a hidden neuron $\mathbf{z}_1$, and an output y_1. By plotting the level of activity generated at the hidden GaRBF neuron against a range of corresponding values at the inputs, a Gaussian-shaped surface space is produced.

The centroid of the bell-shaped Gaussian surface is located at a point in the input plane defined by the points on the hidden neuron's input space. The width of the bell-shaped surface is determined by the value of a $\boldsymbol{\sigma}$ parameter associated with the hidden neuron. The bell-shaped surface decays in a radial manner, equally in all directions out from the centroid. The amplitude of the bell-shaped surface measured at the hidden neuron is unity. This is then adjusted during training by the values of the weights on the hidden neuron's output links, which may be either positive or negative and of any magnitude.

During training, the neural network generates surfaces that approximate the desired function by means of a set of training samples, and provides an accurate generalization at interpolated points. These surfaces are a complete description of the neural network's answers to all variations of the problem it is trained to solve. Since an output neuron merely integrates all incoming values, it can be seen that the surface it produces is a simple approximate combination of the amplitude-adjusted Gaussian-shaped surface produced by the hidden neurons. A GaRBF neural network with a single hidden neuron would generate surfaces comprising a single bell-shaped surface, a GaRBF neural network with two hidden neurons would generate surfaces composed of two bell-shaped surfaces, and so on. This concept can be extended to any number of hidden GaRBF neurons although visualization becomes impossible beyond three dimensions.

Clearly, the more GaRBF hidden neurons incorporated in a network, the more convoluted can be the surfaces produced at the outputs from the network. The bell-shaped Gaussian function gives the highest output when the input is close to its center and decreases monotonically as the distance from the center increases. The distance is defined by the Euclidean distance. The training in a GaRBF network, or configuring the whole network, is done by finding the centers, widths, and the weights connecting hidden nodes to the output nodes.

C. Learning Paradigm

The proposed GaRBF learning paradigm consists in appropriately defining a function to satisfy the interpolation condition, $f(x_i) = y_i$ with $(i = 1, 2 \cdots m)$, where m is the total number of training patterns and (x_i, y_i) is the ith training pair. The transfer function of the ith GaRBF neuron in the hidden layer is of the form,

$$\mathbf{z}_i(x) = r\left(\sum_{i=1}^{n} (x^j - \boldsymbol{\rho}_i^j)^2 / (\boldsymbol{\sigma}_i^j)^2\right),$$

where $\mathbf{z}_i(x)$ is the ith output of the neuron in the hidden layer. The argument x shows its explicit functional dependence on x; x^j is the jth element of the input vector, x of dimension l, $x = [x_1, x_2, \ldots, x_l]^T$; $r(\bullet)$ is a radial basis function which is chosen in this research to be the Gaussian function (exponential function) of the form,

$$\mathbf{z}_i(x) = \exp\left(-\sum_{i=1}^{n} (x^j - \boldsymbol{\rho}_i^j)^2 / (\boldsymbol{\sigma}_i^j)^2\right),$$

where $\boldsymbol{\rho}_i^j$, also of dimension l, called the center of the ith GaRBF neuron, is the jth element of bias vector with the components corresponding to those of x; and the positive scalar $\boldsymbol{\sigma}_i^j$ is the jth element of the width vector $\boldsymbol{\sigma}_i$ for the ith neuron. Both $\boldsymbol{\rho}_i$ and $\boldsymbol{\sigma}_i$ may be different for different neurons. A reason for choosing the exponential function is a proof [23, 67, 72, 77] showing that it is in a class of functions possessing the "best approximation property." This ensures that there exists a set of weights that approximates the desired function better than any other set, an attribute not shared by the sigmoidal functions commonly used in networks trained by backpropagation. Denoting y_i as the output of the ith neuron in the output layer of a GaRBF network, its transfer function is simply the weighted sum of the outputs from the hidden layer expressed as

$$y_i = \sum_{j=1}^{n} w_{ij} \mathbf{z}_j(x),$$

where w_{ij} is the weight from the jth GaRBF neuron in the hidden layer to the ith linear neuron in the output layer; and n is the number of GaRBF neurons in the hidden layer. The foregoing is clearly a linear operation, and with m such linear neurons in the output layer, the transfer function can be rewritten in the following matrix form,

$$y = \mathbf{W}\mathbf{z}(x),$$

where $y = [y_1, y_2, y_3, \ldots, y_m]^T$ is called the output vector of the GaRBF net; $\mathbf{z}(x) = [\mathbf{z}_1(x), \mathbf{z}_2(x), \mathbf{z}_3(x), \ldots, \mathbf{z}_n(x)]^T$ is called the output vector of the hidden layer; and $\mathbf{W}$ is an $m \times n$ weight matrix with w_{ij} being its ijth element given as

$$w_{ij} = \begin{bmatrix} w_{11} & w_{12} & \cdot & \cdot & w_{1n} \\ w_{21} & w_{22} & & & \cdot \\ \cdot & & \cdot & & \cdot \\ \cdot & & & \cdot & \cdot \\ w_{m1} & \cdot & \cdot & \cdot & w_{mn} \end{bmatrix}.$$

It can effectively decompose all the parameters in the GaRBF neural network into two main parts: namely, the matrix W containing all the weights of the neural network, and the vector $\mathbf{z}(\bullet)$ containing all the architectural parameters such as the number of neuron (grid points) n, the center vectors ($\boldsymbol{\rho}_i$), and the width vectors ($\boldsymbol{\sigma}_i$). The GaRBF neural network is used for nonlinear experimental data analysis, prediction, and inverse modeling because of its universal approximation property which is able to predict the future based on the past observations which are corrupted with noise.

Using the preceding notations, this property states that for any error ε and an arbitrary nonlinear continuous function y [where $y = f(\bullet)$] on a compact set S, there always exist a weight matrix W and a vector $\mathbf{z}(x)$, all of finite dimensions, such that: the maximum absolute value of the actual minus predicted must be less than the desired errors. So,

$$\max_{x \in S} |f(x) - \mathbf{Wz}(x)| < \varepsilon.$$

This property translates into

$$\begin{aligned} x = x(t) = [&y(t), y(t-1), y(t-2), \ldots, y(t-k+1), \\ &u(t), u(t-1), \ldots, u(t-l+1)], \\ y = y(&t+1), \end{aligned}$$

the existence of a weight matrix $\mathbf{W}$ and a structural vector $\mathbf{z}(x)$, both with finite dimension, is guaranteed that any real-world system can be estimated on its region of operation space S in the form,

$$y_{t+1} = \mathbf{Wz}(x_t),$$

within the given estimation error tolerance ε, and the weights can be updated as in [95],

$$\mathbf{W}_{t+1} = \mathbf{W}_t - \frac{\beta e_t \mathbf{z}(x_t)}{1 + \mathbf{z}^T(x_t)\mathbf{z}(x_t)}.$$

Accordingly, learning in the adaptive Gaussian radial basis function neural network is equivalent to finding a surface in a multidimensional space that provides a best fit to the training data, with the criterion for "best fit" being measured in some statistical sense such as the mean squared error. Correspondingly, generalization is equivalent to the use of this multidimensional surface to interpolate the test data. It is in this sense that the adaptive GaRBF neural network offers a model structure for representing nonlinear prediction, sensitivity analysis, and inverse modeling.

The property of localized universal approximation of the GaRBF neural network ensures that it will not produce a high output for the samples which are far away from the centroids. This helps to reduce the extrapolation errors which occur when the test data fall beyond the range of the training data and are misclassified. Moreover, each hidden node represents a small region in the feature space, that is, the effect of each hidden unit is completely local. In addition, the GaRBF neural network has a structural feature of linear-in-the-weights as depicted in Eq. (6). This feature relates the weights directly to the output error and thus allows relatively simple and stable weight updating formulas to be constructed. These characteristics enable the GaRBF neural network to generalize extremely well, even in complicated tasks such as prediction, sensitivity analysis, and inverse modeling.

X. ALGORITHM FOR ADAPTIVE GaRBF NEURAL NETWORK

Existing theory on radial basis function approximation suggests that center $\boldsymbol{\rho}_i$ and width $\boldsymbol{\sigma}_i$ are closely related to the concept of data cluster an unknown function y where $y = f(\bullet)$ on compact set S. In this proposed framework, n is interpreted as the number of data clusters with center and width ($\boldsymbol{\rho}_i$ and $\boldsymbol{\sigma}_i$), the covering range of the ith cluster over a compact set S. The spatial Fourier analysis constitutes a theoretical framework for configuring GaRBF neural networks on a compact set S. By confining the function approximation to within compact set S and properly truncating an unknown function $f(\bullet)$ on set S, it can be shown that all the structural parameters in $\mathbf{z}(\bullet)$ including n, center $\boldsymbol{\rho}_i$, and width $\boldsymbol{\sigma}_i$ of a GaRBF neural network can be determined directly from a fine enough uniform grid (data clusters) drawn on compact set S for a given approximation error ε. The specific approach proposed is constructed in two basic steps:

(a) Adaptive architecture generation. A so-called GaRBF nominal rectangular grid is simply set by choosing a set of grid sizes, Δ_j (*delta*) $(j = 1, 2, \ldots, mk + ql)$ to cover the whole $(mk + ql)$-dimensional space that contains S. In addition, a forgetting process is introduced whereby selected neurons will be eliminated from the model structure if they have not been updated by the input for a given period of time.

(b) Adaptive error reduction. The sizes of the nominal grid are adjusted to be finer if the initial sizes do not allow the combined architecture formation and weight updating processes to achieve the target error within a prescribed period of time. After the adjustment, the architecture generation will proceed again with the finer nominal grid.

A. Neuro-Dynamics Initialization

The adaptive neural network procedure starts with the existence of a compact set S as the region of operation for $y_{t+1} = [y_t, y_{t-1}, \ldots, y_{t-k+1}, u_t, u_{t-1}, \ldots, u_{t-l+1}]$ needs to be assumed. Except for its existence, neither the size nor the shape of S is required. Next is to define an initializing nominal grid on the whole $(mk + lq)$-dimensional linear space with a prescribed set of grid sizes Δ_j and, consequently, $\boldsymbol{\sigma}_j$ using the rules given in $\boldsymbol{\sigma}_i^j \in [\frac{2}{3}\Delta_j, \Delta_j]$ (based on heuristics) for $i = 1, 2, \ldots, n$

and $j = 1, 2, \ldots, mk + lq$. Initially, the GaRBF neural network is set up with the required number of input and output neurons, but with no hidden neurons. The input is used to select the neurons on the nominal grid to gradually build the GaRBF neural network model. Each hidden GaRBF neuron is then added and trained by the proposed algorithm until the surface generated at an output fits the points marked by the training patterns to within a predefined level of accuracy.

B. Adaptive Architecture Generation Phase

For each input $x_t = [y_t, y_{t-1}, \ldots, y_{t-k+1}, u_t, u_{t-1}, \ldots, u_{t-l+1}]$ the so-called central grid-point $\tilde{\boldsymbol{\rho}}_i$ which is a vector of integers, is calculated by dividing the jth component of x_t by Δ_j, and by rounding the result to the nearest integer. With $\tilde{\boldsymbol{\rho}}_i$ and γ, the set S_t (local neuron set) can be determined. The weight updating at time t will thus only be performed on the neurons in S_t. Another set S_d (structural neurons set) which is empty initially is defined. After the weight updating, the neurons in S_t will join those in S_d to form an updated S_d. The set S_d is in fact the partial model at any time instance as shown in Fig. 14.

C. Adaptive Architecture Deletion Phase

The neuron will be eliminated from S_d if its weight has not been updated for a period equal to or greater than the deletion period T. Clearly, this process forms the model structure by putting together the local characteristics of an unknown real-world system exposed by the input updating sequence. With a forgetting process, a nonuniform grid will be developed which will place more neurons in certain areas and fewer neurons in certain other areas in compact space S depending on particular input updating history.

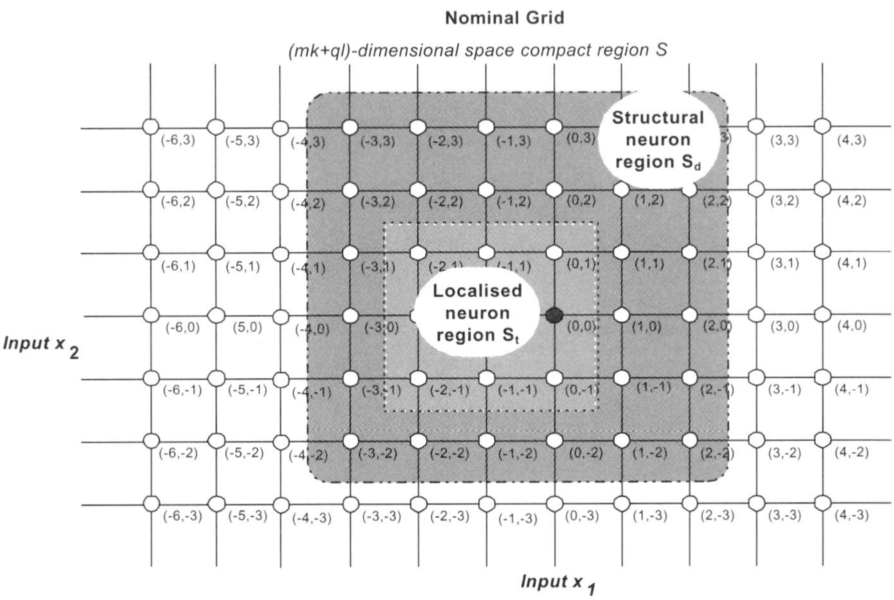

FIGURE 14 Adaptive partial model.

D. Adaptive Error Reduction

When the initial choice of Δ_j is too large, the error is not likely to decrease to the given limit within a prescribed adaptation period τ. Then the grid adaptation is activated to modify the nominal grid as follows:

> The fineness of the nominal grid is doubled by halving the grid sizes Δ_j. Thus, the new grid will have the grid size $\Delta_j/2$ in the jth dimension. As shown in Fig. 15, this process does not change the original nominal grid, thus leaves the structural neurons already present in S_d intact. After the adaptive error reduction, another round of architecture generation will be activated. The whole process repeats until the error drops within the prescribed limit.

E. Summary of Adaptive GaRBF Neural Network Algorithm

Step 1. Initialize all neurodynamics parameters to zero. Define an initializing nominal grid on the whole $(mk + lq)$-dimensional linear space with a prescribed set of grid sizes Δ_j. Determine $\boldsymbol{\sigma}_j$ using the rules given in $\boldsymbol{\sigma}_i^j \in [\frac{2}{3}\Delta_j, \Delta_j]$ for $i = 1, 2, \ldots, n$ and $j = 1, 2, \ldots, mk + lq$. The initial setting of Δ_j can incorporate any prior knowledge about the unknown solutions. Otherwise, they can be arbitrarily chosen. Choose structural radius $0 \leq \gamma \leq 3$, deletion period T (chosen to be between 15 to 20 times of the discrete time steps), and the adaptation period τ (recommended at least 10 times of T). Reset structural neuron set S_d so that it contains no element initially.

Step 2. For each training pattern, use the localized sampling to present a pair of input and output samples

For each incoming data x_t at time t,

For each processing neuron units j determine the central neuron $\boldsymbol{\rho}_t$ (calculated by dividing the jth component of x_t by Δ_j, and rounding the result to the nearest integer) determine the current neuron set S_t

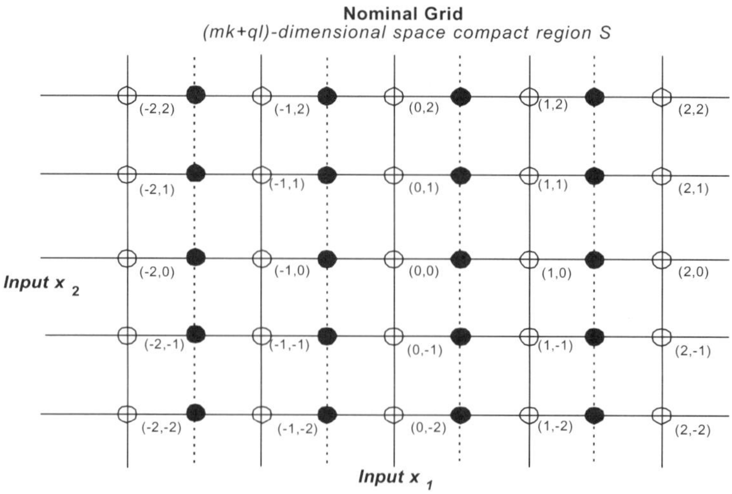

FIGURE 15 Halving of nominal grid size.

The weight updating at time t will thus only be performed on the neurons in S_t. After the weight updating, the neurons in S_t will join those in S_d to form an updated S_d. The set S_d is in fact the partial model at any time instance.

Step 3. For each processing neuron unit j

{Form the partial model $\tilde{y}_{t+1} = \mathbf{W}_t \mathbf{z}(x_t)$ for the neurons in S region,

and use $\mathbf{W}_{t+1} = \mathbf{W}_t - \dfrac{\beta e_t \mathbf{z}(x_t)}{1 + \mathbf{z}^T(x_t)\mathbf{z}(x_t)}$ to carry out weight update for

the partial model},

where β is a positive constant such that $0 < \beta < 2$ and $e_t = \tilde{y}_t - y_t$.

Step 4. Update S_d using S_t as follows: Remove all the neurons in S_d that have not got their weights updated for a prescribed period T, and complete $S_d = S_d U S_t$.

Step 5. Reset S_t to an empty set. Compute: $MSE = \frac{1}{2}\sum(x_{\text{actual}} - x_{\text{predicted}})^2$. If the error is not below the prescribed limit after the period τ, then invoke the structure adaptation procedure to half the sizes of the nominal grid (grid size $\Delta_j/2$ in the jth dimension), and go back to Step 2 to let the error decrease until convergence criterion. The whole process repeats until the error drops within the prescribed limit.

XI. TRAINING AND APPLICATION

The proposed adaptive GaRBF neural network has two operating modes (as shown in Fig. 16):

(a) Supervised training phase, which includes both training and testing phases, where the parameters of the adaptive GaRBF neural network are set to minimize the average error between the actual output and the desired output over the vectors in a training set.
(b) Application phase where the neural network is used for sensitivity analysis (e.g., hypothesis testing), optimization, forward prediction, and inverse modeling of the experimental design problems as well as for decision support.

The data sample size usually includes both training and test data patterns or samples. These training and testing data are developed from a combination of specific data collection strategies such as historical data, analytical simulation, observational studies, and experimental studies. These data are usually available in one form or another. Figure 17 shows a schematic of the data collection approaches.

Initially the neural network is trained using the training data samples by building the network up in stages, training one hidden neuron at a time. It is important to note that in the beginning of training, the weights are randomly assigned, unless otherwise specified. This means that the minimization of the error function begins at a random point in the terrain determined by the weights, and searches for the "valley" of the terrain by the gradient descent method. The point where the training process is to stop is when the desired error is achieved. This means that the

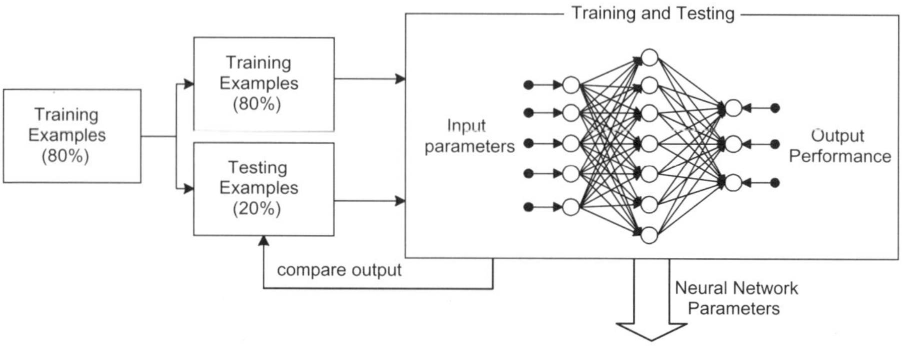

FIGURE 16 Supervised training and testing data size.

stopping criterion depends on the error desired, that is, the error tolerance criterion. A small error will provide better generalization, but will increase training time.

After training, the test data samples are used to check whether the samples have produced parsimonious models which generally perform well (within the error tolerance criterion specified). The test subset is used for evaluation of the performance of the model (testing its ability to generalize correctly). The benchmark to determine whether a retraining of the network to achieve better generalization results depends on the test performance. This testing process involves predicting the output values, and compares it with actual unused output values. If the predicted error of testing is less than the desired error within the error tolerance criterion specified, then the trained neural network is acceptable. When the testing is satisfactory, the test data samples and the training data samples are combined and the adaptive neural network is retrained on all the data samples to give the best model.

Figure 18 shows the iterative procedure taken for obtaining a "learned" network given the data available and the problem specification. Additionally, Fig. 19 shows a sample printout from the training process. For the adaptive GaRBF neural network architecture where the number of hidden neuron units is determined not

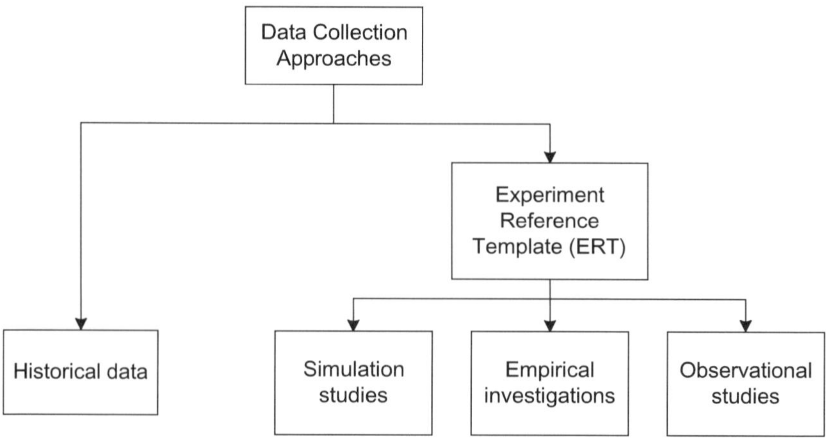

FIGURE 17 Data collection approaches.

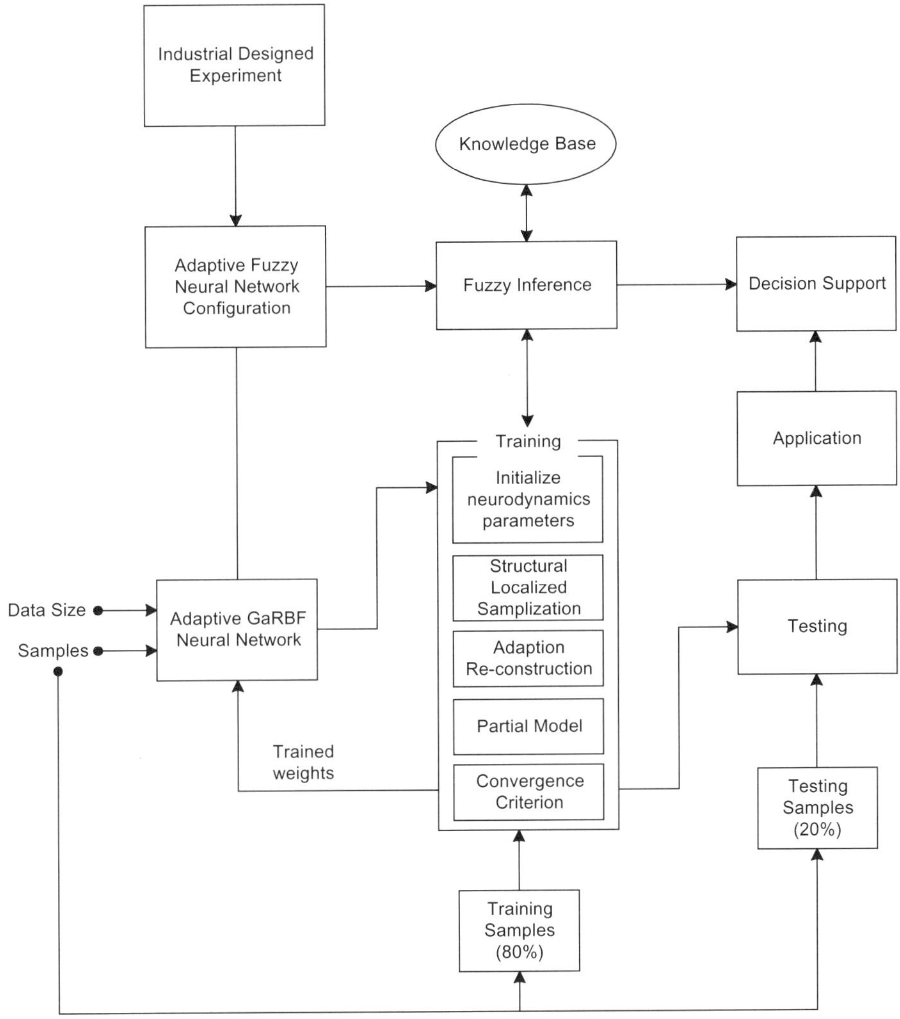

FIGURE 18 Iterative procedure for a learned adaptive GaRBF neural network.

only by the data size, and input–output requirements (problem specification) and localized sampling initially, but also by the iterative improvement due to adaptive re-construction. Training where the weights are determined by stopping the training after the desired error tolerance criterion is achieved, or by a certain number of epoch cycles and after checking the testing results.

A. Forward Prediction

After training and testing, the adaptive GaRBF neural network can be used for forward predictions of output performance, without having to do extensive experiment. This can easily be achieved by keying in the desired input parameters, the adaptive neural network will compute and will automatically predict and will present an optimized output performance within the specified error tolerance criterion. This

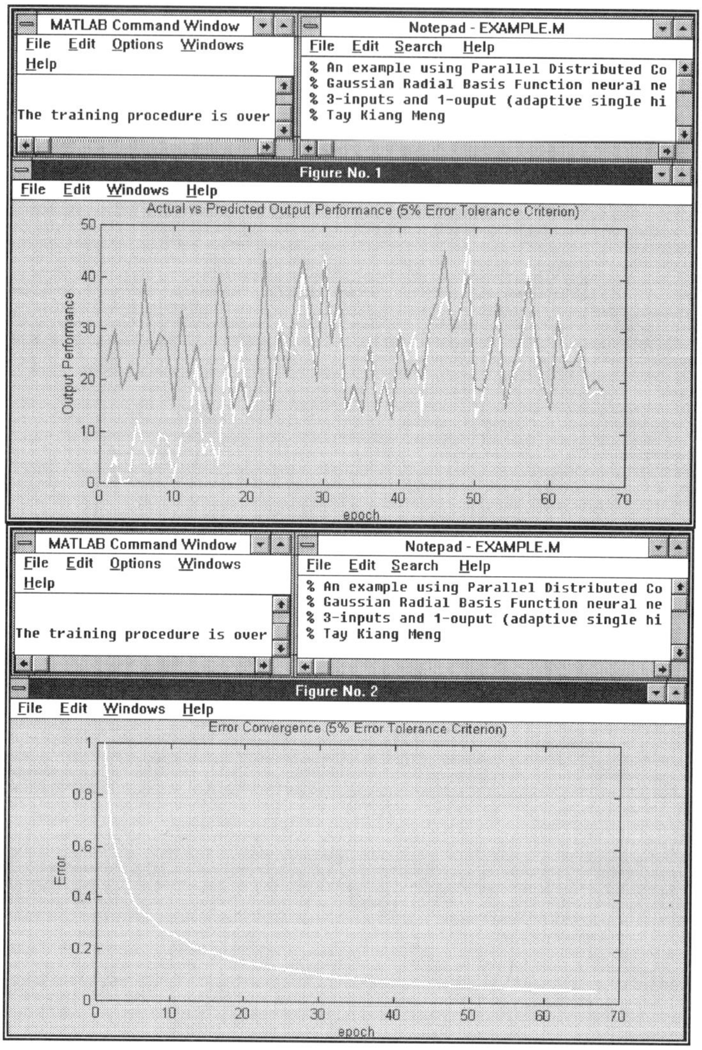

FIGURE 19 Sample printout of the training process—actual (solid line) versus predicted (dotted line).

is equivalent to the optimization process in the Taguchi methods and the response surface methodology. The novel idea behind this is to generate and to probe the entire solution space of the topographical neural map for the experimental design problem which can be modeled to any degree of detail (depends on the error tolerance criterion). With this information, engineers and managers can identify and can solve any experimental design problems as well as provide for decision support. A sample printout of the forward prediction is shown in Fig. 20.

B. Sensitivity Analysis

When the neural network is trained and able to generalize well to the required error tolerance criterion, the neural network system can then be used for sensitivity analysis such as quick hypothesis testing, parameters identification, fine tuning of

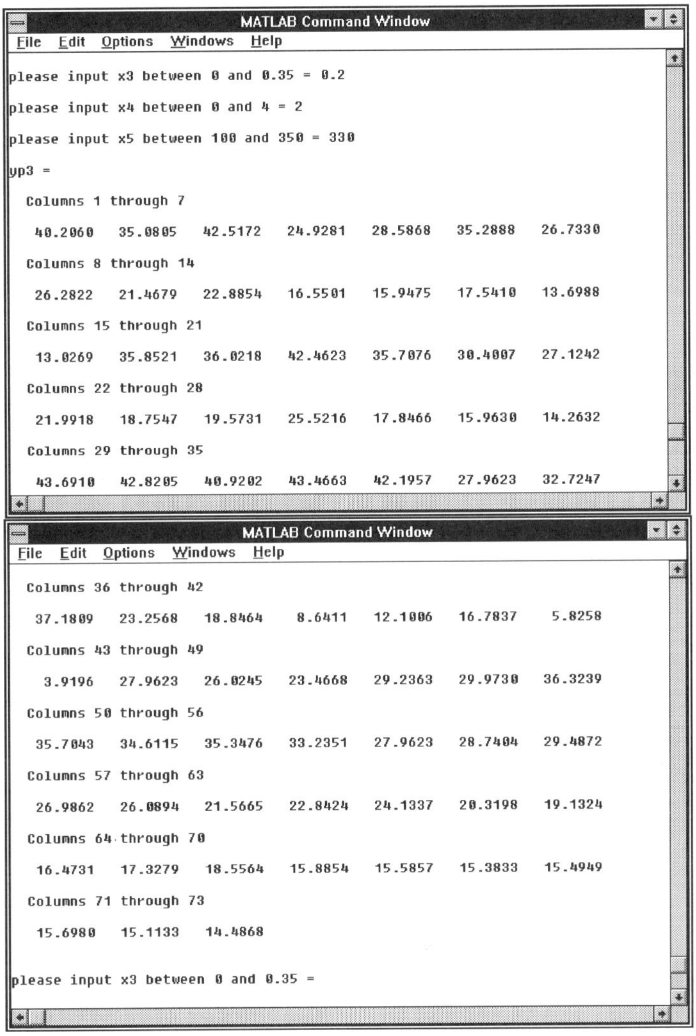

```
MATLAB Command Window
File  Edit  Options  Windows  Help

please input x3 between 0 and 0.35 = 0.2

please input x4 between 0 and 4 = 2

please input x5 between 100 and 350 = 330

yp3 =

  Columns 1 through 7

   40.2060   35.0805   42.5172   24.9281   28.5868   35.2888   26.7330

  Columns 8 through 14

   26.2822   21.4679   22.8854   16.5501   15.9475   17.5410   13.6988

  Columns 15 through 21

   13.0269   35.8521   36.0218   42.4623   35.7076   30.4007   27.1242

  Columns 22 through 28

   21.9918   18.7547   19.5731   25.5216   17.8466   15.9630   14.2632

  Columns 29 through 35

   43.6910   42.8205   40.9202   43.4663   42.1957   27.9623   32.7247
```

```
MATLAB Command Window
File  Edit  Options  Windows  Help

  Columns 36 through 42

   37.1809   23.2568   18.8464    8.6411   12.1006   16.7837    5.8258

  Columns 43 through 49

    3.9196   27.9623   26.0245   23.4668   29.2363   29.9730   36.3239

  Columns 50 through 56

   35.7043   34.6115   35.3476   33.2351   27.9623   28.7404   29.4872

  Columns 57 through 63

   26.9862   26.0894   21.5665   22.8424   24.1337   20.3198   19.1324

  Columns 64 through 70

   16.4731   17.3279   18.5564   15.8854   15.5857   15.3833   15.4949

  Columns 71 through 73

   15.6980   15.1133   14.4868

please input x3 between 0 and 0.35 =
```

FIGURE 20 Sample printout of forward prediction.

input parameters for optimum output performance. By perturbing the input parameters by a small amount (the perturbation should be consistent with the nature of the parameters), the testing data or even the training data can be used to predict the sensitivity of the parameters in response to the change in the input conditions. The perturbation can affect one parameter at a time, or a few parameters at a time. The change in the output can be averaged to reflect the sensitivity or for hypothesis testing. Judging from the amount of the change, hypotheses about the effect of the change in parameters on the output value can be verified. A sample printout of the sensitivity analysis is shown in Fig. 21.

Partial analysis can be used to determine if any of the input parameters has a nonlinear relationship with the output variable. The input parameters that are deemed important can be identified by (hypothesis testing) perturbing these param-

Perturb Input Parameter C	-10%	-5%	0%	5%	10%	Remarks
Level1	135	143	150	158	165	A=0.2
Output Performance	29.50	28.70	28.00	27.00	26.10	B=2
% Change of Output Level1	5.36%	2.50%	0.00%	-3.57%	-6.79%	
Level2	180	190	200	210	220	
Output Performance	24.10	22.80	21.60	20.30	19.10	
% Change of Output Level2	11.57%	5.56%	0.00%	-6.02%	-11.57%	
Level3	225	238	250	263	275	
Output Performance	18.60	17.30	16.50	15.90	15.60	
% Change of Output Level3	12.73%	4.85%	0.00%	-3.64%	-5.45%	
Level4	270	285	300	315	330	
Output Performance	15.70	15.50	15.40	15.10	14.50	
% Change of Output Level4	1.95%	0.65%	0.00%	-1.95%	-5.84%	

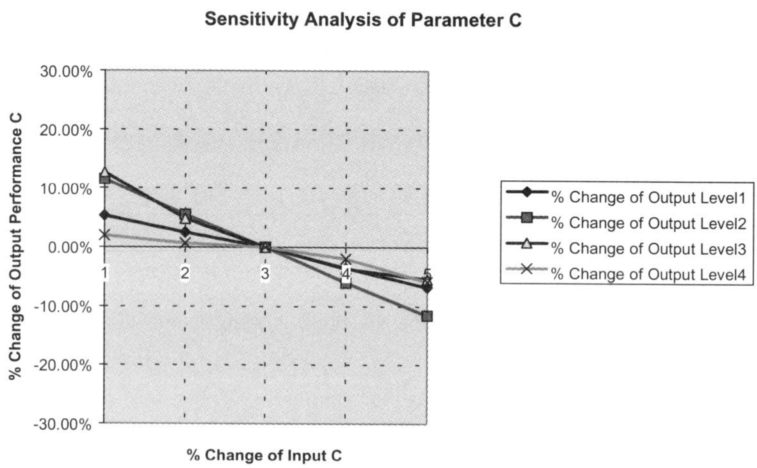

FIGURE 21 Sample printout of the sensitivity analysis.

eters for different ranges of values of these parameters to obtain the corresponding output changes; and then plot output changes against the changes of these parameters. This is the sensitivity analysis of using the GaRBF neural network model of the relationship between input parameters and output performance. The sensitivity analysis can also be done for a combination of input parameters to examine the interactions among parameters.

A simplified and quick way of testing a hypothesis is to test by comparing the output performance of the neural network generated by the input data containing the original value of the parameters and the new increased or decreased value of the variables, respectively. In addition, only data points whose tested mean squared error (MSE) are low is selected. This is to ensure that when there is a change in the output, one can be sure that it is not due to the discrepancy between the targeted output and the output obtained from the network as a result of the input data set. Among the parameters which have a negligible effect on

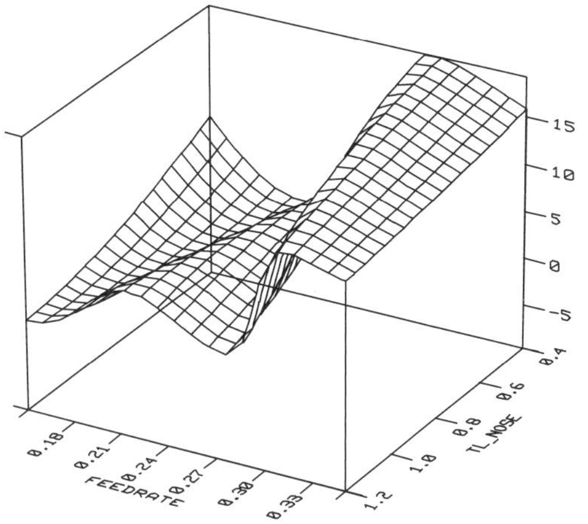

FIGURE 22 Sample printout of optimization surface.

the model, and those which have a significant effect on the output performance measure are identified. These parameters, called adjustment factors, are now the basis for further performance gain while retaining the robustness of the design. The output performance is "tuned" to bring the value of its performance measure closer to target by properly setting the adjustment factors. This is equivalent to the Taguchi data analysis.

C. Inverse Modeling and Optimization

The idea is to invert the generation of a solution of the space topographical neural map using the output performance to drive the adaptive GaRBF neural network so as to estimate (predict) the input parameters. Similarly, the adaptive GaRBF neural network can generate and can probe the entire solution space of the topographical neural map which is equivalent to performing a full factorial experiment without further extensive experimentation. The final application for the users will only involve the keying in of the required output performance, the adaptive GaRBF neural network will compute and will automatically predict the appropriate input parameters within the specified error tolerance criterion. A sample printout of the optimization surface is shown in Fig. 22.

XII. MAIN AREAS OF APPLICATION

The proposed software model (Gaussian radial basis function) is a powerful method with a definite range of applicability in manufacturing research. It greatly accelerates the development and evaluation process for empirical data analysis, predictions, and inverse modeling, allowing experimentation and optimization that would not be practical. In addition, its rapid training makes it suitable for situations where adaptive incremental learning is necessary. In a larger framework, the main areas of application for the proposed scheme are:

(a) Multiresponse experimental design and analysis. In the nonlinear functional relationship $y = (x_1, x_2, \ldots, x_n)$, the nonlinear functional form f is unknown or not well understand in a certain range of the input parameters, $x_1, x_2, \ldots, x_n$.
(b) Nonlinear problem modeling, prediction, inverse interpolation, and chaotic time-series forecasting.
(c) Empirical model building and parameter estimation or identification, and possibly data mining for experimental design or predictive learning problems.

The software can be used for pre-processing, screening, modeling post-processing, optimization, and sequential experimentation as well as decision support for both offline or online. Many of the issues addressed, however, can also apply to new products development and manufacturing processes or research and development (R&D) and to various additional experimental goals, such as optimization and robustness studies as well as decision support. The proposed approach is particularly appropriate for complex nonlinear multiresponses experimental investigation (both discrete and continuous) and for people with limited experience in designing experiments. Thus, it should be of value to practitioners of experimental design and analysis, and could facilitate more effective applications of experimental design and analysis by novice users. [For actual usage and application of software see [95].

XIII. IMPLICATION OF THE ADAPTIVE NEURAL NETWORK APPROACH FOR EXPERIMENTAL DESIGN AND DECISION SUPPORT

Given the potential advantages of a neural network in predicting and modeling the results of experimental design, the case with which it can be used to capture the nonlinear relationship, and to conduct a sensitivity analysis, predictions, or inverse modeling, based on data, it would be interesting to contemplate the possible incorporation of neural networks in a decision support framework such as the one depicted in Fig. 23. It is noted here that such a framework can be included as a module in the model base of a complete intelligent experimental design system, along with other modules such as a quantitative forecasting module or an expert system module. No mention is made here of the data base and the user interface associated with the intelligent experimental design system, which are beyond the scope of this research.

There are four blocks in this methodology that are interlinked. The first block consists of a network architecture block where a PDC adaptive GaRBF neural network architecture is chosen. The second block is a training block where the neural network is trained using the training set of data. The training stage should end as approximately indicated by the error converging result to the desired level. The third block is the testing block where the testing set of data is used for a generalization test. If the result is not satisfactory, a different neuro-dynamics configuration can be chosen, or the same network is used, while a different random starting point of training is used, or a different breaking point of training is used. This is

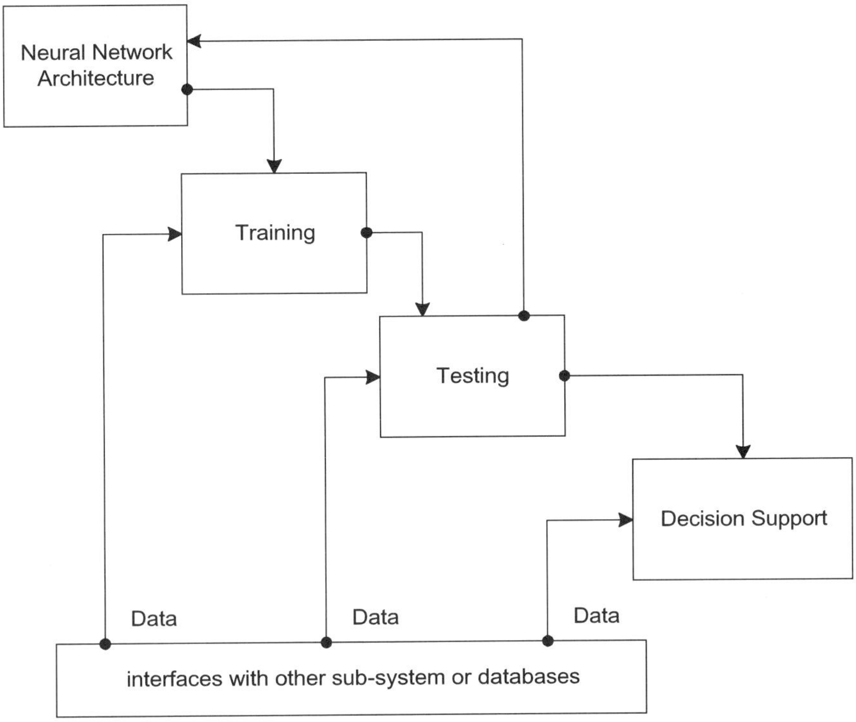

FIGURE 23 Neural network for experimental design and decision support framework.

the iterative training process (until the network is satisfactorily trained). The fourth block is the decision support block, where given the satisfactorily trained neural network, a bunch of causal relationships can be studied which leads to strategies, and the input data can be perturbed to see how the neural network responds, or strategies can be thus evaluated, through partial–sensitivity analysis.

It should be noted that the first three blocks can be "hidden" from the users. Perhaps with the help of an expert system, or a knowledge-based component, the iterative search for a suitable network configuration or an optimal training–testing result for the network can be taken care of automatically without human intervention. The engineer then simply makes use of the trained network.

Another possible use of expert systems would be in the choice of a suitable module in the model base for the end user depending on the needs and the availability of information. The concept of comparative modeling, enabling users to have access to different modeling techniques within a single system, would be applicable here. It should also be noted that the data can come from other systems–modules within the model base or databases associated with the decision support system. For example, the network can draw the result of a forecasting system or historical data or online data as an input to the network. The interface with a database either directly or via network would provide the neural network with up-to-date decision support.

The prototype adaptive fuzzy neural network once trained and tested, can generate and probe the entire solution space of the topographical neural map for the experimental design problem which can be modeled to any degree of detail (depends on the error tolerance criterion). The advantages of incorporating the adaptive fuzzy neural network for experimental design and decision support lie in the ease with which the adaptive fuzzy neural network can conduct sensitivity analysis such as hypothesis testing and partial analysis, predictions, and inverse modeling between the input and output factors. This allows users to understand the effect of change to one or more input parameters (sensitivity analysis) and the general contribution of one of the parameters in the performance of the output (partial analysis). In addition, the neural network can also be used to predict input values or forecast output values with additional emphasis on the inverse modeling. In addition, with this information and knowledge, the engineers and managers can identify and solve any experimental design problems as well as provide for decision support. The prototype demonstrated that the adaptive fuzzy neural network has remarkable generalization (interpolation) capabilities when trained with the same sparse array of data as used in the Taguchi methods.

XIV. CONCLUSION

A new concept necessary for experimental design and decision support is presented. Traditionally, statistical techniques have been applied to experimental design, but the analysis of the results is difficult, and requires restrictive assumptions for the problem to be analytically formulated, or a prohibitively large computational effort. These drawbacks lead to the application of a combination of other methods or tools such as genetic algorithms, neural networks, fuzzy logic, machine learning, etc. A number of concepts which include the surface approximation, sampling, universal approximation, and fuzzy neural networks were discussed. The innovative use of these concepts conceived two key ideas, that is, localized sampling and adaptive reconstruction. These two key ideas are the main learning engine and allow an experimental design and decision support model to grow and reconstruct by learning novel features from the localized input and output sequence samples. These proposed concepts are able to provide a nonlinear, model-free, multivariate surface data fitting learning algorithm, which automatically determines the functional relationship between inputs and outputs directly from data without a hypothesized functional form. In addition, under these concepts, it has been shown that both neural networks and fuzzy systems offer the property of universal approximation. They are therefore ideal for solving and representing experimental design problems which provide a means to decision support. The relation between neural networks and fuzzy systems offers a link which connects two seemingly different research areas.

The new concept was implemented which includes Taguchi's ideas of robust designs through fractional factorial orthogonal designs for data collection, but excludes awkward and technically (statistically) troublesome tactics in existing experimental design methodologies, by incorporating adaptive neural network data analytic approaches. The new proposed method can be used for pre-processing, screening, modeling, post-processing, optimization, and sequential experimentation as well as decision support for both product development and manufacturing processes, offline or online. Many of the issues addressed, however, can also apply to new products development and manufacturing processes or research and development (R&D) and to various additional experimental goals, such as optimization and robustness studies as well as decision support. The proposed approach is particularly appropriate for complex nonlinear multiresponses experimental investigation (both discrete and continuous) and for people with limited experience in designing experiments. Thus, it should be of value to practitioners of experimental design and analysis, and could facilitate more effective applications of experimental design and analysis by novice users.

The most novel feature of the proposed intelligent software is its ability to, in a universal integrated way, facilitate the combined use of Taguchi quality engineering with adaptive neural network analysis to model empirical investigation and decision support characterized by complex nonlinear interactions involving discrete and continuous variables. As compared to the classical and Taguchi methods of experimental design and analysis, the proposed approach can, under certain conditions:

(a) Achieve full factorial design performance with small fractional factorial designs.
(b) Accommodate a large number of input variables at many different levels.
(c) Model many output responses concurrently, that is, multiresponse experiment and provide more complex nonlinear models for the data.
(d) Use for comparison, hypothesis testing, sensitivity analysis, prediction, inverse modeling, and decision support by judiciously manipulating the input end and output end.

The proposed software described is powerful and provides a framework which can be used in the virtual reality of experimentation and investigation. It will help to integrate and to manage the ingredients of good experimental design and analysis activities by bridging the gap between domain and statistical knowledge with neural network learning capabilities. Furthermore, it help engineers to understand and to implement good decision making for real-world problems. Good decision making is based on trustworthy data, which in turn are derived from an intelligent experimental system, which provides a basis for generating a learning tool to acquire experimental knowledge.

XV. SYMBOLS AND ABBREVIATIONS

ERT	Experiment reference template
GaRBF	Gaussian radial basis function
DOE	Design of experiment
q and m	Dimensions of input and output, respectively
k and l	Order of input and output, respectively
OA	Orthogonal array
Δ	Delta grid size
df	Degrees of freedom
exp	Exponential function
e_t	Error at time t
ε	Error tolerance
$f(\cdot)$	Continuous function

$f(\mathbf{W}, x)$	Approximate continuous function expressed by weight (W) and by input (x)
γ	Structural radius
T	Deletion period
τ	Adaptation period
$\lim_{t\to\infty}$	Limit when time approaches infinity
MSE	Mean squared error
$\boldsymbol{\sigma}_i$	Width of GaRBF
$\boldsymbol{\rho}_i$	Center of GaRBF
$\tilde{\boldsymbol{\rho}}_i$	Central grid point
S	Compact set
S_t	Local neuron set
S_d	Structural neuron set
β	Positive constant
W	Weight matrix
μ	Mean response
$\mathbf{z}_i(x)$	Output of Gaussian function

APPENDIX A. PROOF OF PROPERTIES OF THE SCHEME

A. Adaptive Weight Adaptation and Convergence Analysis

From the preceding discussion, given the existence of a compact surface of operation S for an unknown real-world problem described by an unknown underlying function in a one-dimensional real discrete time series of the form:

$$y_{t+1} = f(y_t, y_{t-1}, \ldots, y_{t-k+1}, u_t, u_{t-1}, \ldots, u_{t-l+1}). \tag{1}$$

The unknown nonlinear function $y = f(\bullet)$ is required to meet two conditions which are essential for the proposed GaRBF approximation methodology. First, the function is required to have a unique solution for any set of initial conditions, and second, the function should be continuously differentiable and should be time invariant (does not contain time-varying coefficients).

With the preceding discussion on the structural formation scheme described in the preceding section, a nominal grid needs to be laid down as a grid for S. Using $\tilde{y}_{t+1}$ to denote the neural model estimate of y_t, and using the grid built earlier, the following adaptive neural model is formulated by substituting the nonlinear function $f(\bullet)$ with the neural network,

$$\tilde{y}_{t+1} = \mathbf{W}_t\mathbf{z}(x_t) + \text{error}, \tag{2}$$

where $\mathbf{W}_t$ is the weight matrix at t, then with proper choices of n, p_i, and $\boldsymbol{\sigma}_i$, there must exist a weight vector $\mathbf{W}$ (where W is unknown) such that the relationship is

$$y_{t+1} = \mathbf{W}\mathbf{z}(x). \tag{3}$$

The Gaussian radial basis function is typically governed by two bodies of mathematics, mainly global stability and convergence. The global stability is defined as the eventual stability of neuron activation from any initial inputs, while convergence is defined as a sequence of numbers x_n that tends to a limit x,

$$\lim_{n\to\infty} x_n = x.$$

The level of convergence in training is monitored using a measure known as mean squared error (MSE) which is based on the error correction learning method of gradient descent [Haykin (1991)] given by

$$\text{MSE} = \frac{1}{2}\sum(x_{\text{actual}} - x_{\text{predicted}})^2. \tag{4}$$

B. Derivation of Stable Weight Updating Algorithm

A stable weight updating algorithm (given a real discrete time-series nonlinear problem) to obtain the weight matrix, $\mathbf{W}$ by minimizing an output error, ε related criterion is derived as

$$y_{t+1} = f(y_t, y_{t-1}, \ldots, y_{t-k+1}, u_t, u_{t-1}, \ldots, u_{t-l+1}), \tag{5}$$

where y_t is the response at time t, u_t is the input at time t, $f(\bullet)$ is the nonlinear function with unique solutions and time invariant k and l are positive integers.

Using the GaRBF neural network as a general description with

$$\begin{aligned} x &= (y_t, y_{t-1}, \ldots, y_{t-k+1}, u_t t, u_{t-1}, \ldots, u_{t-l+1}), \\ y &= y_{t+1}, \\ y_{t+1} &= \mathbf{Wz}(x). \end{aligned} \tag{6}$$

Let the weight updating rule at any instance be constructed as

$$\begin{aligned} \tilde{y}_{t+1} &= w_t\mathbf{z}(x_t) + e_t, \\ \tilde{y}_{t+1} &= w_t\mathbf{z}(x_t) + (1-a)e_t, \\ \tilde{y}_{t+1} &= \text{estimate of } y_t, \end{aligned} \tag{7}$$

where a is a constant. Subtracting (5.13) from (5.12), the error equation is given by

$$\begin{aligned} \tilde{y}_{t+1} - y_{t+1} &= \{w_t\mathbf{z}(x_t) - \mathbf{Wz}(x)\} + (1-a)e_t, \\ e_{t+1} &= \Delta w_t\mathbf{z}(x) + (1-a)e_t, \\ e_{t+1} - e_t &= \Delta w_t\mathbf{z}(x) - ae_t, \end{aligned} \tag{8}$$

where $e_t = \tilde{y}_t - y_t$, $\Delta w_t = w_t - \mathbf{W}$. For the error-correction learning rule, the general weight updating algorithm is given by

$$w_{t+1} = w_t - \eta e_t\mathbf{z}(x), \tag{9}$$

where η is the learning rate. The projection method is used for modifying the weight updating when the GaRBF neurons are not adequate or when the parameters (centers and widths) are not properly set. Then,

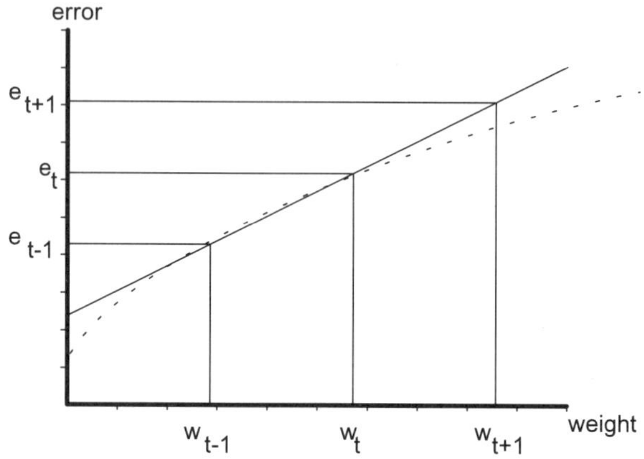

$$\frac{w_{t+1} - w_{t-1}}{e_{t+1} - e_{t-1}} = \frac{w_t - w_{t-1}}{e_t - e_{t-1}}. \tag{10}$$

Forcing $e_{t+1} = 0$,

$$\frac{w_{t+1} - w_{t-1}}{-e_{t-1}} = \frac{w_t - w_{t-1}}{e_t - e_{t-1}},$$

$$w_{t+1} - w_{t-1} = \left(\frac{w_t - w_{t-1}}{e_t - e_{t-1}}\right)(-e_{t-1}),$$

$$w_{t+1} = w_{t-1} + \left(\frac{\Delta w_{t-1}}{\Delta w_{t-1}\mathbf{z}(x_{t-1} - ae_{t-1}}\right)(-e_{t-1}),$$

$$w_{t+1} = w_{t-1} - \left(\frac{\Delta w_{t-1} e_{t-1}}{\Delta w_{t-1}\mathbf{z}(x_{t-1}) - a[-(\Delta w_{t-1}/\mathbf{z}(x_{t-1}))]}\right).$$

Re-arranging and generalizing it with β and a=1, the adaptive weight updating algorithm is given by

$$w_{t+1} = w_{t-1} - \frac{\beta e_{t-1}\mathbf{z}(x_{t-1})}{1 + \mathbf{z}(x_{t-1})\mathbf{z}^T(x_{t-1})}. \tag{11}$$

Therefore, defining $e_t = \tilde{y}_t - y_t$ to be the estimation error at time t, and when the error approximates to zero, $w_{t-1} = w_t$; thus the weight updating algorithm becomes

$$w_{t+1} = w_t \left\{\frac{\beta}{1 + \mathbf{z}^T(x_t)\mathbf{z}(x_t)}\right\}[e_t\mathbf{z}(x_t)], \tag{12}$$

where β is a positive constant such that $0 < \beta < 2$. The proof of the properties of the scheme is shown in Appendix A.

It should be noted that in the preceding equations that all the Gaussian functions $\mathbf{z}_i(\bullet)(i = 1, 2, \ldots, n)$ in the vector $\mathbf{z}_i(\bullet)$ are centered at the grid-points of the nominal grid for S. Although $\tilde{y}_{t+1} = \mathbf{W}_t\mathbf{z}(x_t)$ and $\mathbf{W}_{t+1} = \mathbf{W}_t - \beta e_t\mathbf{z}(x_t)/(1 + z^T(x_t)\mathbf{z}(x_t))$

are built directly on the nominal grid, the nature of the Gaussian functions can be used to show that they can equally be treated as defining the adaptive partial model and the weight adaptation on S_t. This is because since all the $z_i(\bullet)$ whose centers are far enough from x_t(γ *grid-points away*) will have negligible values, they can be omitted from the weight updating algorithm. The same observation applies to the weight adaptation formula. In this case, Eq. (12), can be seen as describing the weight updating operations for the neurons in S_t. This important observations analyze the convergence property of the complete adaptive structure and the weight adaptation scheme by examining $\tilde{y}_{t+1} = \mathbf{W}_t\mathbf{z}(x_t)$ and $\mathbf{W}_{t+1} = \mathbf{W}_t - \beta e_t\mathbf{z}(x_t)/[1 + \mathbf{z}^T(x_t)\mathbf{z}(x_t)]$ directly thus simplifies the analysis considerably.

The weight initialization scheme is specific to the particular neural network model chosen. However, in many cases, initial weights are just randomized to small real numbers. The learning rule is one of the most important attributes to specify a neural network. The learning rule determines how to adapt connection weights to optimize the network performance. It indicates how to calculate the weight adjustment during each training cycle. However, the rule is suspended after training is completed.

When the neural network is used to solve a problem, the solution lies in the activation levels of the output units. Then, starting with some arbitrary or random weight setting, the neural network is trained to adapt itself to the characteristics of the training instances by changing weights inside the network. In each training cycle, an instance is presented to the network. It generates an output vector, which is compared with the desired output vector (if available). In this way, the error for each output unit is calculated and then used to update relevant weights. In a multilayer network, the errors of hidden units are not observed directly but can be estimated with some heuristic. Each weight change is hoped to reduce the error. When all instances are examined, the network will start over with the first instance and repeat. Iterations continue until the system performance (in terms of the error magnitude) has reached a satisfactory level.

In the adaptive framework, the dimension of equation $y_i = w_{ij}\mathbf{z}_j(x)$ can be seen as gradually growing through time embedding naturally the robustness issue in the convergence process. The proposed parallel distributed computational model (Gaussian radial basis function) is a powerful method with a definite range of applicability in manufacturing research. They greatly accelerate the development and evaluation process for experimental design and decision support, allowing experimentation and optimization that would not be practical. Also, their rapid training makes them suitable for situations where adaptive incremental learning is necessary.

C. Proof of Properties of the Scheme

LEMMA 1. *The parallel distributed computational Gaussian radial basis function neural network defined by* $\tilde{y}_{t+1} = \mathbf{W}_t\mathbf{z}(x_t)$ *and* $\mathbf{W}_{t+1} = \mathbf{W}_t - \beta e\mathbf{z}(x_t)/[1 + \mathbf{z}^T(x_t)\mathbf{z}(x_t)]$ *has the following properties.*

(a) $\|\mathbf{W}_t - \overline{\mathbf{W}}\| \leq \|\mathbf{W}_{t-1} - \overline{\mathbf{W}}\|$.

(b) $\lim_{\to\infty} |e|/\sqrt{1 + \mathbf{z}^T(x_t)\mathbf{z}(x_t)} = 0$.

Proof 1. We have

$$\mathbf{W}_{t+1} = \mathbf{W}_t - \frac{\beta e_t \mathbf{z}(x_t)}{1+\mathbf{z}^T(x_t)\mathbf{z}(x_t)},$$

$$\mathbf{W}_{t+1} - \mathbf{W}_t = -\frac{\beta e_t \mathbf{z}(x_t)}{1+\mathbf{z}^T(x_t)\mathbf{z}(x_t)},$$

$$\mathbf{W}_t - \mathbf{W}_{t-1} = -\frac{\beta e_{t-1} \mathbf{z}(x_{t-1})}{1+\mathbf{z}^T(x_{t-1})\mathbf{z}(x_{t-1})}.$$

Consider the scalar function, $V_t = \|E_t\|^2 = E_t(E_t)^T$ with $E_t = \mathbf{W}_t - \overline{\mathbf{W}}$ at $t = 1, 2, 3, \ldots, m$. Then,

$$\begin{aligned}
E_t - E_{t-1} &= -\frac{\beta e_{t-1} \mathbf{z}(x_{t-1})}{1+\mathbf{z}^T(x_{t-1})\mathbf{z}(x_{t-1})},\\
V_t - V_{t-1} &= E_t(E_t)^T - E_{t-1}(E_{t-1})^T\\
&= (E_t - E_{t-1})(E_t + E_{t-1})\\
&= (E_t - E_{t-1})(E_t - E_{t-1})^T + (E_t - E_{t-1})(2E_{t-1})^T,\\
V_t - V_{t-1} &= (E_t - E_{t-1})(E_t - E_{t-1})^T + (E_t - E_{t-1})(2E_{t-1})^T\\
&= \left[-\frac{\beta e_{t-1} \mathbf{z}(x_{t-1})}{1+\mathbf{z}^T(x_{t-1})\mathbf{z}(x_{t-1})}\right]\left[-\frac{\beta e_{t-1} \mathbf{z}(x_{t-1})}{1+\mathbf{z}^T(x_{t-1})\mathbf{z}(x_{t-1})}\right]^T\\
&\quad + \left[-\frac{\beta e_{t-1} \mathbf{z}(x_{t-1})}{1+\mathbf{z}^T(x_{t-1})\mathbf{z}(x_{t-1})}\right]^T [2E_{t-1}]^T
\end{aligned}$$

From $\tilde{y} = \mathbf{W}_t \mathbf{z}(x_t)$ and $e_{t-1} = E_{t-1}\mathbf{z}(x_{t-1})$;

$$\begin{aligned}
V_t - V_{t-1} &= \left[\frac{\beta^2 (e_{t-1})^2 \mathbf{z}(x_{t-1})\mathbf{z}^T(x_{t-1})}{\{1+\mathbf{z}^T(x_{t-1})\mathbf{z}(x_{t-1})\}^2}\right] + \left[\frac{2\beta (e_{t-1})^2}{1+\mathbf{z}^T(x_{t-1})\mathbf{z}(x_{t-1})}\right],\\
(E_t - E_{t-1})(E_t - E_{t-1})^T &= \left[\frac{\beta^2 (e_{t-1})^2}{1+\mathbf{z}^T(x_{t-1})\mathbf{z}(x_{t-1})}\right]\left[\frac{\mathbf{z}(x_{t-1})\mathbf{z}^T(x_{t-1})}{1+\mathbf{z}^T(x_{t-1})\mathbf{z}(x_{t-1})}\right],\\
(E_t - E_{t-1})(E_t - E_{t-1})^T &\le \left[\frac{\beta^2 (e_{t-1})^2}{1+\mathbf{z}^T(x_{t-1})\mathbf{z}(x_{t-1})}\right],\\
V_t - V_{t-1} &\le \left[\frac{\beta^2 (e_{t-1})^2}{1+\mathbf{z}^T(x_{t-1})\mathbf{z}(x_{t-1})}\right] - \left[\frac{2\beta (e_{t-1})^2}{1+\mathbf{z}^T(x_{t-1})\mathbf{z}(x_{t-1})}\right]\\
&= [-\beta(2-\beta)]\left[\frac{(e_{t-1})^2}{1+\mathbf{z}^T(x_{t-1})\mathbf{z}(x_{t-1})}\right] \le 0 \quad \text{for } 0 < \beta < 2.
\end{aligned}$$

The preceding equations hold only when error $(e_{t-1} = 0)$ implies that the value of β, E_t is strictly less than E_{t-1} for all t when the error is nonzero.

By introducing the Lyapunov function, $V_t = \sum_{i=1}^{m} V_t = \sum_{i=1}^{m} \|E_t\|^2$ for the combined error system,

$$\left\{\begin{aligned}
e_{t-1} &= E_{t-1}\mathbf{z}(x_{t-1}),\\
E_t &= E_{t-1} - \left[\frac{\beta (e_{t-1})\mathbf{z}(x_{t-1})\mathbf{z}^T(x_{t-1})}{1+\mathbf{z}^T(x_{t-1})\mathbf{z}(x_{t-1})}\right]
\end{aligned}\right\}.$$

Obviously $V_t \le 0$ and $V_t - V_{t-1} = \sum_{i=1}^{m} V_t - V_{t-1} \le 0$, therefore it can be concluded that $V_t = \|\mathbf{W}_t - \overline{\mathbf{W}}\| \le V_{t-1} = \|\mathbf{W}_{t-1} - \overline{\mathbf{W}}\| \le V_0 = \|\mathbf{W}_0 - \overline{\mathbf{W}}\| \Rightarrow$ inequality (i) is thus proven.

Proof 2. From

$$\left\{ \begin{array}{l} [-\beta(2-\beta)]\left[\dfrac{(e_{t-1})^2}{1+\mathbf{z}^T(x_{t-1})\mathbf{z}(x_{t-1})}\right] \le 0 \\ \lim\limits_{\to\infty} \sum\limits_{k=1}^{t} [-\beta(2-\beta)]\left[\dfrac{(e_{k-1})^2}{1+\mathbf{z}^T(x_{k-1})\mathbf{z}(x_{k-1})}\right] \le 0 \end{array} \right\}.$$

It can be concluded that

$$\lim_{t\to\infty}\left[\frac{(e_{k-1})}{1+\mathbf{z}^T(x_{k-1})\mathbf{z}(x_{k-1})}\right] = 0 \qquad \text{for all } i.$$

D. Error Convergence Proof

The preceding schemes provide the convergence theorem: The PDC adaptive GaRBF neural network formula $\tilde{y}_{t+1}\mathbf{W}_t\mathbf{z}(x_t)$ and $\mathbf{W}_{t+1} = \mathbf{W}_t - \beta e_t \mathbf{z}(x_t)/[1 + \mathbf{z}^T(x_t)\mathbf{z}(x_t)]$ guarantee that $\lim_{t\to\infty} |e_t| = 0$.

From

$$\lim_{t\to\infty} \sum_{k=1}^{t} [-\beta(2-\beta)]\left[\frac{(e_{k-1})^2}{1+\mathbf{z}^T(x_{k-1})\mathbf{z}(x_{k-1})}\right] \le 0,$$

if t approaches infinity ∞, $\lim_{t\to\infty} |e_t| = 0$.

This theorem concludes that the proposed PDC adaptive GaRBF neural network algorithm will converge to zero.

APPENDIX B. DESIGN OF EXPERIMENT SOFTWARE

1. Alligator Technologies: Fourier Perspective III.
2. AT&T MAnufacturing Systems: AT&T Quality Workbench Robust Design Expert.
3. Aviar Software: NESTED.
4. BBN Software Products Division: RS Series, BBN/Catalyst.
5. Catalyst, Inc.: Catalyst/DOE.
6. Compusense: Computerized Sensory Analysis.
7. Randall F. Culp: SADIE.
8. Experience in Software, Inc.: The Idea Generator Plus, Project Kickstart.
9. GR Technologies, Inc.: QC-PRO Design of Experiments.
10. Paul Hertzier & Co., Inc.: QA/S.
11. Imaging Technology Inc., ITEX-ALIGN, ITEX-ANALYZE, ITEX-OCR.
12. Internation Qual-Tech, Ltd.: Discovery, Optimization, ESPC.
13. Interpharm Software Systems Inc.: PREDICTOR.
14. Joiner Associates, Inc.: Jass.
15. JUSE-QCAS/NIMAC America: JUSE-QCAS II.

16. John A, Keane and Associates: QMS Programs/ISO 9000 Compliance Group, QMS Programs/Aerospace-Defense Compliance Group.
17. Lionheart Press, Inc.: Quality Control and Industrial Experiments, Parameter and Tolerance Design.
18. MIXSOFT Mixture Experiment Software: MIXSOFT.
19. NCSS: NCSS.
20. Newport Corp.: CAD-ASSISTANT, Computerized Optics Catalog.
21. OLIS: On-Line Instrument Systems, Inc.: OLIS Spectroscopy Operating System, OLIS STopped-flow Operating System.
22. PQ SYstems, Inc.: DOEpack Version 2.0.
23. Process Design and Control, Inc.: Design of Experiments Package.
24. The Product Integrity Co.: Statistical Engineering.
25. Productivity Enhancements: Verstat.
26. Productivity Management Consultants: Turbo Statistics.
27. QINAS, Inc.: Design Cube, SIM Q, SIM Q-Custom.
28. Qualitron Systems, Inc.: DoES.
29. Quality America, Inc.: DOE-PC IV.
30. Quality Concepts, Inc.: TADA! Experimental Design.
31. Quality Consultants & Computer Sales: TQA Software.
32. Quality Engineering Services: The Taguchi Expert Version 1.2, The Taguchi Expert and Simulator Version 2.0.
33. Quality Information Systems: Search, Simulate.
34. Quality Resources: STAT-PAK II.
35. Quality Resources International: STSC-Statgraphics 5.0.
36. Rapid Data: Design of Experiments.
37. Responsible Management Inc.: OATS 2.0.
38. Rochester Institute of Technology: Quality Engineering by Design.
39. SAS Institute Inc.: The SAS System, JMP software.
40. Schmidt/Launsby Consulting: Q-Edge.
41. Scientific Computing Associates: SCA Quality Improvement Package.
42. Software Technology: Advanced Gage Control 5.2.
43. Sof-Ware Tools: Lab Partner.
44. Solution Specialists: Plastic Injection Simulation.
45. Spentech: QARMS.
46. STAT-EASE: Design-Ease, Design-Expert RSM, Design-Expert Mixture.
47. Statistical Graphics Corp.: STATGRAPHICS 5.0.
48. Statistical Programs: EXPERTiMENTAL DESIGN, SIMPLEX-V, SCREEN.
49. Statware, Inc.: statit.
50. Stochos, Inc.: Factor Extractor.
51. SYSTAT, Inc.: QCSTAT.
52. Technicomp, Inc.: DOE/Target.
53. Teque, Inc.: SPC-Plus.
54. TPG, Inc.: TSS.
55. Ultramax Corp.: ULTRAMAX.
56. Williams & Associates: Quality Fielder-Statistics.
57. Tom Woods, Inc.: SPVR.
58. Zimm-Tech Inc.: Signal-Graphics II.

REFERENCES

1. Baldi, P. Computing with arrays of bell-shaped and sigmoid functions. In *Advances in Neural Information Processing Systems*, (R. P. Lippmann, J. E. Moody, and D. S. Touretzky, Eds.), Vol. 3, pp. 735–742. Morgan Kaufmann, San Mateo, CA, 1991.
2. Bates, D. M. and Watts, D. G. Multiresponse estimation with special application to linear systems of differential equations. *Technometrics* 7:329–339, 1985.
3. Bendell, A., Disney, J., and Pridmore, W. A. *Taguchi-Methods: Applications in World Industry*. IFS Springer-Verlag, Kempston, 1989.
4. Bisgaard, S. Quality engineering and Taguchi methods: A perspective. *Target* (Oct):13–19, 1989.
5. Bishop, C. Improving the generalization properties of radial basis function neural networks. *Neural Comput.* 3(4):579–588, 1991.
6. Box, G. E. P. Signal-to-noise ratios, performance criteria and transformations. *Technometrics* 30:1–31, 1988.
7. Box, G. E. P. and Jones, S. S. An investigation of the method of accumulation analysis. *Total Quality Manage.* 1:101–113, 1990.
8. Box, G. E. P., Bisgaard, S., and Fung, C. An explanation and critique of Taguchi's contributions to quality engineering. *Int. J. Quality Reliability Manage.* 4:123–131, 1988.
9. Box, G. E. P., Hunter, W. G., and Hunter, J. S. *Statistics for Experimenter—An Introduction to Design, Data Analysis and Model Building*, Wiley, New York, 1978.
10. Box, G. E. P., Hunter, W. G., MacGregor, J. F., and Erjavec, J. Some problems associated with the analysis of multiresponse data. *Technometrics* 15:33–51, 1973.
11. Broomhead, D. S. and Lowe, D. Multivariable functional interpolation and adaptive networks. *Complex Syst.* 2:321–355, 1988.
12. Chen, S., Cowan, C. F. N., and Grant, P. M. Orthogonal least squares learning algorithm for radial basis function networks. *IEEE Trans. Neural Networks* 2(2):302–309, 1991.
13. Cover, T. M. Geometrical and statistical properties of systems of linear inequalities with application in pattern recognition. *IEEE Trans. Electron. Comput.* 14:122–132, 1965.
14. Cybenko, G. Approximation by superpositions of a sigmoidal functions. *Math. Control, Signals Syst.* 2:303–314, 1989.
15. Derringer, G. and Suich, R. Simultaneous optimization of several response variables. *J. Quality Technol.* 12:214–219, 1980.
16. Donohue, D. L. and Johnstone, I. M. Projection-based approximation and a quality with kernel methods. *Ann. Statist.* 17(l):58–106, 1989.
17. Dyn, N. Interpolation and approximation by radial and related functions. In *Approximation Theory* (C. K. Chui, L. L. Schumaker, and D. J. Ward, Eds.), Vol. VI, pp. 211–234. Academic Press, New York, 1991.
18. Fisher, R. A. *Statistical Methods for Research Workers*. Oliver & Boyd, Edinburgh, U.K., 1930.
19. Fisher, R. A. *Design of Experiment*. Oliver & Boyd, Edinburgh, U.K., 1966.
20. Fukushima, K., Miyake, S., and Takayuki, T. Neocognitron: A neural network model for a mechanism of visual pattern recognition. *IEEE Trans. Syst., Man, Cybern.* SMC-13:826–834, 1983.
21. Funahashi, K. I. On the approximate of continuous mappings by neural networks. *Neural Networks* 2:183–192, 1989.
22. Gale, W. A. and Pregibon, D. REX: an expert system for regression analysis. In *Proceedings of the COMPSTAT 84,* Physica-Verlag, Prague, pp. 242–248, 1984.
23. Girosi, F. On some extensions of radial basis functions and their applications in artificial intelligence. *Comput. Math. Appl.* 24(12):61–80, 1992.
24. Girosi, F. and Anzellotti, G. *Rates of Convergence for Radial Basis Functions and Neural Networks. Artificial Neural Networks with Applications in Speech and Vision*. Chapman & Hall, London, 1993.
25. Grossberg, S. Nonlinear neural networks: Principles, mechanisms, and architectures. *Neural Networks* 1:17–61, 1988.
26. Gunter, B. H. A perspective on Taguchi methods. *Quality Progress* 6:44–52, 1987.
27. Gupta, M. M. Fuzzy logic and neural networks. In *The Tenth International Conference on Multicriterion Decision Making,* Taipei, July 19–24, 1992, pp. 281–294.
28. Gupta, M. M., Kiszka, J. B., and Trojan, G. M. Multivariable structure of fuzzy control systems. *IEEE Trans. Syst., Man, Cybern.* 16:638–656, 1986.

29. Hamada, M. and Wu, C. F. J. Discussion of testing in industrial experiment with ordered categorical data. *Technometrics* 28:295–301, 1992.
30. Hartman, E. J., Keeler, J. D., and Kowalski, J. M. Layered neural networks with Gaussian hidden units as universal approximations. *Neural Comput.* 2(2):210–215, 1990.
31. Hasting, W. F. and Oxley, P. L. B. Predicting tool life from fundamental work material properties and cutting conditions. *Ann. CIRP* 25:55–61, 1976.
32. Hecht-Nielsen, R. *Neurocomputing*. Addison-Wesley, Reading, MA, 1990.
33. Hill, W. J. and Hunter, W. C. A review of response surface methodology: A literature review. *Technometrics* 8:571–590, 1966.
34. Hoadley, A. B. and Kettenring, J. R. Communications between statisticians and engineers/scientists. *Technometrics* 32:1–9, 1990.
35. Hornik, K., Stinchcombe, M., and White, H. Multilayer feedfoward networks are universal approximators. *Neural Networks* 2:359–366, 1989.
36. Hunter, J. S. Statistical design applied to product design. *J. Quality Technol.* 17:210–221, 1985.
37. Joglekar, A. and Kackar, R. Graphical and computer aided approaches to plan experiments. In *Transactions of the 1988 Annual Quality Congress,* American Society for Quality Control, 1988, pp. 45–55.
38. Jokinen, P. A. On the relations between radial basis function networks and fuzzy systems. In *Proceedings International Joint Conference on Neural Networks,* Baltimore, MD, June 7–11, 1992, pp. 1123–1128.
39. Kackar, R. N. Off-line quality control, parameter design and the Taguchi method. *J. Quality Technol.* 17:176–188, 1985.
40. Kackar, R. N. and Shoemaker, A. C. Robust design. A cost-effective method for improving manufacturing processes. *AT & T Techn. J.* 65(2):39–50, 1986.
41. Kadirkamanathan, V., Niranjan, M., and Fallside, F. Sequential adaptation of radial basis function neural networks and its application to time-series prediction. In *Advances in Neural Information Processing Systems* (R. P. Lippmann, J. E. Moody, and D. S. Touretzky, Eds.), Vol. 3, pp. 721–727. Morgan Kaufmann, San Mateo, CA, 1991.
42. Kaufmann, A. and Gupta, M. M. *Introduction to Fuzzy Arithmetic: Theory and Applications*, 2nd ed., Van Nostrand-Reinhold, New York, 1991.
43. Khuri, A. I. A test for lack of fit of a linear multiresponse model. *Technometrics* 27:213–218, 1985.
44. Khuri, A. I. and Conlon, M. Simultaneous optimization of multiple responses represented by polynomial regression functions. *Technometrics* 23:363–375, 1981.
45. Khuri, A. I. and Cornell, J. A. *Response Surfaces*, Dekker, New York, 1987.
46. Kohonen, T. *Self-Organizing and Associative Memory*, Springer-Verlag, Berlin, 1988.
47. Kohonen, T. and Ruohonen, M. Representation of associated data by matrix operators. *IEEE Trans. Comput.* 22:701–702, 1973.
48. Kolen, J. F. and Goel, A. K. Learning in parallel distributed processing networks: Computational complexity and information content. *IEEE Trans. Syst., Man, Cybern.* 21(2):359–367, 1991.
49. Kosko, B. Fuzzy knowledge combination. *Int. J. Intell. Syst.* 1:293–320, 1986.
50. Kosko, B. Adaptive inference in fuzzy knowledge networks. In *Proceedings of the IEEE First International Conference on Neural Networks,* Vol. II, 1987, pp. 261–268.
51. Kosko, B. *Neural Networks for Signal Processing*. Prentice Hall, Englewood Cliffs, NJ 1992.
52. Kusaba, I. Statistical methods in Japanese quality control. Societas Qualitatis 2, Union of Japanese Scientists and Engineers, 1989.
53. Lapedes, A. and Farber, R. How neural nets work. Los Alamos National Laboratory, Los Alamos, NM, 1988.
54. Lee, N. S., Phadke, M. S., and Keny, R. S. An expert system for experimental design: Automating the design of orthogonal array experiments. In *ASQC Transactions of Annual Quality Congress,* Minneapolis, 1988, pp. 45–49.
55. Leon, R. V., Shoemaker, A. C. and Kackar R. N. Performance measures independent of adjustment: an explanation and extension of Taguchi signal-to-noise ratio. *Technometrics* 29:253–285, 1987.
56. Leonard, J. A., Kramer, M. A., and Ungar, L. H. Using radial basis functions to approximate a function and its error bounds. *IEEE Trans. Neural Networks* 3(4):624–627, 1992.

57. Linden, R. J. P., Renes, W. A. and Rademaker, O. PRIMAL: A package for real-time interactive modeling, analysis and learning. *Benelux Quart. J. Automat. Control* 29(1):1–9, 1988.
58. Lippmann, R. A critical review of neural network pattern classifiers. In *Proceedings of the IEEE Workshop on Neural Networks for Signal Processing*, Princeton, 1991, pp. 266–275.
59. Ljung, L. Issues in systems identification. *IEEE Contr. Syst.* 1:25–29, 1991.
60. Logothetis, N. Off-line quality control and ill-designed data. *Quality Reliability Eng. Int.* 3:227–238, 1987.
61. Logothetis, N. and Wynn, H. P. *Quality through Design: Experimental Design, Off-Line Quality Control and Taguchi's Contributions*. Clarendon, Oxford, U.K., 1989.
62. Logothetis, N. and Haigh, A. The statistical flexibility of Taguchi method in the optimization of multi-response processes. *Professional Statist.* 6(7):10–16, 1987.
63. Lorentz, G. G. *Approximation of Functions*. Chelsea, New York, 1986.
64. Meeker, W. Q., Hahn, G. H., and Feder, P. I. A computer program for evaluating and comparing experimental designs and some applications. *Amer. Statist.* 29(1):60–64, 1975.
65. Montgomery, D. C. *Design and Analysis of Experiments*, 3rd ed., Wiley, New York, 1991.
66. Montgomery, D. C. Using fractional factorial designs for robust design process development. *Quality Eng.* 3(2):10–20, 1992.
67. Moody, J. and Darken, C. Learning with localized receptive fields. In *Proceedings of the 1988 Connectionist Models Summer School* (D. Touretzky, G. Hinton, and T. Sejnowski, Eds.), pp. 133–143. Morgan Kaufmann, San Mateo, CA, 1988.
68. Moody, J. and Darken, C. Fast learning in networks of locally-tuned processing units. *Neural Comput.* 1(2):281–294, 1989.
69. Morrison, D. F. *Multivariate Statistical Methods*, 2nd ed., McGraw-Hill, New York, 1976.
70. Nair, V. N. and Pregibon, D. A data analysis strategy for quality engineering experiments. *AT&T Tech. J.* 65(3):73–84, 1986.
71. Narendra, K. S. and Parthasarthy, K. Identification and control of dynamical systems using neural networks. *IEEE Trans. Neural Networks* 1:4–27, 1990.
72. Park, J. and Sandberg, I. W. Universal approximation using radial-basis-function networks. *Neural Comput.* 3(2):246–257, 1991.
73. Pedrycz, W. *Fuzzy Controls and Fuzzy Systems*, Wiley, New York, 1989.
74. Phadke, M. *Quality Engineering Using Robust Design*, Prentice Hall, Englewood Cliffs, NJ, 1989.
75. Pignatiello, J. J. and Ramberg, J. S. Discussion of off-line quality control, parameter design, and the Taguchi method. *J. Quality Technol.* 17(4):151–162, 1985.
76. Plackett, R. L. and Burman, J. P. The design of optimum multifactorial experiments. *Biometrika* 33:305–325, 1946.
77. Powell, M. J. D. Radial basis functions for multivariable interpolation: A review. In *Algorithms for Approximation* (J. C. Mason and M. G. Cox, Eds.) pp. 143–167. Clarendon, Oxford, U.K., 1987.
78. Quinlan, J. *Product Improvement by Application of Taguchi Methods*, ASI Inc., Dearborn, MI, 1985.
79. Ranjit, R. A Primer on the Taguchi Method. *Competitive Manufacturing Series.* Von Nostrand-Reinhold, New York, 1990.
80. Ranky, P. G. Real time quality control loops in CIM environment. In *Proceedings of the International Conference on Automated Inspection and Product Control.* IFS, Bedford, 1987, pp. 45–62.
81. Robinson, S. L. and Miller, R. K. *Automated Inspection and Quality Assurance*, ASQC Quality Press, New York, 1989.
82. Ross, P. J. *Taguchi Techniques for Quality Engineering*, McGraw-Hill, New York, 1988.
83. Rumelhart, D. E. and McCleland, J. L. *Parallel Distributed Processing*, MIT Press, Cambridge, MA, 1986.
84. Saba, A. and Keeler, J. D. Algorithms for better representation and faster learning in radial basis function networks. In *Advances in Neural Information Processing Systems* (D. S. Touretzky, Ed.), Vol. 2, pp. 482–489. Morgan Kaufmann, San Mateo, CA, 1990.
85. Sarajedini, A. and Hecht-Nielsen, R. The best of both worlds: Casasent networks integrate multilayer perceptrons and radial basis functions. In *International Joint Conference on Neural Networks,* Baltimore, MD, June 7–11, 1992.
86. Schneiderman, A. M. Optimum quality costs and zero defects: Are they contradictory concepts? *Quality Progress* 11:28–31, 1986.

87. Seber, G. A. F. *Multivariate Observations*, Wiley, New York, 1984.
88. Simpson, P. K. Fuzzy min-max neural networks-Part 1: Classification. *IEEE Trans. Neural Networks* 3(5):776–786, 1992.
89. Speclit, D. F. A general regression neural network. *IEEE Trans. Neural Networks,* 2(6):568–576, 1991.
90. Sullivan, L. P. The power of Taguchi methods. *Quality Progress* 20:15–20, 1987.
91. Taguchi, G. *System of Experimental Design*, Vols. 1 and 2, Unipub–Kraus, New York, 1987.
92. Taguchi, G. and Wu, A. *Introduction to Off-Line Quality Control.* JQCA, Japan, 1985.
93. Taguchi, G. and Konishi, S. *Taguchi Methods: Orthogonal Arrays and Linear Graphs: Tools for Quality Engineering*, ASI, Dearborn, MI, 1987.
94. Taguchi, G. and Phadke, M. S. Quality engineering through design optimization. In *IEEE Globecom 1984 Conference,* Atlanta, GA, Vol. 3, 1984, pp. 1106–1113.
95. Tay, K. M. An adaptive fuzzy neural network approach to the design of industrial experiment and decision support. Ph.D. Thesis, Brunel University, Uxbridge, Middlesex, UB8 3PH, U.K., 1995.
96. Vining, G. G. and Myers, R. H. Combining Taguchi & response surface philosophies: A dual response approach. *J. Quality Technol.* 22:38–45, 1990.
97. Wang, L. X. Fuzzy logic are universal approximators. In *Proceedings of the IEEE International Conference on Fuzzy Systems,* San Diego, 1992, pp. 1163–1170.
98. Welch, W. J., Yu, T. K., Kang, S. M., and Stack, J. Computer experiments for quality control by parameter design. *J. Quality Technol.* 22:31–37, 1990.
99. Weymaere, N. and Martens, J. P. A fast and robust learning algorithm for feedforward neural networks. *Neural Networks* 4(3):361–369, 1991.
100. Widrow, B. Learning phenomena in layered neural networks. In *Proceedings of the IEEE First International Conference on Neural Networks,* 1987, pp. 411–430.
101. Widrow, B. The original adaptive neural network broom balancer. In *Proceedings of the First International Symposium on Circuits and Systems,* 1988, pp. 351–357.
102. Wild, R. H. and Pignatiello, J. J. Jr. An experimental design strategy for designing robust systems using discrete-event simulation. *Simulation* 57(6):358–368, 1991.
103. Wu, C. F. J., Mao, S. S., and Ma F. S. SEL: *A Search Method Based on Orthogonal Arrays. Statistical Design and Analysis of Industrial Experiments.* Dekker, New York, 1990.
104. Yamakawa, T. A fuzzy inference engine in nonlinear analog mode and its application to a fuzzy logic control. *IEEE Trans. Neural Networks* 4(3):233–242, 1993.
105. Zadeh, L. A. Fuzzy sets. *Inform. Control*, 8:338–353, 1965.
106. Zadeh, L. A. Toward a Theory of Fuzzy Systems. *Aspects of Networks and Systems Theory,* Rinehart and Winston, New York, 1971.
107. Zadeh, L. A. Outline of a new approach to the analysis of complex systems and decision process. *IEEE Trans. Syst., Man, Cybern.* 3(1):28–44, 1973.
108. Zimmermann, H. J. *Fuzzy Set Theory and Its Applications*, Kluwer Academic, Dordrecht, 1991.

6

A MODEL-BASED EXPERT SYSTEM BASED ON A DOMAIN ONTOLOGY

YOSHINOBU KITAMURA
MITSURU IKEDA
RIICHIRO MIZOGUCHI

The Institute of Scientific and Industrial Research, Osaka University, Osaka, 567-0047, Japan

I. INTRODUCTION

Although a lot of expert systems have been developed, one of the major short-comings of current knowledge engineering is lack of reusability and sharability of

Expert Systems, Edited by Cornelius T. Leondes, Volume 1

ISBN: 0-12-443881-4 / $35.00

knowledge [1]. One of the main reasons for the lack of reusability is that assumptions and performance of knowledge are not explicit. For example, when we make a model of a power plant by configuring components, it is based on specific concepts such as connection. Because the meaning of "connection" is not explicit, it is not clear whether heat transfer with radiation through the atmosphere is included. As a consequence, when someone wants to reuse the model for a diagnosis task, how does he or she know the model is appropriate for his or her purpose? Thus, model assumptions are indispensable to reuse. However, such assumptions rarely are explicit.

The expectation that the concept of ontology will play an important role in realizing knowledge sharing and reuse is widely shared by many researchers in the field. Ontology is an explicit specification of conceptualization [2] and it provides a primitive vocabulary for knowledge-based systems [3]. It can represent explicitly design rationales behind models and reasoning engines in model-based systems.

Domain ontology refers to explicit specification with respect to the target domain. A domain ontology plays two roles [3]. One is to provide vocabulary for model representation to capture the domain and to exhibit underlying assumptions and decisions; the other is to define performance specification of a reasoning system by representing the class of problems to be solved and requirements for the reasoning. Such explicit specifications facilitate reusability of models.

This chapter, which consists of the following five parts, discusses ontologies for model-based systems, and shows examples of our ontologies and reasoning system.

1. An introduction to ontology engineering. We introduce ontology engineering directed at a basis of modeling knowledge [3]. The definition of ontology and its role are discussed.
2. An ontology of time. We discuss an ontology of time concepts in qualitative reasoning systems [6]. Causality with time plays a crucial role in human understanding of the behavior of physical systems. A lot of research has been carried out on qualitative reasoning systems for causal understanding (e.g., [4, 5]). Little, however, is known about the temporal meaning of causal relationships generated by qualitative reasoning systems. With a goal toward explicit description of time concepts that underlie the models and the causal reasoning engines, we propose a causal time ontology that defines a set of general time concepts in qualitative models. These general concepts are called *causal time scales* [6], and allow us to specify the temporal performance of the engines and to identify a general causal reasoning scheme together with a sophisticated feedback analysis.
3. Design of a reasoning system. On the basis of the ontology, we show how the modeling schemes and the reasoning procedures of causal reasoning systems are determined according to the given requirements. As an example, we use our causal reasoning system [7, 8], which has been developed to deal with causal relations than more finely grained conventional systems.
4. An ontology of fluid systems. We discuss a domain ontology of fluid systems such as power plants that targets an explicit description of the design rationales of model-based reasoning systems [8]. That is, the concepts that capture the fluid systems and the causal characteristics of fluid-related components are discussed.

5. Application. An application of the reasoning system and the domain ontology to a heat transportation subsystem of a power plant is presented [8].

In this chapter, we do not discuss formal ontology based on axiomatization. Instead, we aim at getting agreement on the content and the terminology.

II. INTRODUCTION TO ONTOLOGY ENGINEERING

This section briefly introduces ontology engineering as a basis of modeling knowledge. For more details on ontology engineering, see [3].

In the history of artificial intelligence (AI), we can identify two types of research: form oriented and content oriented. The former deals with logic and knowledge representation; the latter concerns knowledge content. Form-oriented research has dominated AI research to date. However, content-oriented research increasingly has been gathering attention because a lot of real-world problems, such as knowledge reuse, facilitation of agent communication, media integration through understanding, and large-scale knowledge bases, require not only advanced theories or reasoning methods, but also sophisticated treatment of the knowledge content. Content-oriented technologies are powerful, but ad hoc, and because of this, content does not accumulate very well.

What we need for the future is a theory for content that will enable us to systematize and accumulate knowledge, that is, ontology engineering. Ontology engineering is a research methodology that gives us a design rationale for a knowledge base, kernel conceptualization of the world of interest, and strict definition of basic meanings of basic concepts together with sophisticated theories and technologies that enable the accumulation of knowledge that is essential for modeling the real world.

A. What Is an Ontology?

Three simple definitions of ontology follow.

1. Ontology is a term in philosophy and its meaning is “theory of existence.”
2. In AI, ontology is defined as “an explicit specification of conceptualization” [9].
3. In the knowledge base (KB) community, ontology is defined as “a theory/system of primitive vocabulary/concepts used for building artificial systems” [10].

In the simplest case, an ontology looks like a taxonomy. However, it is more than a taxonomy. It is a set of axioms that specify the meanings of concepts and the relationships among them. Designing an ontology requires a view toward helping to articulate concepts with appropriate attributes that underlie the world of interest. Viewed from another standpoint, an ontology is a shared understanding of conceptualization among human and computer agents, that is, a picture that is understood by both humans and computers.

B. Roles of an Ontology

An ontology can be used at various level of utility as follows:

Level 1: A vocabulary for communication among distributed agents.
Level 2: A taxonomy of concepts.
Level 3: A conceptual schema of a relational database that uses structural information about the concepts and the relationships among them. Conceptualization in a database is nothing other than a conceptual schema. Data retrieval from a database is performed easily when there is agreement on its conceptual schema.
Level 4: Hierarchical indices for information retrieval.
Level 5: A thesaurus.
Level 6: A meta model for a certain knowledge base (knowledge-based system in the case of task ontology).
Level 7: Transformation of databases by considering the differences in meaning of conceptual schemata. This requires not only structural transformation, but also semantic transformation.
Level 8: Reusing knowledge in a knowledge base.
Level 9: Reorganizing a knowledge base.

An ontology plays the following crucial roles:

Meta Model. The meta model view of the role of an ontology is important. Assume you are building a model of a certain thing. The model is described in terms of a set of terms or concepts. An ontology gives you the design rationale needed in the modeling together with a theory of the terms or concepts you use, which shows that an ontology is a meta model.

Design Rationale. Another important role of an ontology is to explicate implicit conceptualization and design decisions of a knowledge base which often called the design rationale. To reuse knowledge in a knowledge base, we have to know the underlying conceptualization that reflects the assumptions and requirements made in the problem solving using the knowledge base. Although many KBs have been built to date, no such information has been described. Using ontologies as design rationale information in knowledge bases will contribute to reuse of the knowledge bases and will serve as backbones of knowledge bases. Future knowledge bases should be built with explicit representation of ontologies.

Standardization. Needless to say, industries have attained their current high productivity due to standardization of components, say, bolts and nuts. It is a pity that we have no such standardized components in knowledge base technology. To model target objects, such components would help a lot to facilitate model-based problem solving. An example is standardization of a pipe and pumps in qualitative modeling of a plant that represent enterprise ontology and task ontology.

III. A CAUSAL TIME ONTOLOGY [6]

A. Motivation and Goals

Causality with time plays a crucial role in human understanding of the behavior of physical systems. Human recognition of causal relationships is based on recognition of time delay (i.e., time interval) between the cause and the effect. Little is, however, known concerning the temporal meaning of causal relationships generated by reasoning systems, that is, how long (or fast) the time interval is in the causal relationships in real physical behavior as discussed in [11]. There are two explanations for this lack. First, there are many modeling techniques and representations, each of which implicitly implies several temporal relationships among variables in the models. Second, such models are interpreted by the reasoning engines on the basis of their own time concepts that their reasoning procedures can support.

For example, using the same qualitative differential equations, QSIM [12] and the causal ordering procedure proposed in [5] generate different causal relations with different temporal meanings. (Strictly speaking, Iwasaki's procedure needs additional information.) The reason for this difference is that the reasoning engines have different time concepts that the reasoning procedures support. As a consequence of the implicit existence of several time concepts, the temporal meaning of generated causal relations is not clear for users of reasoning engines.

The goal of this ontology is to reveal the structure of causal time that underlies the qualitative models and the causal reasoning engines. This ontology defines 13 general time concepts in qualitative models that are called *causal time scales* and are shown in Table 1. The causal time scales generalize time concepts described in previous frameworks [4, 5, 12–15]. Each causal time scale associated with a modeling technique represents a temporal granularity and/or an ontological viewpoint.

In terms of causal time scales, we can explicitly specify the following temporal meanings of models or causal reasoning engines.

- Temporal meanings of causal relationships.
- Temporal performances of the reasoning engines.
- A general causal reasoning scheme.
- Sophisticated analysis of feedback.

First, causal relations generated by the reasoning engines can be categorized into one of the causal time scales. For example, causal relations generated by QSIM are categorized into the causal time scale named *Ta*3, which represents the time concept associated with the mathematical integral operation. On the other hand, some of the relations generated by the causal ordering procedure are categorized into the time scale *Ta*2 which is a finer-grained time concept than *Ta*3.

Second, the causal time scales enable us to specify the performances of reasoning engines with respect to causal ordering that are called *causal time resolutions*. In this example, the time resolution of the causal ordering procedure is finer than that of QSIM. The time resolutions of other reasoning methods will be discussed later.

Third, we also identified a general and primitive reasoning scheme that can describe essential parts of the conventional reasoning methods. Fourth, fine-grained time scales enable sophisticated analysis of causality in the feedback loop so that less ambiguous causal ordering is obtained.

TABLE I The Causal Time Scales

(a) Direct modeling
- $ca1$: changes of parameter values
- $Ta1$: *mutual dependency time scale*
- $ca2$: A set of inherently simultaneous equations are satisfied
- $Ta2$: *dependency time scale*
- $ca3$: A set of constraints are completely satisfied
- $Ta3$: *integral time scale*
  - $Ta3p$: Integral-from-equality time scale
  - $Ta3i$: Integral-to-equality time scale
- $ca4$: A set of parameters reaches equilibrium
- $Ta4$: *equilibrium time scale*

(b) Time constant modeling
- $Tb1$: *a faster mechanism time scale*
- $cb2$: A faster mechanism reaches equilibrium
- $Tb2$: *A slower mechanism time scale*
- $cb3$: A slower mechanism reaches equilibrium

(c) Component structure modeling
- $Tc1$: *intracomponent time scale*
- $cc2$: All parameters in a component are satisfied
- $Tc2$: *intercomponent time scale*
- $cc3$: All parameters in a global structure are satisfied
- $Tc3$: *global time scale*
- $cc4$: All parameters in the whole system are satisfied
- $Tc4$: *the whole system time scale*

(d) Modeling of periods of interest
- $Td1$: *initial periods time scale*
- $cd1$: The first event happens on a time scale
- $Td2$: *intermediate transitional time scale*
- $cd2$: The last event happens on a time scale
- $Td3$: *final periods time scale*

B. Theoretical Foundation

In our causal time ontology, behavior over time generated by the reasoning engine is represented in terms of events and links among the events, in a way similar to the history model [16]. An event $e \in E$ represents instantaneous changes of qualitative values of parameters and their resultant values at a time point. Changes of quantitative values are assumed to be continuous and differentiable. A new event e_2 is generated by applying an operators $o \in O$ to an old event e_1 according to the model M. A link $l_1 \in L$ between e_1 and e_2 represents a causal relationship according to the model M. There is a time interval t_1 between e_1 and e_2 that corresponds to the causal relationship l_1. The time interval t_1 includes not e_2, but e_1. The roles of operators $o \in O$ are to propagate changes and to generate new events, time intervals, and, hence, partial temporal relationships. Note that the symbol t always represents not a time point, but a time interval herein. Although events correspond to time points, we concentrate on time intervals in which changes propagate.

The causal time ontology provides categories of such time intervals, called *causal time scales*. A causal time scale represents a concept of time interval for propagation of effect. The notation $\tau(l) = T$ denotes that a time interval t of a

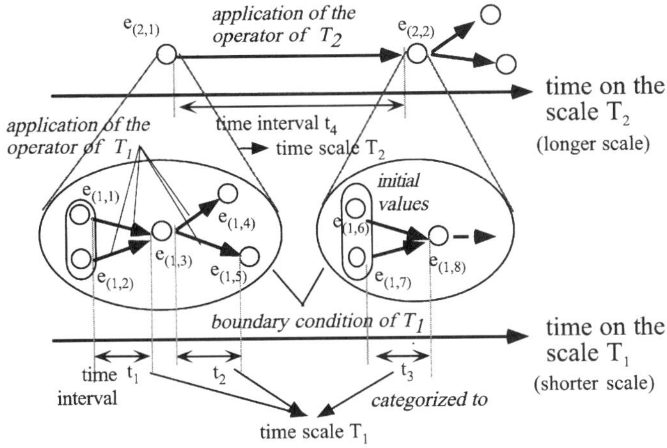

FIGURE 1 Relationship between the two time scales.

causal relationship l is categorized into a time scale T. We can say that the causal relationship l is represented on the time scale T.

The ordinal relationship $T_1 \prec T_2$, which represents that a time scale T_1 is shorter (finer grained) than T_2, is defined as

$$T_1 \prec T_2 \quad \longleftrightarrow \quad \forall t_1 \in T_1, \forall t_2 \in T_2, \, t_1 < t_2.$$

In other words, T_1 represents faster events than T_2 does. This relationship is transitive. The relationship between T_1 and T_2, where $T_1 \prec T_2$, is shown in Fig. 1.

When a certain condition becomes true in the reasoning process on a shorter time scale T_1, the reasoning shifts to a neighboring longer time scale T_2. Such a condition is called as a *boundary condition* of T_1 or a *precondition* of T_2. The set of events grouped by the condition $e_{(1,1)}, e_{(1,2)}, \ldots, e_{(1,4)}$ in T_1 is treated as the instantaneous events $e_{(2,1)}$ in T_2. Then the *reasoning operator* of T_2 is applied to the event $e_{(2,1)}$. Each time scale has an operator. The resultant values in T_2 can be treated as the initial values in T_1. The same concept applies to $T_0 \prec T_1$ cases recursively. In summary, a time scale T can be defined by a tuple of three elements, $\langle \mathrm{Pc}, \mathrm{Op}, \mathrm{Bc} \rangle$, where the abbreviations denote a precondition, an operator, and a boundary condition, respectively. The elements of T_1 are denoted by $T_1 : \mathrm{Pc}$, $T_1 : \mathrm{Op}$, and $T_1 : \mathrm{Bc}$, respectively.

The relationships l generated by the reasoning engine do not always make sense from a physical viewpoint. There exist such cases where a link l represents an operational order that is not justified in the physical sense. To clarify *the physical meaning* of the causal relationships, we will discuss two aspects of the physical meaning of each time scale, that is, *interval meaning* and *ordinal meaning*. The former represents a physical justification of the existence of time intervals on the time scale. The latter justifies the order of events on the time scale.

C. Causal Time Scales

This section defines 13 causal time scales as shown in Table 1. The time scales are classified into four categories, each of which represents a modeling technique together with particular modeling rationales. *Direct modeling* describes models that use mathematical differential equations, which directly represent dynamic behavior over time. *Time constant modeling* qualitatively categorizes the time constants for modeling of phenomena. *Component structure modeling* introduces the concept of "component" and is aimed at causal relationships that reflect the physical structures of the target systems. The *modeling of periods of interest* such as initial responses allows the reasoning engine to neglect changes of no interest. The notation *Tx#* denotes a time scale, where x denotes a category (a, b, c, or d) and the number # represents ascending order in each category. In Table 1, each condition denoted by the notation *cx#* represents the boundary condition of the time scale listed above it and the precondition of the time scale listed below it.

1. Direct Modeling

In direct modeling, temporal characteristics of the phenomena are represented directly by the mathematical aspect of the models. The precondition of the time scale $Ta3$ is that a set of parameters are *completely satisfied*, where every parameter in the set has values that satisfy all constraints. When the condition holds, the reasoning engine applies the integral operator and hence generates a new event. The integral operator embodies the qualitative mean value theorem $x_{\text{new}} = x_{\text{old}} + dx/dt$ [4]. The time intervals between the old events and the new events are categorized as $Ta3$:*integral time scale*. The time in QSIM [12] corresponds to $Ta3$. Furthermore, $Ta3$ is categorized into two types: $Ta3p$ and $Ta3i$. The former represents the time intervals for integration from the same value as the landmark values to the interval of the landmark values. The latter represents the time intervals from the interval to the landmark values. $Ta3p \prec Ta3i$ holds.

On the other hand, until a set of parameters is completely satisfied, the time intervals are categorized to $Ta2$:*dependency time scale*. The precondition of $Ta2$ is that a set of inherently simultaneous equations be satisfied. The inherently simultaneous equations, borrowed from [4], are such simultaneous equations that cannot be solved by substitution alone. The time scale of the causal ordering theory [5] corresponds to $Ta2$. Until the inherently simultaneous equations are satisfied, the time intervals are categorized to $Ta1$:*mutual dependency time scale*. Although this time scale has the previously mentioned interval meaning, it has no ordinal meaning. On the other hand, $Ta2$ and $Ta3$ can have both kinds of physical meaning. When a set of parameters achieves its equilibrium, the reasoning shifts to $Ta4$:*equilibrium time scale*.

For example, consider a simple system modeled by a direct model $y = x - z$, $dz/dt = y$. A variable takes one of the three qualitative values [+], [0], or [−], where the landmark value is 0. In the initial state, all variables takes [0] except for a disturbance $x = [+]$. Figure 2 shows causal relationships generated with $Ta2$, $Ta3$, and $Ta4$. In this case, the method of constraint satisfaction is simple propagation of values. First, the value of y becomes greater than 0 (denoted by $[0] \rightarrow [+]$ in the figure) according to $y = x - z$, $x = [+]$, and $z = [0]$. Next, the value is propagated to the derivative of z (denoted by dz in the figure). At this point, every parameter has values that satisfy all constraints (the precondition of $Ta3$). Then the reasoning shifts to the longer time scale $Ta3$. On the scale $Ta3$, the integral operator is applied to z; then z becomes greater than 0. Next, on $Ta2$, the new value of z is propagated to y and so on. In the case that the system achieves

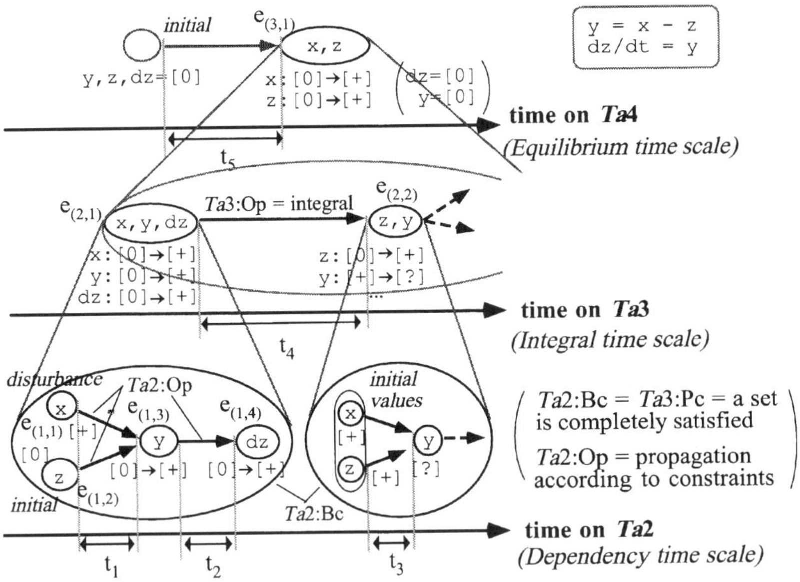

FIGURE 2 Relationship among time scales *Ta2* ≺ *Ta3* ≺ *Ta4*.

its equilibrium, an event $e_{3,1}$ is generated on the time scale $Ta4$. Note that there is no causal relationship between y and dz (i.e., both events happen at the same time point) on the time scale $Ta3$, whereas the change of y causes the change of dz after a small time interval t_1 on the time scale $Ta2$.

When model builders describe a phenomenon in terms of differential equations, the modeling rationale is to capture dynamic changes in the transitional behavior in $Ta3$ to its equilibrium. In general, this implies that the time interval to achieve equilibrium is longer than the other phenomena.

2. Time Constant Modeling

To represent differences in time constants, this modeling technique divides the target system into parameter sets where the time intervals to achieve equilibrium $Ta4$ are extremely different from each other. In such a model, the (relatively) faster mechanism first reaches equilibrium on the time scale $Tb1$. Then the reasoning shifts to the time scale $Tb2$. This kind of modeling is found in [13] and [14]. It has an advantage in reasoning efficiency because of separation of the reasoning space.

3. Component Structure Modeling

Component structure modeling divides the whole system into subparts according to component structures based on the device ontology [4]. In this chapter, devices in the minimum grain size are called components. $Tc1$ represents internal behavior in components, whereas $Tc2$ represents behavior between neighboring components. Interactions between the global structures that contain components are represented by $Tc3$. Those interactions between more coarse-grained global structures are also represented by $Tc3$. $Tc4$ represents the fact that the whole system eventually reaches equilibrium. The ordinal relationships among these time scales reflect structural distances.

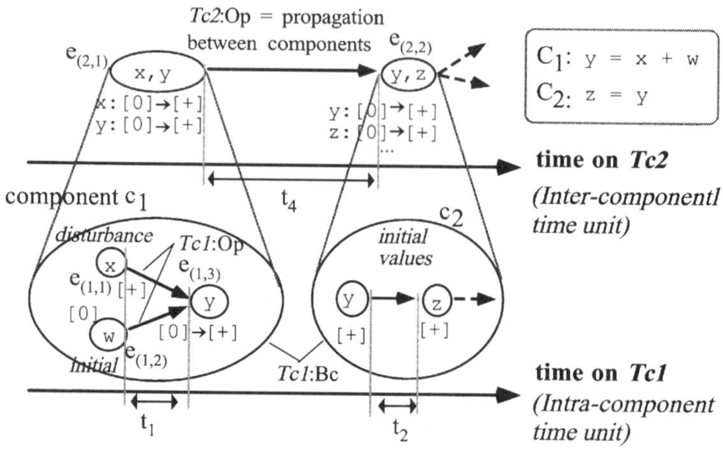

FIGURE 3 Relationship between time scales $Tc1 \prec Tc2$.

Figure 3 shows an example of causal relationships in the local components c_1 and c_2. Given the disturbance $x = [+]$ in c_1, the values within c_1 are changed by intracomponent propagation. Then, on the scale $Tc2$, the values of y are propagated to c_2.

Although $Tc2$ and $Tc3$ have interval meaning, the connection information alone cannot give them ordinal meaning. We will discuss additional knowledge for ordinal meaning later. On the other hand, $Tc1$ has no physical meaning in any sense. This modeling technique implies such modeling rationales that the causal relationships should reflect functioning components and the medium flow along the structures.

4. Modeling of Periods of Interest

Modeling of periods of interest allows the reasoning engine to treat only particular temporal periods of interest such as initial behavior. The time scales do not constrain length, but do constrain the number of time intervals. For example, QUAF [15] reasons only the initial changes $Td1$ and the final responses $Td3$ without the intermediate transient behavior. This technique contributes to disambiguation of reasoning results and avoids reasoning costs.

D. Causal Time Scales in Reasoning Systems

Let us characterize some of the existing reasoning systems in terms of the causal time scales. In general, a time resolution of a reasoning system is specified by a set of combinations of the primitive time scales discussed thus far. The notation $T_1 : Tx_1 \& Tx_2$ denotes that the time scale T_1 consists of Tx_1 and Tx_2. Table 2 shows the time scales that can be treated by some conventional qualitative reasoning systems. For example, QSIM [12] can cope only with behavior in $Ta3$, because it uses only mathematical differential equations and adopts a kind of generate-and-test method for constraint satisfaction. Thus, no causal relationship among transitional behavior to $Ta3$ is identified. The time of QSIM corresponds to $Ta3$. QSEA [14, Chap. 7] treats only equilibrium states represented by $Ta4$. The time-scale abstraction [14, Chap. 12] is the kind of time-scale modeling represented by

TABLE 2 Causal Time Scales in Reasoning Systems

QSIM [12]	$T1_{qs}$:$Ta3$ $T2_{qs}$:$Ta4$
QSEA [14, Chap. 7]	T_{qa}:$Ta4$
Time scale [14, Chap. 12]	$T1_{ts}$:$Ta3$ & $Tb1$, $T2_{ts}$:$Ta4$ & $Tb1$, $T3_{ts}$:$Ta3$ & $Tb2$, $T4_{ts}$:$Ta4$ & $Tb2$
QUAF [15]	$T1_{qf}$:$Ta3$ & $Td1$, $T2_{qf}$:$Ta3$ & $Td3$
Mythical time [4]	$T1_{mt}$:$Ta1$ & $Tc1$, $T2_{mt}$:$Ta1$ & $Tc2$, $T3_{mt}$:$Ta3$ & $Tc4$
Causal ordering [5]	$T1_{co}$:$Ta2$, $T2_{co}$:$Ta3$
Abstraction [13]	$T1_{ab}$:$Ta2$ & $Tb1$, $T2_{ab}$:$Ta3$ & $Tb1$, $T3_{ab}$:$Ta2$ & $Tb2$, $T4_{ab}$:$Ta3$ & $Tb2$

Tb. QUAF [15] reasons only the initial changes $Td1$ and the final responses $Td3$ on the integral time scale $Ta3$.

The method proposed in [4] can generate causal relationships in the more finely grained time scale $Ta1$, which is called mythical time, on the basis of the concept of device. Causal relationships in $T1_{mt}$, however, do not always have the physical meaning because $T1_{mt}$ consists of $Ta1$ and $Tc1$. On the other hand, to give the ordinal meaning to $T2_{mt}$, de Kleer and Brown [4] employed general heuristics that represent physical intuitions. The causal relationships they generated are ambiguous, however, due to the arbitrariness of heuristics application.

The causal ordering theory [5] derives causal relationships in $Ta2$, where the ordinal meaning represents mathematical dependency. The theory, however, does not try to derive the relationships in $Ta1$. Two abstraction techniques that correspond to Tb are also discussed.

E. Primitive Reasoning Scheme

The primitive reasoning scheme of a reasoning system can be specified by the set of time scales that the system can cope with. Let TS be such a set and let E_c be a current set of events to be carried out. The generic reasoning scheme for a current time scale T_c and neighboring time scales T_1 and T_2, where $T_1 \prec T_c \prec T_2$, is defined as follows:

1. In the time scale T_c, if an event $e_1 \in E_c$ satisfies the precondition T_c:Pc, the operator T_c:Op is applied to e_1, and then a new event e_2 and a new link l between e_1 and e_2 are generated. $\tau(l) = T_c$ holds.
2. The reasoning process shifts to the shorter time scale T_1. $T_c \leftarrow T_1$ and $E_c \leftarrow e_2$, and it goes to step 1 recursively, where the symbol $\leftarrow$ denotes subsitution.

3. If e_2 does not satisfy the boundary condition T_c:Bc, go back to step 1 and $E'_c \leftarrow E_c - \{e_1\} + \{e_2\}$.
4. If e_2 satisfies the boundary condition T_1:Bc, the reasoning process shifts to the longer time scale T_2. All events in T_c are transferred to the event e_3 in T_2. Go to step 1 recursively.

The reasoning process starts with the minimum time scale $T_{\min}$ in TS, given the initial value E_c. This reasoning process repeats recursively until the boundary condition of the maximum time scale holds. There are such cases when $T_{\min}$ needs a special operator to satisfy the precondition of $T_{\min}$.

The reasoning processes of conventional systems can be explained by their time scales shown in Table 2. For example, the reasoning method called time-scale abstraction [14, Chap. 12] starts with the minimum time scale $T1_{ts}$. Since $T1_{ts}$ contains $Ta3$, the operator for $T1_{ts}$ is the integration. (Strictly speaking, the operator of QSIM is not identical with integration. It represents possible transitions over time for reasoning efficiency.) When the boundary condition of $T1_{ts}$ becomes true, that is, the faster system reaches equilibrium, the reasoning process shifts to $T2_{ts}$. Because the system is in equilibrium, no reasoning is carried out in $T2_{dx}$. Then the reasoning process in $T3_{ts}$ starts and then the slower behavior is generated. In principle, the reasoning process at $T3_{ts}$ returns to the shorter time scales $T1_{ts}$ and $T2_{ts}$. In this case, however, because $T2_{ts}$ is in equilibrium and hence has no more events, only checks of values are needed. The primitive scheme of the algorithm shown in [14] is identical to the one given here.

The reasoning result consists of a set of events E and a set of links L, each of which has a time scale $T \in TS$ associated with it, where $\tau(l) = T$. If there is a (transitive) causal relationship between e_1 and e_2, then $\tau(e_1, e_2)$ denotes the time scale that represents the time interval between e_1 and e_2, and is defined as

$$\tau(e_1, e_2) = \max_{l \in Le} \tau(l),$$

where $L_e \subset L$ consists of the links between e_1 and e_2. This definition implies that a chain of time intervals represented by a time scale can be represented by the same time scale. In other words, time intervals on a time scale T_1 can never become long enough to be categorized into time scales longer than T_1. In the cases of no causal relationship, if $\tau(e_0, e_1) \prec \tau(e_0, e_2)$, where e_0 represents the last common event (i.e., the junction event), we can say only that e_1 happens before e_2. If not, there is no temporal order between such events.

F. Feedback and Causal Time Scales

Phenomena where the effect of a parameter event is eventually propagated to the parameter itself are called as feedback. The time delay along the feedback loop plays a crucial role in human understanding of feedback. For example, in cases where the time delay along a feedback is very short and the modeler has no interest in the transitional behavior of the feedback, there is no need to generate causal relationships among events in the feedback loop and trace the changes of parameter values. Therefore, the reasoning engine can treat feedback according to the following heuristics.

Feedback Heuristics. Whether or not a phenomenon is recognized as feedback depends on the time delay for the propagation loop according to the predefined threshold values T_{s1} and $T_{s2} \in TS$. Let L be a set of the links contained in the propagation loop and let T_l be the time scale for the time delay along the loop.

1. If $T_l \preceq T_{s1}$, then the phenomenon is not treated as feedback. The order of events in L has no physical meaning. If the new value after the feedback is different from the original value, the situation is viewed as a contradiction at the same time point.
2. If $T_l \succ T_{s1}$ and $T_l \preceq T_{s2}$, then the phenomenon is treated as *semi*feedback. The order of events in L has physical meaning. If there is a conflict between the old and the new values, then the new value is neglected.
3. If $T_l \succ T_{s2}$, then the phenomenon is treated as feedback. The order of events in L has physical meaning. The values will be changed after the feedback.

The last scenario corresponds to usual feedback. The first two scenarios can be paraphrased as "the feedback is virtual, produced by the sequential operations of the reasoning method" and "there is no feedback that suppresses the original change instantaneously," respectively.

IV. DESIGN OF A REASONING SYSTEM

This section discusses design processes for causal reasoning systems based on the causal time ontology. We show how the modeling scheme, the constituents of the models, and the reasoning procedure are determined according to the required temporal granularity. In this section, we use our causal reasoning system [7, 8] as an example, which was developed to target causal relationships more finely grained than the conventional systems.

A. Required Time Scales

The system is designed to derive causal relationships based on the device ontology. The target systems are fluid-related systems such as power plants. The system is concerned with flow rate, pressure, and heat of fluid, assuming the fluid is incompressible. The requirements are reusability of models and disambiguation of reasoning results. Table 3 shows the requirements for causal relationships to be generated and their time scales. For example, to cope with global phenomena such

TABLE 3 Requirements for Causal Relationships

Required causal relationships	Time scales
Interaction among components	$Tc2$
Global phenomena (heat)	$Tc3$
Globally simultaneous phenomena (flow)	$Tc3$ & $Tb1$
Dependency relationships	$Ta1, Ta2$
Dynamic behavior	$Ta3$
Initial and final response	$Td1, Td3$

TABLE 4 Time Scales of Our Reasoning System

Name of time scale	Definition
$T1$: intraComponent	$Ta1/2$ & $Tb1/2$ & $Tc1$
$T2$: interComponent	$Ta1/2$ & $Tb2$ & $Tc2$
$T3$: Global	$Ta1/2$ & $Tb2$ & $Tc3$
$T4$: Globally simultaneous	$Ta1/2$ & $Tb1$ & $Tc3$
$T5$: Integral	$Ta3$ & $Tb2$ & $Tc3$
$T6$: Partial equilibrium	$Ta4$ & $Tb2$ & $Tc3$
$T7$: Complete equilibrium	$Ta4$ & $Tb2$ & $Tc4$

$T1 \prec T4 \prec T2 \prec T3 \prec T5 \prec T6 \prec T7$

as changes in temperatures caused by global heat balances, a hierarchical structure ($Tc3$) is needed. There are also cases where changes in nonneighboring components are simultaneous; these changes are called *globally simultaneous phenomena.* For example, on the assumption that fluid is incompressible, the flow rate of such fluid at each component changes at the same time. Thus, a time scale that is a combination of $Tc3$ and $Tb1$ is needed.

As a result of design decisions regarding how to cope with the required primitive time scales shown in Table 3, the set of time scales shown in Table 4 are determined. First, it is assumed that there is only one level of faster mechanisms in terms of equilibrium equations. Thus, $T4$:*globally simultaneous time scale* consists of $Ta1$ or $Tb2$ & $Tb1$ & $Tc3$, and the intercomponent phenomena ($T2$) and integration ($T5$) are in $Tb2$. Next, as a reflection of no interest in the transient behavior of the intercomponent phenomena, the $T2$:*intercomponent time scale* is represented by equilibrium equations, i.e., $Ta1$ or $Ta2$. Last, although the $T1$:*intracomponent time scale* can represent not only faster mechanisms, but also slower mechanisms, $T1 \prec T4$ holds because $Tc1$ in $T1$ represents finer-grained changes. Because $T4$ represents almost simultaneous phenomena, $T4 \prec T2$ holds.

Moreover, the reasoning engine has some assumptions. First, we assume that the target system has a normal equilibrium state without any perturbation. The behavior represents a response to perturbation to the normal equilibrium. A parameter takes one of three qualitative values related to the deviation from a normal value that is defined as a permitted range of the parameter in the normal equilibrium. The [+] ([−]) represents a quantity greater (less) than the normal value. [0] represents a quantity equal to the normal value. Next, it is required that the reasoning engine can infer only the initial changes ($Td1$) and the final responses ($Td3$), and skip the transient behavior in $Td2$. Last, we assume that all constraints are continuous.

B. Required Constituents of the Model

The set of time scales as the performance specification of a reasoning engine governs the constituents of the model. In other words, the model should have contents that give physical meaning to the causal relationships to be generated. Table 5 shows the modeling schemes of the system for each time scale. For example, to skip from the transitional behavior ($Td2$) to the equilibrium state ($Td3$&$Ta4$), it is necessary to know whether or not the behavior will reach equilibrium, i.e., so-called stability of equilibrium [14], is needed.

TABLE 5 The Modeling Scheme

Time scales	Modeling scheme
$Tc1, Tc2$	Components and connections between ports
$Tb1, Tb2$	Description of time scale of mechanisms
$Td2, Td3$	Stability to equilibrium of parameters
$Ta1\&Tc2$	Causal specification

C. Causality of Components

A main issue to discuss for causal ordering based on the device ontology is what model contents give physical meaning to the causal relationships among components ($Tc2$). As discussed thus far, additional knowledge is needed. Considering components have their own causal characteristics, our approach is to explicitly describe inherent causal properties of each parameter in components, called *causal specifications*, context independently. Such properties, however, are prone to depend on context as discussed in [4]. To help capture causal properties independent of context, we have identified three categories of causal relationships within a component: *isolated internal causality, external causality*, and *combined internal causality*. The isolated internal causality represents such causal relationships that a change of a parameter in a component causes a change in another parameter in the component through events in the components. The external causality is concerned with direct interactions between connected components. In the case of the combined internal causality, the causal chains between cause and effect include events in other components. Causal specifications from the viewpoint of isolated internal causality are context-independent.

D. Model Representation

The overall structure of the system is represented by a combination of component models and connections on the basis of the device ontology [4]. A component model consists of (1) a set of parameters, (2) constraints over parameters, (3) ports for connections, (4) *causal specifications* that represent causal properties of the component, and (5) a *time scale* of phenomena.

Constraints are described in terms of qualitative operators and parameters. $D(p)$ represents a derivative of a parameter p with respect to time. It takes one of the three qualitative values [+], [−], or [0], which correspond to the sign of the derivatives. The integral equation $p_{(t+1)} = p_{(t)} + D(p)_{(t)}$ holds. Constraints $\exists \ell$, $D(p)_{(t)} = [0]$ mean that the parameter converges to the equilibrium state. A parameter can belong to some ports for connections among components. The connection information is represented by relationships between the ports. There are global constraints that have connections to local components.

A causal specification of a parameter represents the possibility of acting causal roles using the following two flags.

Cause (C): Changes of the value of the parameter can cause changes of values of other parameters in the component through events within the component.

Effect (E): Changes of the value of the parameter can be caused by changes of values of other parameters in the component through events within the component.

A causal specification takes one of the three values, $C\tilde{E}$, $\tilde{C}E$, and CE, where the tilde (˜) is a negation symbol. If a parameter exists whose change affects the value of the parameter under consideration, then the flag E is associated with the parameter under consideration, and if a parameter exists whose value is affected by that of the parameter under consideration, then the flag C is associated with the parameter under consideration. If there is no such parameter, $\tilde{C}$ ($\tilde{E}$) is associated. Parameters with a constant value have $C\tilde{E}$ as a causal specification. For example, on the assumption that the resistance R is not changed by heat, a resistance R in an electric circuit will have $C\tilde{E}$. The values of such parameters are changed only by influences of other components and/or factors external to the model of the system such as faults. Thus, a parameter is *exogenous* [13] to the model of the target system if and only if it has $C\tilde{E}$ as a causal specification and has no connection with other components. The exogenous parameters are candidates of the faults in the diagnostic tasks.

To cope with global phenomena, global constraints over local components are described. Such global constraints are justified by general properties of the physical entity such as heat and fluid. Whereas such properties are specified by physical laws and the generic topologies of connections among components such as a loop, they can be prepared beforehand for each generic topology as a part of the domain ontology. For example, such a general property for the generic loop topology holds in which changes of the temperatures in a loop are caused by the difference between the inflow and the outflow of thermal energy according to the law of heat conservation. Global constraints are instantiated according to concrete configurations.

Time scales of phenomena enable the reasoning engine to distinguish *globally simultaneous* phenomena such as changes of the flow rate of incompressible fluid as $T4$. The global constraints that represent such phenomena are called *globally simultaneous constraints* and are marked with "simultaneous." Other constraints and local component models are marked with "not simultaneous."

E. Reasoning

The reasoning method is based on the primitive reasoning scheme discussed before. Given an initial event, intracomponent reasoning at the minimum time scale $T1$ is initiated to determine values of other parameters in the component. In general, the intracomponent reasoning is invoked when changes are propagated from other components. The operator in $T1$ is an evaluation of constraints according to the causal specification. If a value of a parameter marked with $C\tilde{E}$ is not determined by other components, it can be assumed to remain an old value in the precedent state. Next, the intercomponent reasoning in $T4$ globally propagates events to other components. Then the reasoning shifts to the longer time scales $T2$, $T3$, and $T5$, similarly. The reasoning of feedback is based on the feedback heuristics. In our system, because a part of the causal relations in $T1$ have no physical meaning and $T4$ represents a very fast mechanism, the threshold values T_{s1} and T_{s2} are set to $T1$ and $T4$, respectively.

V. AN ONTOLOGY OF FLUID SYSTEMS

This section describes a domain ontology of fluid systems such as power plants based on the kernel ontologies discussed thus far. The ontology concerned with flow rate, pressure, and heat of fluid assumes the fluid is incompressible. On the basis of device ontology [4], we view the model of the whole of the target system as consisting of a set of component models and information about connections among them.

A. Causality of Fluid

The concept of *total continuity* allows us to capture the causality of incompressible fluid. Total continuity of a component indicates whether all amounts of fluid entering the component flow out continuously. For example, relief valves and tanks do not satisfy total continuities and are called *partially continuous* fluid components. The whole system can be decomposed into *totally continuous fluid subsystems*, each of which has only one partially continuous fluid component working as a source of flow. From the viewpoint of the total continuity, we can identify the causality of flow rates at components. In a totally continuous fluid subsystem, flow rate does not change at a totally continuous fluid component, because such change contradicts the assumption that fluid is incompressible. All the fluid-related components in plants are classified into two categories, flow-supplying components and flow-receiving components, according to their ability to change flow rates. Flow-supplying components do not satisfy total continuities and can change flow rates, whereas flow-receiving components, which include pipes and flow valves, do satisfy total continuity. Pumps do satisfy total continuity, but, as an exception, can change flow rate, because pumps suck the fluid.

It is desirable for a causal relationship to consist of internal events in a component and to affect a unique qualitative value. This type of relationship is called *locally deterministic*. According to the local determinism, pressure drop is more important than pressure in the ontology. Pressures are determined not locally, but globally by a balance of the whole system. Therefore, the causal specifications of pressure drop and pressure in flow-receiving components are $\widetilde{C}E$ and $C\widetilde{E}$, respectively.

B. Time Scales and Global Constraints

Ideally, the flow rates of incompressible fluid at all components in a totally continuous fluid subsystem change simultaneously. Therefore, constraints that concern flow rate are global and simultaneous. Pressure drop and pressure are also global and simultaneous. On the other hand, heat flows between neighboring components if we assume there is no emission of heat. In the case of global loop structures, however, global constraints additionally hold that represent the law of heat conservation relative to the thermal energy of a molecule of fluid circulating in the loop. The global constraints that concern heat are not simultaneous, because it takes time for the molecules to circulate in the loops.

Such global constraints are specified by physical laws and the generic topologies of connections among components such as the loop. They can be prepared beforehand for each generic topology as a part of the domain ontology. The following global constraints hold generally for totally continuous fluid subsystems that form loop structures.

Heat Conservation Law: The variation in temperature at each component in the loop is positively influenced by the difference between the inflow and the outflow of thermal energy.

Flow Rate: All flow rates of incompressible fluid at components in the subsystem are same. They are simultaneous.

Pressure Drop: The sum of pressure drops of flow-receiving components in a subsystem equals the sum of pressure drops of flow-supplying component in the same subsystem. They are simultaneous.

Pressure: Pressures at components are determined according to all pressure drops in the subsystem. They are simultaneous.

Global constraints are instantiated according to concrete configurations.

C. Models of Fluid-Related Components

1. Pump

A pump is one of the flow-supplying components. It has some relationships with power supply, pressure head, and flow rate. The pressure head is equal to the total pressure drop of the flow-receiving components according to the global constraints concerning pressure drop. The causal specification of the flow rate is $\tilde{C}E$ and that of the pressure head is $C\tilde{E}$. Thus, changes in the total pressure drop cause changes in the flow rate and the power supply. The changes depend on the characteristics of the pump. If the pump is of "pressure-compensative" type, that is, it controls the flow rate to maintain constant power supply, the causal specification of the power supply of the pump is $C\tilde{E}$. In this case, the causality of the pump can be recognized as "a pump controls the flow rate according to the total pressure drop and the power supply." Note that the pump is not an ideal flow supplier.

2. Flow Valve

A flow valve without any drain is one of the flow-receiving components. It has the following parameters: available flow area that can be changed by hand, flow rate through the valve, inlet pressure, outlet pressure, and pressure drop between inlet and outlet. The causal specification of the area is $C\tilde{E}$ and that of flow rate is $C\tilde{E}$; those of pressures and pressure drops are $C\tilde{E}$ and $\tilde{C}E$, respectively. Thus, in the case where the valve is closed a bit by hand, a change of area causes a change not of the flow rate, but of the pressure drop. The change is propagated to the pump (a flow-supplying component) and then it may or may not cause a change of flow rate according to the characteristics of the pump. If the flow rate changes, that is, if the pump tries to compensate for increased load by changing the flow rate, it causes a decrease of the flow rate at the flow valve. Recognition that "a flow valve changes flow rate" is the direct association from the viewpoint of combined internal causality. Because this relationship depends on the characteristics of the pump, it is not reusable.

VI. APPLICATION TO A POWER PLANT [8]

This section describes the application of our method to a nuclear power plant. To concentrate on the behavior of the flow of thermal energy and the fluid, we built a model of the heat transportation system of the power plant. Figure 4 shows an outline of the system. The plant transports thermal energy generated in the reactor vessel (RX) into the open air through two heat exchangers (IHX and AC). Because this is a test plant, it has no power generator. The system has two subsystems (called A and B), each of which has two loops (called primary and secondary) in which the coolant circulates.

The model of the whole system consists of 27 components, 143 parameters, and 102 constraints. Major components and parameters are shown in Fig. 4. A component model is an instance of a component class, such as heat exchangers and pumps. The component class models are based on the domain ontology of fluid systems. Figure 5 shows the qualitative model of the heat exchanger in the primary loop in the subsystem A (called IHXa); Fig. 6 shows that of the pump (called P1a). According to the ontology, the pump changes the flow rate by reacting to changes in the power supplied to the pump and the total pressure drop along the loop. The 16 global constraints are derived according to the four global properties of heat and fluid of the domain ontology. Figure 7 shows a heat conservation law in the primary loop of subsystem A.

Table 6 shows the simulation results. Given one of the five anomalous perturbations in the topmost row, the reasoning engine determines values of the other parameters when the system eventually reaches the heat-balanced state. The numbers associated with the qualitative values represent causal orders. The value denoted by the question mark (?) represents ambiguous values. All results in the table correspond to results of a domain expert. Although results when the system is subjected to decrease of the power supplied to pump 2b (P2b) are ambiguous, domain experts cannot determine the value without *quantitative* values of the flow rate.

Figure 8 shows part of the causal relationships generated by the reasoning engine in the case of decreasing the power supplied to P1a. When the power supply `Power` takes [−], the reasoning engine derives the flow rate `Flow` = [−] in $T1$ (see sequence 2 in Fig. 8) by introducing an assumption that the difference of the pressure of the pump `Pio` specified as $\widetilde{CE}$ is [0]. The change of `Flow` is propagated to the all components in LOOP1a (i.e., IHXa, RX, and V1a) simultaneously in $T4$ by the globally simultaneous constraint concerning flow rate. In each component, each pressure drop decreases (sequence 4) because pressure drop is proportional to flow rate. Then the total pressure drop along LOOP1a changes to [−] by the globally simultaneous constraint concerning pressure drop. Because the `Pio` of the pump equals the total pressure drop, `Pio` = [−] is derived (sequence 5) and then the assumed value, so-called feedback, is dismissed. Then the value of `Flow` becomes ambiguous (sequence 6) because `Power` = [−] and `Pio` = [−]. Note that multiplication has the same effect as addition because the qualitative values represent deviation from a normal value, not sign. Whereas the time delay along the feedback loop is $T4 + T1 + T4 + T1$, which represents instantaneous phenomena, according to the heuristics (i.e., there is no instantaneous feedback), the system obtains `Flow` = [−], which matches reality (sequence 7). The decrease of the

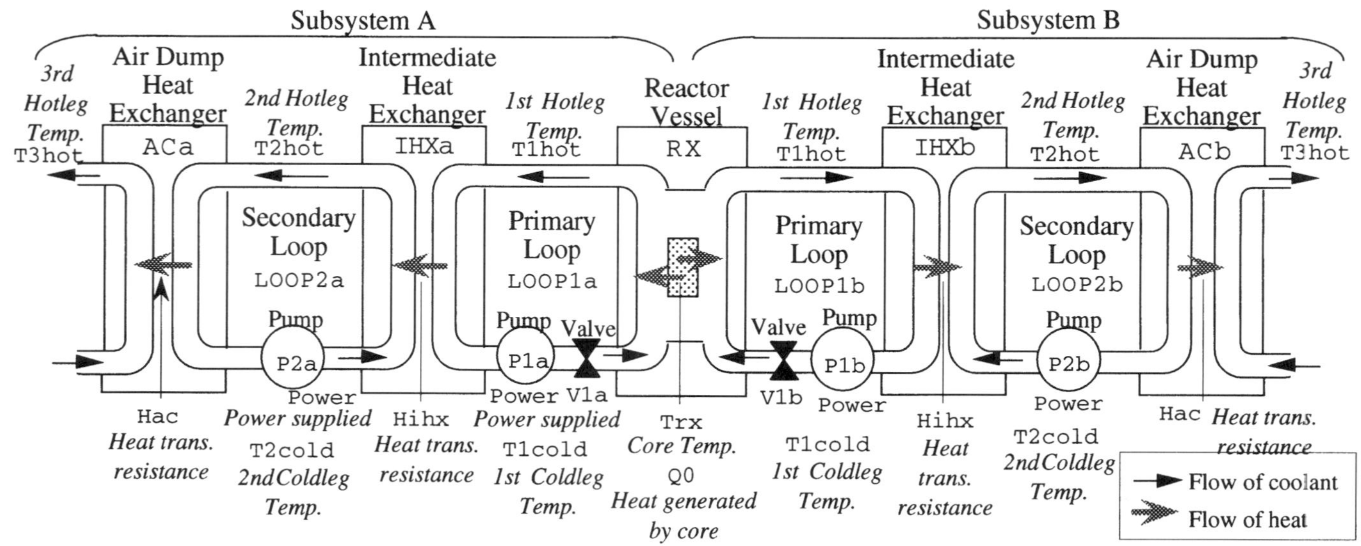

FIGURE 4 Outline of the heat transportation system.

pressure drop in RX, on the other hand, is propagated to the other pump, P1b (sequence 5). This causes an increase of the flow rate in LOOP1b. Moreover, in RX and IHXa, the decrease of the flow rate of LOOP1a also causes changes in the temperatures of the coolant (sequence 4). Because these changes are not simultaneous (i.e., in $T2$), they are propagated to other components after simultaneous phenomena (sequence 8).

Figure 9 shows the causal relationships when the heat transfer resistance Hihx of IHXa decreases. (In contrast with the result shown in Table 6, Fig. 9

Name: IHXa
Time-Scale: not-simultaneous
Ports:

symbol	*connected comp.*	*connected port*
in1	RX	out1a
out1	P1a	in
in2	P2a	out
out2	ACa	in1
heat1	LOOP1a_HEAT	out
heat2	LOOP2a_HEAT	in
flow1	LOOP1a_FLOW	rst2
flow2	LOOP2a_FLOW	rst1
dp1	LOOP1a_DP	rst2
dp2	LOOP2a_DP	rst1

Parameters:

symbol	*description*	*causal spec.*	*port*
T1hot	1st Coolant inlet Temp.	$C\tilde{E}$	in1,heat1
T1cold	1st Coolant outlet Temp.	$\tilde{C}E$	out1,heat1
T2cold	2nd Coolant inlet Temp.	$C\tilde{E}$	in2,heat2
T2hot	2nd Coolant outlet Temp.	$\tilde{C}E$	out2,heat2
Q12	Heat transported to 2nd coolant	CE	heat1, heat2
Hihx	Heat trans. resistance.	$C\tilde{E}$	
Flow1	Flow rate of 1st coolant	$C\tilde{E}$	flow1
Flow2	Flow rate of 2nd coolant	$C\tilde{E}$	flow2
P1io	Pressure drop of 1st coolant	$\tilde{C}E$	dp1
P2io	Pressure drop of 2nd coolant	$\tilde{C}E$	dp2

Constraints:

```
Q12 = Hihx * ((T1hot + T1cold)/2
                - (T2hot + T2cold)/2)
Q12 = Flow1 * (T1hot - T1cold)
Q12 = Flow2 * (T2hot - T2cold)
P1io = Flow1
P2io = Flow2
```

FIGURE 5 Qualitative model of IHXa.

Name: P1a
Time-Scale: not-simultaneous
Port:

symbol	*connected comp.*	*connected port*
in	IHXa	out1
out	V1a	in
flow	LOOP1a_FLOW	driver
dp	LOOP1a_DP	driver

Parameters:

symbol	*description*	*causal spec.*	*port*
`Power`	Power supplied	CE	
`Flow`	Flow rate	$\tilde{C}E$	flow
`Pio`	Difference of pressure between inlet and outlet	$C\tilde{E}$	dp
`Tin`	Coolant Temp.(inlet)	$C\tilde{E}$	in
`Tout`	Coolant Temp.(outlet)	$\tilde{C}E$	out

Constraints:

```
Power = Flow * Pio
Tin = Tout
```

FIGURE 6 Model of the pump in LOOP1a.

Name: LOOP1a_HEAT
Time-Scale: not-simultaneous
Port:

symbol	*connected comp.*	*connected port*
in	RX	heata
out	IHXa	heat1

Parameters:

symbol	*description*	*causal spec.*	*port*
`Q01`	Heat transported from RX	$C\tilde{E}$	in
`Q12`	Heat transported to IHX	$C\tilde{E}$	out
`T1hot`	Coolant Temp.(hotleg)	$\tilde{C}E$	in,out
`T1cold`	Coolant Temp.(coldleg)	$\tilde{C}E$	in,out

Constraints:

```
D(T1hot) = Q01 - Q12
D(T1cold) = Q01 - Q12
```

$\exists t,\ \mathtt{D(T1hot)}_{(t)} = [0]$
$\exists t,\ \mathtt{D(T1cold)}_{(t)} = [0]$

FIGURE 7 Model of LOOP1a with respect to the heat conservation law.

TABLE 6 Results of Qualitative Simulation

		RX Q0 [+]	IHXa Hihx [-]	ACb Hac [-]	P1a Power [-]	P2b Power [-]
	Trx	(1)+	(2)+	(3)+	(1)+	(2)+
A	T1hot	(1)+	(2)+	(3)+	(1)+	(2)+
	T1cold	(2)+	(1)+	(4)+	(1)−	(3)+, (4)?
	T2hot	(2)+	(1)−	(4)+	(1)−	(3)+, (5)?
	T2cold	(3)+	(2)−	(5)+	(2)−	(4)+, (6)?
	T3hot	(3)+	(2)−	(5)+	(2)−	(4)+, (6)?
B	T1hot	(1)+	(2)+	(3)+	(1)+	(2)+
	T1cold	(2)+	(3)+	(2)+	(2)+	(1)+, (4)?
	T2hot	(2)+	(3)+	(2)+	(2)+	(1)+, (5)?
	T2cold	(3)+	(4)+	(1)+	(3)+	(1)−, (6)?
	T3hot	(3)+	(4)+	(1)−	(3)+	(1)−, (6)?

shows the result in the case where the system has only subsystem A without subsystem B.) First, in IHXa, the reasoning engine derives T1cold = [+] and Q12 = [−] (sequence 2 in Fig. 9). The value of T1cold is propagated to RX through P1a and V1a. Then T1hot = [+] and Q01 = [0] (sequence 8) are derived in RX. When Q01 = [0] and Q12 = [−] are propagated to LOOP1a_HEAT (sequence 9), D(T1hot) = [+] and D(T1cold) = [+] are derived (sequence 10). These adjustments mean that the temperatures in the loop are increasing in *T*3 due to the difference between the inflow (Q01) and outflow (Q12) of thermal energy. Following a long enough time in *T*6 after the occurrence of an anomaly, the loop achieves an equilibrium state and, hence, the temperatures are stable. Thus, although Q12 becomes ambiguous (sequence 12), the reasoning engine obtains Q12 = [0] in the equilibrium state in *T*6 (sequence 14). This reasoning result shows that the increase of the temperatures of LOOP1a compensates for the decrease of the heat transfer resistance of IHXa, and then the temperatures of LOOP2a equalize to normal val-

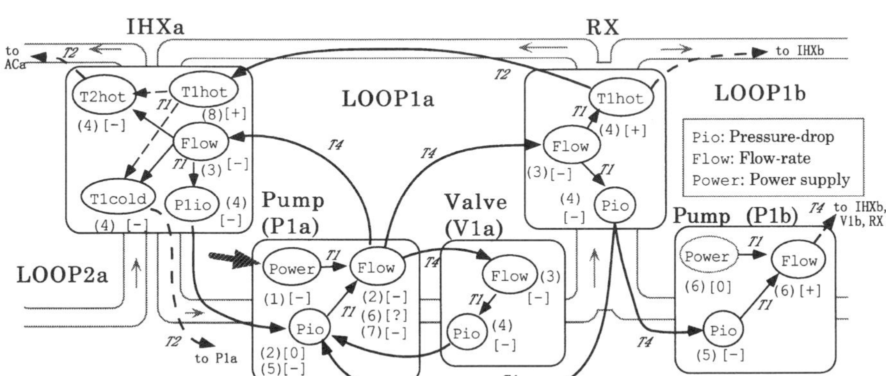

FIGURE 8 Part of the causal relationships in the case of decreasing power supplied to P1a.

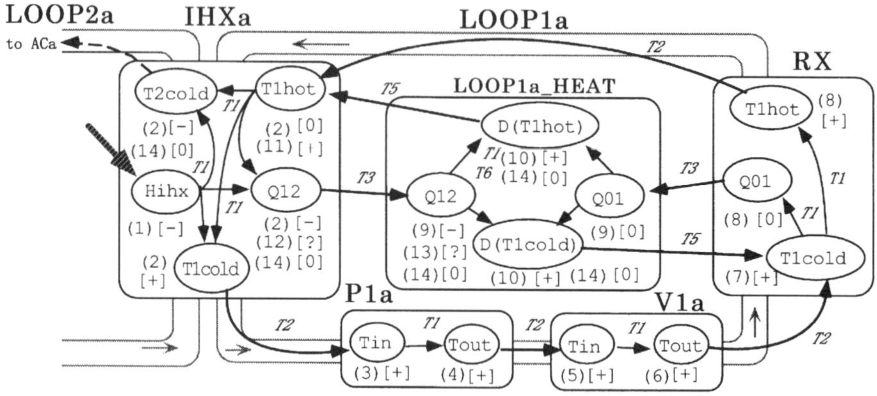

FIGURE 9 Part of the causal relationships in the case where the heat transfer resistance of IHXa decreases (without subsystem B).

ues. (In the case where the system also has subsystem B, these phenomena do not happen as shown in Table 6.)

VII. RELATED WORK

The time concept in QSIM was discussed by Kuipers [14] from the mathematical viewpoint, which is categorized into *Ta* or *Tb*. The article by Iwasaki and Simon [13] shows a causal ordering theory for hierarchical sets of variables and discusses how to generate such hierarchical sets according to time scale and strength of interaction among variables. The causal time ontology allows us to clarify the rationales that underlie such sets from the physical viewpoint.

Ontologies of time itself have been discussed elsewhere such as by Allen [17], who identified primitives for representing time itself and categorized logical relationships between them. The causal time ontology provides cognitive categories of time intervals from the viewpoint of causal ordering of physical systems.

Although de Kleer and Brown [4] and Top and Akkermans [18] identified general causal properties of devices, causal relationships generated by their methods are ambiguous in the case of inherently simultaneous equations. The TQ analysis of Williams [19] provides heuristics to analyze limited kinds of feedback according to time delay. A part of our causal specification ($\widetilde{CE}$) corresponds to the descriptions of "exogenous parameters" [13] of each component. In Forbus [16] and Washio [20] described causal properties of physical processes. Our global constraint about heat corresponds to an energy constraint [21] (a global filter) for QSIM.

VIII. SUMMARY

We have proposed a causal time ontology that contains the set of causal time units shown in Table 1 and is used to uncover the relationship between the time intervals for propagation of change and the modeling rationales. Some conventional reasoning systems have been characterized with respect to causal ordering using the time units shown in Table 2. Furthermore, the design rationales and the time resolution or our reasoning system have been presented (the summary is shown in Tables 3–5).

We confined the topic to continuous changes. A discrete model of a phenomenon is often the result of modeling according to such rationale that the phenomenon is extremely faster than other phenomena, as discussed in [11] and [22]. Such discrete models can be viewed as the results of other kinds of temporal modeling techniques discussed in this article. Investigation of such discrete changes remains as future work.

ACKNOWLEDGMENTS

The authors thank Shinji Yoshikawa and Kenji Ozawa from Power Reactor and Nuclear Fuel Development Corp. (currently Japan Nuclear Cycle Development Institute) and Munehiko Sasajima from ISIR, Osaka University (currently Toshiba Corporation) for their help and comments on building the power plant model.

REFERENCES

1. Musen, M. A. Dimension of knowledge sharing and reuse. Technical Report KSL-91-65, Knowledge Systems Laboratory, Stanford University, 1991.
2. Mars, N. J. I. (Ed.). *Towards Very Large Knowledge Bases*. IOS Press, Amsterdam, 1995.
3. Mizoguchi, R. and Ikeda, M. Towards ontology engineering. In *Proceedings of Pacific Asian Conference on Expert Systems*, 1997, pp. 259–266.
4. de Kleer, J. and Brown, J. S. A qualitative physics based on confluences. *Artif. Intell.* 24:7–83, 1984.
5. Iwasaki, Y. and Simon, H. A. Causality in device behavior. *Artif. Intell.* 29:3–32, 1986.
6. Kitamura, Y., Ikeda, M., and Mizoguchi, R. A causal time ontology for qualitative reasoning. In *Proceedings of The Fifteenth International Joint Conference on Artificial Intelligence*, 1997, pp. 501–506.
7. Kitamura, Y., Sasajima, M., Ikeda, M., Yoshikawa, S., Indou, A., Kakusyo, R., and Mizoguchi, R. A method of qualitative reasoning for model-based problem solving and its application to a nuclear plant. *Expert Syst. Appl.* 10(3/4):441–448, 1996.
8. Kitamura, Y., Ikeda, M., and Mizoguchi, R. A qualitative reasoning based on an ontology of fluid systems and its evaluation on a power plant. In *Proceedings of The Fourth Pacific Rim International Conference on Artificial Intelligence*, 1996, pp. 288–299.
9. Gruber, T. A translation approach to portable ontology specifications. In *Proceedings of Japan Knowledge Acquisition for Knowledge-Based Systems Workshop*, 1992, pp. 89–108.
10. Mizoguchi, R. Knowledge acquisition and ontology. In *Proceedings of The First International Conference on the Building and Sharing of Very Large-Scale Knowledge Bases (KB&KS '93)*, 1993, pp. 121–128.
11. Iwasaki, Y., Farquhar, A., Saraswat, V., Bobrow, D., and Gupta, V. Modeling time in hybrid systems: How fast is "instantaneous"? In *Proceedings of The Fourteenth International Joint Conference on Artificial Intelligence*, 1995, pp. 1773–1780.
12. Kuipers, B. J. Qualitative simulation. *Artif. Intell.* 29:289–338, 1986.
13. Iwasaki, Y. and Simon, H. A. Causality and model abstraction. *Artif. Intell.* 67:143–194, 1994.
14. Kuipers, B. J. *Qualitative Reasoning*. MIT Press, Cambridge, MA, 1994.
15. Rose, P. and Kramer, M. A. Qualitative analysis of causal feedback. In *Proceedings of Ninth National Conference on Artificial Intelligence, American Association for Artificial Intelligence*, 1991, pp. 817–823.
16. Forbus, K. D. Qualitative process theory. *Artif. Intell.* 24:85–168, 1984.
17. Allen, J. F. Towards a general theory of action and time. *Artif. Intell.* 23:123–154, 1984.

18. Top, J. and Akkermans, H. Computational and physical causality. In *Proceedings of the Twelfth International Joint Conference on Artificial Intelligence*, 1991, pp. 1171–1176.
19. Williams, B. C. Qualitative analysis of MOS circuits. *Artif. Intell.* 24:281–346 (1984).
20. Washio, T. Causal ordering methods based on physical laws of plant systems. Report NRL-033, MIT, Cambridge, MA, 1989.
21. Fouché, P. and Kuipers, B. J. Reasoning about energy in qualitative simulation. *IEEE Trans. Syst., Man, Cybern.* 22(1):47–63, 1992.
22. Nishida, T. and Doshita, S. Reasoning about discontinuous change. In *Proceedings of Sixth National Conference on Artificial Intelligence, American Association for Artificial Intelligence*, 1987, pp. 643–648.

7

INTELLIGENT SYSTEM CONTROL: A UNIFIED APPROACH AND APPLICATIONS

HUI-MIN HUANG
HARRY SCOTT
ELENA MESSINA
MARIS JUBERTS
RICHARD QUINTERO

Intelligent Systems Division, National Institute of Standards and Technology, Gaithersburg, Maryland 20899

Expert Systems, Edited by Cornelius T. Leondes, Volume 1

ISBN: 0-12-443881-4 / $35.00

I. INTRODUCTION

Software architecture and its associated engineering methodology are among the predominant factors that determine the success and the performance of large, complex, intelligent, real-time control systems. These systems may contain many subsystems that execute in a distributed environment. The subsystems may execute independently, yet communicate with the rest of the system in a defined and integrated manner so that the entire system pursues its overall goals. The subsystems may be implemented with different planning and control strategies and yet communicate through standard interfaces that are consistent with the rest of the system. The control system may be reconfigured, in that subsystems may be taken offline for maintenance or integrated online for particular jobs or missions. In addition, information is becoming a critical piece in current and next-generation system control. In the manufacturing environment, part models, process plans, and production statistics are just a few of the many pieces of information that need to be computerized, organized, and interfaced to allow easy and timely access so that system goals can be achieved and desirable performance can be delivered. All of these requirements call for an architecture that is scalable and open, incorporating a standard interfacing method [1].

It is desirable to have an architecture that allows developers to employ innovative solutions that may be based on AI techniques such as case-based reasoning, neural nets, fuzzy logic, or reactive behavior for the individual subsystems. The architecture should also allow a hybrid construct [2] that combines discrete-event components such as finite state automata [3] or Petri nets and continuous-time-based components such as adaptive and learning control [4]. To address these issues systematically, it is desirable to employ a particular type of architecture, reference model architecture, that provides generic system static and dynamic models yet integrates individual component solutions.

Researchers have been addressing certain aspects of these system problems, including flexible manufacturing systems (FMS) [5], hybrid systems [2], intelligent control [6, 7], and open system architecture [8, 9]. Lima and Saridis [10] described a learning stochastic automata based intelligent control system. Antsaklis and Passino, in a chapter of [6], described a hierarchical control architecture that emphasizes successive delegation of duties from higher to lower levels. Meystel, in another chapter of [6], described a nested hierarchical control theory that included the concept of treating design and control as a design–control continuum. Acar and Özgüner [11] provided an architecture that organizes the system into a multiresolutional hierarchy by identifying its components and examining the physical relationships among them.

The High Performance Computing and Communications (HPCC) program was formally established following passage of the High Performance Computing Act of 1991 by Congress. That program has been organized more recently into the Computing, Information, and Communications (CIC) Research and Development program. The Systems Integration for Manufacturing Applications (SIMA) program [12] is an activity under one of the major components of the CIC. Since 1994, the SIMA program has partially funded work on the development of a standard reference model architecture for the control of complex, intelligent systems. This effort builds on earlier related work in several projects at the National Institute of Standards and Technology dating back to the early 1980s and leverages current efforts in other programs.

In particular, besides the Real-time Control System architecture described in this chapter, NIST efforts have included developing the Manufacturing Systems Integration (MSI) architecture [13] and the Quality in Automation (QIA) architecture [14]. Each of these was developed with specific attention given to different areas of application in the manufacturing domain. For example, MSI focused on manufacturing activities above the shop floor. Application of QIA concepts focused on problems of in-process and process-intermittent inspection on machine tools.

The NIST Intelligent Systems Division (ISD), under the leadership of Dr. James Albus, has been developing, evolving, and applying a reference model architecture called the NIST Real-time Control System [15] for the last two decades. This RCS is the ISD's proposed solution to the aforementioned issues and requirements. RCS is a hierarchical control structure with each level assigned specific responsibilities. Controllers are employed at each level capable of performing designed behaviors to fulfill the level's responsibilities. The authors will describe the methodology and show how to apply RCS to control system design. There have been earlier reports describing various states of the architecture and its applications [16–21]. The authors describe some advances in the architecture and the methodology.

A key to the development methodology is a consistent software engineering paradigm to facilitate the realization of RCS applications. Since RCS emphasizes controlling engineering systems to perform physical work, RCS prescribes a behavior- or task-oriented system design and analysis [21]. Object-oriented (OO) paradigms [22–25] are emerging as a major methodology for system development. Although there are skeptics, it is generally believed that these object-oriented paradigms provide several significant advantages over some traditional methods, such as structured design and analysis and information engineering in that OO paradigms focus on the depiction of the real world. This makes the OO paradigms consistent with RCS. The authors will address the object aspects of RCS.

Knowledge engineering is an important issue in the field of expert systems. Knowledge engineering may include the processes of acquisition, perception, organization, management, and inference to support decision making. The RCS reference model provides a mechanism to support all these processes. The RCS methodology focuses on a knowledge-based system development procedure. During operations, the RCS-based systems exercise all these processes to perform desired behaviors.

The authors will describe three case study control systems with two objectives in mind. First, the descriptions progressively demonstrate the richness of the RCS architecture, from a generic process template based system to real-time rich sensing and planning systems. Second, the case studies describe the evolution and the road map of the methodology, from finite state machine models to process and interface definitions and to a project plan for fully exercising the architecture and methodology. Case study I is a submarine automation demonstration system project, which is one of the first test cases for the methodology. In this project, most of the behaviors are modeled as state diagrams at the system development stage. This project provides a base execution model for RCS applications.

Case study II applies RCS to the manufacturing domain. An instantiation of RCS, called the Intelligent Systems Architecture for Manufacturing (ISAM) [26, 27], is applied to the overall SIMA project. A NIST testbed called the National Advanced Manufacturing Testbed (NAMT) [28] is used for implementing and testing the prototype systems. In this case study, more RCS capabilities are planned to be implemented, including real-time planning and rich sensory interaction. The ultimate resulting system would exercise the full architectural capability. The project also calls for specifying processes and interfaces, based on the reference model, to facilitate architectural implementation and integration. This specification process will involve industrial and other government agencies' efforts and results. The results will facilitate component technology integration in the architectural framework.

Case study III applies RCS to the intelligent autonomous vehicles domain, ranging from the Army's Next-generation Unmanned Vehicle (XUV) to the U.S. Department of Transportation Crash Avoidance program. 4-D/RCS, an instantiation of RCS [29], has been created for these purposes. The implementation effort will leverage the ISAM project results. Full RCS capability is anticipated in the resulting control systems.

II. THE RCS REFERENCE MODEL

A close study of complex systems, including human reasoning processes, manufacturing systems, and military command structures, reveals some common principles of intelligent processing and control. RCS is based on a generalization of these principles.

A. A Node

The basic operating unit in RCS is a node, or control node, as shown in Fig. 1. The model contains a behavior generation (BG) function that makes decisions

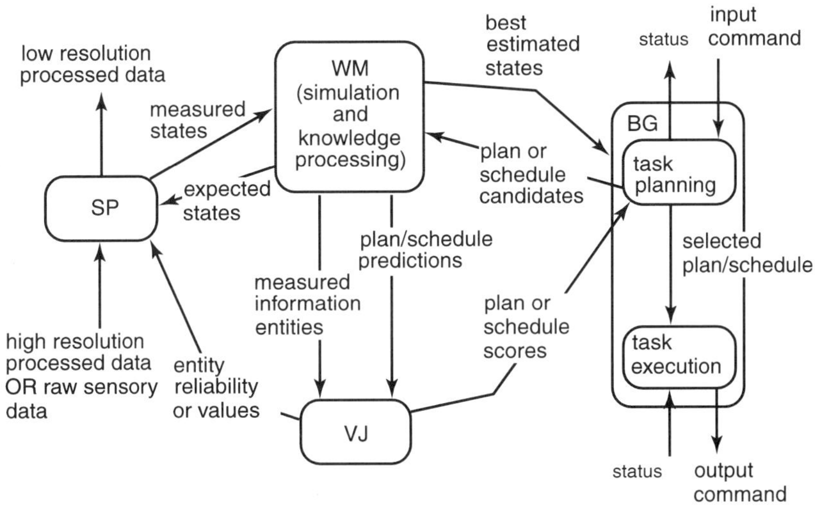

FIGURE 1 An RCS node.

based on the received task commands and on the current state of the world. BG is supported by world modeling (WM), value judging (VJ), and sensory processing (SP) functions [1, 19].

BG employs a task planning function that generates a set of possible plans or schedules. WM simulates these candidates and generates the predicted results. VJ uses a set of cost functions to judge the simulation results and provides the values of these schedule candidates for the BG planning function to determine a final schedule for execution. Note that a schedule is the timing or ordering specifications for a plan [29].

SP processes sensory data and generates measured states for the system. Particular data sets may require different processing algorithms or different gain values for the selected algorithms. The selection process may involve WM and VJ, as the left side of Fig. 1 shows. Figure 1 also shows that SP processes data from lower levels at higher resolutions (with more detail but with narrower scope) and outputs data to higher levels at lower resolutions (with less detail but larger scope).

B. Multiple Resolutions

RCS is a hierarchical architecture that focuses on modeling systems through spatial and temporal decompositions. Higher levels operate in a state space with larger spatial and temporal span but coarser resolution. Rules that guide the hierarchical decomposition with respect to resolution of space and time are based on control theory and biological evidence. In his "Outline for a theory of intelligence," Albus [30] proposed a principle that states:

> In a hierarchically structured, goal-driven, sensory interactive, intelligent control system architecture:
>
> 1. control bandwidth decreases about an order of magnitude at each higher level,
> 2. perceptual resolution of spatial and temporal patterns decreases about an order of magnitude at each higher level,

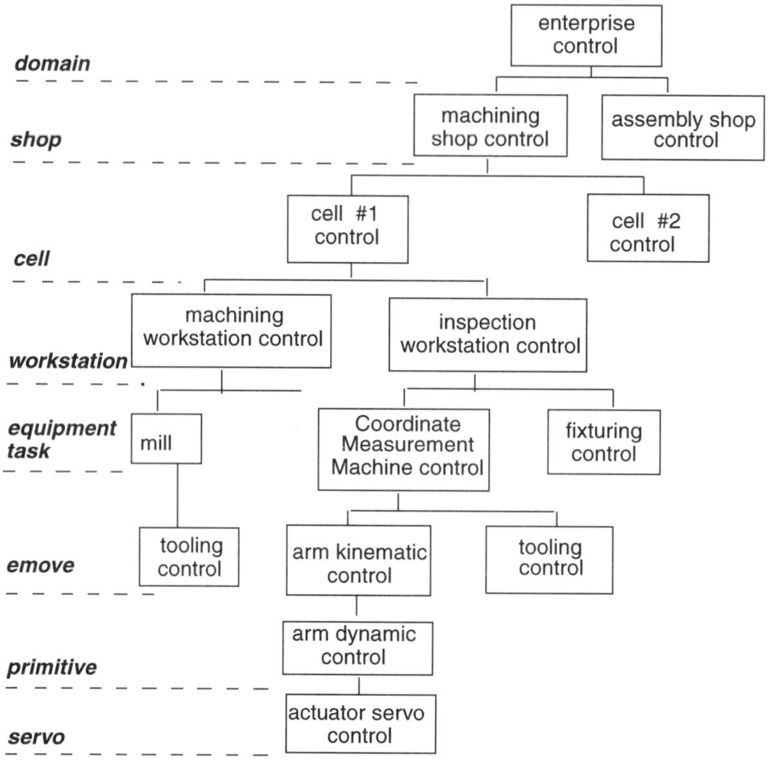

FIGURE 2 RCS control levels based on the principle of multiple levels of resolutions.

3. goals expand in scope and planning horizons expand in space and time about an order of magnitude at each higher level, and
4. models of the world and memories of events decrease in resolution and expand in spatial and temporal range by about an order of magnitude at each higher level.

By following these guidelines, the RCS methodology has a sound basis for decomposing a system at its constituent, resolution levels. RCS provides as many control levels as required to cover the scope of individual problems. These levels form a smooth transition of spatial and temporal resolution from the highest to the lowest levels. Figure 2 illustrates an application of these levels to a manufacturing facility. The levels include application domain (the highest), shop, cell, workstation, equipment, elementary move [or emove (kinematic)], primitive (dynamic), and servo. See [1, 17] for a detailed description of these levels. Each level may have zero or multiple control nodes (except for the highest level, which has one node) all using the same model as described in Section II.A. At each level of the hierarchy, the control for individual and collective physical entities, such as robots, vehicles, workstations, manufacturing shops, and robotic motors, are modeled. Note that if the implementation problem were for the control of a machining center only, then the upper levels of control would become unnecessary.

These guidelines also help operators to understand and anticipate the way a high-level goal can be decomposed into low-level detailed behavior.

C. Behavior and Behavior Generation

RCS applies to intelligent systems that make decisions and perform physical work in real-time. Therefore, behavior, describing actions, as opposed to data, is the most critical aspect driving the control system design. Albus and Meystel [31] defined behavior as "an ordered set of consecutive or concurrent changes among the states registered at the output of the system or subsystems." In a complex system, agents or subsystems are capable of performing certain behaviors. A mechanism is required to coordinate the individual behaviors to form system behavior. This mechanism does not necessarily have to be external to the agents, but can be embedded within the agents themselves and manifest itself as "cooperation."

In RCS, agents or nodes generate behavior through planning and execution processes. The objective of the generated behavior is to command and coordinate the subbehaviors of all the nodes' subordinates. The system behavior may be initiated when a user enters a high-level goal. An incoming task for a manufacturing system may be to "complete the product order." The activity of the highest level node is to decompose the order into the language of the next lower-level group of nodes and assign and schedule the involved groups.

The workstations decompose their received tasks into the languages of their subordinate individual pieces of equipment. The equipment decomposes the incoming tasks into "elementary moves" that are (or are equivalent to) a series of physical motions of the equipment to achieve the task goals. The elementary moves are further decomposed into "primitives" that are (or are equivalent to) dynamic motion commands for the equipment. Finally, the primitives are decomposed at the servo level into the electrical or mechanical signal commands for the equipment actuators.

Manufacturing orders are completed through this behavior generation process that results in the desired machine actuation. Refer to [1, 17] for a detailed description of these levels.

Note that object-oriented techniques also use the term behavior but in a different context [22]. In this chapter the term behavior refers to the definition given here.

D. Behavior as a Principle of Abstraction

Abstraction is defined as denoting the essential characteristics of an object that distinguish it from other objects, while suppressing nonessential details. Different types of abstractions are described in various OO paradigms, including object, class, data, function, and process [22]. The abstraction relationship among objects within a system leads to system hierarchies.

RCS views goal-oriented behaviors as the most important aspect of an intelligent system. Therefore, RCS uses behavior analysis to derive control system hierarchies. Each control node is highlighted with a finite number of tasks that it can perform. This may be referred to as the *task abstraction* or *behavior abstraction*.

E. Organization and Command Authority

Modeling a system through the combination of the multiple levels of resolution and behavior generation concepts forms a control hierarchy. Figure 2 gives an example.

These concepts further establish a relationship of command authority within the control hierarchy. The superior control nodes command the subordinate nodes. The subordinates report back the status of command execution.

F. Object-Oriented Perspectives: Control Nodes and Mapping Behavior to Node Hierarchy as a Means of Encapsulation

Encapsulation publicizes the interface of a model and hides the implementation (procedures and internal data). An RCS hierarchy is composed of the control nodes with a generic functional model as described in Section II.A. The generic control node is considered one of the base types of objects. Additional base types are also being developed [32]. Nodes at different control levels are derived from this base type when extra characteristics that are specific and necessary are added.

In a class declaration within an object-oriented model, the interface is in the public portion and implementation is in the private portion of the model [22]. In RCS, the task structure is integrated with the node hierarchy. Each node has a set of tasks that it is capable of performing. An input command set, corresponding to the task set, is used by the node's superior to command the node's behavior. In the same manner, the node's behavior results in the generation of subcommands for its subordinates.

In this way, in RCS, the nodes' behavioral capabilities are encapsulated via the task set that it is capable of processing. A given node within an RCS hierarchy needs to be aware only of its immediate subordinates' interfaces. It does not need to be concerned about how the subtasks the node passes down are carried out or if the subtasks are further decomposed.

G. Operator Interface

RCS is generic in that it supports a full range of system operation modes, from teleoperation to autonomous. An operator interface is allowed at every level and at any node to facilitate these modes.

1. Basic Principles

Our basic principles for operator interface design are as follows:

- to have a well-defined overall structure and well-defined roles for individual operators;
- to integrate with the system control;
- to integrate with the current operating environment;
- to provide a systematic model of conducting man-in-the-loop control and migrating legacy subsystems;
- to match user requirements and expertise;
- to allow emergency procedures;
- to optimize both real-time performance and operator work load;
- to inform intuitively, in real-time, and to provide as much information as operators require, without overloading;
- to support system service and development, including testing and simulation.

2. Operator Levels of Commanding Authority

To support hierarchical real-time control, in RCS, operator interface functions are divided into six types of levels of commanding authority. Specific applications may not contain all the levels. From the highest to the lowest levels of authority, the level types are as follows:

Level 6: Application domain level operator. This is the highest level. The operator enters and monitors the overall command for the entire control system. In Case Study I, Section IV, the command controller operator belongs to this level.

Level 5: Group level operators. They handle control activities involving either multiple coordinated control entities or multiple coordinated groups of control entities. For example, machines, material handlers, and/or vehicles are often grouped according to the degree of coordination necessary to accomplish a set of tasks. The operators would be interacting with such groups at this level.

Level 4: Equipment or task level operators. These operators deal, through their corresponding controllers, with the control activities of individual major physical entities, such as a single machine or vehicle.

Level 3: Elementary move (emove) or subsystem level operators. The operators may monitor or command such elementary move control activities as avoiding obstacles and kinematic limits, including, in Case Study I, the possible instability of the submarine caused by large bubble (pitch) angles. At this level, an operator is interacting with a major subsystem of a larger machine or vehicle.

Level 2: Primitive (prim) level operators. At this level, an operator might be interacting to control dynamic motions of machine appendages, perhaps setting machine acceleration or directing motion in a particular direction.

Level 1: Actuator level operators. Through their corresponding controllers, these operators deal with direct environmental interaction, by controlling the electrical and mechanical signals that drive the movement of individual actuators toward the goals.

This hierarchical organization also allows a problem with a high level of abstraction to be logically and smoothly transitioned to a set of subproblems with lower levels of abstraction. In this way, the operator interface for a complex problem can be shared by a set of operators with well-defined and limited responsibilities. The operators may act on different levels of abstraction at different times by controlling the modes of operator interaction.

III. RCS METHODOLOGY—THE DEVELOPMENT PROCESS

A. Behavior Orientation, Object Orientation, and Data–Function Orientation

Behavior is considered part of an object's model in most of the object-oriented methods. For example, Coad and Yourdon [24] describe parameters, such as frequency and location, that control a radar system's behavior. Shlaer and Mellor [25] describe real-world things as having stages in their behavior patterns. However, the distinction is, in OO methods, objects are the defining element and "behavior is a part of objects." The RCS methodology is "behavior-oriented." Behavior is the most critical aspect in the control system software. The analysis of behaviors and tasks drives the system development effort while the related physical subsystems or components serve as a part of the constraints for the analysis.

From a global perspective, the system behavior determines an RCS hierarchy and the underlying control flow. In RCS, developers typically analyze and identify system behavior before designing control nodes, or "objects," to perform the behavior. This concept has not been emphasized in most object-oriented methods. We believe that this behavior orientation could significantly strengthen the general object-oriented methods, particularly in the large, complex, real-time control problems dealing with physical tasks where the RCS architecture excels.

In the RCS methodology, the analysis of data and data processing are driven by the task performance requirements. Data and processors are also organized to support task performance.

B. The Methodology Steps

RCS is intended for systems that generate intelligent behaviors to achieve desired goals. The first issue in the system development effort is understanding the problem area; i.e., what is the physical operating environment for the system to be developed and how will the system operate in that environment. The RCS methodology prescribes a behavior analysis and scenario development process to address this first issue. The development process is shown in Fig. 3. Designers may develop the operational scenarios through reviewing literature, such as operating manuals, and through interacting with domain experts. The latter is the most effective to obtain first-hand knowledge. Among the RCS applications, in the submarine automation project, the researchers interacted with several retired submarine commanders throughout the project period. In the NAMT Inspection Workstation project, the researchers interviewed shop floor inspectors. In the Army Next Generation Unmanned Vehicle Demo III project, the researchers coordinated with the Army Mounted Maneuver Battlefield Laboratory (MMBL) in Ft. Knox, Kentucky. The details are described in later sections.

In the behavior analysis and scenario development process, the system goals and functional requirements are analyzed in terms of how the users expect to use the systems and what they expect the systems to perform. Goals drive behaviors and scenarios. Behaviors and scenarios define system requirements, including those of subsystems, information, communication, and integration. This behavior analysis process is constrained by factors including conformance to standards, legacy system compatibility, technology limitations, and programmatic requirements.

In the behavior analysis process, the "action verbs" in scenario descriptions are identified as task commands. The task commands are structured, using the multiple resolution principle, as described in Section II.B, as task trees. These task commands and parameters serve as the vocabulary to model the intelligent behavior of the control system.

Correlating the reference model with the task knowledge results in a control hierarchy. Iterations are required to obtain a control hierarchy with an appropriate

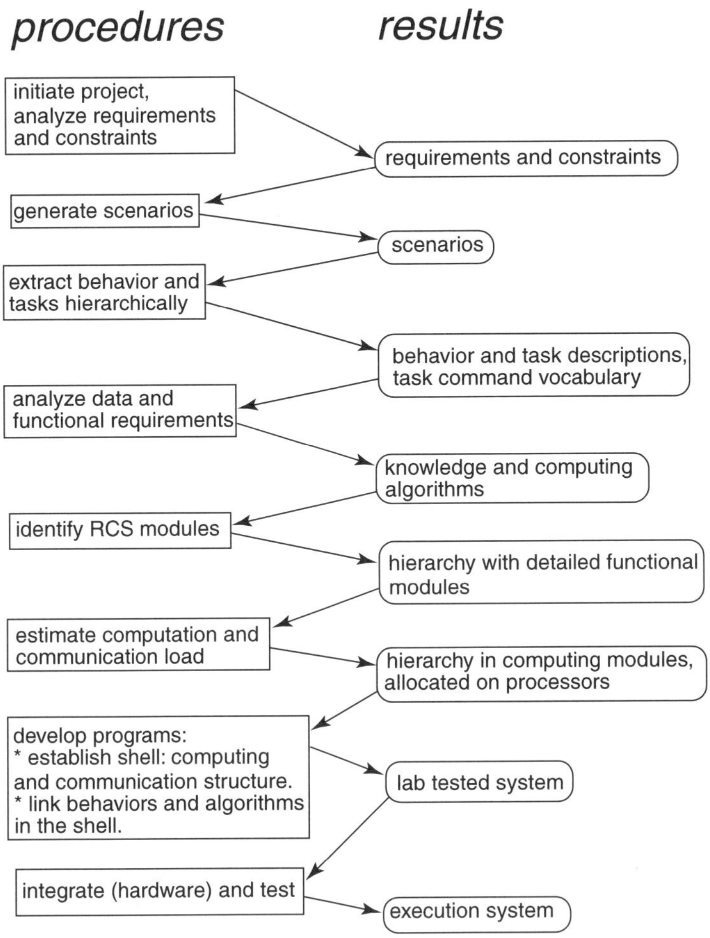

FIGURE 3 RCS development process.

number of control levels and nodes and to map the task trees onto the hierarchy at the appropriate levels of abstraction.

The task knowledge is further analyzed to identify the explicit data, communication, and computation requirements. It is emphasized that only explicitly and specifically stated requirements can be programmed into executable software. This process also scopes the system capability in the sense that the developers must determine how high a priority it is to implement a particular task and whether the task performance is autonomous, semiautonomous, or manual. To execute a task, developers determine whether a certain piece of information is provided a priori or generated online. Next, the developers must determine which sensors, processing algorithms, computing platforms, and databases to use.

For example, in a manufacturing scenario that involves a machining sequence, one issue is whether a schedule is generated offline for selection and interpretation into the machine native language by the machine controller, or, alternatively, whether the schedule is to be generated by an on-board, real-time, planning system that operates on, for example, a computer-aided design (CAD) model of the part.

In a military scenario, when multiple next generation unmanned vehicles are to perform a reconnaissance, surveillance, and target acquisition (RSTA) mission, the developer needs to determine whether an area map is given, and at what resolution, or whether the vehicles are to build the map as they survey the area. The differences would affect the sensor selection and other design decisions.

The results of this scenario-development and behavior-analysis process include the design of a control hierarchy, the input and output of each node in the hierarchy, the behavior of the nodes, and all the processing and data requirements. These results are organized per RCS reference model.

Computation and communication load is estimated to form computing processes. A template-based approach is used to first build a system shell for the hierarchical control nodes before knowledge, processing modules, and behavior modules are linked in the shell. Laboratory and field tests are performed and results are used to modify the behaviors, the processing algorithms, and the computation and communication load distribution among the computing processes.

C. Behavior Analysis, Scenario Development, and Domain Expert Interaction

In a military scenario, a behavior to be analyzed would be for the XUV scout platoon to "Establish Observation Post", in which the first subactivity is to "Receive Mission". The RCS developers determine that the mission statement would be implemented as a task command in the control hierarchy. In preparing interactions with a crew of Army soldiers, the developers must be prepared to explore, or verify, with the soldiers the data included in the mission statement. The developers are to generate a list of questions to stimulate the interactions, to catalyze the soldiers' stories, and to maximize the scenario descriptions useful to system development. The questions related to the mission statement may include the following:

- The mission statement may list named areas of interest (NAIs). What are the purposes and how are they specified?—The answer is that the upper level commanders would identify areas that potentially contain useful features as NAIs. For example, areas containing rough terrain may be good for defensive purposes. NAIs are specified with four coordinates to enclose the interested areas.
- The mission statement may list observation post (OP) sites. Is it sufficient to describe them as a list of coordinates? Is there any other information that needs to be specified, such as time to reach the sites? What are some considerations in selecting an OP?—The answers are the following: An OP can be specified via either coordinates or landmarks. Additional information is often required when an OP is assigned. Timing constraints are critical when fire suppression at a certain time on the OP is planned. The upper level commander must associate this information with the OP for the XUV to avoid the fire. Some considerations for selecting an OP are whether it is cleared, it allows an escape route, and it supports the planned areas of advances (AOAs).

On the opposite side of the interaction, architectural developers may provide soldiers some flavor of how the behaviors may be implemented, such as: The section level behavior generation planner module may contain a main flow chart describing the "Establish Observation Post" activity. At various steps in the flow chart, the planner queries the map and the knowledge base (both are parts of the world model) to either make a decision or invoke a specific planner. For example:

Query WM⟨Has area been cleared?⟩

⟨Yes⟩ (1) Invoke "formation planner" to determine a formation for the vehicles to proceed.
(2) Invoke "path planner" to generate waypoints for the vehicle formation to follow.

⟨No⟩ (1) Invoke "path planner" to generate coordinated vehicle paths to conduct area reconnaissance.
(2) Command vehicles to conduct certain RSTA subsystem activities, including target identification.
(3) Command vehicles to conduct certain weapon subsystem activities, including preparing for fire suppression support.

The section level would have an executor for each vehicle in the section. The executors execute the generated schedules containing steps involving various vehicle behaviors (navigation, RSTA, etc.).

All of the proposed activities need to be verified with or obtained from the soldiers to be credible. Some consensus can be reached as to steps that are essential and must be implemented, or are less significant and designated for future expansion.

The results of this scenario-development and behavior-analysis process include the design of a control hierarchy, the input and output of each node in the hierarchy, the behavior of the nodes, and all the processing and data requirements. Later sections provide implementation examples.

D. Structuring Behaviors in Hierarchy

Scenarios are described in a natural language form. The next step toward a computational system in the RCS methodology is to structure the descriptions hierarchically. The following example (see Fig. 4) illustrates the process.

In a manufacturing inspection scenario [33], the current activity is to perform system initialization to prepare for inspection tasks. The initial control hierarchy has been drafted (see the bottom of the drawing for the middle levels of the entire hierarchy). The workstation (WS) receives a "initForInspect" command. The first subtask that WS decomposes for the subordinates, Measurement (MS) and Fixturing (FX), is "equipSetup". The arrowhead pointing downward shows the command process. MS and FX decompose their received task command but such activities are omitted from the diagrams. MS and FX report to WS a "Done", illustrated by an upward arrowhead, when the subtasks are completed. In WS, the next step for initialization is "calibrateCMM" (coordinate measuring machine), for MS only. MS decomposes the task into a sequence of subtasks, including "calibrate Reference Sphere" and "calibrate Probe", for its Tooling subordinate. These activities

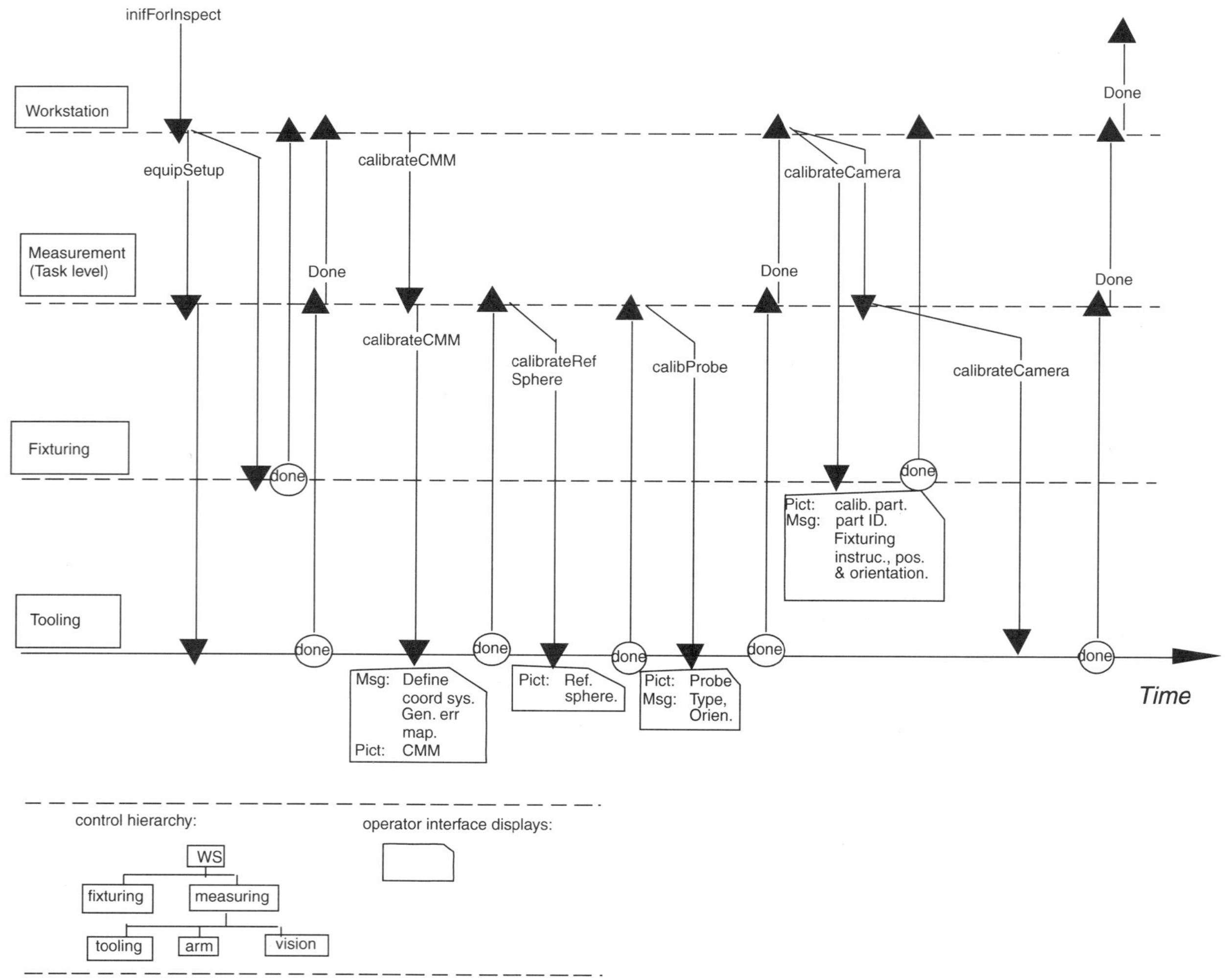

FIGURE 4 Mapping behavior on hierarchy.

include aligning all the coordinates and using the reference ball to calibrate the probe on the CMM. See [33] for a detailed explanation of these activities. In performing these activities, the Tooling operator is given instruction displays as an aid. The displays include what to do (to define the coordinate system) and how to do it (orientation of the probe). Pictures provide further assistance.

Once Tooling and MS are done with calibrating the CMM, WS issues the final activity for the initialization task, "calibrate Camera". Once the "Done" is rippled back from the low levels to WS, it sends a "Done" to its superior.

The later sections on implementation cases use either this method as is or a modified version to perform RCS development.

E. Template-Based System Implementation

In RCS, control nodes perform designed behaviors. The generic structure of the control nodes warrants the creation of process-template sets for the control nodes and their submodules. As such, the control nodes are designed via the behavior paradigm and yet implemented in an object-oriented notion. The generic command and status communication protocol in the RCS hierarchy warrants a separate set of templates.

1. Functional View, Multiple Granularity, and Current Scope

Figure 5 shows a generic processing view of an RCS control node. The approach is to group the boxes to form process templates. For example, there may be a node template. There may also be templates for individual node functions, such as behavior generation and sensory processing. Figure 6 illustrates this effect. The granularity depends on applications, as the templates would be further derived

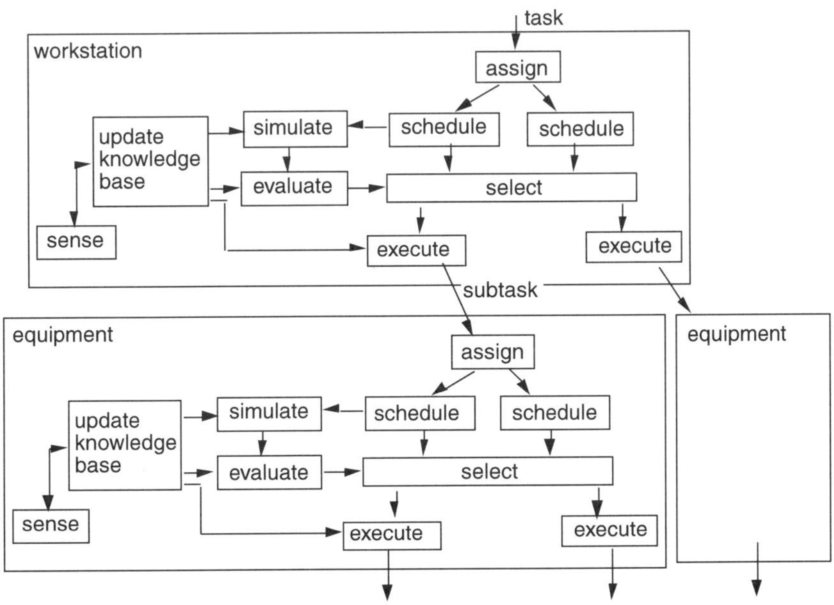

FIGURE 5 Functional Layout of RCS Process templates.

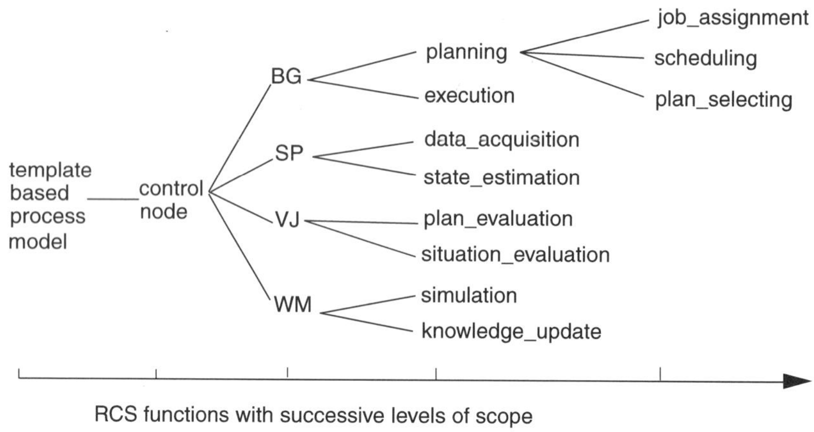

FIGURE 6 Process templates may cover different functional scopes of RCS node.

and instantiated at different control levels and applications. The algorithms in the templates may be different. The behavior generation functions may be suitable to be modeled using a finite-state-machine-based process template. Such a finite-state-machine (FSM) model may not be suitable for a knowledge-base maintenance function. See [29] for a description of the sensory processing template.

In software implementation of a control hierarchy, the nodes and their functions are grouped, according to computation and communication load distribution, to form independent computing processes. All the control nodes should contain all the functions as described in Fig. 5. In a situation when a control node performs a significant amount of planning and scheduling work for a number of subordinates, the node's job assignor (JA), schedulers (SC), plan selector, simulator models, and state estimation algorithms may all be complex and executed independently in a distributed environment. When a particular planning algorithm calls for intensive communication among the JA, SC, simulation, and value judgment modules, they may be grouped as an independent computing process, which is referred to as a planning process in this chapter. Note that this chapter focuses on the behavior generation process templates. The sensory processing and world modeling aspects are left for future development.

2. Base-Class Generic Process Template

The template approach has been an evolutionary process in the NIST Intelligent Systems Division. An earlier paper [17] described a previous implementation. Here we describe the latest [34]. Figure 7 shows the generic process template, which, in the context of C++, is called a base class. The template describes the basic processing flow of most of the RCS modular computing processes, or abbreviated as processes. The arrows indicate the process' communication, based on a nonblocking command and response protocol. This template is further expanded to form specific RCS functions, such as the finite-state-machine-based execution model, the planner (PL) template, and the executor (EX) template. The next section describes the template expansion process, as a part of the methodology, whereas the later case-study descriptions show the template expansion results.

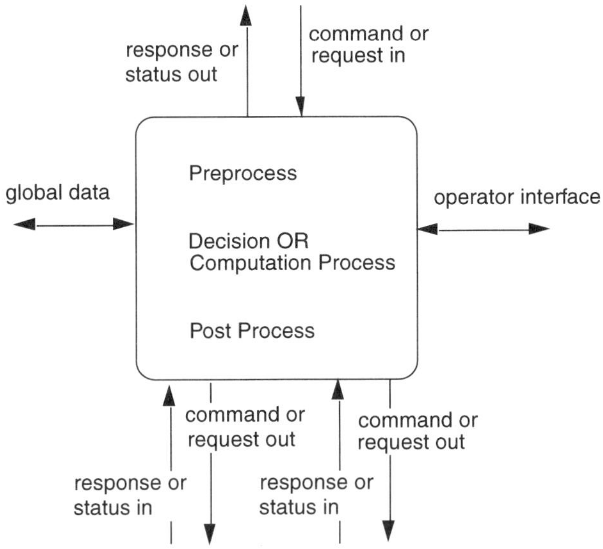

FIGURE 7 A base class independent process generic process template.

In the base-class, generic, process template, a process has the following communication channels:

- a pair of command input and status output channels to the superior processes;
- as many pairs of command output and status input channels as the number of subordinate processes the process has;
- a pair of operator input–output channels;
- As many data read–write channels as necessary to support the decision-making process.

This model is consistent with RCS that addresses the one-writer multiple-reader paradigm for each data entity.

This process executes the following functions:

- Preprocessing:
  - Read in required globally shared data. Read input data from all the coordinating processes, typically including the superior and subordinate processes and the operators. The Internet or any network may be used to implement the operator interface function to facilitate distributed system activities.
  - Evaluate thresholds, flags, or status or process any other necessary prerequisites to support the following computing process.
- Computing or decision process:
  - Invoke a computing algorithm based on the world state and the execution status of the subordinates. In the situation where this base class is used to implement finite state machines, this process would select and execute a state table. The first implementation case, in a later section, will describe this FSM model in further detail.

- Postprocessing:
  - Write decisions (subtask commands) to subordinate processes. Write to operator when required. Post global data. Post responses or status reports to superior or upstream process in general.
- Support facility:
  - Real-time performance algorithms compute features such as the percentage of the total execution time that is spent on particular states. An operator interface function allows accessing the command and status communication channels to monitor input and output.

3. Command and Status Templates

RCS prescribes a command and status execution model. Each command is associated with a serial number. The subordinates who receive the commands are to verify the numbers against the numbers associated with the last received commands. The subordinates then echo the current serial numbers back. The superior is to verify the echoed numbers to determine whether its commands have been successfully received.

In addition to the echo, the subordinates also send the superior the information on command execution status: executing, done, or error. In a finite-state-machine execution model, the subordinates also send the state number information to indicate the particular segments of the state tables that the subordinates are executing.

The authors use a set of base classes [34] as the templates for implementing system command and status messages. This serial-number-and-echo model is also extended to general request-and-response activities among the node processes. Note that the message implementation must use the same communication system as in the generic process base class.

4. Template Inheritance

The RCS methodology employs multiple layers of inheritance [23] for the templates. A base-class, generic-process template establishes the communication and processing flow. These properties are inherited to form the executor and planning templates. The executor contains the additional functionality of invoking emergency action when normal execution fails. The planning template contains the additional functionality of handling the planning horizon. These two templates are further inherited when they are used by specific applications. Figure 8 shows this effect. In this way, common RCS characteristics are implemented consistently. This method also reuses common code systematically.

The base-class, process template is also used to implement a finite-state-machine model. This model reads all of its inputs in the preprocessing section of the template. The decision process selects and uses a state table or graph to decide its next state and performs its data processing based on the computed state transition. The postprocessing writes all of its outputs and waits for all its next execution cycle, which is usually based on a time-based execution clock.

5. Generic Shell: Using Templates to Build RCS Nodes and Functions

Developers use the templates to build their applications. The process templates contain standard RCS interface channels. When implementing a node or a function, for example, the machining control node planning module shown in Fig. 9 as the

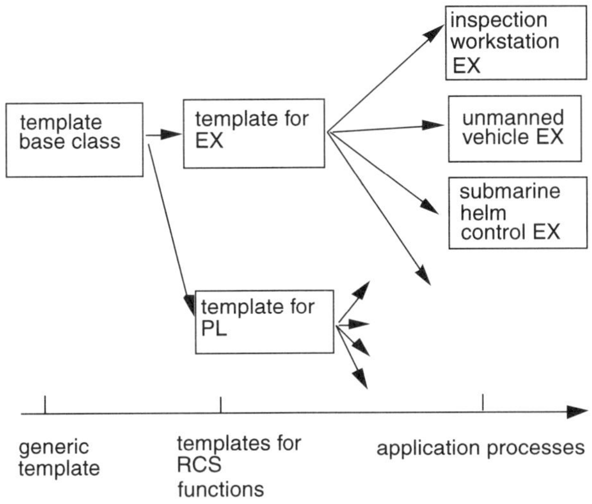

FIGURE 8 Templates inherit common RCS characteristics.

"mc PL/Sim/VJ/PS" box, the developers specify this box's interfacing modules. The interfacing modules include the workstation, "mc SPWM" (sensory processing and world model), "mc EX Motion", and "mc EX Tooling", These modules are connected via the generic interfaces as provided in the base-class, process template. The developers, then, specify the data that go across each of the interface lines. The following is a list of RCS interfaces being used and yet evolving:

- The PL/Sim/VJ/PS sends a schedule to EX. The schedule can be a manufacturing process schedule, a navigation path for mobile robots, a pointer to a state graph, etc.

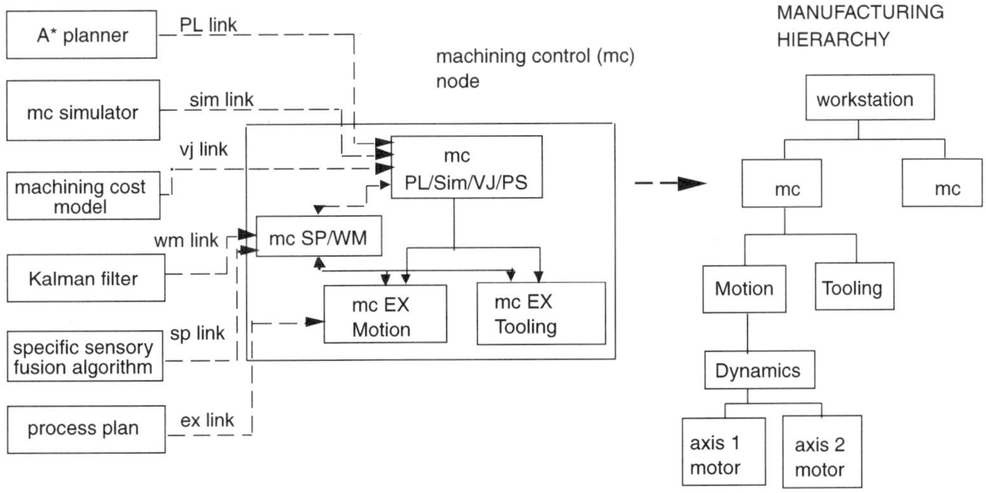

FIGURE 9 Applying templates to system architectural implementation.

- The EX sends a task command to the subordinate PL. The subtask command is typically a step in the schedule. The EX may send more than one schedule step to meet the subordinate's planning-ahead requirements.
- The SPWM sends supporting data to PL and EX. PL and EX may require the same types of data but PL requires the data that apply through the planning horizon whereas EX may need the data applied to the current time. In a manufacturing environment, a planner may need to know whether the resources are available for the next X minutes in order to generate a schedule for the X minutes, whereas an EX needs to know whether the resource is available right now in order to control the next plan step. In a path planning situation, the PL and EX may need map data or obstacle lists.

A linking facility is employed to allow specific algorithms to be integrated to perform required functions. A control module template is associated with a linker template that lists the kinds of software library or processing algorithms that the control module may need. A PL template typically links different types of software from what an EX does. In a UNIX operating system environment, the linking procedure is done via the Makefile facility. In the Fig. 9 example, the planner module employs an A^* search-based planner [35], shown in dotted lines. The EX may also link in a pregenerated, state-table-based plan for execution. These are shown as dashed lines. The linking process also facilitates code sharing.

Developers can apply the process templates at an early stage and construct a skeleton control hierarchy capable of interfacing, linking, and executing individual component technologies. This is called the generic shell for the targeted control system. This shell serves as the backbone for the system operations. The developers construct a control-node "shell" and the control-hierarchy "shell" by specifying the interfaces, shown in Fig. 9 as connecting the solid lines, and by identifying the required algorithms, shown in Fig. 9 as connecting the dashed lines. Note, again, that the authors plan to revisit, in the future, the issue of implementing the SPWM process template.

6. Combining Behavior-Oriented, Object-Oriented, and Functional Decomposition Paradigms

The method described in the preceding section shows how RCS applies the three prominent system development paradigms: a behavioral orientation drives system analysis and design; an object orientation facilitates software design and implementation; and a functional view describes control nodes explicitly and in detail. Finally, in system operations, behaviors are generated by objects serving as system control nodes.

7. Analysis and Implementation Structure

The RCS methodology proposes a generic and comprehensive logical structure to facilitate analysis and implementation. This structure identifies and integrates the following five hierarchies: control, simulation, animation, operator interface (OI) for control, and OI for simulation, as seen in Fig. 10. The reasons for requiring these hierarchies are as follows:

The control hierarchy performs real-time system control to accomplish missions. The lowest level nodes send electrical, hydraulic, or mechanical

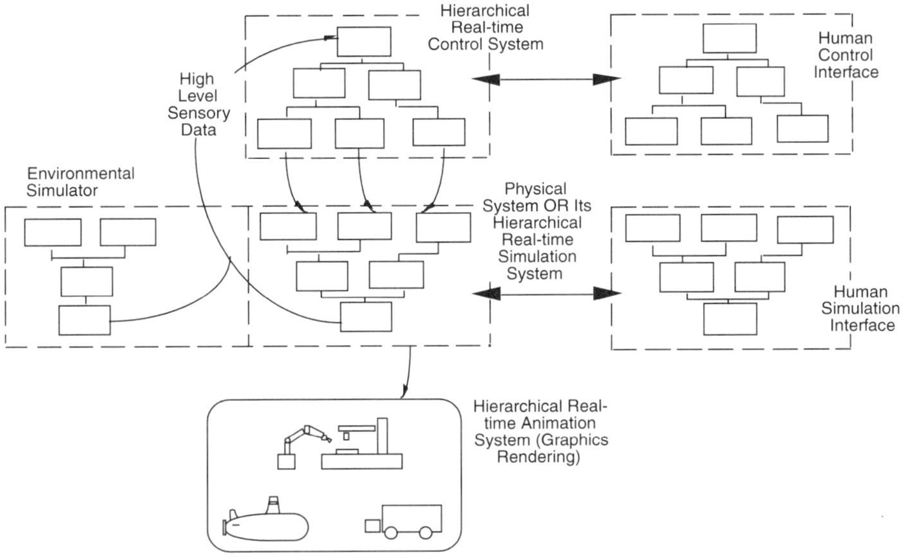

FIGURE 10 A software structure for analysis and implementation.

control signals to physical actuators. However, there are many situations in which simulation is either extremely useful or typically required. The situations include laboratory development, testing, training, and maintenance functions. Inside the control nodes, simulation is also used to facilitate planning.

Simulation may take a different context or cover a different scope in these different situations. Simulators typically employ kinematic or dynamic models of the physical systems to be controlled or of other environmental objects that are within the controlling scope. At different hierarchical control levels, control nodes output task commands at different levels of abstraction and anticipate effects at the corresponding levels of abstraction. Therefore, it is beneficial to have the simulation also hierarchically structured to provide the anticipated effects. The lowest level simulator nodes, that is, the actuator simulators, receive control signals and compute the mechanical movements of each actuator. The next higher level simulation nodes integrate the simulated actuator movements and compute the system dynamics. The same process continues up the simulation levels that correspond to the control levels. As such, the resulting simulated states at different levels can be fed back to the higher levels of the control hierarchy via the simulated sensors.

The environmental simulation is treated in the same manner.

Animation performs a graphic rendering of the simulation results, at, or close to, real-time. The animator may also be hierarchically structured to form a close correspondence to the simulator. Animation does not compute the dynamic nor kinematic behaviors of the objects.

The RCS architecture specifies that all the nodes permit operator interaction. This is why, in Fig. 10, the OI is described as a one-to-one correspondence to the control and simulation hierarchies. Note that this shows a functional relationship. In implementation, it is possible not to follow the one-to-one relationship. A single operator may use a keyboard as the input device to interact with multiple control nodes. In case study I, the authors demonstrate that an operator display interacts with multiple nodes.

We also propose a logical distinction between the control and the simulation OI. Control OI may allow switching among multiple control modes: manual, autonomous, or semiautonomous. It may allow a control override from an operator in emergency situations. Simulation OI involves setting up parameters or triggering external events for the simulator software to generate desired simulation behavior. This simulation OI capability allows us to test the performance of the control systems.

IV. CASE STUDY I, FINITE STATE MACHINES, SIMULATOR TEMPLATES, AND OPERATOR INTERFACE FOCUSED IMPLEMENTATION

RCS has been applied to many control systems [21, 36–40]. In this section, the authors describe the submarine automation demonstration system project that was supported by the Defense Advanced Research Projects Agency (DARPA) Maritime Systems Technology Office. This project was one of the first test cases for the development steps described in Section III. The software demonstration system contains multiple levels in its control hierarchy, simulation, and animation [18, 41]. The authors studied and extended the base-class, process template to all these software aspects, that is, control hierarchy, operator interface, simulation, and animation.

Submarines often conduct missions in hostile and uncertain environments in both peacetime and wartime. Crew members routinely make critical decisions at many levels of authority in a coordinated and concurrent fashion while the submarine is underway. A huge volume of information, including sensory data, mission and systems status, a priori knowledge, and mission requirements, must be processed, organized, and made available to support the decision-making process in real-time. In today's submarines most of the information produced by the sophisticated submarine subsystems is manually organized, evaluated, and communicated between watchstations by crew members. As submarine subsystem technology has advanced, crew size and, in turn, submarine size have increased to handle the information processing load. Therefore, the current challenge is how to process and communicate the information in a smarter and more efficient way without increasing crew size. The ultimate challenge is crew size reduction. As the United States is trying to realign its economic and defense priorities, cost effectiveness and operational efficiency are vital to the strength of its defense forces. Automation, computer, and control system architecture technologies have advanced enough to meet these challenges.

This project demonstrated, in simulation, automatic maneuvering and engineering service systems for a 637-class nuclear submarine. The maneuvering system involved steering, trim, depth, and propulsion control. A rudimentary engineering service system demonstrated the ship's ability to respond to a casualty report. Ventilation lineup's are reconfigured in real-time. Sophisticated maneuvers were performed to clear baffles, to raise the depth to enable the diesel engine to perform emergency ventilation, and to engage the ship's emergency propulsion control. Human–computer interaction was described in detail.

In this project, all the behaviors are described as state diagrams and tables at the system development stage except for ice avoidance capability. Therefore, the template utilization is limited to a finite-state-machine model. The other RCS functions, such as sensory processing, world modeling, and ice avoidance planning, are embedded in the base-class, process template as an implementation simplification.

A. Scenarios

ISD researchers collaborated with retired submarine commanders to develop the demonstration scenarios. Based on the preestablished goals of the simulated submarine, they described, in detail and in every aspect, how a submarine would operate to achieve the specified goals. The following are some of the guidelines used to maximize the relevant knowledge captured from the domain experts. The developers did not impose any structural constraints during their descriptions. The commanders were encouraged to use the submarine terminology. The main role of the developers at this stage of interaction was to be goal driven, to be intelligent listeners, and to ask stimulating questions sparsely to catalyze their stories.

A brief introduction of the submarine mechanisms is given first to facilitate understanding.

1. Maneuvering Mechanisms

A submarine has a number of mechanisms for hydrodynamic control of its depth, buoyancy, orientation, and speed (see Fig. 11). The authors briefly introduce a selective set of them:

- main ballast tanks;
- variable ballast tanks;
- fairwater or sail planes;
- stern planes;
- rudder planes;
- propulsion mechanisms.

The sailors use the main ballast tanks (MBTs) for gross control of the ship's buoyancy, specially for submarine submerging and surfacing. If the six tanks are

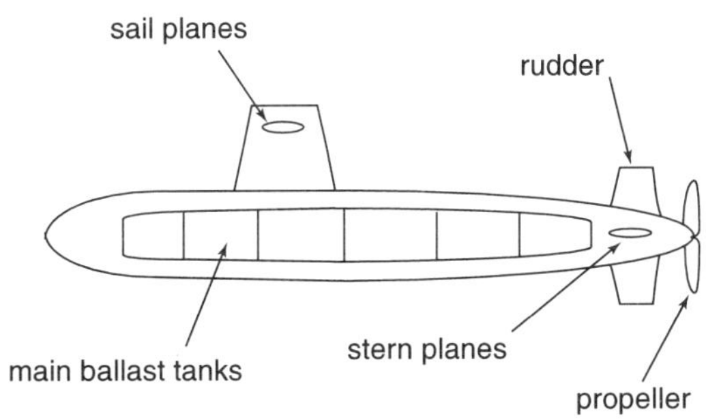

FIGURE 11 Submarine hydrodynamic control mechanisms.

flooded (completely filled), the submarine gains negative buoyancy and the ship submerges. If the tanks are blown (emptied), the submarine gains positive buoyancy and surfaces. The tanks are blown by admitting high-pressure air through valves at their tops. Conversely, they are flooded by allowing the air at the top of the tanks to leave through the vent valves while seawater floods through ports at the bottom of the tanks. The submarine may gain its neutral buoyancy when the MBTs are full and the variable ballast tanks are at their prescribed levels.

The variable ballast tanks are used for small adjustments in buoyancy and orientation. "Variable ballast" as used in this paper refers to any of the following tanks: forward, aft, water round torpedo, auxiliary, and depth control. An example of buoyancy control via variable ballast follows. At greater depths the pressure of the water outside the vessel is much higher and causes the pressure hull to contract. The weight of the ship remains the same; however, the volume of the water it displaces decreases. The result is negative buoyancy and the ship will start to sink. Blowing water from the variable ballast tanks, which decreases the weight of the ship, may be sufficient to stabilize the submarine's buoyancy. The variable ballast tanks are also utilized for trim–orientation control. Weight distribution in a submarine may change after it has been at sea for some time; for example, the supplies that were brought on board might be consumed, which results in a change in forward-and-aft weight distribution. Specifically, the submarine will experience a downward pointing pitch (the bow will be at greater depth than the stern). Water may be transferred between the forward and aft trim tanks to resolve the imbalance.

The fairwater or sail planes are located on the conning tower and have a range of $\pm 22^\circ$. The stern planes are located at the rear of the submarine and have a range of $\pm 27^\circ$. These planes are used for depth control, either in combination or separately. Their distance from the center of mass provides a means for changing the pitch of the submarine. The rudder provides a means for steering the submarine left or right with limits on its range of $\pm 37^\circ$.

The turbine is the main propulsion mechanism, which enables the submarine to travel "ahead" at a commanded speed. A DC motor provides propulsion power during emergency situations.

2. Traverse through Bering Strait Scenario

In this demonstration scenario, a 637-class submarine traverses the Bering Strait in stealth mode. Much of the travel will be under ice, which creates a need for obstacle avoidance to be resolved by the control hierarchy. Fluctuations in water density may require maneuvering mechanism adjustments. The submarine encounters changes in seawater density at freshwater runoffs, where rivers of fresh water cause the water density to drop suddenly. The drop in the density of the seawater will cause the ship to have negative buoyancy and it will start sinking.

3. Open Sea Maneuver and Casualty Responses Scenario

In this demonstration scenario, the submarine is conducting a submerged transit of the open ocean at its standard speed (15 knots, or 7.7 m/s) and at a keel depth of 120 m. A watchstander—a submarine term meaning a crew member who is assigned to a designated onboard location, which itself is called a watchstation, to perform prespecified duties—informs the maneuvering room on the sound powered phone circuit that there is fire in the lower level engine room. The fire is reported to be in the vicinity of the main lubrication (lube) oil pumps. The Engineering Officer of the Watch (EOOW) passes the word to the Officer of the Deck (OOD) in the control room on both the sound powered phones and the intercom announcing system.

The OOD directs the ballast control panel (BCP) operator to pass the word on the general announcing system (1MC), "Fire in the engine room. All hands on EABs" (emergency air breathing system masks), and to sound the general alarm. The OOD completes the following actions for coming to periscope depth:

- clearing baffles;
- checking for sonar contacts, close contacts;
- slowing and changing depth (ahead one-third, keel depth 18 m);
- raising the periscope.

Upon hearing the general alarm the crew proceeds to their assigned general emergency (battle) stations; relief of the section watchstanders occurs.

The damage control party fights the fire in the engine room. On indication of decreasing main lubrication (lube) oil pressure, the EOOW recommends to the OOD that propulsion be shifted to the emergency propulsion motor (EPM) to secure the main lube oil to the propulsion turbines.

The OOD orders, "All stop, shift propulsion to the EPM." The shaft rotation is stopped and the clutch is used to disengage the shaft from the turbines and the EPM circuit breaker is closed. The EOOW reports to the OOD that he is prepared to "answer bells on the EPM." The OOD orders "Ahead two-thirds," which maintains enough speed for depth and steering control. The EPM operator operates the hand wheel to control the EPM and increase the motor speed to ahead two-thirds.

The damage control party reports to the EOOW that "The fire is out, the reflash watch is stationed." The EOOW relays this word to the OOD. The OOD directs the word to be passed "Prepare to emergency ventilate the engine room with the diesel." The BCP selects the ventilation lineup, setting it to emergency ventilate the engine room using the diesel engine. When the lineup is proper, the BCP operator reports to the OOD "Prepared to emergency ventilate the engine room with the diesel." The OOD directs "Commence snorkeling." The diesel engine is started and emergency ventilation of the engine room is commenced to remove the smoke and noxious gases from the engine room. The OOD directs that the atmosphere analyzer be used to sample the engine room atmosphere. The atmosphere sample shows that the carbon monoxide level in the engine room is 800 ppm. The ballast control panel operator uses the ventilation control panel to determine that with this level of carbon monoxide (CO) and ventilation configuration, it will take 80 minutes to reduce the CO level to an acceptable 5 ppm.

As the emergency ventilation of the engine room with the diesel continues, the atmosphere throughout the ship is checked in several locations. In areas where the atmosphere analyzer shows normal conditions, the OOD grants permission for the removal of emergency air breathing system masks (EABs). When the atmosphere in the engine room reaches acceptable conditions the OOD will order "Secure emergency ventilation of the engine room with the diesel, recirculate." The BCP operator will use the ventilation control panel to line up for normal submerged ventilation. The OOD will order "Secure from General Emergency. Secure from fire in the engine room." The normal underway watch section will resume the watch. The diesel engine and generator will continue to be used to supply power for the emergency propulsion motor until the main lube oil system is again ready to supply lubrication to the turbine bearings. When the main lube oil system is restored, the turbines are warmed up with steam, the EPM is ordered to "All stop" and then the clutch reengages the turbine and the shaft. The EPM circuit breaker is opened. Propulsion orders are again answered using the main engines and propulsion turbines.

B. Behavior Analysis

Developers follow the scenarios and identify the events and entities including control system tasks, simulation events, and involved control nodes. These events and entities are put, in order, on the appropriate parts of the logical structure as described in Fig. 10. This results in a system analysis diagram as shown in Fig. 12. The tasks and events correspond to the verbs of the scenario descriptions. The control nodes correspond to, but are not equal to, the sailors performing the operations as stated in the scenario descriptions. In the scenario, the first event that occurred was a report on a lube oil fire. In the system design, this malfunction should be initiated by an environmental simulator operator interface (OI, see Fig. 13 for the implemented OI). Once the simulator receives the trigger, the smoke generation simulator ramps up the smoke contamination values. Following the arrows on the diagram, the control system employs a ventilation subsystem sensor that detects the contamination and reports it to the engineering system node. In this exercise, the scenario description is mapped onto the complete software system structure.

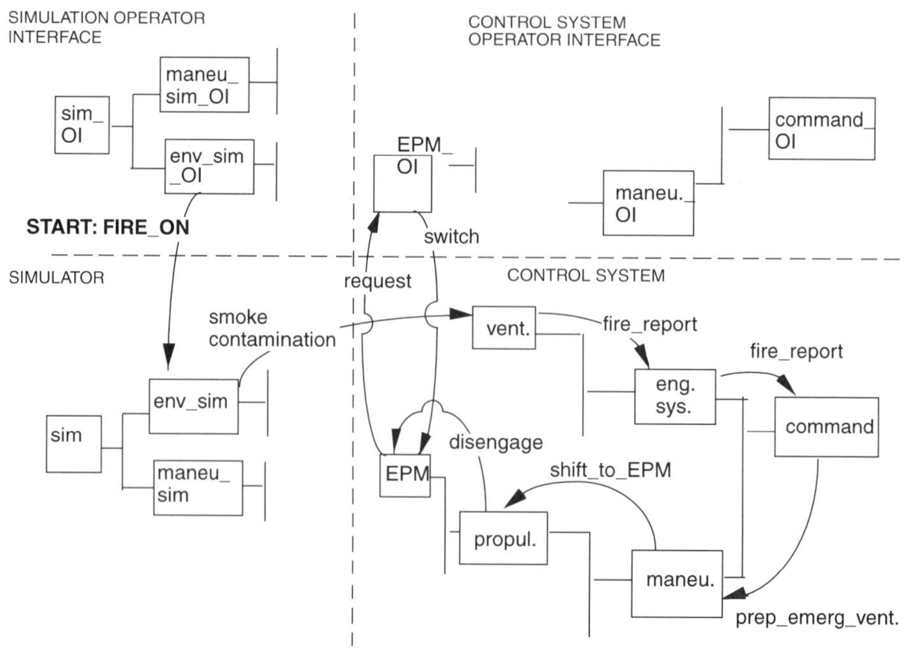

FIGURE 12 Task analysis diagram.

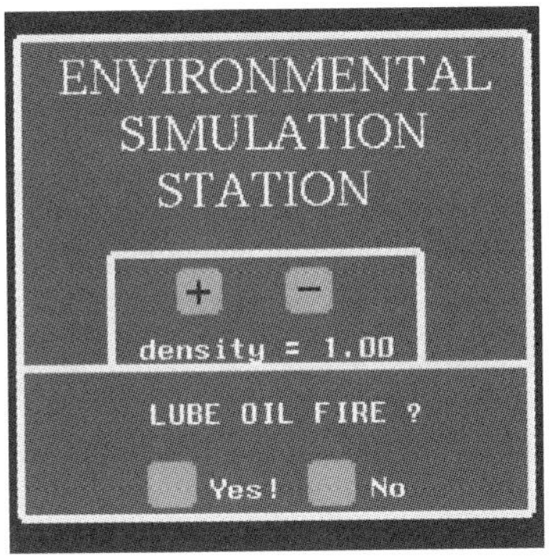

FIGURE 13 Environmental simulation operator interface.

The developers then model, via state diagrams, the sentences in the scenarios with which the verbs are associated. The state-diagram-development process also reveals the data and the data processors that are required to support the state transition processes. These state diagrams and data processors are associated back with the node tasks. The control system behavior generator process selects and executes proper state diagrams based on the system goals and the environmental situations.

Figure 14 shows the resulting control hierarchy. Figures 15 and 16 show the resulting task structures. RCS is scalable. Therefore, systems can be expanded or reduced. The shaded control nodes are added at a late project period to support the newly required open sea maneuver scenario.

A task tree provides a structure for organizing the system knowledge. The two task trees support the two scenarios, while task behaviors are shared for different scenarios when applicable. Multiple, higher plans may require the same set of lower

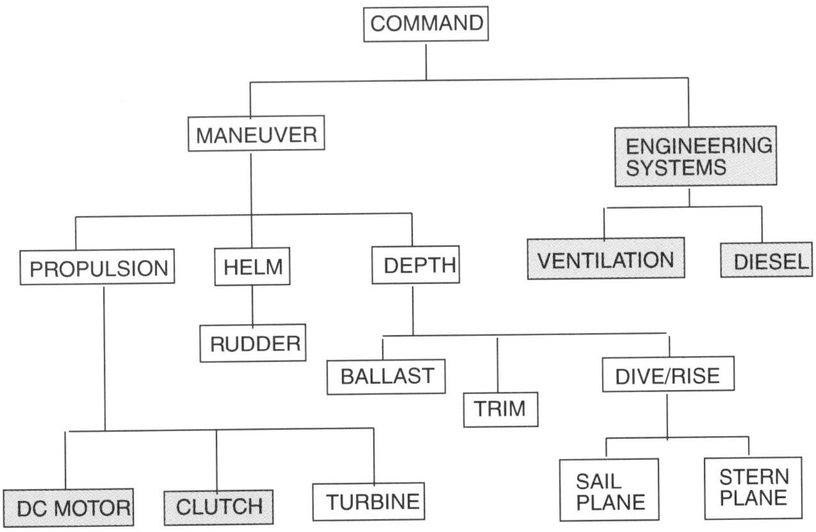

Note: The controllers in the shaded boxes are developed for the Demo#5 purposes.

FIGURE 14 Submarine automation RCS control hierarchy.

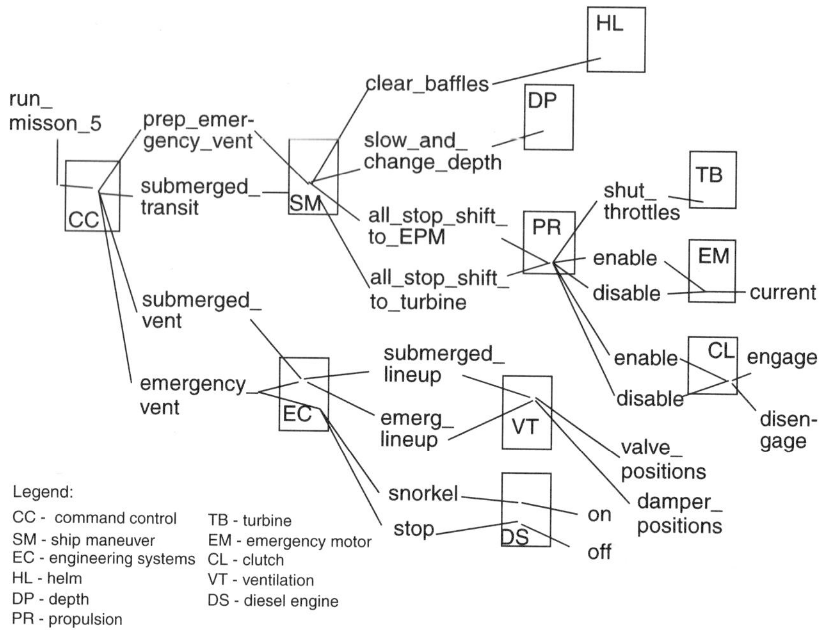

FIGURE 15 Submarine automation task tree for casualty scenario.

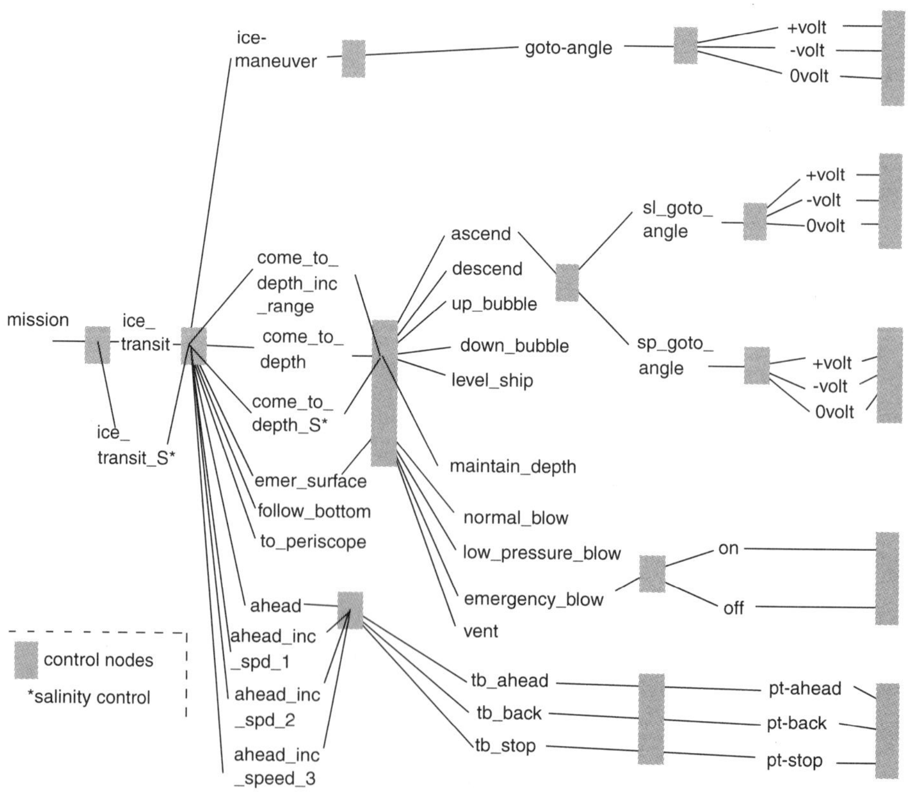

FIGURE 16 Submarine automation task tree for maneuvering and iceberg avoidance scenario.

level plans. In these cases, the capability to avoid resource contention problems should be carefully built into the appropriate plans.

C. Illustrative Behavior Descriptions

Behaviors for all the tasks shown in the task trees have been developed. This section describes two of them in detail to illustrate the development effort.

1. Command Level

From Fig. 17, the Run_Mission command is decomposed into Prep_emergency_Vent, Submerged_Transit, Submerged_Vent, and Emergency_Vent commands. When the mission command is received, the command controller (CC) enters the state S1. The submarine transits toward the next waypoint with CC ordering the ship's maneuver (SM) controller to execute the Submerged_Transit command and the engineering system controller (EC) to execute the Submerged_Vent command for normal open sea operations, see Fig. 15. CC is in the state S2 waiting for the execution status coming back from SM and EC. States S1 and S2 describe a feedback control loop for CC under normal conditions. Once all the waypoints are reached, the submarine completes its mission and CC would be in the (done) state.

When a fire is reported, CC changes the normal behavior by ordering SM to Prep_emergency_Vent, which includes activities such as Clear_baffles by SM. Once SM is done, CC enters S3 and orders EC to perform emergency ventilation. EC reconfigures the ventilation system (called lineup in submarine terms) and uses the diesel engine to snorkel. Once the contaminants are vented and the atmosphere

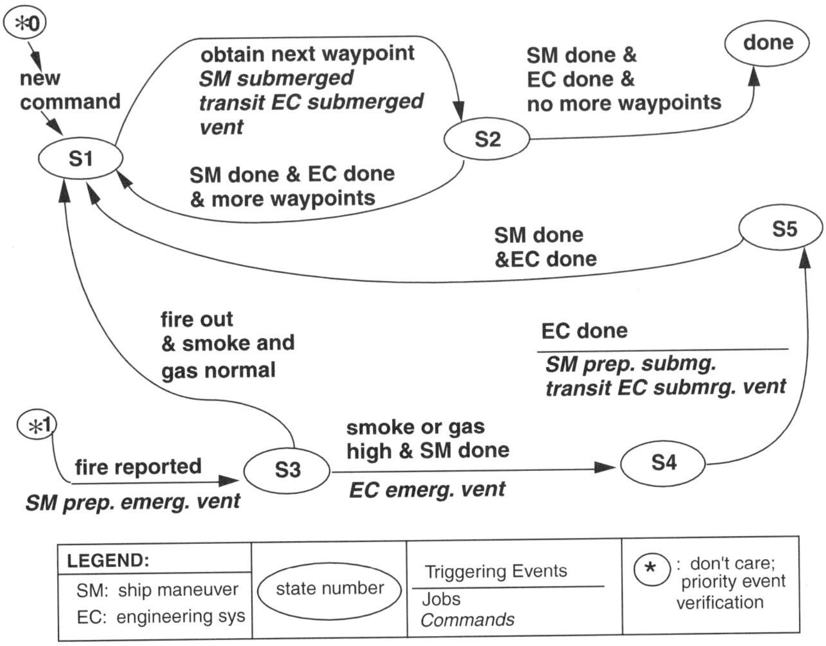

FIGURE 17 A mission plan for the command controller.

is safe for breathing, CC enters (S4) and orders SM and EC to prepare to resume the normal open sea transit, S1 and S2.

The Run_Mission task has been explicitly decomposed and described using this state diagram, Fig. 17. The same process is applied to each command on the task tree. This plan defines the initial state, the goal state, and all the intermediate states for the command controller during the execution of this command. In addition, all the required data, computation jobs, operator input, and subordinate status requirements are identified. This information enables the development of the associated sensory processing, world models, and human interface processes.

2. Helm Control and Illustrative Result

The helm controller is solely responsible for the ship heading control. It receives the ICE_MANEUVER command and a next goal position from its superior, from which a desired course is computed (*0 and Evt0 in Fig. 18). The required rudder angles are computed based on the course control error. If no obstacle (mainly ice keels) exists, the helm controller will send the computed rudder angles to its subordinate, the rudder controller, to approach the goal position (Evt3, Evt4, and Evt5 in the figure).

In this example, the helm controller employs a cerebellar model articulation controller (CMAC) sensory processing algorithm [42] for evaluating the existence of the ice problem. Sonar data contain ice obstacle detection. The CMAC receives the data, generalizes for an estimated ice distribution map, stores the map in the

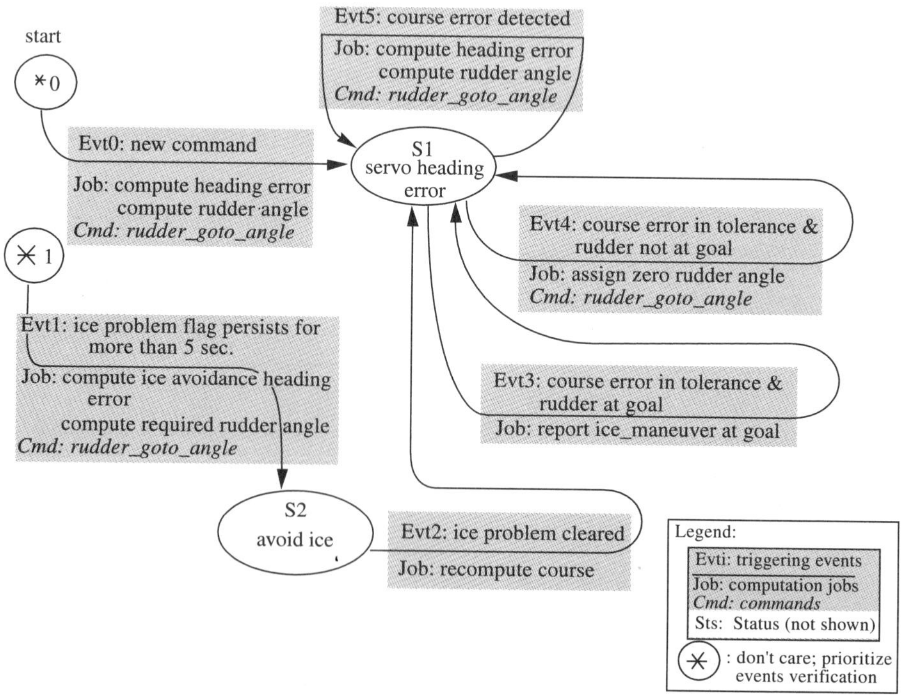

FIGURE 18 The helm control plan.

control world model, and computes an ice avoidance recommended heading by taking into account the desired course. Inside the helm controller, an ice_problem flag is raised if the CMAC recommendation differs from the desired course (Evt1 in the figure). The persistence of the ice problem for a predefined period of time warrants the specification of a "don't care state (*1)". The desired course will be omitted temporarily and the rudder controller will be given an ice avoiding rudder angle (Evt1). A new course toward the original goal must be computed after the ice has been avoided (Evt2). Under the no-ice situations, the CMAC recommendations will be consistent with the desired course.

The computation of the desired rudder angles depends on the heading error. As the error reduces to within some precalculated tolerance, a zero angle command must be sent in advance (before the heading error reaches zero) to account for the inertia of the submarine motion. An "ice_maneuver_at_goal" status would be reported (Evt3) to the ship's maneuver controller once helm and rudder are within the specified tolerances. The helm controller continues in state S1, monitoring any possible heading deviation or the occurrence of the ice problem.

The rudder controller always receives a GOTO_ANGLE command together with a target angular value resulting in a typical loop implementation. Simulated +VOLT, −VOLT, and 0VOLT signals are sent to the rudder simulator to generate the corresponding rudder angles.

As described in [1], one important feature a designer may discover as he steps from the higher levels down to the lower levels in an RCS hierarchy is the transition of coordinate systems from global systems with coarse resolutions to local systems with finer resolutions. The helm controller refers to headings, a measurement global to the world, whereas rudder refers to rudder angles, local to the submarine center line. The output of the rudder controller, the voltage signals, is local to the electromechanical rudder mechanism.

Figure 19 illustrates a simulated execution of a scenario. The 637 class submarine transits through a section of Bering Strait that has ice problems. The planned path, shown as the dark line segments, is generated offline and given to the controller prior to the transit. The islands, land, and Article Circle shown in the figure are, as such, not directly within the scope of this helm control illustration. The ice keels are generated randomly, in their sizes and shapes, and continuously (described also in Section IV.F.5) throughout the paths. The actual paths of the submarine are shown in the light lines, which are jagged due to the local ice-avoidance activities. The box around the submarine is called its moving haven, meaning that the submarine is allowed to stay anywhere within the given area, but not outside it.

D. Software Structure

This implementation employed a software structure as shown in Fig. 20. Later sections describe each hierarchy, including its development—how templates are applied—and capability.

- The *RCS control hierarchy* (upper left in Fig. 20) executes the plans to perform real-time automatic control of ship maneuvering. Section IV.B described the specific nodes. The finite-state-machine-based process

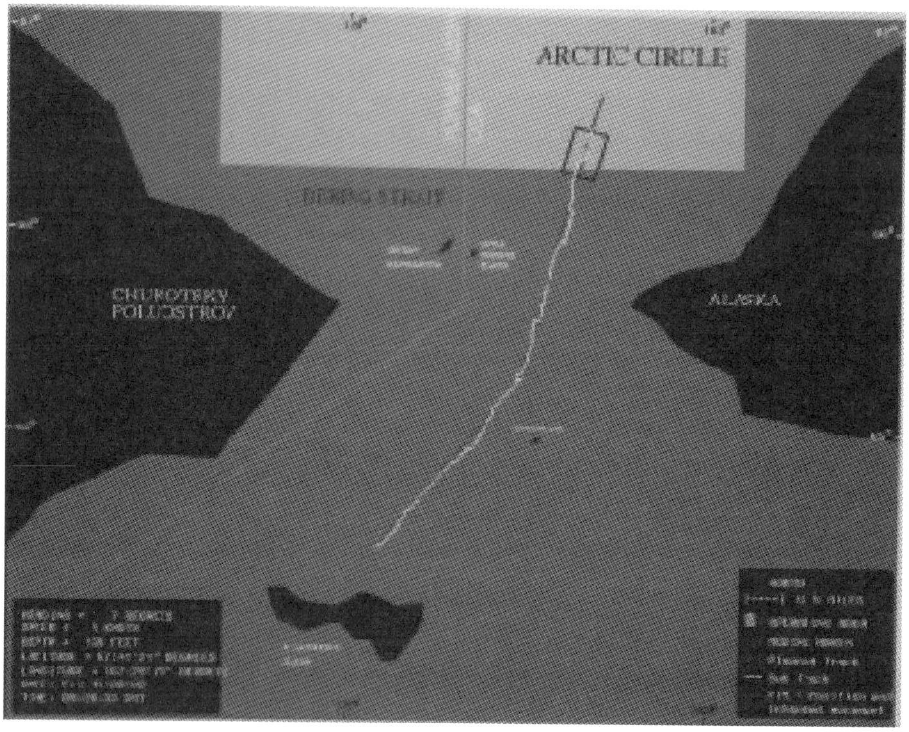

FIGURE 19 Resulting path control in simulated environment.

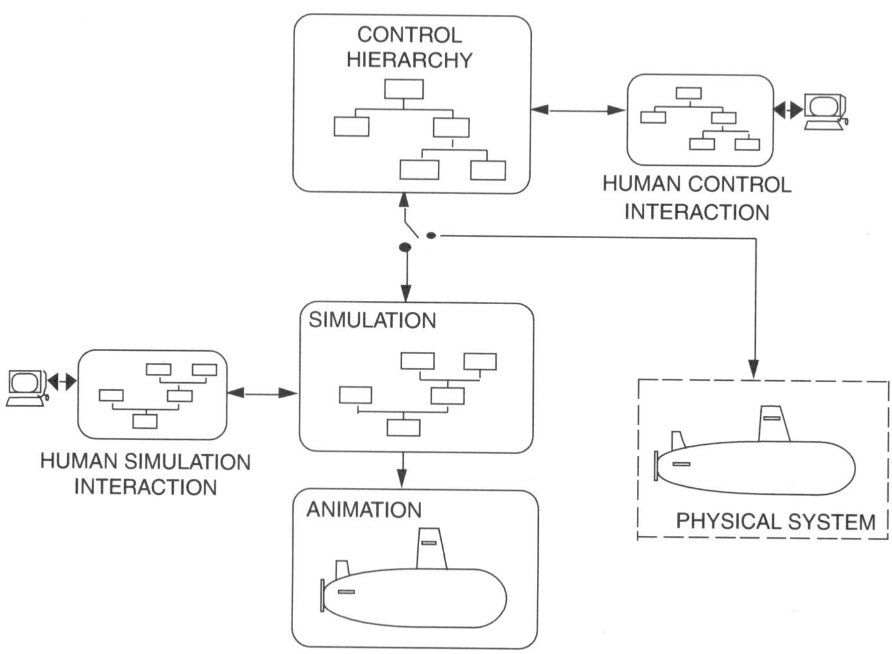

FIGURE 20 Comprehensive software structure.

template is used to implement the control nodes. Each node receives a command from its superior and selects an appropriate state table-based plan for execution.
- The *human interface hierarchy to RCS* (upper right in the figure) serves as the interface between the RCS hierarchy and various kinds of human operators who access system data and perform interactive control and system maintenance.
- The *simulation hierarchy* receives actuator commands and computes ship dynamics. Environmental objects and phenomena of concern are also simulated.
- The *human interface hierarchy to the simulator* (lower left in the figure) allows the operator to change the simulation (including ship or environmental) setup to test the responsiveness of the RCS ship maneuvering system. System servicers may utilize this interface for maintenance and upgrade.
- The *animator* (the lowest segment in the figure) paints pictures in real-time on a graphic display based on the data computed in the simulation software.

The other four hierarchies all use the same format as the controller template. They all execute via the command and status paradigm. The entire RCS system results in five parallel sets of concurrent hierarchical execution.

Two distinct world models are used, one for the control system and one for the simulation, respectively. Each contains a set of state variables, dynamic models, and/or geometry models to represent the world.

E. Finite State Machine Based Process Template

The authors applied the base class, process template to implement the controller nodes. Behaviors were embedded in the decision process of the template in the form of state tables, as shown in Fig. 21. The control hierarchy executes as a set of finite state machines.

The base class, process template was used in a specific way to form the finite state machine execution model, as the following describes:

- Preprocessing:
  - Read task command input from the superior. Read operator requests. Read in the globally shared data required for decision process. Read status reports from the subordinates.
  - Compute state values or evaluate event triggers from the following input data sets: environmental states, previous states for this node, states of other coordinating nodes, and required thresholds.
- Decision process:
  - Select a new task plan (state graph or table) if necessary and make a next state decision based on the latest task command input from the superior, opcrator requests, current world state, and subordinate execution status.
- Postprocessing:
  - Write subtask commands to subordinates. Write to operator if necessary. Post WM data. Post status reports to superior. Collect performance data.

All the controllers in the control hierarchy are implemented using this template.

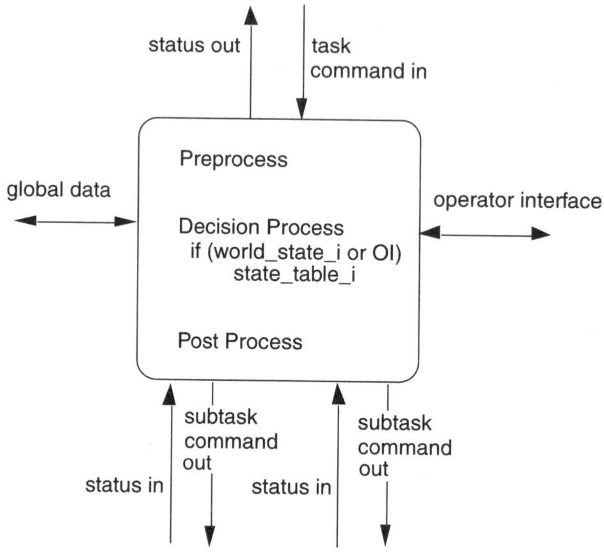

FIGURE 21 Finite-state-machine-based process template.

F. Simulation: Template and Implementation

1. The Structure

The simulator hierarchy is shown in Fig. 22. This hierarchy is developed to fit directly in the bottom of the RCS control hierarchy, Fig. 14. The RCS actuator controllers send commands to their respective simulators. The lowest level simulators compute the actuator movements accordingly and send the computed values back to the original controllers via the simulated sensors. The same values also are used by the ship simulator (i.e., the values are copied to the simulation world model) for the computation of the ship dynamics. The simulated ship state is fed back to the required higher level RCS controllers via another set of simulated sensors.

2. Sensor

The sonar simulator sends the data to the helm control sensory processing routines. The submarine is equipped with 14 forward-looking sonars. Sonar data are simulated by extending 14 lines, each simulating a sonar pinging in its fixed direction relative to the ship's center line, from the ship to the full sonar operating range (approximately 900 m, or 3000 ft). Intercepts with the simulated ice-keels are collected as sonar detections.

3. Actuators

The template for the ship system simulator, shown in Fig. 23, assumes the same format as the generic base-class, process template. During execution, the simulator processes copy the commands from the actuators stored in the global memory and the current actuator position values stored in the simulation world model. The simulators then compute new actuator position values according to the incoming commands. At the post processing phase, the simulators copy the values back to both the simulator world model and the global memory interface buffers.

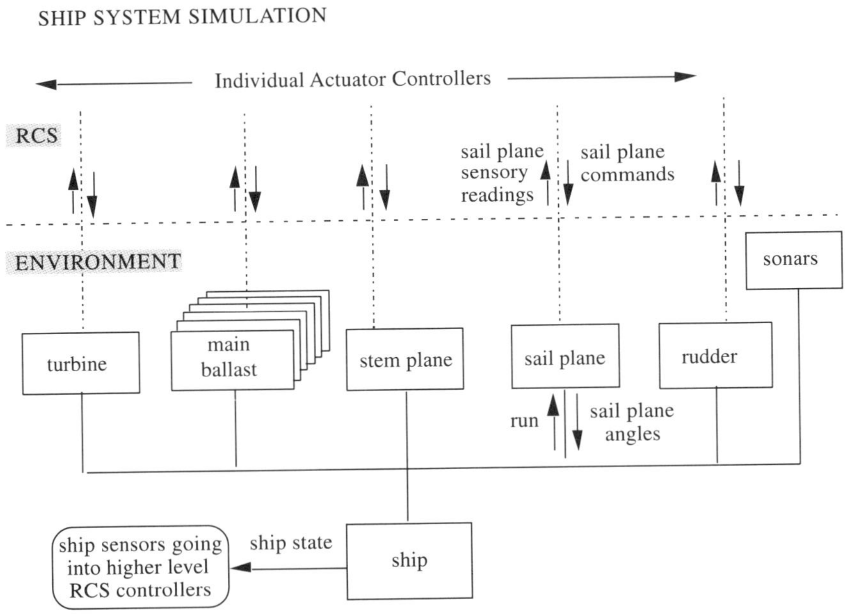

FIGURE 22 The simulation hierarchy.

This information is consumed by the sensory processing function of the control hierarchy and by the high level simulation.

These simulated actuators do not perform any closed loop control function but their corresponding controllers do. The desired actuator positions are used by the lowest level RCS controllers. The actuators normally receive and respond to

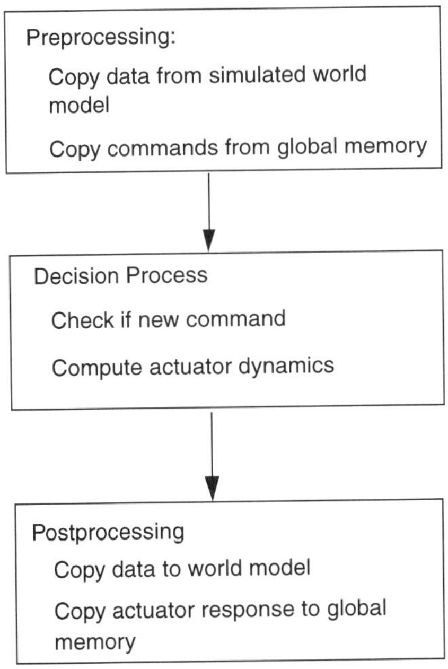

FIGURE 23 Actuator simulator template.

commands such as ON, OFF, +VOLT, −VOLT, 0VOLT, etc. Dynamic models typically exist in the simulators to translate those commands to actuator positions.

4. Physical System

The template for the ship system simulator, shown in Fig. 24, assumes the same format as the base-class, process template. In execution, this simulator module first copies in its incoming "commands," an initialization or execution. The module then copies in all the data required for simulation, including the current ship state and the computed actuator positions.

The decision processing essentially involves a sequential execution of all the actuator simulators and a computation of the ship dynamics. In this example, the ship dynamics computes the position, speed, depth, bubble angle, and heading for the ship. There are two kinds of ship-depth simulation, namely, the actual depth and the depth that the ship-depth sensor reads. The former is regarded as the environmental simulation, whereas the latter is regarded as the ship simulation.

5. Environmental

The environmental simulation contains ice keels, sea bottom and depth, and seawater density. The ice keel and sea bottom profiles were generated using fractals [43], which allowed a complex structure of indefinite size and extent without the need for long and complex mappings. They are generated prior to test runs. The

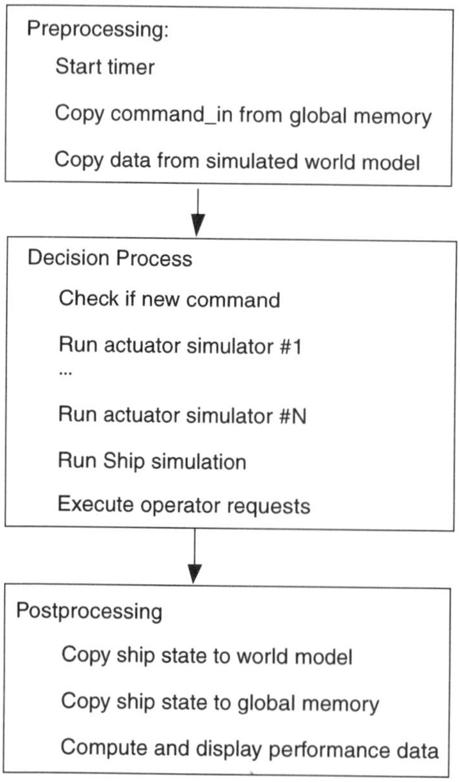

FIGURE 24 The ship system simulator process template.

seawater is simulated in terms of fresh water runoff's, the true ship depth, and the water density. Unlike the depth simulation in the ship system, in this environmental simulation the depth model is sensitive to water density changes. Section IV.I, demonstrates the graphic effects.

G. Operator Interface

1. Watchstation Displays: Mapping Control Activities to the Operating Environment to Facilitate Operator Interaction

In the process of upgrading existing systems from manual-operation-dominant to automation and intelligent control, it is beneficial to integrate the technology in an incremental and user-friendly manner. It is beneficial for the operators to be able to relate the new technology to their current operations. Therefore, the authors propose that the logical OI structure must be designed to be compatible with the current submarine operating environment.

The researchers have developed three watchstation, graphic panels to provide the input and output capability for operators during real-time control. The three displays are shown in the three shaded areas in Fig. 25. They correspond to both the layout of actual submarine operational compartments and the RCS control hierarchy.

The three watchstation displays are as follows:

1. the Officer of the Deck watchstation (OOD WS), which serves as the OI of the command and maneuvering controllers of the control hierarchy;
2. the Engineering Officer of the Watch watchstation (EOOW WS), which serves as the OI of the propulsion controller and all its subordinates;
3. the ballast control panel watchstation (BCP WS), which serves as the OI of the engineering systems, ventilation, and diesel controllers.

The operator interface (OI) must display the necessary information for all the controllers, in real-time, to enable the interaction between the control hierarchy and the submarine operators. Note that the objective of the OI is not to mimic the current submarine operating environment. Instead, the number and types of WS displays are determined by considering the following three factors: the operator work load; understandability by and acceptability to the current submarine operation community; the efficiency of hierarchical system control.

The OOD WS, illustrated in Fig. 26, displays the crucial maneuvering data for the OOD, including (from left to right) the bubble angles, the heading and speed, and the depth. The WS also includes two text-based message areas: the left side showing the command that the command controller is outputting (for maneuver) and the right side showing the announcement that the controller is making. When a lubrication (lube) oil fire is reported through the commanding channels, the command controller immediately announces the message "ENGINE ROOM FIRE, ALL HANDS ON EABs". Meanwhile, the COMMAND text area starts displaying "PREP FOR EMERGENCY VENT", meaning that the command controller is ordering the maneuver controller to execute the displayed command: to prepare for emergency ventilation.

The Engineering Officer of the Watch watchstation, shown in Fig. 27, employs two buttons for engaging or disengaging the main shaft clutch. This WS also

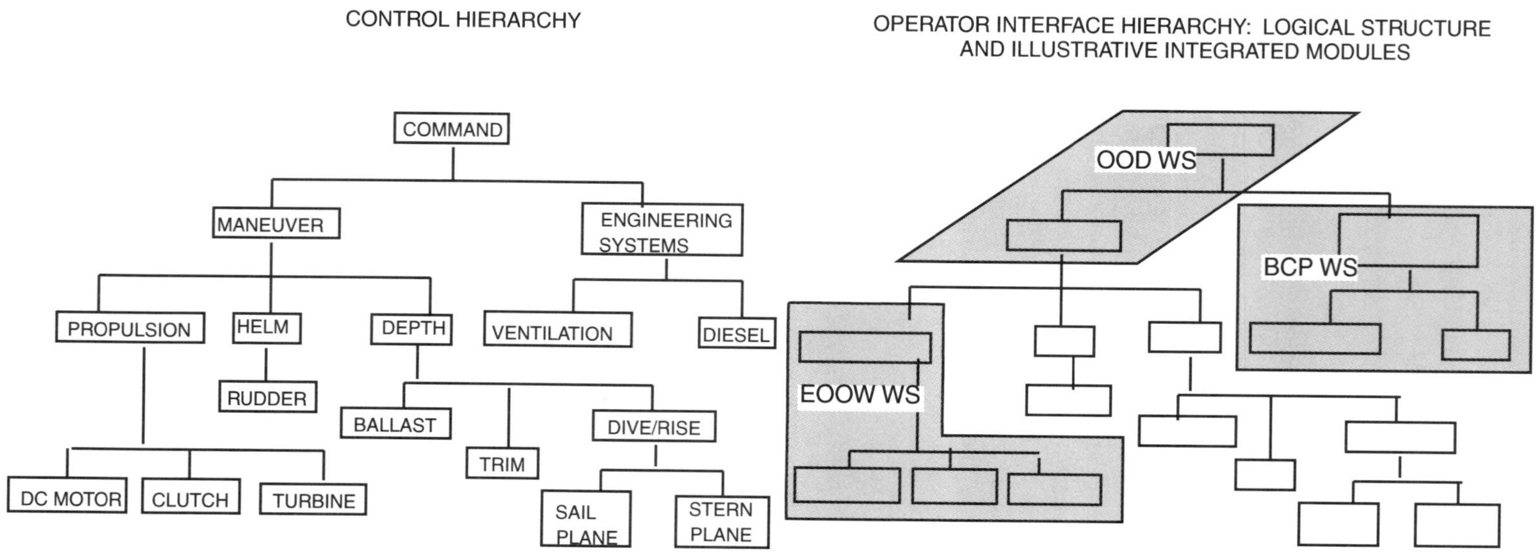

FIGURE 25 Mapping control activities to operating environment to facilitate operator interaction.

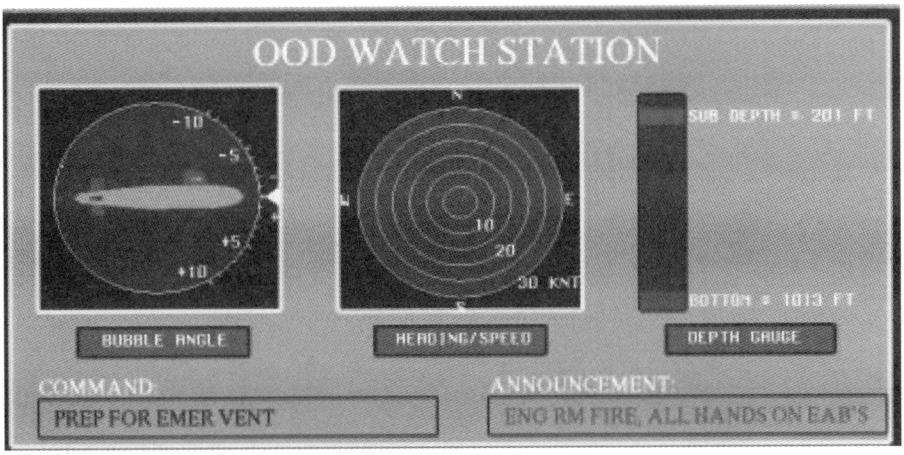

FIGURE 26 The officer of the deck watchstation display.

employs a speed control knob for the emergency propulsion motor. In addition, this WS has two text-based message windows. The command-text window normally displays the command that the propulsion controller is executing. When the propulsion controller requests the operator to perform a command, this command appears in this window. Meanwhile, the window will shade in yellow. The REPORT message window displays useful messages for the Engineering Officer of the Watch operator. In Fig. 27, EOOW must execute a ONE_THIRD_SPEED command, which is a subcommand of the "PREP FOR EMERGENCY VENT" command that Maneuver is executing.

The ballast control panel watchstation, shown in Fig. 28, contains the same types of text-message areas as in the Engineering Officer of the Watch watchstation. The ballast control panel watchstation also includes four atmospheric analyzer displays, the main ballast tank control buttons, and a ventilation lineup display.

At the beginning of the operation, the submarine is conducting an open sea transit. The Officer of the Deck watchstation displays a nominal zero-degree bubble angle, a standard speed, and the nominal keel depth. The ANNOUNCEMENT

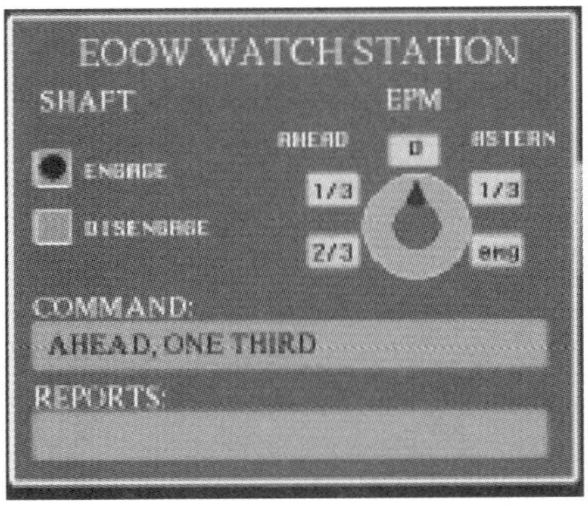

FIGURE 27 The engineering officer of the watch wathcstation display.

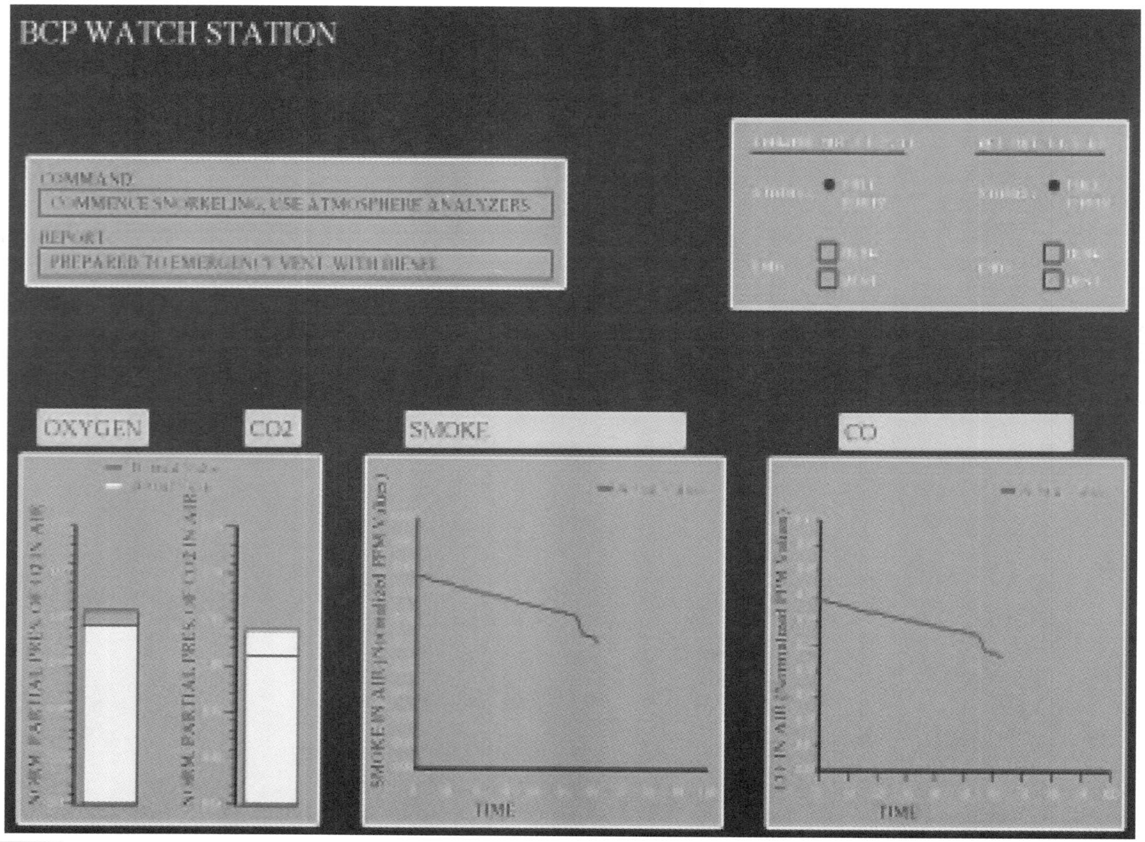

FIGURE 28 The ballast control panel watchstation display.

message window is blank. At the Engineering Officer of the Watch watchstation, the COMMAND window displays a standard speed. Neither the SHAFT nor the EPM button is activated. The atmospheric analyzers in the ballast control panel watchstation display normal levels of oxygen, carbon dioxide, smoke, and carbon monoxide. The ventilation diagram displays normal air circulation.

A lube oil fire is reported through the sensors in both the propulsion and the ventilation control systems. The REPORTS text window in Fig. 26 displays the fire message. The command controller immediately announces the message "ENGINE ROOM FIRE, ALL HANDS ON EABs" through the Officer of the Deck watchstation display. Meanwhile, the COMMAND window starts displaying "PREP FOR EMERGENCY VENT", meaning that the command controller is ordering the maneuver controller to execute the displayed command. Maneuver decomposes this command into three commands: Clear_baffles, Slow_and_Change_Depth, and Shift_To_EPM for its subordinates, as seen in Fig. 15. This task decomposition activity is displayed in the COMMAND window in real-time. In other words, the displayed commands correspond to the actual states that the maneuver controller is in. Meanwhile, the ventilation controller SP and WM algorithms update the abnormal concentrations of the modeled air constituents, namely, oxygen, carbon dioxide, smoke, and carbon monoxide. These data are displayed, in real-time, in the ballast control panel watchstation atmospheric analyzer displays. See Fig. 28.

The ventilation system is reconfigured automatically to prepare for emergency ventilation once the submarine is at periscope depth. Once this command is completed, a message stating "Prepared to emergency ventilate with diesel" will be shown in the REPORT window in Fig. 28. The engineering systems controller then receives a "Commence Snorkeling, Using Atmospheric Analyzers" command, as shown in Fig. 28. The diesel engine extracts and exhausts the contaminated air and takes in the fresh air through the mast extending above the level of the water. This command completes when the atmosphere becomes safe to breathe again. At such point, the command controller orders the submarine to resume the open sea transit.

2. Operator Interface Data Types

This project studied the data types developed for operator interactions with an objective of generalizing and standardizing the interfaces. The following summarizes the results:

- input from the operators: status; command selections; environmental variable settings; and actuator override devices.
- output to the operators: continuous operational data, including ship depth displays and paths; digital operational data, including ship speed displays; discrete activities, such as commands, announcements, watchstation reports; operator input requests; schematic diagram; errors and recommendations; controller performance, such as execution time; and debug data, including command or status, world data.

3. Levels of Operator Involvement during Operations

RCS allows operators to be involved in system operations at varying degrees. In this application, the researchers started experimenting with five degrees of "access control," giving the operators from the least to the most amount of authority to interact with individual controllers in the hierarchy (this also provides a systematic model of conducting man-in-the-loop control and migrating legacy subsystems):

- monitor, or be informed;
- respond to system requests;
- alter system behavior by issuing new commands;
- use manual override;
- modify system, or reconfigure control hierarchy.

Operator access control should be applied to both the controllers and the tasks. Each controller in the hierarchy has a logical operator interaction function with assigned degrees of operator access control. Each step in a task plan may be assigned certain degrees of operator access control. For example, operator intervention may not be allowed during the execution of a safety-related task. Our experiments focused on applying the operator interaction to controllers. Further research is required to integrate these two aspects.

The authors use a two-dimensional matrix to describe how the access control is applied to the hierarchy, as shown in Fig. 29. Monitoring is the default degree of authority, which is available to all the operators.

The next unit on the horizontal axis, "respond to system requests", does not allow operators to interrupt system operations. The system design does not allow the propulsion operator to issue new commands. Rather, the operator is only authorized to perform requested actions, such as CHANGE_TO_EPM, as shown in Fig. 30. The operator, then, manually disengages the main turbine shaft, engages

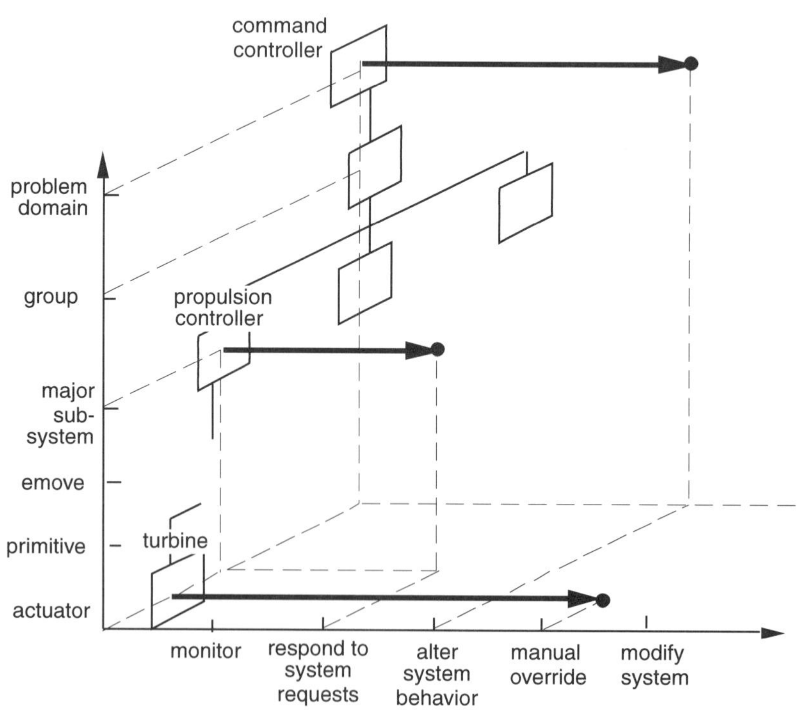

FIGURE 29 Different degree of operator involvement.

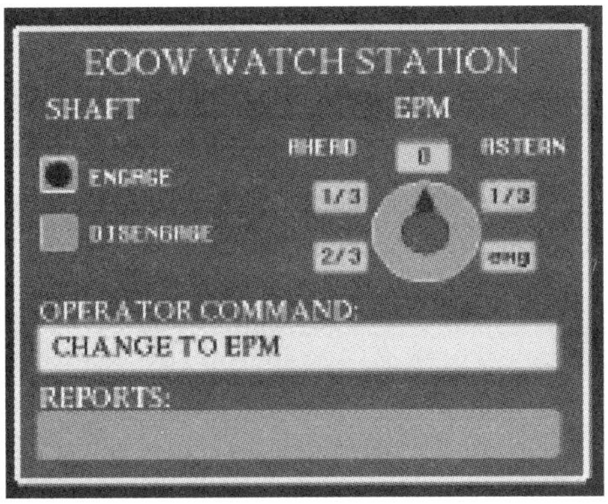

FIGURE 30 Request for operator action.

the EPM shaft, and clicks the button on the display to report the completion. In this case, the operator serves as the EPM controller. This man-in-the-loop control operation also suggests that our method supports integrating the automation technology with legacy systems with manual operations.

Another example of "responding to system requests" is for operators to make decisions for the control system. The submarine may run into some salinity disturbances close to the coast where the depth controller cannot maintain the ship's depth. The error messages and a set of options that involve either sail or stern planes or ballast tanks are displayed for maneuver. Blowing MBTs may be the last resort that disallows the submarine to resubmerge whereas adjusting the planes is the normally selected option. The operator selects the best command for the controller to perform.

The next unit on the horizontal axis, "alter system behavior", means that the operator initiates graceful changes to system operations. In other words, operator commands are integrated with the ongoing system automatic operation. The command controller operator can alter system behavior by issuing a new mission command and having both the new and the existing mission commands scheduled and executed.

The next unit on the horizontal axis, "manual override", means that the operator takes over the control and the automatic control commands are ignored, suspended, terminated, or aborted. The lowest level operators can block the automatic commands and directly manipulate the actuators. When the submarine is about to hit ice keels, the helm operator must be allowed to enter an emergency turning command.

Reconfiguring the control hierarchy means that the operator can realign the command chain of the hierarchy or can expand or reduce the control capability of the controllers. This advanced capability was not implemented.

4. User Expertise and Hierarchical Situation Perception

As stated in our basic principles, operator interface information must meet the user requirements and expertise [44]. All users are unique. They require different types of data. In one respect, data are processed and assimilated according to the levels of the operator command authority.

In the RCS hierarchical environment, different levels deal with events and commands at different resolutions and time scales. Temporal and spatial integration must be performed when lower level information, either discrete events or continuous data, is delivered to higher levels. This integration process creates a different perception. Operators only need to understand the languages describing the situations at two levels of resolution: their own level and the level below.

Figure 31 illustrates this perception process. At the high control level, maneuver is integrating the information received from the three spatially distinct subordinates, propulsion, depth, and helm. At the first instance, propulsion reports that the submarine has achieved the required speed. At the second instance, helm reports that the areas of concern have been cleared of hostile objects. At the following instance, depth reports that the submarine has reached the required depth. Next, propulsion reports that the emergency motor has been engaged. Maneuver summarizes all the information and concludes that it is ready to perform emergency ventilation.

5. Supporting Other System Functions

The focus of this example was on the operators' roles in system control. There are, however, additional types of operators that require control system support, including supporting systems development and service, simulation, and training. A system servicer may prefer to review raw data, as opposed to view concise and processed data often preferred by a control operator.

H. Knowledge Inference

The data that are useful to a submarine control operator may or may not be either useful or sufficient to a system developer or servicer. A system developer or ser-

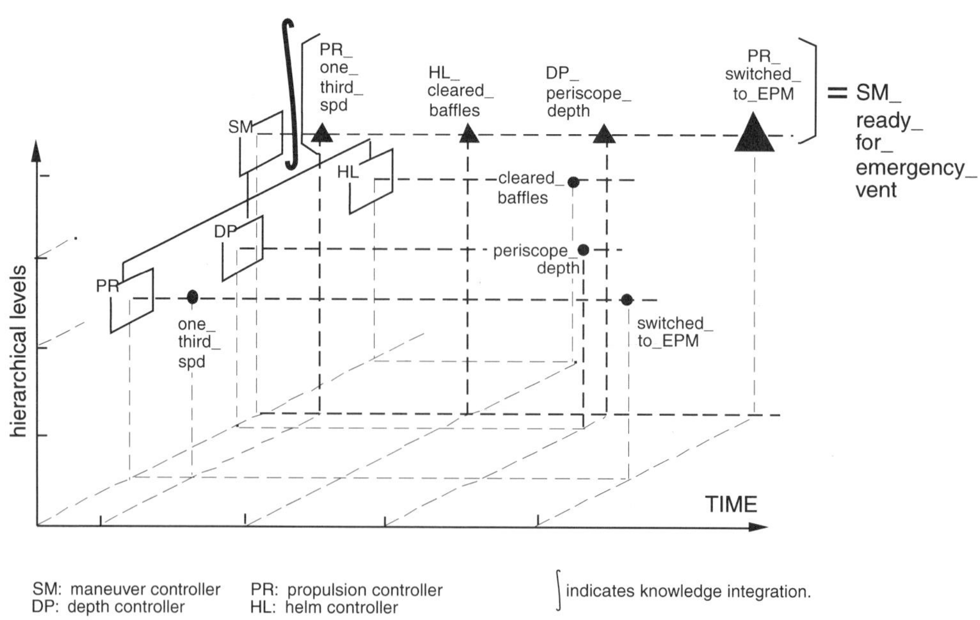

FIGURE 31 Hierarchical situation evaluation.

vicer may need to access computer, machine-level, raw data during the debugging periods. However, in emergency situations, a control operator may not have time to read through all raw data to find out the problems, she or he needs to view concise and processed data. This implementation makes the raw data available, while transforming them to different formats to suit the user needs.

Therefore, knowledge processing is a part of our RCS world modeling functions. The knowledge transformation process can cover several layers of abstractions:

- from raw data to concise data;
- from the raw or concise data to conventional terms that match the operator's expertise (Fig. 32);
- from any of the aforementioned data formats to vocabulary that is consistent with the levels of abstraction in RCS hierarchical control and perception levels.

We have used submarine terms in our vocabulary, including "Fire in engine room, all hands on EABs" and "All stop, shift to EPM". A particular message for a control operator may be an inferenced result of many pieces of raw data.

Note that, although we have made distinctions among these types of data, they are not intended to be hard boundaries. Some concise and processed data may be just as informative to a debugger as to a control operator. These different types of data may also share common criteria. For example, these data should, whenever possible, be displayed graphically to help human dissemination, be displayed in real-time to facilitate situation evaluation, and share a common knowledge base to improve consistency.

I. Animation

Animation performs graphic rendering and allows the users to visualize the actions that the controller takes. Animation enhances the human understandability of a process. A human can comprehend many more variables pictorially than by reading numbers. Because RCS focuses on machines that do work, animating these machines is a logical step. It enables one to debug the algorithms that are used to control the machine and may avoid costly mistakes that occur when transferring software from simulated to real systems.

Figure 33 gives an overview of the demonstration computer screen including operator interface and animation. On the upper portion of the screen display,

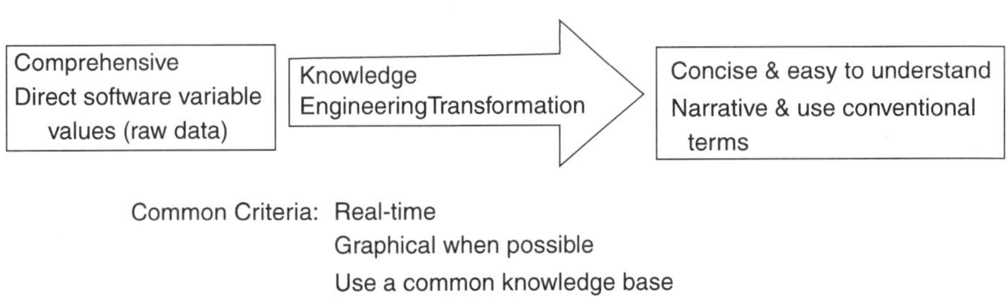

FIGURE 32 Knowledge processing.

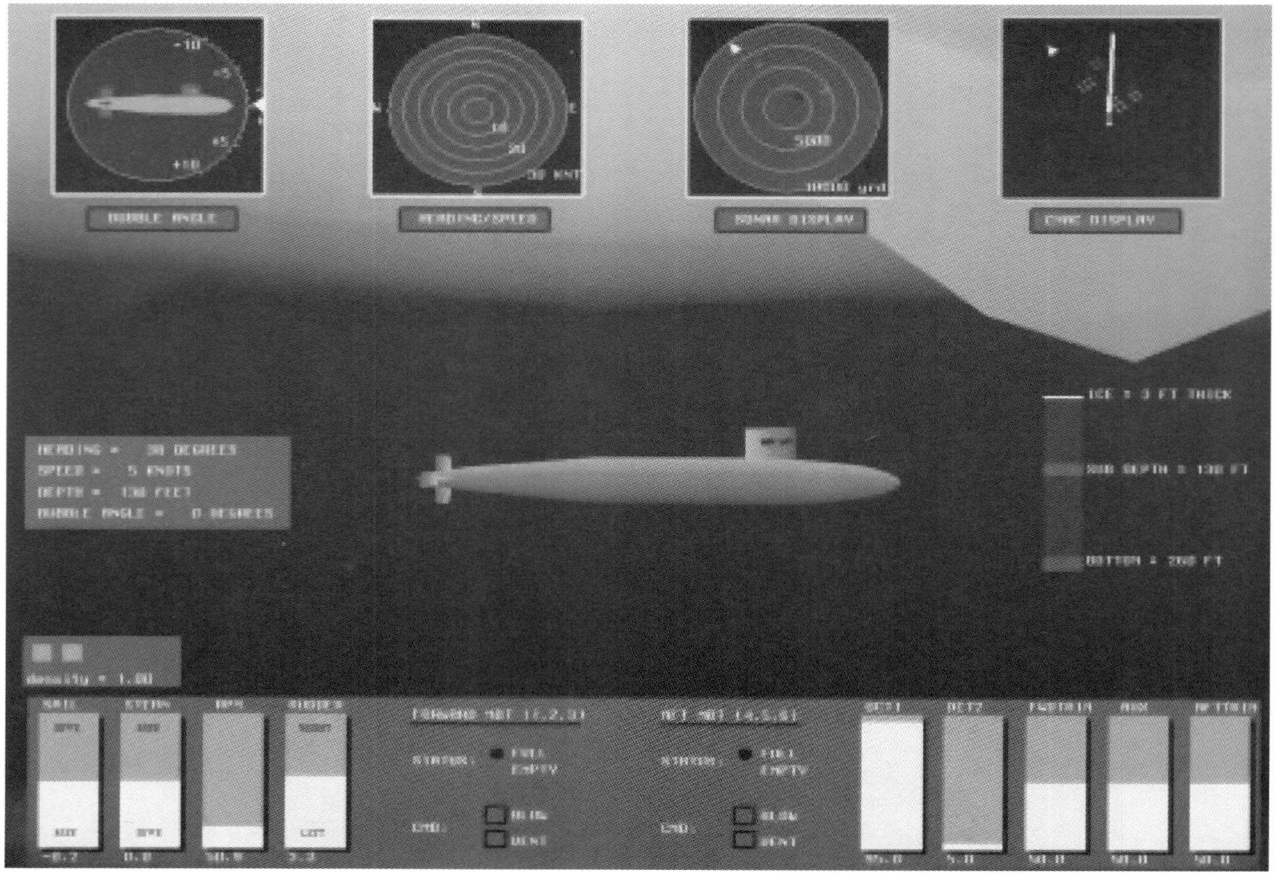

FIGURE 33 Overview display for animation and operator interface.

the ice keel is shown in the background. The foreground consists of four graphic displays: the bubble angles, speed and headings, current sonar detection, and ice map, from left to right. The middle portion of the screen display includes a digital, maneuvering-data display on the left and a depth display on the right. The submarine model was moving by the center of the screen when this snapshot was taken. On the lower portion of the screen display, a water-density simulation button is on the left corner, followed by the slider bars for the stern planes, sail planes, main turbine speed, and rudder, the control buttons and indicators for the main ballast tanks, and the slider bars for the depth control tanks, forward trim tank, auxiliary tank, and aft trim tank. All the displays are updated in real-time.

V. CASE STUDY II, MANUFACTURING DOMAIN, TOWARD IMPLEMENTATION SPECIFICATION AND ONLINE BEHAVIOR GENERATION

Various aspects of RCS have been applied to many manufacturing systems over the last two decades of the 20th century [16, 19, 46]. Under the SIMA program [12], a comprehensive reference model architecture called the intelligent systems architecture for manufacturing [26, 27] is being developed. ISAM intends to integrate RCS with important concepts from MSI [13] and QIA [14], as well as to resolve architectural issues among them where differences exist. The objectives of ISAM include providing a framework for developing standards and performance measures for intelligent manufacturing systems and providing engineering guidelines for the design and implementation of intelligent control systems for a wide variety of manufacturing applications. ISAM is intended to anticipate the future needs of industry.

The implementation of a testbed to evaluate the applicability of the reference architecture is under way. The testbed development effort leverages the work of several industry and government consortia. This ensures attention to current industry issues. These relationships are described briefly in the approach section (Sect. V.A).

These objectives and the approach taken address the NIST Manufacturing Engineering Laboratory (MEL) goals of fostering the development and implementation of advanced manufacturing systems and anticipating and addressing the needs of the U.S. manufacturing industry for the next generation, including measurement techniques and standards.

A. Approach

The authors take the following approach in order to meet the project objectives:

- Specify processes and interfaces based on the ISAM reference model to facilitate architectural implementation and integration. This specification process will take into account industrial and other government agencies' efforts and results.
- Furnish a testbed to facilitate the testing.
- Leverage and integrate component technology, developed in-house or outside, in the architectural framework.

The elements given in the following subsections describe the approach in detail.

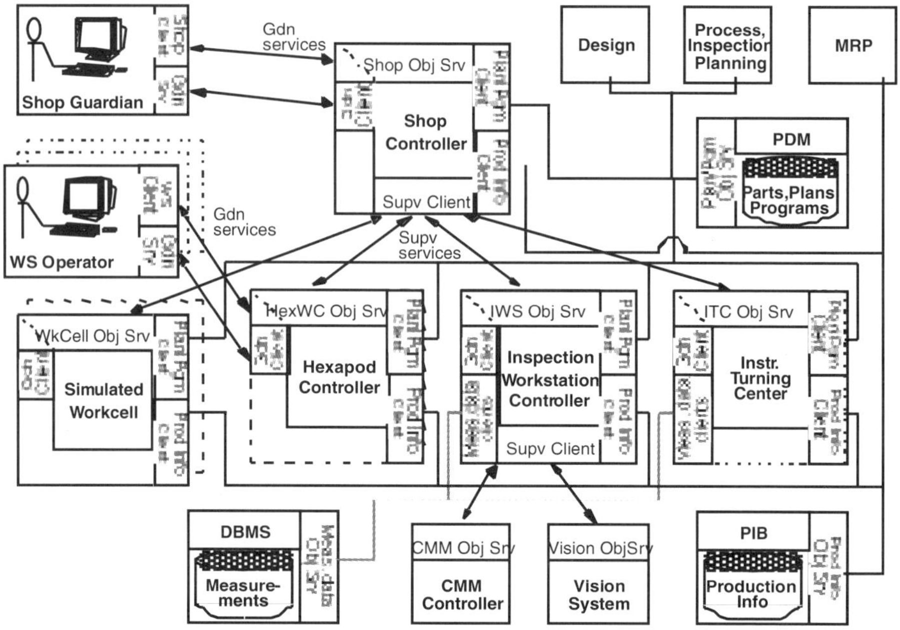

FIGURE 34 NAMT CIM testbed.

1. Generic Shell for ISAM

An ISAM implementation contains many control nodes arranged in a hierarchy. Section III.E.5 described a generic shell approach. In this project, the generic shell effort is to define a software structure, interface definitions, and task frame specifications that permit the core control node model to be standardized to the extent possible for manufacturing applications. As such, the authors are using the template-based approach to examine and develop the software organization and development support for the Behavior generation, world modeling, value judgment, and sensor processing components of a control node and their interfaces. A part of the effort is to tailor the RCS methodology to suit the manufacturing problem domain. In this case the intent is to develop a shell structure that accommodates rich RCS capability, including sensory-interactive, real-time planning.

2. Application Domain: TestBed and Prototype System Design

The ISAM testbed is configured as a part of the NIST National Advanced Manufacturing Testbed [28]. The NAMT is established to allow scientists and engineers from NIST, industry, other government agencies, and academia to work together to solve measurement and standards issues in information-based manufacturing. As a part of NIST's mission, NAMT also develops the needed tests and test methods for industry. Ultimately, the reference model architecture may be tested with the simulated and implemented factory components in the testbed.

NAMT has accommodated multiple subprojects that address different manufacturing issues, and its scope is still expanding. A NIST Computer Integrated Manufacturing (CIM) Framework project [45] investigates a NAMT subarea testbed that is described in a configuration shown in Fig. 34. Many SIMA project elements are to be integrated in this CIM Framework testbed. An inspection workstation and a hexapod controller are to be coordinated by a shop controller. The communication follows a common object request broker architecture (CORBA) client and server model. The shop controller can coordinate additional workstations when scenarios dictate, as the turning center and simulated workstation on the drawing indicate. The shop controller employs an operator interface function called a guardian. Other features shown in the figure include a product database management system (PDM) and production information base (PIB), which are under investigation by other SIMA participants. Manufacturing activities including design, process and inspection planning, and manufacturing resource planning (MRP) may produce information feeding the databases. An initial integration of PDM has been completed in that the shop controller has coordinated the PDM to provide certain inspection instructions to the inspection workstation.

As a starting point of ISAM experiments, the authors have applied the methodology to the chosen inspection workstation (IWS) that is based on a coordinate measuring machine. Choice of this facility permits this project to take advantage of capabilities in advanced inspection currently being developed there under the Next Generation Inspection System (NGIS) [46] program. That project's use of vision- and scanning-probe technologies provides a sensory-rich environment for testing aspects of the architecture. Architectural and inspection (RCS, MSI, QIA, and NGIS) practitioners have joined their efforts in pursuing scenario sets for the activities of the IWS that can exercise the architecture. The first step is to generate a list of capabilities that will sufficiently exercise the architecture. These capabilities include online task planning, processing and handling errors, explicit quality loops, advanced human interaction, interface with legacy software and hardware, simulation, design, plan, and production data interface, administrative functions, learning, multiple simultaneous tasks per node, and interaction between CAD and sensed features.

Activities that required these capabilities are then included in the scenarios. The scenario identifies visible activities and data exchanges that reflect characteristics of typical inspection activities determined through various factory visits. A subset of the activities was used in the initial implementation. See the later section on project development. The scenario serves as an indispensable starting point in the implementation design. From this point, the researchers have been developing task descriptions and task trees, control node hierarchies and state representations for all tasks for each intended testbed mission. Part of this effort is the continued interaction and collaboration with software tool vendors that produce products that may be adapted to assist control system developers in this phase of implementation.

3. Leveraging Component and Interface Technologies

1. The *Enhanced Machine Tool Controller* (EMC) [16] project focuses on the development of implementation infrastructure. Our ISAM implementation heavily leverages their results, including the neutral manufacturing language (NML) communication interfaces, an application programming interface (API) specification, a baseline development environment with a version control mechanism, Internet-based operator interfaces, and advanced control system diagnostic capabilities.

2. *OMAC/TEAM message definition efforts*—the Open, Modular Architecture Controller (OMAC) users group [47] and the Department of Energy (DOE) Technologies Enabling Agile Manufacturing (TEAM) programs [48] have been working on API message definitions for manufacturing. These specifications support communication between control nodes, and, therefore, facilitate open architectures. A member of the ISAM Reference Model Architecture project team actively participates in that effort and applies and extends applicable results to the APIs used in the IWS testbed implementation.
3. *Planning* at an ISAM node is conducted in the behavior generation module. An extensive study of planning–scheduling algorithms has been performed and performance experiments have been conducted. The current effort involves integrating the algorithms in the planner template, as described in Section V.B.3. Further work to develop standard interfaces to planners, plan simulators and evaluators, and schedulers is needed. These interfaces are to be tested in the IWS testbed. Issues in discrete event planning are also being examined.
4. A focus on *feature-based control* involves applying part features described in solid models in STEP form to machining operations. Initial developments are being extended to the inspection domain.
5. *World modeling and CAD*—this effort seeks to formalize world modeling definitions within the generic process template and to design possible API access for world model information. Experiments are planned for an integration of product data and CAD API's with inspection controller code. This work will also include developing knowledge base entities of ISAM that include task frames, command frames, plans, algorithms, and resources.
6. The *operator interface* work includes integrations of various operator interface technologies, including Java-based tools. This work also includes the analysis of operator interface specification requirements with respect to the ISAM generic shell, world model, and MSI guardian. These tools and requirements are being investigated by many SIMA activities and outside researchers, which this project plans to leverage.

B. Methodology Development: Generic Shell, Interface Definitions, and Task Execution

The base-class, process template and the experience gained from the first case study provide a solid foundation for the authors to take the step to develop the next generation process templates that provide richer RCS capabilities. However, before launching the development effort, the authors conducted a detailed investigation of the internal execution activity of an RCS control hierarchy to gain insights into how the template-based systems work.

1. An Internal Execution Model of an RCS-Based Manufacturing Workstation

A detailed understanding of the internal execution activity of an RCS-based control hierarchy is desirable before designing such control systems. This analysis reveals design details such as the intermodule interaction requirements and modular synchronization requirements. The authors performed an analysis on an example manufacturing workstation. Time-lines are used to step through the scenarios and reveal the execution details. The result exemplifies an RCS execution model, as the following describes:

The control hierarchy consists of the following:

- WS (workstation) has two subordinates, R (robot) and M (milling machine). See Fig. 35.
- WS contains a control node that contains an SC (scheduler) and EX (executor) pair for each of WS's subordinates. The other planning supporting functions such as simulation and value judgment functions are assumed.
- M employs a dual-station pallet and is able to switch among tasks.
- R has a single end-effector and performs one task at a time.

The scenario as described in the control system execution time-line, shown from the top down in Fig. 36, is as follows:

- WS receives a task W1, W1 = make_part_p1 (DL1). DL1 indicates a deadline.
- WS-JA assigns scheduling jobs for SC-M and SC-R, the schedulers for the two subordinate equipment units.
- The two SCs coordinate, via communicating each one's timing constraints, to generate robot part fixturing schedules and milling machine machining schedules. The schedulers may retrieve process plans as a priori knowledge and schedule the plan steps. The outcome includes two schedules, schedule-R and schedule-M.
- The two EXs receive the schedules and execute the steps according to the time.
- As WS is executing the first step of W1, (W11), the second task, W2, arrives, W2 = make_part_p2 (DL2). The two schedules are to decompose W2 and the subtasks are interleaved within the original schedules based on equipment availability. The results are two modified schedules, schedule-R2 and -M2.

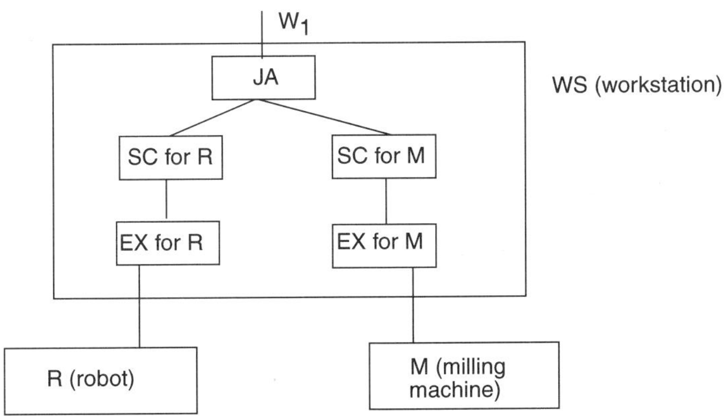

FIGURE 35 RCS-based manufacturing workstation example.

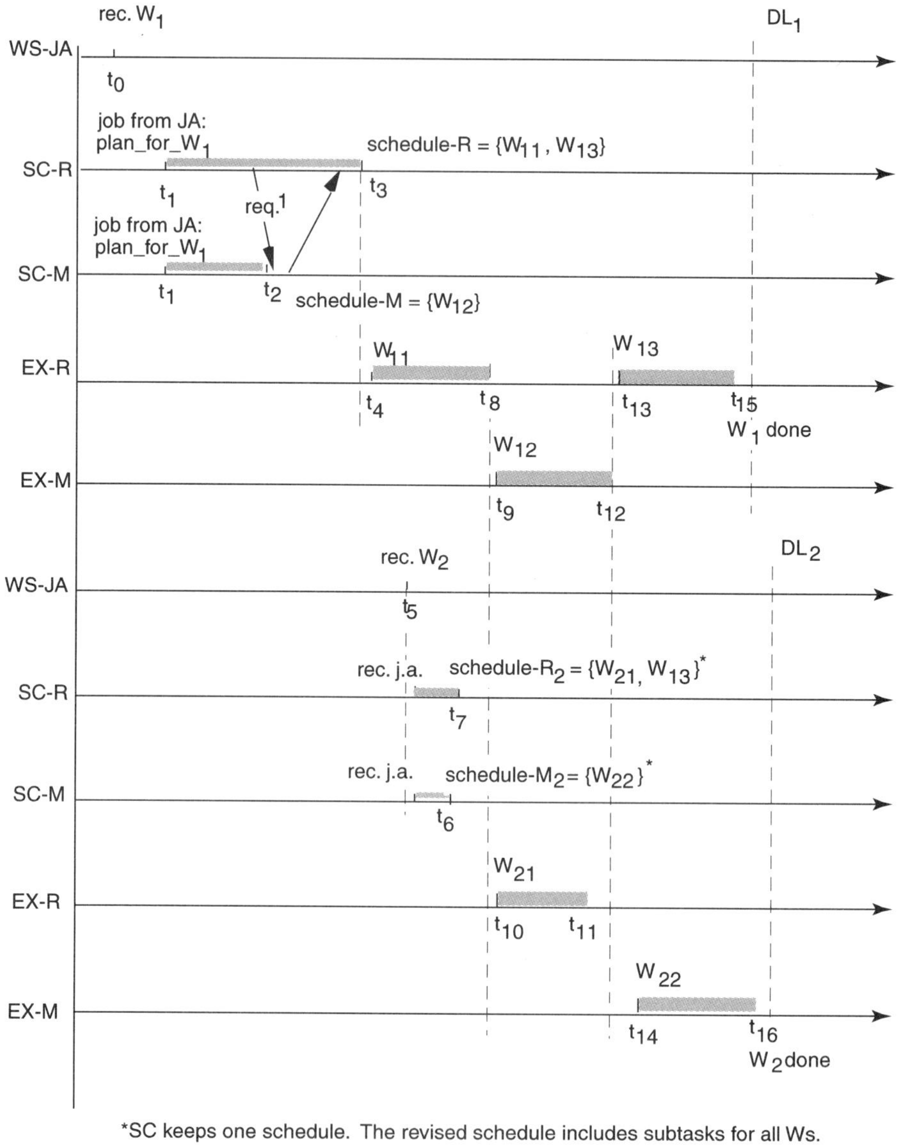

FIGURE 36 Time-line-based RCS hierarchy internal execution model.

- The two EXs continue executing the schedules one step at a time regardless of whether the schedules have been modified.
- If W2 has the highest priority, then an exception procedure may be devised to suspend or abort the original schedules associated with W1 and the scheduling and the execution of W2 takes place immediately.

The first important notion is that only one schedule is maintained for a subordinate controller. The superior controller may handle multiple tasks by interleaving the subtasks for the multiple tasks in one schedule to maximize the subordinate equipment utilization. As the time-line chart illustrates, the two workstation tasks, W1 and W2, may or may not complete in accordance with their arriving order.

The second is that the planning or scheduling process does not wait until the generated plan is completely executed. Rather, the planner (JA and SC) replans concurrently as the generated plan is being executed. The planner appends the generated schedules to the specified planning horizons. At each planning cycle, which may or may not be synchronized with the execution cycle, the planner evaluates the current world state and the future goal state and modifies the schedules when necessary.

2. Executor Template

The base-class, process template is extended, using the object-oriented inheritance concept, to build the executor template. The EX template is further instantiated in the ISAM implementation as well as in other applications. This is a part of the RCS methodology effort to provide generic implementation tools and to standardize the processing and interfacing models. See Fig. 37.

Each executor contains a plan buffer that is loaded via interfacing with the plan selector function in the planning process. The plan consists of two parts: (1) a trajectory of planned actions interleaved with (2) a corresponding trajectory of planned states (or subgoals).

In addition to the plan, each executor also receives input in the form of estimated (or predicted) state feedback via sensory processing and world modeling modules. Status to and from peer EX modules provide the basis for coordination between the EX modules. EX compares the difference between the estimated (or predicted) state feedback and the current planned subgoal and either performs feedback control to compensate for errors or invokes emergency actions when the errors are too large for the employed control laws.

3. Planner Template

The base-class, process template is extended, using the object-oriented inheritance concept, to build the planner template. Figure 38 provides a simplified view of the planning process as defined in [1]. In this simplification, the job assignment and scheduling functions are combined to reduce communication load. Note that, if any of these functions becomes computationally intensive, they may be separated into individual computing processes.

Tentative schedules are generated through the node's plan horizon. Simulation and value judgment functions are called to determine the best schedule. Plan selection chooses the best plan and sends it through the plan buffer in the EX module. The EX may report errors caused by executing earlier generated schedules. The planner will correspondingly replan. If the planner has replanned a particular task for too many times (beyond the designed threshold), an error flag will be generated for the superior node.

4. Interface Definitions

The developers describe the interfacing method with respect to the templates. The method covers both within a node and between the nodes. ISD has implemented generic command and status base classes as a part of the RCSLIB library [34]. Our interface data structures inherit and expand from these base classes.

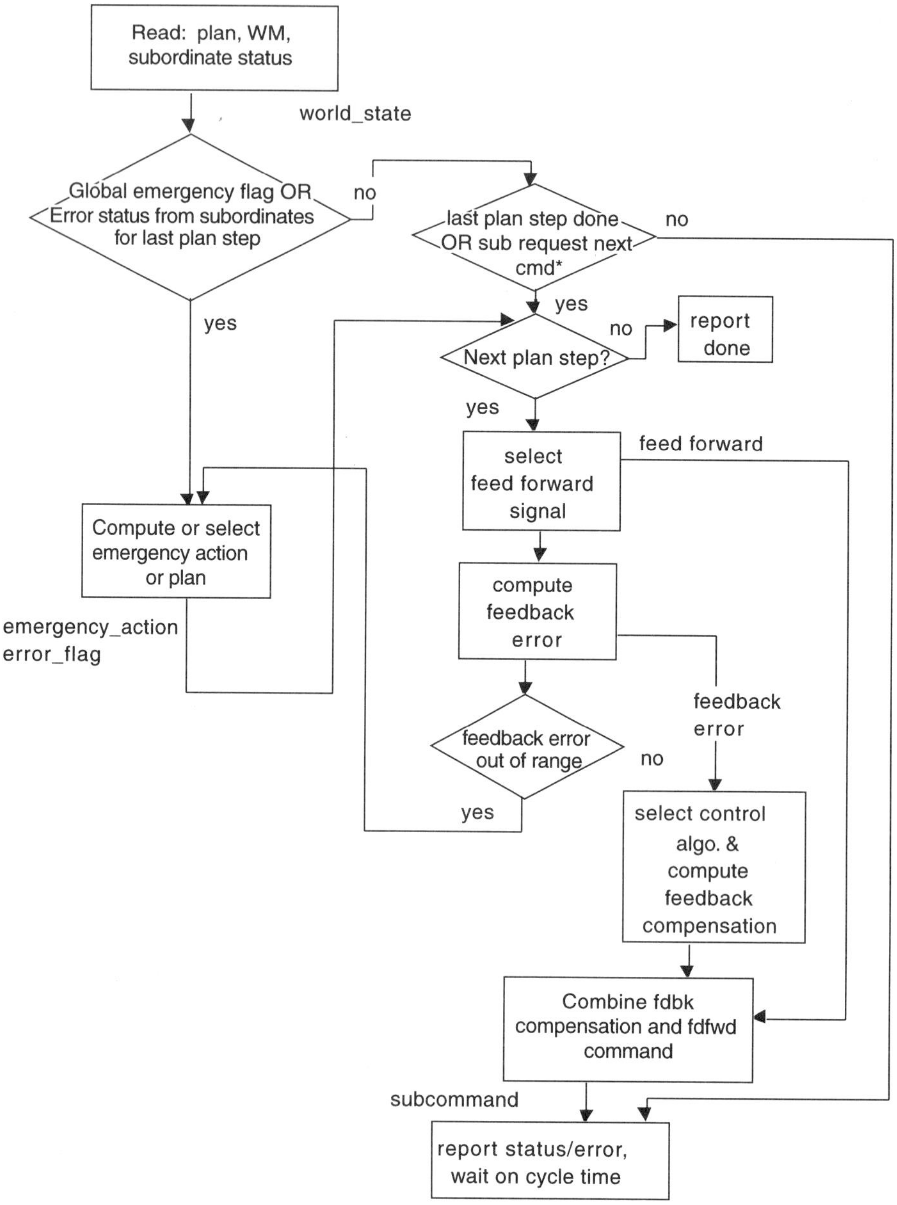

FIGURE 37 Internal functional flow of executor template.

1. The PL/Sim/VJ/PS may send EX an "Execute (schedule)" request (a general sense of command). This request data structure contains a serial number, as inherited from the base class. The schedule can be implemented as pointers to state graphs, inspection plans, or any other manufacturing process schedules. The schedule can also be waypoint arrays of a navigation path for a material handling robot cart. The EX reports, via the information slots defined in the base status class, the

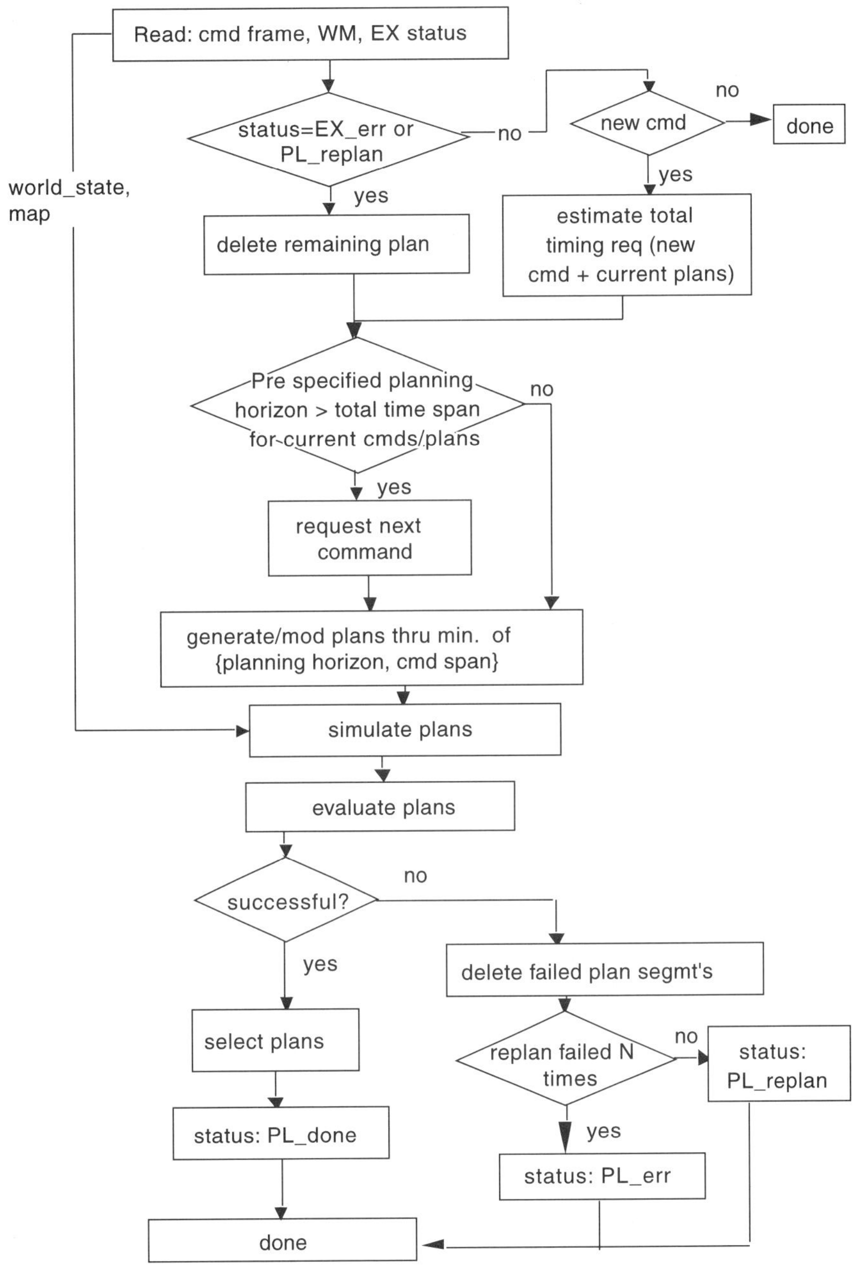

FIGURE 38 Internal functional flow of planner template.

serial number echo, the status, and state number. The PL/Sim/VJ/PS uses this report to adjust the planning activity: to abort and replan, continue updating the generated schedule, etc.

2. The interface between EX and the subordinate PL/Sim/VJ/PS is implemented as a set of task commands and is application specific. The commands include "Goto (goal)", "Load_part", and "Inspect_part

(inspection program)". The data structures for the command frame inherit a serial number and may be appended with a goal, a pointer to a file describing part loading instructions, and methods to retrieve inspection plans from the databases, respectively. The EX may send more than one goal point to meet the subordinate's planning-ahead requirements.

3. The interface with SPWM is under investigation in the area of providing CAD data. Currently SPWM supplies the BG templates with state information.

C. Initial Application System: Inspection Workstation

1. Behavior Generation

In the NAMT Next Generation Inspection Workstation testbed [28], a system goal given to the workstation from the highest level, shop, could be "Inspect_part", as shown at the top of Fig. 39. The shop may retrieve the instructions from a product database management (PDM) system, which may require WS to interpret the inspection instructions. WS decomposes this command to "Place_part" and "Load_probe" for measurement (MS) and fixturing (FX). MS decomposes and issues a subcommand for tooling to perform the probe loading process. FX and tooling are performed by human operators at this stage. Therefore, displays are designed to show the instructions for the operators.

The performance of this goal can involve a series of subbehaviors including a series of "Inspect_feature"s that the workstation would assign the CMM equipment controller to perform and a series of corresponding "place/fixture_part"s for the fixturing controller. The two subordinates need to coordinate. The performance of inspecting a specific feature can involve a series of even lower level "Go_to_point" subbehaviors to be conducted by the inspection probe controller. These subbehaviors are further decomposed until individual motor behavior is generated. This results in the actuation of the hardware components to achieve the goal within a given tolerance. The inspection data may be recorded, reported, and processed at multiple levels of hierarchy to form different perceptions of the inspection results.

Figure 40 further maps the behaviors onto the RCS functional modules.

2. Inspection Workstation Control System Implementation

The authors applied the methodology to the inspection workstation (IWS) of the NAMT. Figure 41 shows the control hierarchy and the command interfaces. Figure 42 shows the internal functionality of some of the control nodes in detail. The primitive (Prim) and servo levels handle low-level motion control. These levels and the elemental move (emove) level were adopted from the existing NGIS implementation [49] and are considered legacy subsystems.

The emove level also contains a node for tool changing. The tool changing activities are performed by a human using an operator interface computer screen. The operator reads the commands and instructions on the screen, acts on them, and reports the status, via the screen, to the control system to close the control loop.

The task level contains control nodes to support the measurement subsystem and the fixturing subsystem of the workstation. These nodes each contain a PL and an EX process. PLs employ interpreters to interpret pregenerated plans that are coded in an industrial standard language called DMIS (dimensional measuring

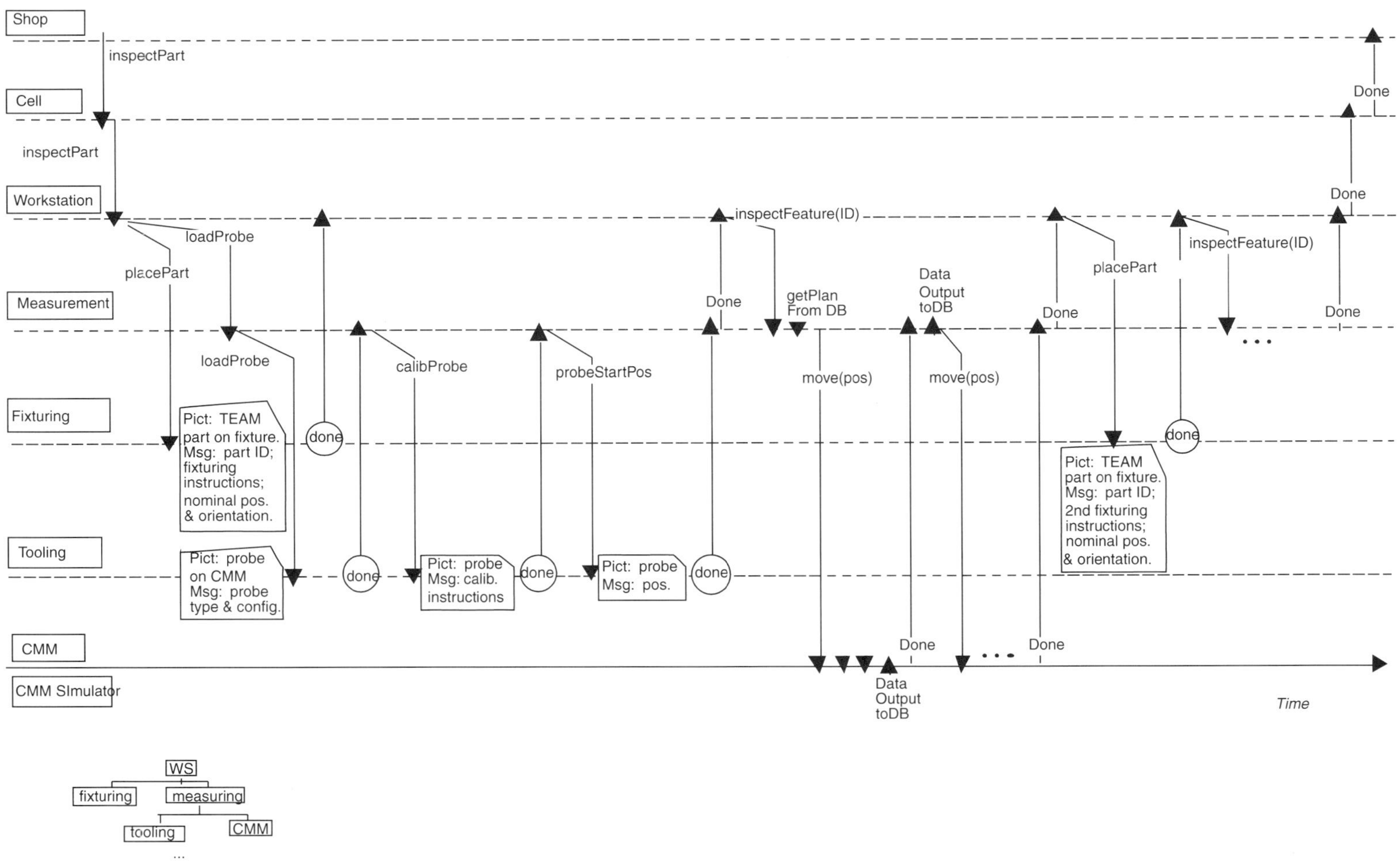

FIGURE 39 Inspection behavior analysis.

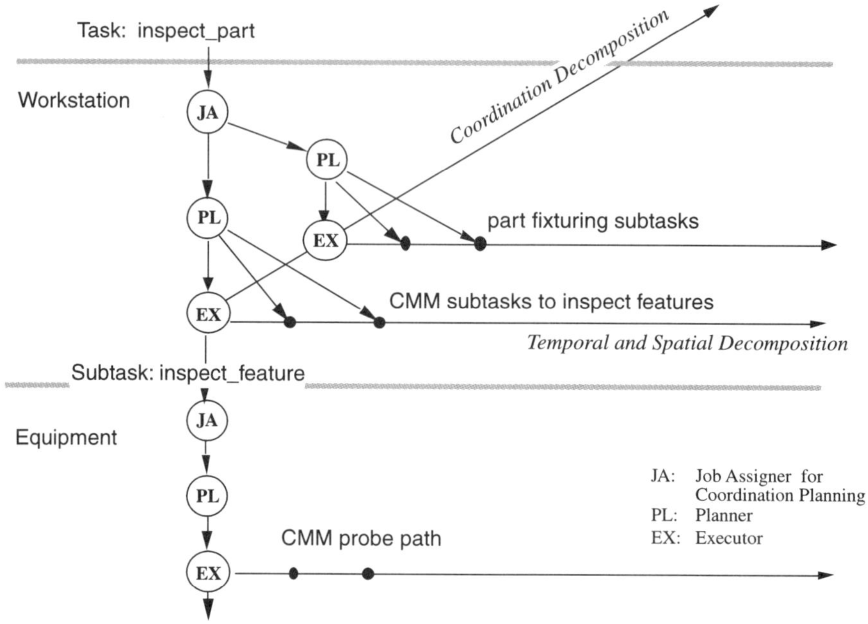

FIGURE 40 Mapping behavior on RCS modules.

interface standard). This configuration demonstrates ISAM's capability of adapting industrial practices into intelligent manufacturing. The fixturing node handles loading, unloading, and refixturing parts. In this implementation, these are executed by a human.

The workstation level control node accepts jobs from the shop level and coordinates the activities of the measurement and fixturing nodes to carry out the job on a particular part lot. In the recently completed integration, the shop controller has coordinated the PDM to provide certain inspection instructions to the inspection workstation. The PL module for this control node interprets the workstation inspection plan and sends the decomposed fixturing instructions and part feature inspection schedules, as described in the previous behavior analysis section, for the two task level subordinates.

A workcell node resides above the workstation node. This node converts and decomposes a highest level incoming job, implemented via a CORBA protocol, to the IWS native communication protocol, implemented via the EMC NML. This setup demonstrates ISAM's capability to integrate heterogeneous manufacturing subsystems.

The shop level obtains orders from its operator interface, that is, the guardian, and plans the jobs for the subordinates accordingly.

Figure 43 shows the hardware configuration for the initial testbed implementation. It illustrates the computing hardware and the mapping of the previously described control nodes into the hardware. Also shown is the physical configuration of the communications connections, via Ethernet or shared memory mechanisms. (Bit3 is a commercial product used to provide shared memory-like communication between backplanes.) Items indicated in parentheses are part of the existing NGIS

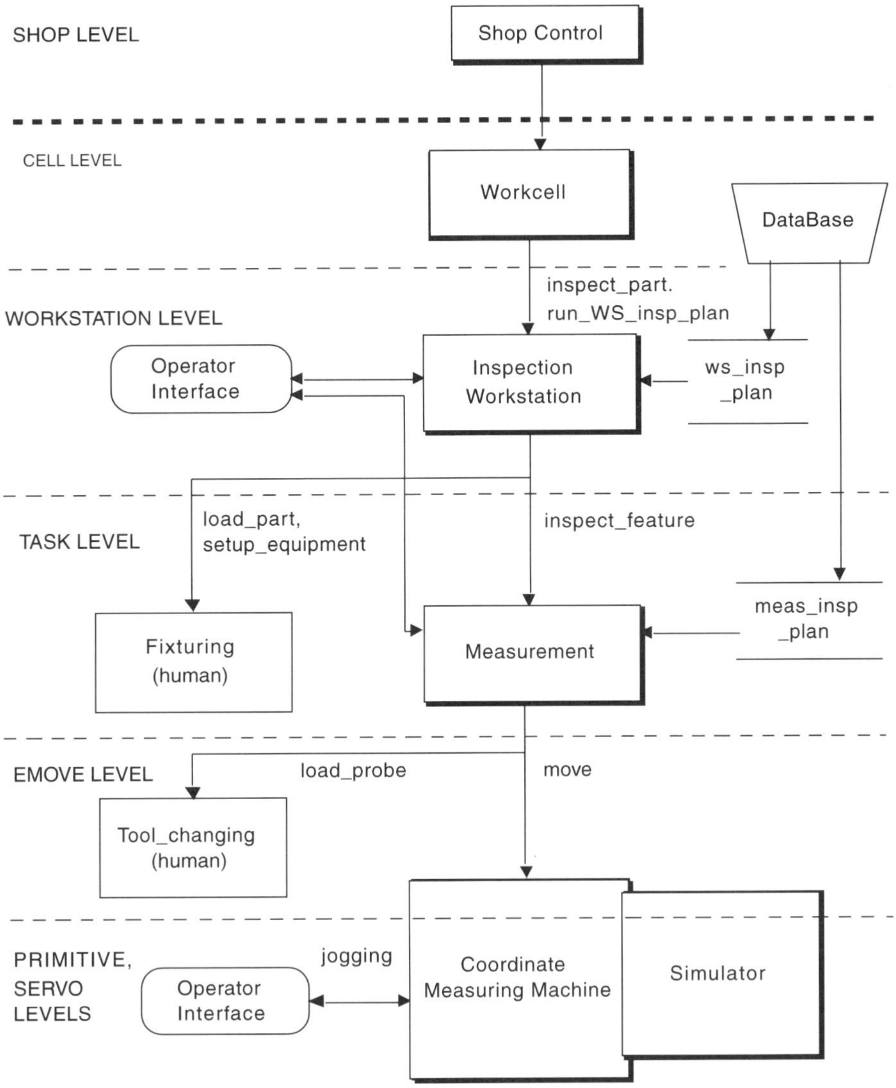

FIGURE 41 Inspection workstation.

configuration, but are not used in the initial implementation described here. They are required for support of the vision system and various inspection probes and their interfaces.

VI. CASE STUDY III, INTELLIGENT AUTONOMOUS VEHICLES, EXERCISING FULL ARCHITECTURAL CAPABILITY

Open system architecture standards are needed for industries that develop intelligent mobile vehicle systems for military security and surveillance and intelligent transportation systems applications. The need is for standard interfaces that facil-

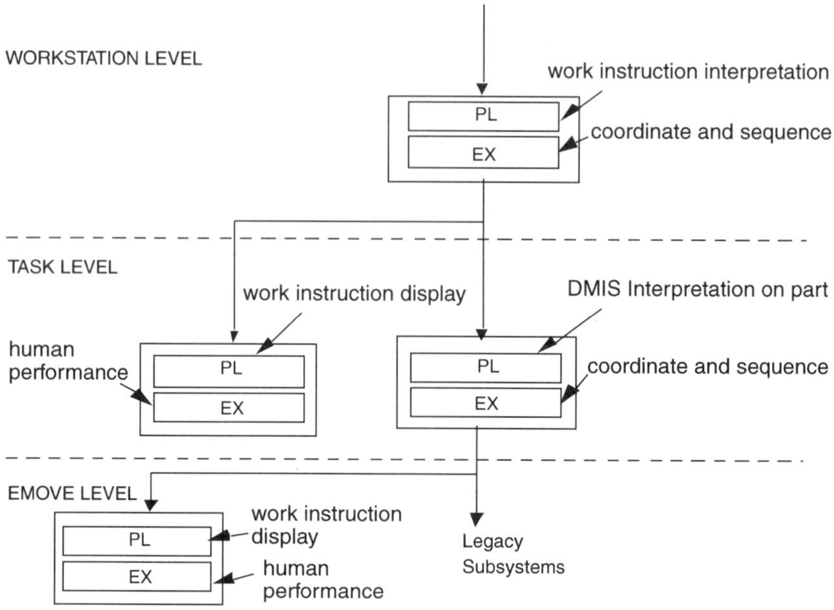

FIGURE 42 Internal functionality of the implemented control nodes.

itate the development and use of commercially available "plug-and-play" components and, in turn, help to reduce cost and development time for system deployment and improvements.

In addition to defining interfaces for subsystems and components, there is also a need for the development and demonstration of intelligent vehicle controllers through the use of advanced, core technology being developed at universities, government labs, and in industry. The United States Army, a major user of the intelligent autonomous vehicle systems that it is considering deploying these systems in the battlefield, has identified technology development needs for such systems. These include reliable obstacle detection, tracking, and recognition; more mobile off-road performance; night and all-weather operations; more autonomous tactical behaviors; and single and multiple vehicles.

The emerging industries and the users need measures of performance for evaluating the technology being developed for intelligent mobile systems. Rapid technology evolution, driven by the availability of compact, low-cost, high performance computers and new advanced sensor systems, requires the evaluation of autonomous and semiautonomous control systems with intelligent behaviors. The National Highway Traffic Safety Administration (NHTSA) recognizes the need for evaluating advanced technology for intelligent transportation systems (ITS) and has sponsored work in ISD to develop a real-time measurement and roadway calibration system to evaluate on-vehicle crash avoidance systems for highways. In addition, NIST, as part of the Department of Defense (DOD) program to develop technology for next generation unmanned ground vehicles, is being asked to develop measurement systems and conduct tests for evaluating this technology for military applications.

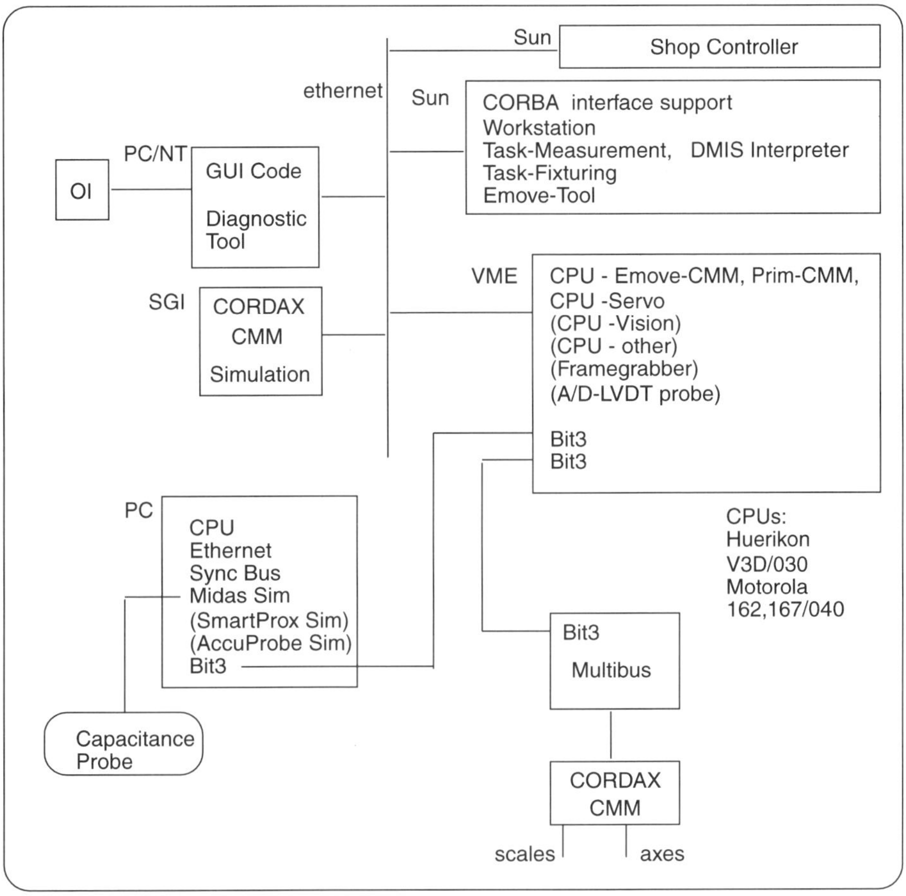

FIGURE 43 ISAM testbed current hardware configuration.

Central to all these issues is the need for an open and standard architecture that allows the integration and exercise of all the advanced component technologies. An instantiated version of RCS, called the 4-D/RCS reference model architecture [29], has been under development as a solution. This development is a jointly sponsored effort that leverages technology from the NIST Intelligent Machines Initiative program and support from the following other agency programs: the Army Research Lab (ARL) Demo III Unmanned Ground Vehicles (UGV) program, the Next Generation Autonomous Vehicle Navigation Control System (AUTONAV) research project between the German Ministry of Defense and the U.S. DOD and the AUTONAV/Department of Transportation (DOT) Crash Avoidance program. This section describes an approach for implementing the architecture and some initial results.

A. Scenario Development

As the earlier cases, the scenarios for this project are being developed via interactions with the Army personnel and the other participating government laboratories. An illustration is given:

The scout platoon leader has been told by his commander to expect the enemy beyond Dogwood Hill. The platoon orders its two sections to establish an observation post on Dogwood Hill. Establishing an observation post means finding one or more locations from which the vehicles can survey an area visually, or through the use of other sensors, while being concealed or covered from sight by the enemy. Cover means being hidden from ground vehicles. Concealment means being hidden from air vehicles. Initial planning is done using a map of the area that contains elevation contour lines and features, such as roads and water. A section contains a leader, and one or more soldiers, all traveling in a single vehicle.

Given this mission, the platoon leader divides the relevant map area into two sectors that are assigned to the two sections. The two sectors are parallel tracts along which the sections plan their motion toward their destination. The sections are assigned code names "Alpha" and "Bravo." A rough trajectory for each section vehicle is derived, based on map elevation and features. Consideration is given to cover and concealment. In a "bounding overwatch" movement, one vehicle travels ahead while the other one looks for enemies from a fixed position. Each vehicle travels to locations that provide a view of the forward area from a covered position. When the moving vehicle reaches its next location, it notifies the overwatching vehicle, which then commences travel, after notifying the other vehicle. The platoon leader may receive these communications as well, which occur over the radio. The rear vehicle moves to a location ahead of the other vehicle until it reaches its chosen next overwatch position. This movement continues until both vehicles have attained their final observation positions.

A narrative of the "establish observation post" scenario could evolve as follows:

1. The battalion commander sends instructions to the platoon commander to establish an observation post at Dogwood Hill by 15:00. Some military information may also be conveyed, such as the latest estimate of enemy positions and direction of movement. A named area of interest (NAI) is defined beyond Dogwood Hill. An NAI defines a region on a map that is to be given particular attention during a mission.
2. The platoon commander (PC) acknowledges receipt of instructions and intention to carry those out.
3. The PC reviews the mission with two section leaders, George and Jerry. Together, they look at a map of the area leading up to Dogwood Hill. The map contains elevation contours and feature information such as tree stands, roads, streams, lakes, and other bodies of water. The resolution of the map is typically fairly low, for example, 100 m. Using his knowledge of other battlefield information (e.g., enemy and friendly locations) and expertise in spatial reasoning with two-dimensional maps, the PC subdivides the corridor of approach toward the observation area into two roughly parallel ribbons. Terrain features, such as water, and elevation contours guide the division between the two. He will also mark the map

with other military information, such as line of departure, avenue of approach for the enemy, and phase lines.

4. The PC establishes coarse-resolution paths for the two sections. He looks for paths that take advantage of cover, such as behind hills or through stands of trees. He avoids wide-open areas and impassable areas. He also strives to place the vehicles at locations from which they can observe as much as possible in front of themselves without revealing themselves. Using criteria such as coverage, concealment, traversability, and visibility, a rough trajectory with possible stopping locations for overwatching is sketched on the map for each corridor. The two trajectories have to be coordinated, because one vehicle must be stopped and overwatching while the other one is moving forward. The moving vehicle must be given a reasonable goal location to stop so that the other vehicle can begin its motion. "Reasonable" is determined from years of experience and training and is based on ensuring that the stationary vehicle does not lose visual contact with the moving vehicle and other criteria.
5. The PC gives orders to two section leaders: goal of mission, mission parameters, individual corridors, path to travel, and suggested stopping points. The overall spatial scope of the mission covers a distance of about 10 km. The width of the sector being covered by the two sections is about 500 m.
6. The PC assigns George the Alpha (left) corridor.
7. The PC assigns Jerry the Bravo (right) corridor.
8. George and Jerry acknowledge that they understand the mission and parameters.
9. A rehearsal of the mission takes place using the map. The soldiers in both sections watch while George and Jerry place microvehicles at the determined locations and simulate the coordinated movements.
10. George and Jerry move the vehicles to the line of departure at 15:40 and radio that they are in position.
11. The PC radios that the mission may begin.
12. George (the Alpha section) radios that he is starting movement.
13. George moves toward the first selected overwatch position for his side. He moves in a manner dictated by the terrain and the enemy location. The navigator uses a map with mission markings on it, along with landmark recognition and a global positioning system (GPS) to direct the vehicle along its assigned path. Other constraints for movement are:
    (a) Move as quickly as possible.
    (b) Select your path so that you are not visible by the enemy.
    (c) Keep your sensors pointed so that the targeted area is always covered.
    (d) Avoid "flanking" the enemy; that is, do not expose your flank to them.
    (e) Select your next location by assessing the terrain and features in the near range (50–1000 m).
    (f) Assess upcoming terrain and features by performing "military cresting." Military cresting is slowly creeping up a hill until only sensor(s) peer over the crest of the hill. One of the soldiers in the vehicle may stand up and look through binoculars and notify the driver when to stop. Using the sensing capability, which relies primarily on

human vision, assess your next movement point. Back the vehicle up, and go around the hill at a lower elevation, while avoiding flanking.

14. As George approaches his planned stopping point, he refines the final location based on actual conditions: cover and concealment opportunities that were not captured in the maps his platoon leader used.
15. When George reaches his first stopping point, he radios Jerry that he is set.
16. Jerry radios George that he is beginning to move.
17. Jerry moves the Bravo section forward and follows steps 13 and 14 until he has reached his planned stopping point.
18. While the Bravo section is moving, the Alpha section overwatches to the front. George uses whatever sensors are appropriate to look forward as far as possible for potential enemy locations. Techniques for searching are sensor-dependent.
19. When Jerry is in an overwatch position, about 3 km from Dogwood Hill, possible enemy locations are detected by one of his sensors. Per military doctrine, the following immediately occur:
    (a) The other sections and the PC are notified of location and situation via a spot report.
    (b) George and Jerry move their vehicles into overwatch positions. They quickly identify candidate locations in their surroundings that provide cover and concealment. George has to move backward about 600 m to a more suitable place he had noted as he was traveling.
    (c) Any other sections that may be visible from enemy locations(s) move to an overwatch position. These include sections attached to other platoons or battalions.
    (d) All sections that may be able to confirm sightings try to do so and notify the PC and peers of their results.
20. The commander assesses the situation and sends an updated mission to the sections. Instead of proceeding to establish an observation post on Dogwood Hill, they are to remain in overwatch positions and continue sending reports on enemy activities.

B. Control Hierarchy and Task Decomposition

Some key aspects of behavior and task decomposition emerge from this high-level scenario. In the Demo III Program, an autonomous vehicle will fulfill the role of a section. As expected in a military hierarchy, commands flow down from superior to subordinates. Status reports flow back up the command chain. The planning horizons for the platoon level are about an order of magnitude larger than those of the section level (e.g., 10 km versus less than 1 km per section movement). Plans for section paths are planned at the platoon level using coarse data. The sections make extensive use of their sensing systems, especially human vision, for fine-tuning the actual path traveled. Other sensors include GPS and mission-specific ones. Experience, training, and external knowledge bases are essential for making military plans. External knowledge bases include maps and military intelligence. Preprogrammed reactive behaviors are useful in military missions. For example, several behaviors were triggered when potential enemy sightings occurred.

Based on analysis of scenarios like the one above, a control hierarchy emerges. In the control hierarchy under development, Fig. 44, active and passive vision are the primary sensors for performing dynamic image perception analysis during navigation. Other sensors, such as accelerometers, inertial navigation system (INS), and differential global positioning system (DGPS), measure vehicle motion through the environment and provide a basis for precise localization of vehicles, targets, obstacles, and terrain features on a map database. These sensors and their controls form the servo levels of the attention and reconnaissance, surveillance, and target acquisition (RSTA) mission package subsystems.

At the lower levels, including primitive, subsystem, and vehicle, hybrid vision processing involves the fusion of real-time laser range image (LADAR), vision

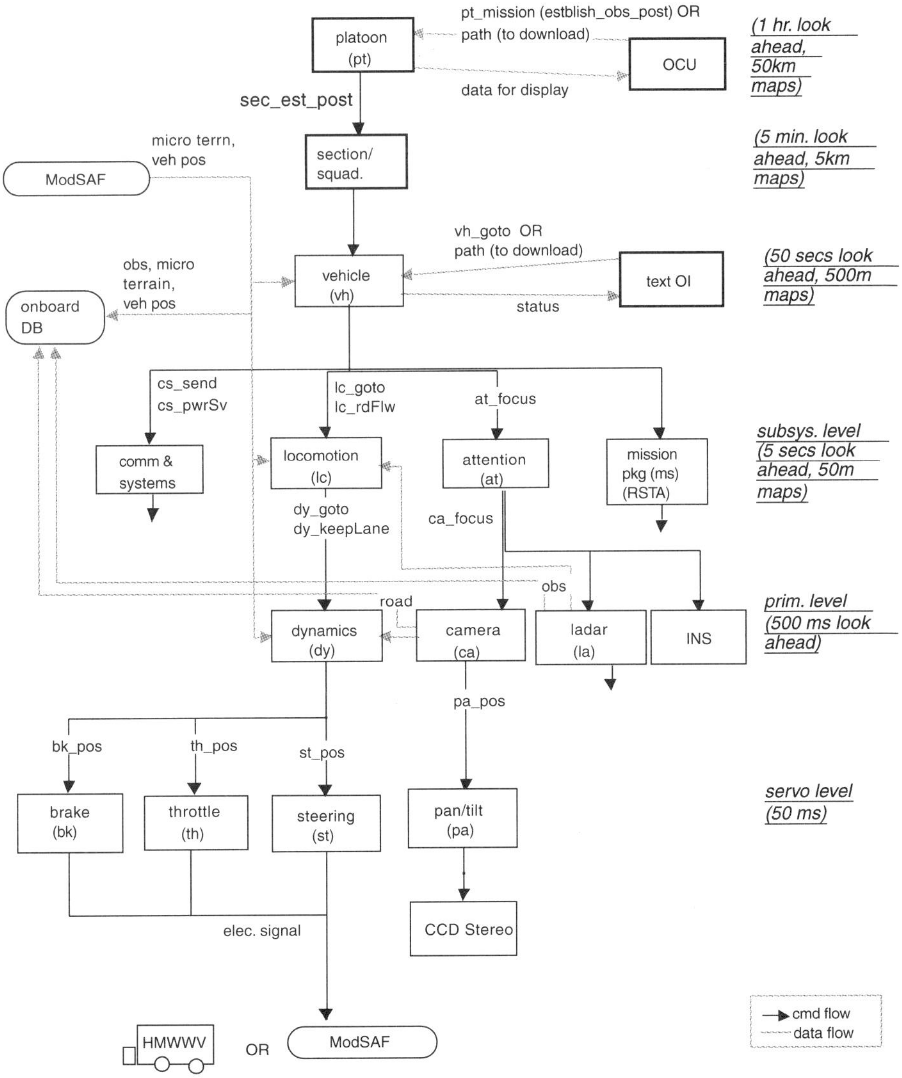

FIGURE 44 Military unmanned vehicle control hierarchy.

image, and inertial navigation system data. Obstacles detected in LADAR images are projected into camera images. The algorithms at these levels perform obstacle detection, recognition, and tracking. The locomotion subsystem uses this information to perform obstacle avoidance and vehicle dynamic control. The locomotion servo control involves such actuators as steering wheel, throttle, and brakes.

The higher levels of the control hierarchy involve a platoon controller that coordinates multiple sections of XUVs in the current Army scout mission scenario configuration. In the DOT programs and others, different vehicle grouping will be devised. A section level controller coordinates multiple vehicles. These high-level controllers take the low-level map data, including terrain, obstacles, and other military information, and derive maps at their own resolutions. The map information is then used for mission planning.

The operator interface function is realized via the operator control units (OCU), which follows the hierarchical construct. The high-level mission simulation will be provided via the Modular Semi-Automated Forces (Mod-SAF) system from the U.S. Army Mounted Maneuver Battlefield Laboratory, Ft. Knox, Kentucky.

Task decomposition is illustrated in Fig. 44. The platoon receives a command to "establish an observation post." The planning process generates the responsibility areas and routes for the subordinate sections or squads. The information is embedded in the command "sc_est_obs". The section–squad planning process generates waypoints that coordinates the overwatch by the two vehicles and sends "goto" commands to the vehicles. The goto command may include responsibility regarding surveying a named area of interest or communication directives. The vehicle controller decomposes this responsibility into subtasks for each of the subsystem controllers. The RSTA mission package will be targeted toward the NAI, whereas the locomotion subsystem will navigate through optimized routes to support RSTA. These subsystem commands are, in turn, decomposed into the actuator commands for locomotion and sensor pointing or adjusting so that the assigned commands can be accomplished.

VII. SUMMARY

We described the hierarchical real-time control systems reference model architecture aiming at designing and developing intelligent control for large and complex engineering systems. RCS is based on several general and fundamental principles of engineering systems. The methodology, or the development process to apply RCS to the system control, is described. This process unifies multiple engineering principles, including the following: multiple spatial and temporal resolutions; behavior-oriented, object-oriented, and functional decomposition.

In the described process, developers arrange controllers in hierarchies according to assigned responsibility and authority. This provides consistent correspondence to both the military chain-of-command and manufacturing system configurations. The developers can easily map current operations, possibly manual, to the automation models. In other words, this feature facilitates incremental upgrade from current manual operations to automatic operations. Operators can easily fit in the RCS hierarchies to perform the designated parts of the system control.

The RCS reference model architecture and methodology provide a simple and systematic mechanism to acquire, describe, and organize domain operational knowledge. The single-node concept improves human understanding of the design.

The process-template-based implementation approach provides a systemwide consistent interfacing infrastructure. This frees up the developers from the infrastructural issues and allows them to focus on individual component technology. Developers can apply the templates at an early stage and construct a control hierarchy capable of interfacing and executing individual component technologies that are linked in. This is called the generic shell for the target control system. This shell serves as the backbone for the system operations. This shell-based approach is generic and applicable to a broad class of complex commercial and military control system applications.

The RCS methodology prescribes modular real-time simulation and animation functions. This facilitates early concept visualization and rapid prototyping that, in turn, reduces development cost.

The authors described three ISD case study control systems. The descriptions progressively demonstrate the richness of the RCS architecture, from a generic-process-template-based system to real-time rich sensing and planning systems. The ultimate goal is to implement the latest control systems that capture the full RCS capability. The case studies also described the evolution and the road map of the methodology, from base-class models to process and interface definitions and to the plan of fully exercising the methodology.

DISCLAIMER

Certain commercial products or company names are identified in this chapter to describe our study adequately. Such identification is not intended to imply recommendation or endorsement by the National Institute of Standards and Technology, nor is it intended to imply that the products or names identified are necessarily the best available for the purpose.

REFERENCES

1. Albus, J. S. and Meystel, A. A reference model architecture for design and implementation of intelligent control in large and complex systems. *Int. J. Intelligent Control and Systems* 1:15–30, 1996.
2. Antsaklis, P. J., Kohn, W., Nerode, A., and Sastry, S. Eds. *Hybrid Systems 11, Lecture Notes in Computer Science Series*, Vol. 999. Springer-Verlag, New York, 1995.
3. Kowal, J. A., *Behavior Models*. Prentice Hall, Englewood Cliffs, NJ, 1992.
4. Astrom, K. J. and Wittenmark, B. *Adaptive Control*. Addison-Wesley, Reading, MA, 1989.
5. Raouf, A. and Ben-Daya, Eds. *Flexible Manufacturing Systems: Recent Developments. Manufacturing Research and Technology Series*, Vol. 23, Elsevier, New York, 1995.
6. Antsaklis, P. J. and Passino, K. M., Eds. *An Introduction to Intelligent and Autonomous Control*. Kluwer Academic, Norwell, MA, 1993.
7. Saridis, G. N. Foundations of Intelligent Controls. In *Proceedings of the IEEE Workshop on Intelligent Control 1985*, pp. 23–28. IEEE Computer Society Press, Washington, DC, 1985.
8. OSACA Project Web Page, http://www.isw.uni-stuttgart.de/projekte/osaca/english/osaca.htm.
9. Albus, J. S., Quintero, R., Proctor, F. M., Michaloski, J. L., Dagalakis, N. G., Tarnoff, N. NIST support to the next generation controller program. NIST Interagency Report NISTIR 4888, Gaithersburg, MD, 1991.

10. Lima, P. U. and Saridis, G. N. *Design of Intelligent Control Systems Based on Hierarchical Stochastic Automata Series in Intelligent Control and Intelligent Automation*, Vol. 2. World Scientific, River Ridge, NJ, 1996.
11. Acar, L. and Özgüner, U. Design of knowledge-rich hierarchical controllers for large functional systems. *IEEE Trans., Syst., Man, Cybern.* 20:791–803, 1990.
12. Barkmeyer, E. J., Hopp, T., Pratt, M., and Runnaudot, G. Background study, requisites, rationale, and technology overview for the Systems Integration for Manufacturing Applications (SIMA) program. NISTIR 5662, Gaithersburg, MD, 1995.
13. Wallace, S., Senehi, M. K., Barkmeyer, E., Luce, M., Ray, S., and Wallace, E. Control entity interface specification. NISTIR 5272, September 1993.
14. Donmez, M. A., Ed. Progress report of the Quality in Automation project for FY90. NISTIR 4536, March 1991.
15. Albus, J. S. Outline for a theory of intelligence. *IEEE Trans. Syst., Man, Cybern.* 21:473–509, 1991.
16. Proctor, F., Michaloski, J., Shackleford, W., and Szabo, S. Validation of standard interfaces for machine control. In *Intelligent Automation and Soft Computing: Trends in Research, Development, and Applications*, Vol. 2. TSI Press, Albuquerque, NM, 1996.
17. Huang, H., Quintero, R., and Albus, J. S. A reference model, design approach, and development illustration toward hierarchical real-time system control for coal mining operations. In *Control and Dynamic Systems, Advances in Theory and Applications,* Vol. 46, pp. 173–254. Academic Press, San Diego, 1991.
18. Huang, H. An architecture and methodology for intelligent control. *IEEE Expert* April 1996.
19. Barbera, A. J., Albus, J. S., Fitzgerald, M. L., and Haynes, L. S. RCS: The NBS real-time control system. In *Robots 8 Conference and Exposition*, Detroit, MI, June 1984.
20. Albus, J. S. System description and design architecture for multiple autonomous undersea vehicles. NIST Technical Note 1251, National Institute of Standards and Technology, U.S. Department of Commerce, September 1988.
21. Quintero, R. and Barbera, A. A software template approach to building complex large-scale intelligent control systems. In *Proceedings of the 8th IEEE International Symposium of Intelligent Control*, Chicago, 1993.
22. Booch, G. *Object-Oriented Analysis and Design.* Benjamin–Cummings, Redwood City, CA, 1994.
23. Rumbaugh, J., Blaha, M., Premerlani, W., Eddy, F., and Lorensen, W. *Object-Oriented Modeling and Design.* Prentice-Hall, New York, 1991.
24. Coad, P. and Yourdan, E. *Object-Oriented Analysis.* Yourdan Press, Englewood Cliffs, NJ, 1991.
25. Shlaer, S. and Mellor, *Object Lifecycles: Modeling the World in States.* Prentice-Hall, New York, 1992.
26. Albus, J. S. Intelligent system architecture for manufacturing. Unpublished, 2001.
27. Huang, H. Intelligent manufacturing system control: Reference model and initial implementation. In *Proceedings of the 35th IEEE Conference on Decision and Control* (CDC), Kobe, Japan, December 1996.
28. http://www.mel.nist.gov/nsmt/.
29. Albus, J. S. 4-D/RCS, a reference model architecture for demo III. NISTIR 5994, Gaithersburg, MD, 1997.
30. Albus, J. Outline for a theory of intelligence. *IEEE Trans. Syst., Man, and Cybern.* 21:473–509, 1991.
31. Albus, J. S. and Meystel, A. Behavior generation: The architectural issues. NISTIR, 1997.
32. Huang, H. and Senehi, K. Task frame conceptual design. NIST ISD internal document, 1996.
33. Horst, J. A. and Scott, H. Scenario for demonstrating the intelligent system architecture for manufacturing (ISAM). NIST ISD internal document, April 1998.
34. http://isd.cme.nist.gov/proj/rcs_lib/.
35. Pearl, J., Heuristics, Addison-Wesley Publishing Company, Reading, MA, 1985.
36. Proctor, F., *et al.* Validation of standard interfaces for machine control. In *Proceedings of the International Symposium on Robotics and Manufacturing-The World Automation Congress '96*, Montpellier, France, May 27–30, 1996.
37. Huang, H., Quintero, R., and Albus, J. S. A reference model, design approach, and development illustration toward hierarchical real-time system control for coal mining operations. In *Control and*

Dynamic Systems, Advances in Theory and Applications, Vol. 46, pp. 173–254. Academic Press, San Diego, 1991.

38. Huang, H. An architecture and methodology for intelligent control. *IEEE Expert* April 1996.
39. Barbera, A. J., Albus, J. S., Fitzgerald, M. L., and Haynes, L. S. RCS: The NBS real-time control system. In *Robots 8 Conference and Exposition*, Detroit, MI, June 1984.
40. Albus, J. S. System description and design architecture for multiple autonomous undersea vehicles. NIST Technical Note 1251, National Institute of Standards and Technology, U.S. Department of Commerce, September 1988.
41. Huang, H. Operator interface and situation perception in hierarchical intelligent control: A case study. In *Combined IEEE International Symposium on Intelligent Control (ISIC), International Conference on Control Applications (CCA) and International Symposium on Computer-Aided Control System Design (CACSD)*, Dearborn, MI, September 16–19, 1996.
42. Albus, J. S. From cerebellar model articulation controller to a reference model for intelligent control. In *Proceedings of the 15th Annual International Conference IEEE Engineering in Medicine & Biology Society*, San Diego, October 28–21, 1993.
43. Lauwerier, H. *Fractals*. Princeton Univ. Press, Princeton, NJ, 1991.
44. Mayhew, D. J. *Principles and Guidelines in Software User Interface Design*. Prentice Hall, Englewood Cliffs, NJ, 1992.
45. Bloom, H. M. and Christopher, N. A framework for distributed and virtual discrete part manufacturing. In *Proceedings of CALS EXPO 96*, October 1996, Long Beach, CA.
46. Nashman, M., Hong, T., Rippey, W. G., and Herman, M. An integrated vision touch-probe system for inspection tasks. Machine Vision Applications, Cleveland, June 1996.
47. http://www.arcweb.com/omac/.
48. http://isd.cme.nist.gov/info/team (Web location for Technologies Enabling Agile Manufacturing (TEAM) application programming interfaces).
49. http://isd.cme.nist.gov/brochure/NGIS.html.

8

REAL-TIME FAULT-TOLERANT CONTROL SYSTEMS

WEI LIU

Department of Automation Engineering, Hebei Institute of Technology, Tangshan, Hebei 063009, People's Republic of China

I. INTRODUCTION

Artificial intelligence and expert systems are currently popular topics in industrial process control because the expert system approach is to take knowledge from

Expert Systems, Edited by Cornelius T. Leondes, Volume 1

ISBN: 0-12-443881-4 / $35.00

human experts and represent it as a knowledge base, which can then be processed to solve difficult problems in the same way the expert would. The development and application of expert systems have moved out of the realm of the computer scientist and into the mainstream of science and engineering research. There are a wide variety of ways that expert system technology can assist the engineering process. Expert systems have found application in many technical domains for troubleshooting processes and systems, planning and training, advising operators and technicians, and a host of other areas. They are regarded as a tool with great potential for improving the efficiency and competitiveness of tuning and service operations in manufacturing. One of the most important areas of research is the application of expert systems to real-time process monitoring and control. It has mainly progressed in two directions. One direction focused on the use of expert systems to guide and automate control system design. The second research direction targeted the use of expert systems as part of the process control system. Expert systems offer a means of incorporating higher levels of intelligence into advanced control systems to make them resilient.

Modern technology is leading to increasingly complex systems with ever more demanding performance goals. In large complex systems such as nuclear power plants and chemical industry plants, the various subsystems fulfill the needs of process control and safety. These systems must have the capability of fault accommodation to operate successfully over long periods of time. Therefore, fault-tolerance in industry is very important from the viewpoint of safety as well as reduced manufacturing costs. In the class of fault-tolerant control systems we admit that one or more key components of the physical feedback system will fail and that this failure can have a significant impact on stability or performance. At the simplest level we can think of sensor and/or actuator failure, while at a more complex level we can think of other system failures, for example, partial structural damage to an aircraft due to a midair collision or weapon damage. In the same vein, we can also worry about computer hardware and software failure. The idea is to design the control system to retain stability and lose performance in a gracefully degraded manner. It may be necessary to reconfigure the control system following the detection of such failures [1].

Mainly there are two research approaches to fault-tolerant control. The first one makes use of passive techniques to deal with faults in the system. Passive techniques of fault tolerance at the sensor or actuator are based on the design of robust controllers that would guarantee performance even with the faults present. Algorithms that guarantee performance have been developed in many disciplines. The other approach is to accommodate faults by active techniques, which are essentially based on a dynamic reconfiguration technique.

A primary feature of any reconfiguration scheme is failure detection and fault diagnosis. Research on fault diagnosis of dynamic systems has been quite active during the last decades. Various methods for fault diagnosis and detection have been presented. Good surveys on this subject, which explain its importance and describe many different applications, can be found in [2–6]. These surveys review a variety of model-free and model-based diagnosis strategies. The model-free methods directly examine the plant measurements for the presence of system anomalies. These diagnostic strategies include limit checking frequency analysis and expert systems. In the limit checking scheme, the magnitude of directly measurable plant signals is monitored for the transgression of fixed thresholds. If exceeded, a failure is declared. A more recent model-free detection method is based on the frequency analysis of plant measurements. Finally, expert systems may be designed to diagnose symptoms using logical rules applied automatically or with human interaction [7].

This chapter is about the application of expert system techniques to industrial process control. A real-time expert-system-based fault-tolerant strategy is proposed for processes with sensor and/or actuator failures. In the strategy, the expert system is used to diagnose the faults, malfunctions, or misoperations in the system and to reconfigure the controller to maintain acceptable system performance in real time, with a combination of formal engineering analysis, mathematical processing techniques, and traditional expert system techniques.

II. REAL-TIME EXPERT-SYSTEM-BASED PROCESS CONTROL SYSTEMS

A. Definition and Advantages of Real-Time Expert System

What are the defining characteristics of a real-time expert system? For an industrial process control system, the most important item is the response time: if events are not promptly handled, the process can get out of control. Thus, the definition of a real-time system is the ability to guarantee a response before a certain time has elapsed, where that time is related to the dynamic behavior of the system. If, given an arbitrary event or state of the system, the system always produces a response by the time it is needed, then the system is said to be real-time. Therefore, the most important feature of a real-time expert system is mostly related to "fast," meaning that a system acquires data quickly, besides the following properties possesed by a general expert system [8]:

a. the ability to explain and justify answers, on the basis of theory, or by citing relevant heuristic rules, or by appeal to past case histories;
b. the closeness of reasoning procedures to those used by human experts;
c. the ability to summarize and point out features of the problem situation that were most important in leading to an answer, including information about which other factors might still have an effect, if they were to become known;
d. the ability to grow gradually by adding new pieces of knowledge, usually in the context of solving an unfamiliar problem.

The advantages of a real-time expert system are significant enough to meet the need for time critical solutions in industrial process control. The principal reason for using a real-time expert system would be to reduce the cognitive load on the operators so as to enable them to be free to take decisions in time-critical emergency situations without the cognitive load on them increasing. Decisions can be obtained more reliably and consistently. Explanation of the final answer is an important side product. A real-time expert system may be appropriate especially when approaches using conventional techniques have failed or are impractical, including problem solving situations where (i) humans are unable to monitor effectively all available information, (ii) those capable of performing the tasks are

TABLE 1 Real-Time Expert System Applications

Area	Discipline	Example
Chemical & biochemical	Fault-tolerant control & fault detection or diagnosis	Yeast fermentation process control [22]
Metallurgical	State prediction & process control	Steel mill soaking pit control [23]
Mechanical	Fault detection & diagnosis	Robotics and automotive [3]
Power system	Operation monitoring & control	Treat alarm messages from 58 substations of a 380/220 kV network [24]
Aerospace	Fault detection & diagnosis	F/A-18 aircraft control [16]

scarce and training new experts is expensive, or (iii) humans cannot provide a control strategy fast enough. Real-time expert-system-based industrial process control strategies can be more easily expandable than conventional control schemes, so that they can be gradually improved as their problem domain evolves. A real-time expert system would automatically tailor itself to changes in the process behavior and faults in the process or control system. Such a system would always maintain the process at the highest level of control under all circumstances. Table 1 gives some successful examples where real-time expert systems have been applied to industrial process control.

B. Components of a Real-Time Expert System

The real-time expert system obtains its knowledge from a knowledge source directly connected to the plant as well as from a global knowledge base and routes this information to a local knowledge database. The key aspects that distinguish real-time expert systems are shown in Fig. 1.

1. Knowledge Acquisition

Human beings gain knowledge in different ways. One way is through direct observation and they draw inferences and conclusions from what they see. Another possibility is indirectly through some kind of tutor (person, book, film, recording, etc.), or through discovery, combining old knowledge in new ways to develop new ideas and hypotheses. A real-time expert system for industrial process control stresses acquiring knowledge from engineers, technological processes, and online input–output data of the plant, and loads it into the computer's memory. The tasks for acquiring knowledge are carried out online and in real time by the user interface in a process control system. The user interface provides a channel through which we can follow up the behavior of the expert system and hence make any necessary modifications of external actions.

2. Knowledge Base

Knowledge representation is a key issue in expert systems. Knowledge representation schemes in artificial intelligence (AI) are prepositional and predicate representations, procedural representations, production systems, semantic nets, and

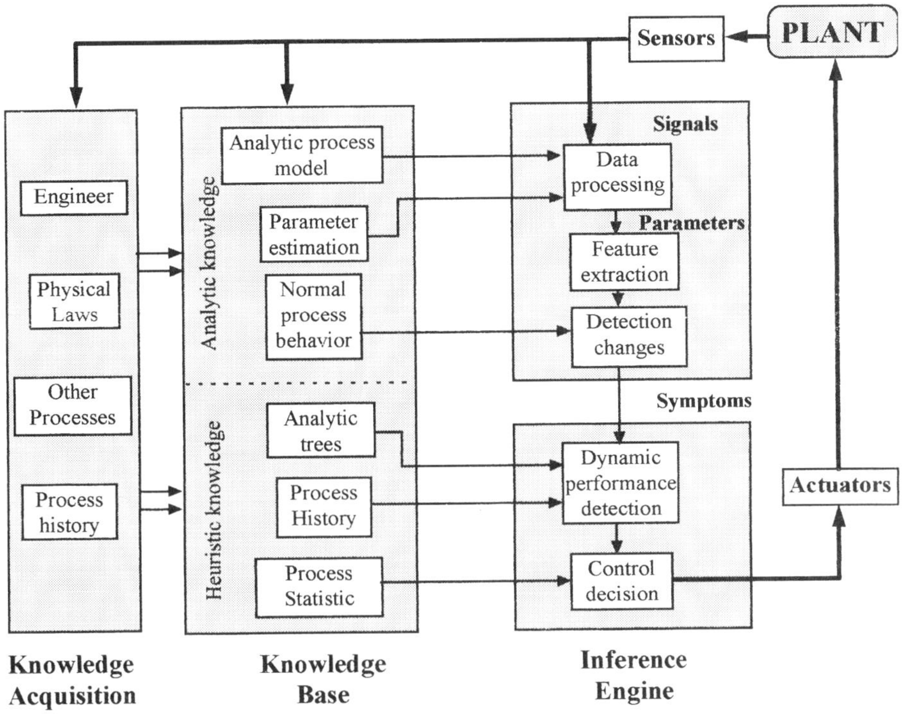

FIGURE 1 Components of a real-time expert system.

frames. The selection of one knowledge representation depends on the particular application intended. A production system representation (rule-based representation) has desirable features for a process control application [9]. For example, in a real-time expert-system-based fault-tolerant process control strategy, the process knowledge base includes two types of knowledge. One is analytical knowledge that consists of analytical process models (e.g., differential equations), estimation methods for parameters and state variables as a basis for feature extraction, and normal process behavior. The second is heuristic knowledge that is constructed by controllers and their parameter trees (connection of process fault symptoms and tailed controllers), historical records (e.g., biomass, substrate, and product concentrations in different culture times in a fermentation process), and process state statistics (e.g., fault and malfunction probabilities). The historical data of a process contain important information about the operation of the process, but they are not in a useful form for understanding the process, and traditional data analysis tools cannot make use of these huge data sets.

3. Inference Engine

An inference engine is a procedure that uses items in the knowledge base of an expert system to draw conclusions and solve problems. Difficulties with real-time application of artificial intelligence include the efficiency of reasoning on the knowledge and the interaction between the symbolic programming environment and the rest of the world, such as the acquisition of measurement data from the plant and the passage of commands to the plant. These methods come from a field where guaranteed response time is not critical. In process control, an important parameter is the sampling period to be chosen. Some action must be taken in the sampling period, whether or not an algorithm or inference engine has concluded that the action is correct. The minimum sampling period that can be used is defined by the amount of time required by the system to make the necessary calculations. The time required by the inference engine to evaluate the knowledge base directly determines the calculation time. Because the process itself and the changing number of inferences has a great influence on which sampling period should be used by the controller, the progressive reasoning principle is very well suited for process control [10]. The implemented reasoning system is generally based on formal classical logic as well as the associated calculations of reasoning and practical implementations and interpretations. The reasoning process is generally problem independent. Here are basic practical reasoning techniques for process control. A good reference for more detail and historical information is the *Handbook for Artificial Intelligence* [8].

C. Building a Real-Time Expert-System-Based Process Control System

Common expert systems enable a computer to solve knowledge-based problem. The problem is fed into the expert system by definite data or facts. The required specific knowledge is stored in a knowledge base, mostly in the form of heuristic knowledge. An inference mechanism then draws conclusions and presents proposed solutions. The computer works with this expert system through an interactive dialog, by presenting different problem data, asking for declarations and for successive conclusions. The common expert system is suited for problems that cannot be solved straightforwardly, because the underlying principles are not known exactly. Therefore heuristic knowledge has to be used, expressed in rules and facts, based on human experience (see [6]).

If the expert system is coupled with the process input or output, a real-time expert-system-based process control system results; see Fig. 2. The real-time expert system is an adjunct to the nominal control structure, which remains the most efficient means of effecting precise control. From this perspective, the expert system performs its decision-making tasks in a concentric *outer loop*; from the expert system perspective, control activity is a *side effect* that supports the decision-making process.

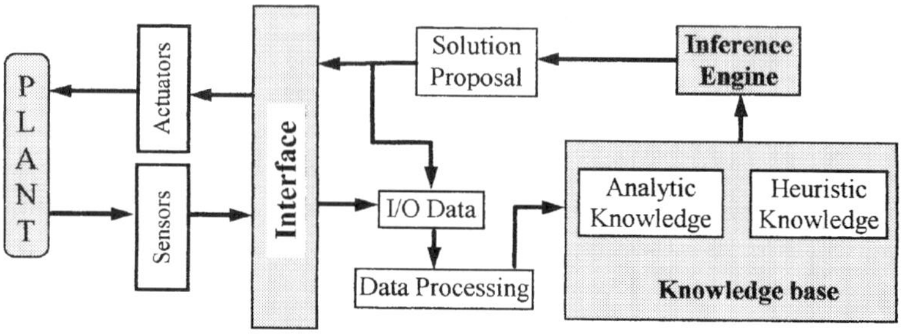

FIGURE 2 A real-time expert-system-based control system.

The expert system offers a useful formalism for fault-tolerant control because it can consider diverse data sources and subproblem abstractions. Failure indicators may be continuous variables generated by measurement or estimation, or they may be discrete variables from online monitors or discrete event models [11].

III. BACKGROUND ON FAULT-TOLERANT CONTROL SYSTEMS

Modern technology is leading to increasingly complex systems with ever more demanding performance goals. These complex systems must have the capability for fault accommodation to operate successfully over long periods of time. Some important industrial processes, for example, nuclear power plants and chemical processes, will require fault detection, isolation, and control reconfiguration that can respond in a short time under adverse conditions. These control systems will allow a plant to maintain adequate levels of performance even with failures in one or more actuators or sensors. Future spacecraft will require higher degrees of autonomous operation that allow for health monitoring and fault tolerance over long periods of time without human intervention [12]. Fault-tolerant control is a topic of immense activity for which a number of different design approaches have been suggested. No attempt is made in this short section to survey all such approaches. Instead, this section concentrates only on some of the structural results obtained in fault-tolerance control for industrial applications such as in the nuclear, chemical, and aerospace industries and discusses some possible approaches for obtaining an effective fault-tolerant controller.

A. Robust Control Strategy

Robust control strives to characterize the uncertainty in the model of the plant to be controlled and to evaluate the degrees of freedom left to achieve the control task within specified bounds. Considerable effort has been made to satisfy the *sine-qua-non* stability robustness requirement, which is to guarantee closed-loop stability under a wide range of plant variations and disturbances that could be due to component failures in either the plant or control system. Bounds under which the stability can be preserved have been derived and a rigorous mathematical theory has been developed to minimize the sensitivity with respect to disturbances and norm-bounded plant uncertainty. The topic of robust control is an extremely active area of research at present, and so it is impossible to include all results and approaches obtained to date. Some literature dealing with various aspects of robust control design by using a number of different approaches may be found, for example, in [13, 14]. In this section, we discuss a robust design scheme that is to find a controller for a given plant such that the resulting controlled system is stable and the error $e(t) \to 0$ as $t \to \infty$ for all $x(t_0) \in R^n$ and for all disturbances and reference inputs satisfying robustness; that is, the given system can be controlled in the desired manner, in spite of the allowable disturbances and changes in the system parameters. The principle of robust control strategy is stated next.

Assume that the controlled plant can be described by the following linear-invariant model:

$$\begin{aligned} \dot{x} &= Ax + Bu + E\omega, \\ y &= Cx + Du + F\omega, \\ e &= y - y_m, \end{aligned} \tag{3.1}$$

where $x \in R^n$is the state vector, $u \in R^m$ is the input vector, $y \in R^p$ is the output vector that is to be regulated, $\omega \in R^l$ is the disturbance vector, which may or may not be measurable, $y_m \in R^p$ is the reference signal vector, and $e \in R^p$ is a vector denoting the error between the output y and the reference input y_m.

It is assumed that the disturbance vector ω satisfies

$$\begin{aligned} \dot{z}_\omega &= A_\omega z_m, \\ \omega &= C_\omega z_\omega, \end{aligned} \tag{3.2}$$

where $z_\omega \in R^{n_\omega}$, the pair (C_ω, A_ω) is observable, and the initial state $z_\omega(t_0)$ may or may not be known. The reference signal vector y_m satisfies

$$\begin{aligned} y_m &= C_m z_m, \\ \dot{z}_m &= A_m z_m, \end{aligned} \tag{3.3}$$

where $z_r \in R^{n_r}$, the pair (C_r, A_r) is observable, and the initial state $z_r(t_0)$ is known.

The robust control design strategy is to construct a controller for (3.1) so that the following hold:

a. The resultant closed-loop system is stable.
b. Asymptotic tracking occurs, that is, $\lim_{t\to\infty} e(t) = 0$ for all $x(t_0) \in R^n$ and for all disturbances and reference inputs satisfying (3.2) and (3.3), respectively, independent of any allowable perturbations in the system parameters. Here the class of *allowable* perturbations could be quite large. A block diagram of the structure of a robust controller is shown in Fig. 3. The robust controller satisfies

$$u(t) = k_1\xi(t) + k_2\eta(t), \tag{3.4}$$

where k_1 and k_2 are gain matrices determined by Lyapunov's stability theory, $\xi(t) \in R^m$ and $\eta(t) \in R^m$ are the outputs of the error compensator and stabilizing compensator defined by

$$\begin{aligned} \dot{\xi}(t) &= \Phi\xi(t) + \theta\, e(t), \\ \dot{\eta}(t) &= \Lambda_1\eta(t) + \Lambda_2\xi(t) + \Lambda_3 u(t) + \Lambda_4 y(t), \end{aligned} \tag{3.5}$$

where Φ, θ, and Λ_i $(i = 1, 2, 3, 4)$ are real constant matrices.

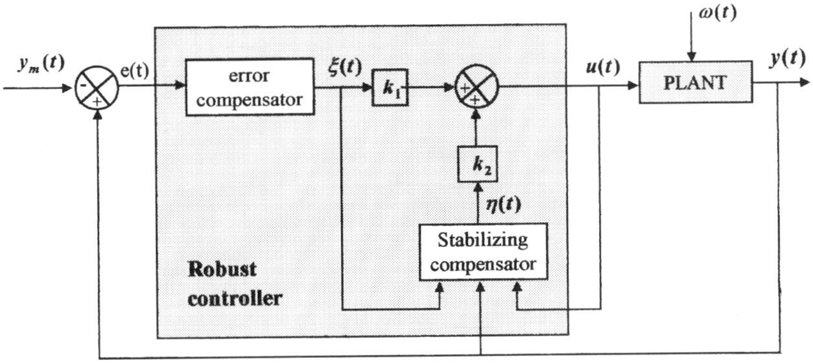

FIGURE 3 A structure of the robust control system.

B. Hardware Redundant Control Strategy

In principle, tolerance to control system failures can be improved if two or more strings of sensors, actuators, and computers, each separately capable of satisfactory control, are implemented in parallel. A hardware redundant control architecture can consist of multiple information processing systems each with the same functional objective. The objective may include the generation of a control signal or the prediction of a process variable. One example of a hardware redundant control systems is multiple sensors measuring the same quantity; the best estimate can be obtained by majority vote. The structure of a hardware redundant control system can be illustrated in Fig. 4.

A voting scheme can be used for redundancy management, comparing control signals to detect and overcome failures. With two identical channels, a comparator can determine whether or not control signals are identical; hence, it can detect a failure but cannot identify which string has failed. In this case, additional online logic is needed to select the unfailed channel for control. When designing a hardware redundant control system, one should consider the following problems: selection logic, nuisance trips, generic failures, reliability of voting or selection units, control force contention, cross-strapping, increased cost and maintenance, number

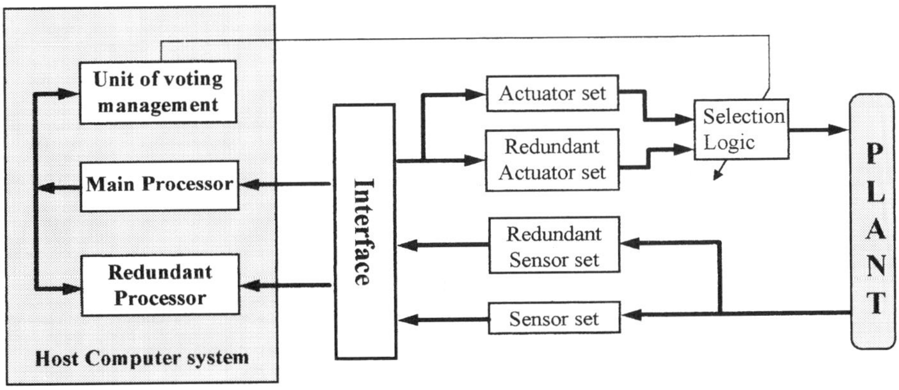

FIGURE 4 A structure of a hardware redundant control system.

of operating channels required for dispatch, and connectors. Fault detection logic must be sensitive to failures yet insensitive to small operational errors, including those due to noncollocation of sensors or actuators. False indications of failure must be minimized to assure that useful resources are kept online and missions are not aborted prematurely.

Hardware redundant control strategy can protect against control system component failures, but it would increase the cost, make maintenance more difficult, and does not address failures on plant components. Furthermore, in the general case, this form of parallelism implies that fault tolerance can only be improved by physically isolating the processors from each other. Software redundant control strategy provides a capability to improve fault tolerance of the control system on the preceding three aspects. It does this with fewer additional components, flexible cross-trapping, and increased computation; therefore, there is greater reliance on the control computer, producing an even greater need for computer reliability.

C. Software Redundant Control Strategy

Hardware redundancy is at the core of most solutions for reliability. However, uninterrupted operation can sometimes be achieved in control systems through redistribution of the control authority between different functioning actuators rather than through duplication or triplication of those actuators. The idea of a software redundant strategy is to utilize different subsets of measurements along with different system models and control algorithms. That is, if a variety of system fault patterns (corresponding fault situations) are possible and some selection of these possible algorithms are simulated based on the particular fault pattern, a decision element will determine the appropriate control algorithm (or appropriate combination of algorithms). When the correct algorithm is determined, the control system can be reconstructed in time against the failures. If the system occurs with the failures, then the control algorithm can be changed with time. The software-based redundancy is also called functional redundancy. It mainly consists of a fault detection or diagnosis unit (for identifying the failed components) and a controller selection logic unit (for making the system adaptation to sensed or estimated failures). The general structure of a software redundant control system can be illustrated in Fig. 5.

In this section, three specific approaches are briefly presented. The first approach uses a single model with adaptive control techniques for updating uncertain system characteristics. The second approach uses fuzzy logical techniques for matching system fault patterns. The third approach uses artificial neural networks for detecting and diagnosing system faults and reconfigurating the controller against the system failures. These control strategies can improve the survival capability of a control system in case of measurement anomalies, and enhances decision making via multiplicity of opinions without the requirement of physical isolation of hardware.

1. Adaptation Control Approach

This approach makes use of the most commonly structured type of uncertainty in which the plant model has a known form, but unknown parameters. The adaptive controller assesses plant and environment variations and then changes its control algorithm correspondingly so as to maintain satisfactory control, which is usually

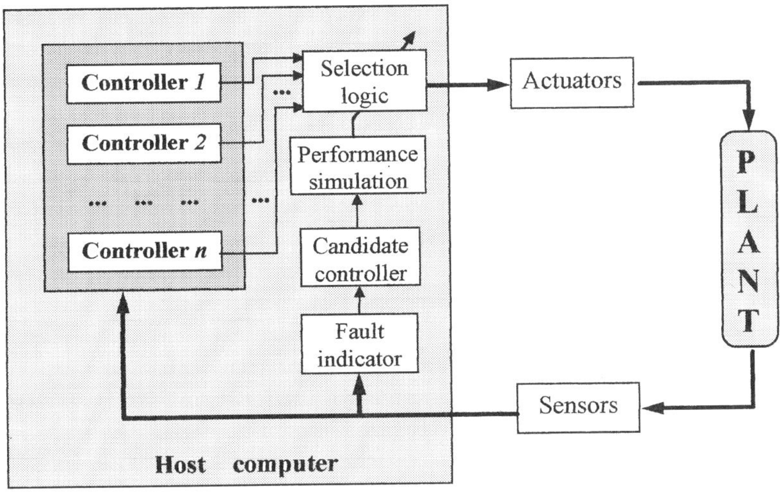

FIGURE 5 The general structure of a software redundant control system.

judged by some performance index. The controller must adapt as rapidly as possible in comparison with the parameter changes of the plant or environment so that it is always at, or nearly at, its most suitable performance.

The performance index is very important in adaptation-based fault-tolerant control systems. It should reflect the effect of system parameters that are likely to vary, so that the adaptive nature can be realized to the full. The controller may also require secondary performance criteria to ensure that the dynamic, transient, and response of the system remain good in the face of maintaining the main performance index as conditions undergo failures. Given a suitable performance criterion the fault-tolerant control system has three major functions to perform. These are the diagnosis of the system failures, the decision in selecting the required control, and the modification of the controller. These three functions are carried out continuously or at selected time internals to allow for unpredictable external influences or unexpected failures occurred in the system. The control scheme is shown in Fig. 6.

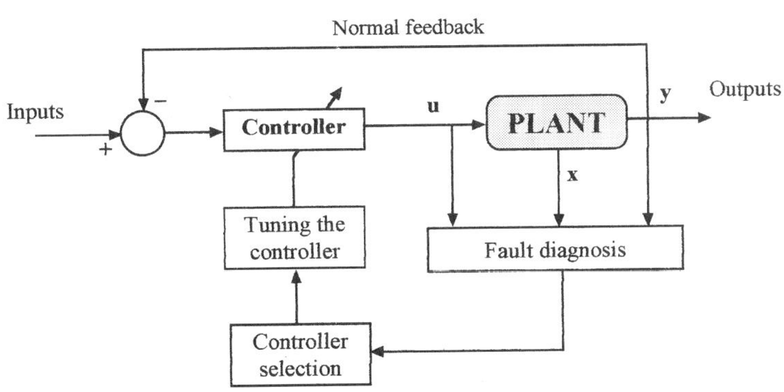

FIGURE 6 An adaptation-based fault-tolerant control system.

A successful example using this strategy was presented by Farid *et al.* [15]. They designed a hybrid adaptive Linear Quadratic control system around the closed-loop system and did the test on the nonlinear model of the F-16 aircraft. The simulation results demonstrated its ability to accommodate control failures and maintain good performance.

2. Fuzzy Logic Approach

Fuzzy logic offers the possibility to express a model qualitatively and to reason with this model qualitatively. Fuzzy-logic-based control has been observed to have excellent robustness characteristics, perhaps because the inherent imprecision, or generality, of the fuzzy decision rules is well suited to imprecise systems whose behavior is known only in large. Hence, fuzzy control systems are able to achieve satisfactory, stable behavior, albeit nonoptimal behavior, over a wide range of system failures.

The main advantage of using fuzzy control is that it is not necessary to have a mathematical model of the observed system. Mathematical models in this research approach are, however, used for simulation purposes. Fuzzy controllers, when compared with the traditional PID controllers in highly nonlinear systems, have often given good results. Recently, fuzzy controllers have been very successful in applications to complex systems. As Zadeh has pointed out, an intelligent control is descriptive and relies on operating experience via a rule-based representation such as fuzzy rules, whereas conventional control is prescriptive and relies on a crisp logic. Thus, fuzzy logic is well suited for the management of uncertainties or failures present in the context of complex behavior that cannot be properly handled by crisp logic [16].

A block diagram of the fuzzy-logic-based fault-tolerant control system is shown in Fig. 7. The controller is composed of two modules, each containing a set of fuzzy rules. The first module receives the signals from the sensors as the input and determines the system-running state as the output. The second module receives the system state information and desired system performance as the input and adjusts the structure and parameters of the controller as the output to ensure the system being in safety and possessing as good performance as possible. In the fuzzy logic-based fault-tolerant control, the algorithm is composed of *if–then*

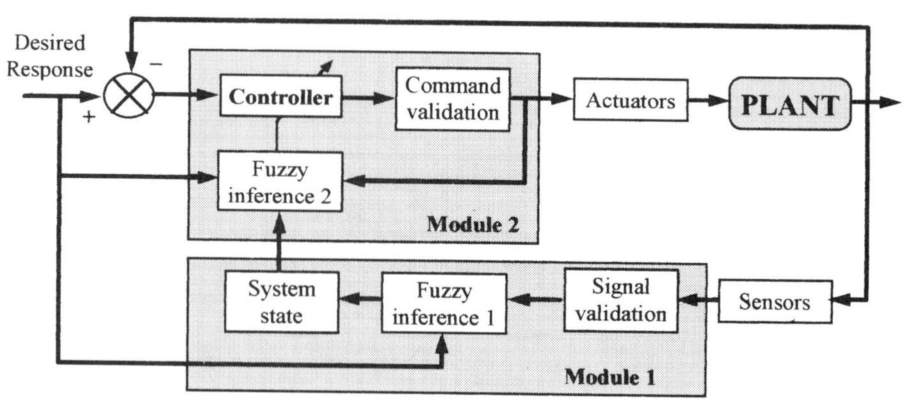

FIGURE 7 A fuzzy-logic-based fault-tolerant control system.

statements. These statements are called *fuzzy rules*. A *fuzzy inference* performs the calculations for control outputs. The literature on fuzzy inferences is extensive and various methods have been proposed. The most commonly used inferance methods in the fuzzy logic applications are *min–max gravity* and *product–sum gravity*.

3. Artificial Neural Network Approach

Artificial neural networks consist of nodes that simulate the neurons and weighting factors that simulate the synapses of a living nervous system. They possess an inherent nonlinear structure suitable for mapping complex characteristics, learning, and optimization. These features have been shown to have considerable potential for fault-tolerant control system design. This fundamental link of neural networks to nonlinear system representation, together with the availability of reliable and inexpensive computing hardware, has resulted in a tremendous growth of research and development in the area [17].

The general idea of using artificial neural network techniques for designing fault-tolerant control system is to recognize process fault patterns and find the structure and parameters of a controller in real time. A multilayer feedforward network can be used for this purpose. The network has an input vector $X = \{x_i\}$, a single output y, and a weight vector $W = \{w_i\}$. The output y equals the sum of input multiplied by the weights and then passed through a nonlinear function, that is, $S(x) = \sum_{i=0}^{n-1} w_i x_i$ and $y(x) = f(s(x))$. The nonlinear function $f(s)$ used here is a sigmoid function. The backpropagation algorithm can be employed to train the network.

The block diagram in Fig. 8 illustrates the fault-tolerant control strategy based on artificial neural networks. The fault detection activity continuously monitors system response and compares the measured system response to models representing a healthy system and specific failure mode systems. The neural network is used to detect faults occuring in the control system and indicate the specific fault characteristics. Based on the process state information, the candidate controller that is predesigned to tailor itself to each anticipated fault condition will be initiated.

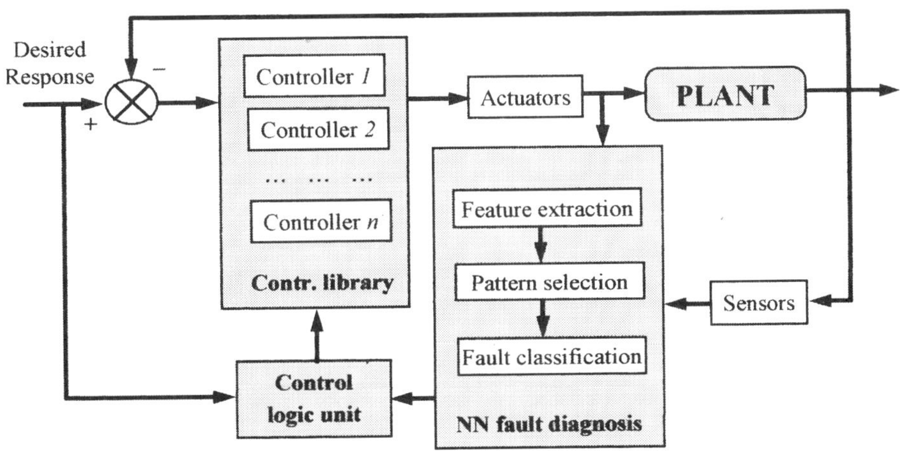

FIGURE 8 An artificial neural-network-based fault-tolerant control system.

IV. FAULT-TOLERANT CONTROL STRATEGY BASED ON THE REAL-TIME EXPERT SYSTEM

A. General Procedure

Fault accommodation is a key aspect of intelligent control. Complex systems require highly sophisticated controllers to insure that demanding performance can be achieved under safe conditions. In the previous section, some fault-tolerant control strategies were briefly given. Two intelligent research approaches have been introduced: fuzzy-logic-based and artificial-neural-network-based control methods. This section focuses on the use of real-time knowledge-based and expert system technology to implement a failure-tolerant control system. Expert system techniques may be used to learn the structure and behavior of the process, to predict the future behavior of the process, and to create algorithms capable of making decisions in real time from online measurement data and the prediction. However, when we need these techniques to solve process control problems, the measurement database must be reduced to a small number of indicators or attributes that provide a sufficiently accurate description of process behavior to allow decisions to be made. Besides, for control engineering purposes, the most important item is the system response time, if events are not promptly handled, the process can get out of control.

In this chapter, a real-time expert-system-based fault-tolerant process control system is described, as shown in Fig. 9. The system is mainly composed of fault detection and diagnosis, real-time simulation and control logic, and controller reconfiguration, which is a combination of formal engineering analysis, mathematical processing techniques, and traditional expert system techniques. The real-time expert system plays an important part in improving dynamic performance and safety of the control system with part sensor and/or actuator failures. It is composed of a database, a fault base, a control architecture base, and an inference engine. The database and fault base contain information about operation and failure states. The control architecture base contains some basic controllers with structures of different types, such as a multiple variable optimum controller, an adaptive controller, a self-tuning controller, a bang-bang controller, and a proportional–integral–differential

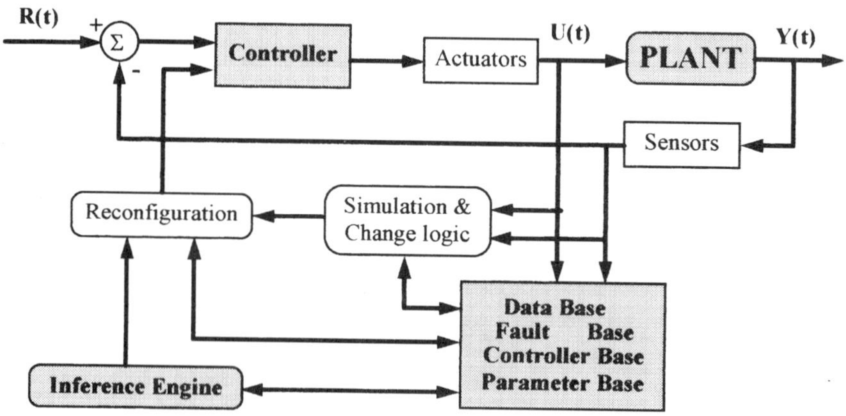

FIGURE 9 The fault-tolerant control system based on real-time expert system.

(PID) controller. The parameter base is the controller parameters that are tailored to the controller for the reconfiguration. The online simulation program is used to predict the control performance of the new controller; therefore, it is a key part of tuning the controller. The control logic is to realize the reconfiguration of the controller, when the simulation part gives the changing signals. The inference engine uses the three bases to configure a controller for the system, about which a real-time decision has been made on whether we should continue to worry about the same performance variables, accepting some performance degradation, or, drastically reducing performance requirements, concentrate on maintaining stability and perhaps afterwards—after the transients have died out—attempt to achieve optimal performance.

B. Structure of the Knowledge Base

In an expert process control system, the knowledge base not only includes the low-level data but also the various problem dependent techniques associated with the processing of the data is naturally unique to every different application. Thus the successful application of the expert systems approach depends on a proper understanding of this knowledge base and its use in relation to an expert system. The knowledge base can be divided into two major categories: (1) knowledge about the particular aspects of the problem (domain knowledge) and (2) knowledge about the problem-solving approaches (metaknowledge).

In the proposed fault-tolerant expert control system, the knowledge base consists of the system database and rule base. The system database is the repository of facts, evidence, hypotheses, and goals. For a process control example, the facts would include static data such as sensor measurement tolerances, operating thresholds, alarm sequencing, plant component configurations, etc. Evidence includes dynamic data such as from sensors, instrument engineering reports, and laboratory and test reports. A practical observation for plant operations is that evidence as just described is typically diverse in type, often noisy, somewhat delayed, possibly incomplete, and sometimes contradictory. An experienced process control engineer has techniques for dealing with this complication. He can develop hypotheses to supplement the current collection of facts. In an expert system, hypotheses are also generated and stored in the database to cope with limitations in known facts or measured evidence. One important class of hypotheses in an expert control system will be the various state and parameter estimates made by parameter estimation algorithm. Including them in the hypotheses acknowledges both that they are derived from evidence and that their derivation is conditioned on other model assumptions.

Goals are other important entries in the database. In an expert control system they usually are both static and dynamic in nature. Static goals include the wide array of performance objectives as to maintain stable operation, find optimal stationary operating points, or determine whether the current control law can be improved. Dynamic goals include those established online, either by external command or from the program itself.

The rule base contains production rules that are typically described as "if ⟨situation⟩ then ⟨action⟩". The "situation" represents facts, evidence, hypotheses, and goals from the database. In a conventional expert system the "action" can be to add a new entry to the database or to modify other entries. In this case the action can also represent activation of a controller or an estimation algorithm. These actions are different from those found in conventional expert systems. The rules may be viewed as functions operating on the state. Because the database is broader in concept than the usual notion of state in control theory, production rules are also richer in content than common transition functions. The rule base is often structured in groups or knowledge sources that contain rules about the same subject. This simplifies the search. The knowledge sources are models for the essential problem elements. In a process control application they include the portion of the operator's skill to be automated, the control and estimation algorithms that may be applied, the appropriate characterization of these algorithms, judgmental knowledge on when to apply them, and supervision and diagnosis of the system [18].

C. Knowledge Acquisition and Knowledge Sources

For expert systems, the process of determining and then encoding into a knowledge base what the expert knows will give the system good performance in the domain. Human beings gain knowledge in different ways. One way is through direct observation—people draw inferences and conclusions from what they see. Another possibility is indirectly through some kind of tutor (person, book, etc.) or through discovery, combining old knowledge in new ways to develop new ideas and hypotheses. Although much of research has been done, no model of human learning has been implemented with a level of performance that even approaches that of a human. This means that we are not yet at the stage in AI development where we can command a computer to gather its own knowledge, so we must gather the information for it, and load it into the computer's memory.

The proposed expert control system contains several special databases. The main bases are the static database, dynamic database, parameter base, performance index base, fault pattern base, and controller base. The detailed descriptions are as follows:

- *The static data source* is a set of limit values such as sensor measurement tolerances, operating thresholds, and alarm sequence. The knowledge is mainly acquired by theoretically modeling the process, analyzing the normal or abnormal process behaviors, making experiments, and interviewing engineers or operators.
- *The dynamic data source* provides a set of external and internal parameters that have symbolic or numerical values. External parameters represent the operation situations and system input and output values, which are updated at every iteration of the control loop. These data are provided online by a computer interface; the interface device is shown in Fig. 10. Internal parameters include system status information, for example, stability and dynamic performance of the controlled process system, which have been obtained by the calculations. Consequently, all internal parameters are initially set to default values.
- *The model parameter source* contains a set of controlled process model parameters that are estimated by an online state and parameter estimation algorithm. Experience with several processes has shown that the estimation of process parameters is very well suited for process fault detection or diagnosis, because they are directly related to many faults; for example, many process faults appear as changes of process coefficients α such as resistance, capacities, inductivities,

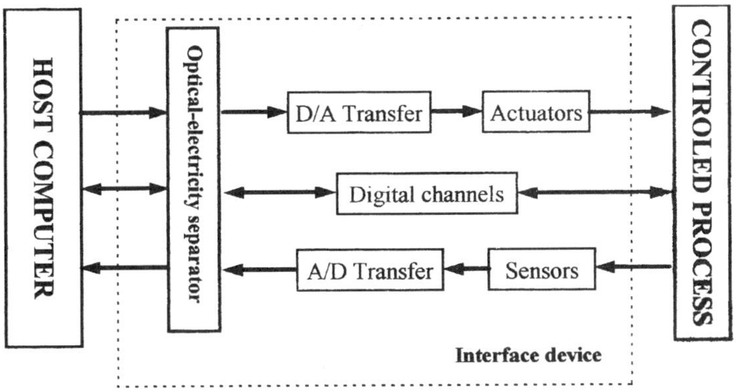

FIGURE 10 Control system interface device.

damping, stiffness, and friction. These process coefficients are contained in the parameters Θ of a process model. However, it is difficult to classify these; that is, the classifier must have the ability to indicate fault size, fault type, and fault location based on the changes of the parameters. A knowledge base method was presented in [6]. In this section, an online least square (LS) estimator is introduced. It is assumed that a process with lumped parameters is described by a linear differential equation,

$$\begin{aligned} y(k) + a_1 y(k-1) + \cdots + a_n y(k-n) \\ = b_0 u(k) + b_1 u(k-1) + \cdots + b_m u(k-m) + \xi(k), \end{aligned} \tag{4.6}$$

that is,

$$\begin{aligned} y(k) = -a_1 y(k-1) - \cdots - a_n y(k-n) \\ + b_0 u(k) + b_1 u(k-1) + \cdots + b_m u(k-m) + \xi(k), \end{aligned} \tag{4.7}$$

where $\xi(k)$ is the equation error.

The recursive LS estimation algorithm is an follows (the recursive calculation procedures are shown in Fig. 11):

$$\Theta(k+1) = \Theta(k) + K(k+1)\big[y(k) - X^T(k+1)\Theta(k)\big], \tag{4.8}$$

$$P(k+1) = P(k) - K(k+1)X^T(k+1)P(k), \tag{4.9}$$

$$K(k+1) = P(k)X(k+1)/\big[1 + X^T(k+1)P(k)X(k+1)\big], \tag{4.10}$$

where

$$\begin{aligned} X^T(k+1) = [-y(k), -y(k-1), \ldots, -y(k-n+1), \\ u(k+1), \ldots, u(k-m+1)], \\ \Theta^T(k) = [a_1, a_2, \ldots, a_n, b_0, b_1, \ldots, b_m]. \end{aligned}$$

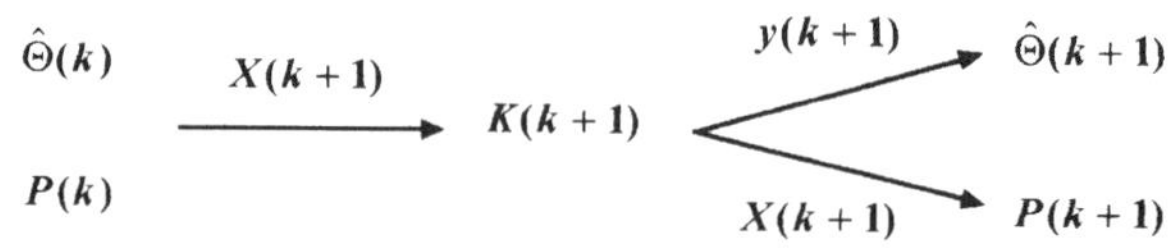

FIGURE 11 Calculation procedures of on-line LS estimator.

• The *fault pattern source* consists of a set of fault situations and misoperations that are selected from the example process. The control system fault patterns are acquired from the experience of the engineers and operators or from specific knowledge about the process. They are also obtained by control engineering practices.

• The *controller parameter source* contains a number of parameters that are tailored to the designed controllers such as proportional–integral–differential controller, robust controller, adaptive controller, etc. They are usually determined by offline simulation analysis; sometimes online adjustments are also made based on real system running conditions.

• The *performance index source* provides two kinds of performance indexes. One is the required system performance given by the designer or user. Most of the requirements are given in the time domain (overshoot, settling time, rise time, etc.). The other is real-time system performance calculated by the online analysis program.

• The *controller structure source* contains several different types of controller, that makes the controlled process performance as good as possible. The controllers in the base are described as follows:

1. The *proportional–integral–differential controller*, also called the three-mode or three-term controller, is quite popular and has no standard form; it can be represented in several ways. A form common in industrial applications is used here, namely

$$G_c(s) = K_c + T_D s + \frac{K_c}{T_I s}.$$

   In this form, K_C represents the proportional term, T_D is the rate time or derivation term, and T_I is the reset time (reciprocal of the integral).
2. *An adaptive controller*, in general, is a controller that adapts to the observed plant behavior. Many adaptive control schemes are available, but only two important strategies are widely used in industrial applications, that is, the self-tuning controller and the model reference adaptive controller (MRAC).
   (i) Self-tuning control is an indirect method in which the process parameters are updated by some learning scheme while the controller parameters are obtained from the solution of a design problem. A self-tuning control system block diagram is shown in Fig. 12. In the system, the controller is designed or the controller parameters are adjusted online.
   (ii) **MRAC** is a direct adaptive control method in which the desired behavior of the plant is given by a reference model. The general

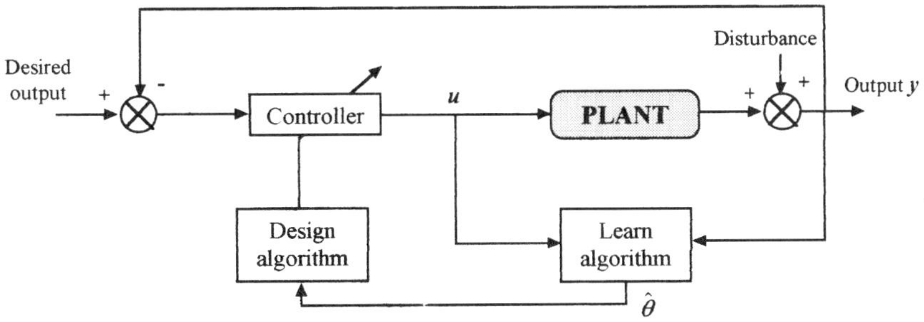

FIGURE 12 Self-tuning control system scheme.

scheme of a MRAC system is illustrated in Fig. 13. The parameters of the controller are directly updated in such a way that the error between the actual plant output y and the model output y_m is minimized.

- The *default source* provides several initial values to the control system programs according to some knowledge about the controlled process. When no information about the process is available a default set of parameters for a worst case situation is used.

D. Knowledge Representation

Knowledge is information about the world that allows an expert to make decisions. This knowledge needs to be represented and employed in a form that can be used for reasoning. The process of representing this knowledge formally is called knowledge representation, which deals with what is known in traditional numerical applications as the database, and in knowledge-based systems as the knowledge base. It can be considered as the description of the problem space, its properties and internal laws.

Knowledge has different forms. It can be certain or uncertain, formalized or unformalized, structured or unrelated, etc., each form having its strengths and weaknesses. The type of knowledge representation that is appropriate in a given situation depends on what sort of knowledge is being represented and how it is to be applied. Many methods for knowledge representation have been proposed. The issues that affect the selection of knowledge representation are the naturalness of

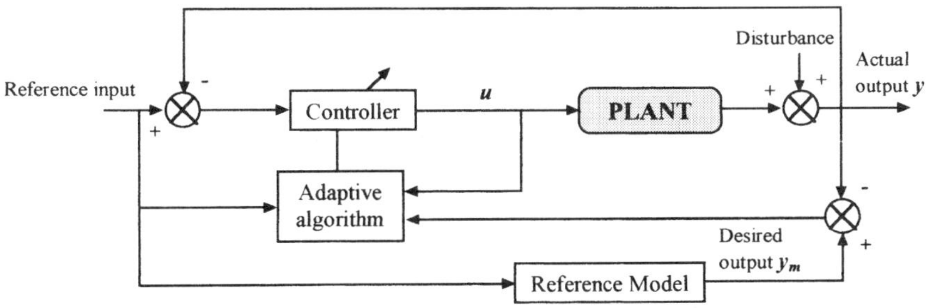

FIGURE 13 Model reference adaptive control system scheme.

representation, efficiency of storage and manipulation, and consistency and compatibility with the rest of the representations in the system. Production rules and frames are used in real-time expert-system-based fault-tolerant control systems.

1. Production Rules

Production rules are expressed in the standard IF–THEN format and are used to represent relationships between facts. Production rules consist of a conditional part and an action part. The conditions of a rule have to be satisfied in order for the rule to act. The actions of a rule execute a series of operations that will modify the state of the problem.

In this chapter, the fault pattern base is composed of the production rules that express the special knowledge about the glutamic acid fermentation process. Each rule can be illustrated as follows.

PREMISE: A. The flow is lower.

B. The pressure of the recycling pipe is higher.

ACTION: The recycling pipe might be blocked.

In the fault pattern base, the interrelated rules form a rule set. The rules are related by the metarule for the reasoning. A piece of the metarule is linked with the system running state information and dynamic data of the process, for example:

RULE 1.

PREMISE: A. The temperature of the fermentor is abnormal.

B. The recycling pump works well.

C. The heat exchanger is fouled.

ACTION: The fault might be in the recycling pipe.

RULE 2.

PREMISE: A. The fermentor works well.

B. The recycling pipe leaks.

C. The recycling pump works well.

ACTION: The heat exchanger is fouled or leaking.

METARULE.

PREMISE: A. The fermentor works well.

B. There are other rules show that the fault might be in fouled heat exchanger part.

ACTION: The rules shown in the premise B might be useless.

To reason about the faults, the system checks the related rules of the set; for example, before calling Rule 1, its premise must be checked piece by piece. Let us assume that A and B are satisfied but C is not satisfied. The system will indicate a rule, for example, Rule 2, that can derive premise C of Rule 1. Then the system will check the premise of Rule 2, etc. This forms a rule chain.

2. Frames

Knowledge representation using frames was first suggested by Minsky. Frames are type of knowledge structure that function like tables or questionnaires and use locations called slots to store attributes. They provide a method of combining declarations and procedures within a single knowledge representation environment. A frame can have any number of attributes or properties attached to it; some of the properties can be relationships. An attribute may have any number of values, that is, no value, one value, or several values. The importance of being able to represent relations is that a given frame can inherit properties (attributes and/or values) from the frames to which it is related. Frames are a convenient and natural way to represent descriptive information, that is, objects, their properties, and their relationships. They also represent very naturally the information carried in hierarchically structured domains.

In the designed fault-tolerant control system, the controller base is a set of controllers with different types of structure. These controller structures are specially designed based on the anticipated failure situations of the process; the goal is to achieve the best dynamic performance under conditions guaranteeing the stability and safety of the whole system. The parameter base contains several parameter sets that are tailored to the controller. Each controller maps a set, while the tuning algorithms are to find the best parameters in the set, so that the dynamic performance of the whole system is the best possible when a fault happens.

Figure 14 shows part of the basic frame hierarchy for the controller structure and controller parameter selection. At the top of the hierarchy is the most general description of the entities, CONTROLLER, and at the very bottom are the descriptions of the actual parameters (e.g., PID controller parameters K_P, K_D, K_I).

Table 2 shows the definition of the frame CONTROLLER, in which the attributes of CONTROLLER are defined with slots. The format used in this chapter

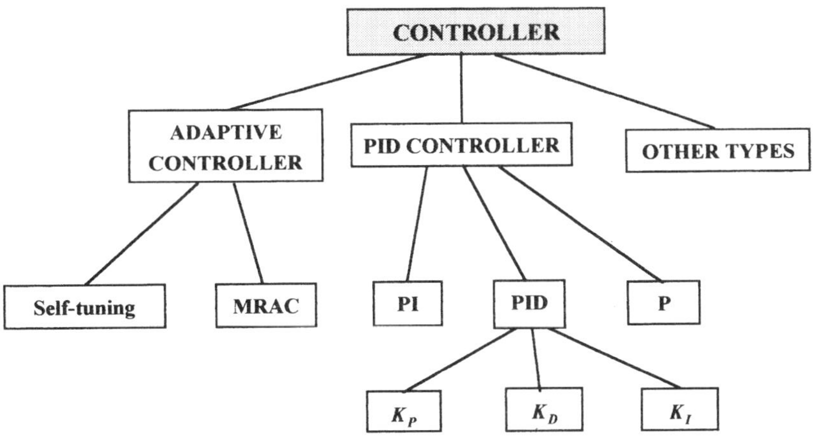

FIGURE 14 The frame hierarchy for CONTROLLER.

TABLE 2 The CONTROLLER Frame

Frame: CONTROLLER
Parents: CONTROL SYSTEM ELEMENT
Children: ADAPTIVE CONTROLLER, PID CONTROLLER, OTHER TYPES
– Slots –
REAL-TIME-SIMULATION: ON
SYSTEM-STATE: NORMAL

to display a frame is the frame name, the frames(s), the child frame(s), and all slot names followed by the slot's default value when it exists. These default values are inherited by the frame's children and are used in the rule inferring at the instance level. If no value is given, the inference engine treats the value as unknown, and if a new value is specified further down the hierarchy, that value is the one used.

Now let us examine the frame hierarchy, starting with one of the CONTROLLER frame's children—PID CONTROLLER (Table 3). CONTROLLER has defined slots that are attributes of all types of controller, for example, all controllers can be shut down. For PID, we add three new slots, system dynamic performance. PID CONTROLLER has child frames representing different types of PID controllers, such as P controller, PI controller, and PID controller (Table 4). By examining the differences of system dynamic performance among controllers, we can use the hierarchy to categorize types of controllers. At each level, new slots and default values will be added.

Because the controller knowledge is represented through frames in the proposed fault-tolerant control system, they should be maintained; for example, slot values should be stored and retrieved whenever required. A search for the slot with the given slot name and frame is done to get the slot value. If it is found, a search for the slot is conducted in the parent frame, and so on further up the inheritance network. This operation is performed until the slot is found or until the root frame is reached. To store slot values into the frame, a similar procedure can be used. The difference is that if the slot has an attached predicate, it is executed first. The value is stored or rejected based on the result of the execution.

E. Inference Engine (Controller Reconfiguration)

The inference engine uses rules and available facts to insert additional facts into the knowledge base When a new fact is placed in the knowledge base and the inference

TABLE 3 Frame PID CONTROLLER

Frame: PID CONTROLLER
Parents: CONTROLLER
Children: P, PI, PID
– Slots –
REAL-TIME-SIMULATION: ON
SYSTEM-STATE: NORMAL
PARAMETER-ESTIMATION:
FAULT-DIAGNOSIS:
DYNAMIC-PERFORMANCE:

TABLE 4 Frame PID

Frame: PID
Parents: PID CONTROLLER
Children: PARAMETER K_P, PARAMETER K_I, PARAMETER K_D
– Slots –
REAL-TIME-SIMULATION: ON
SYSTEM-STATE: NORMAL
PARAMETER-ESTIMATION:
FAULT-DIAGNOSIS:
DYNAMIC-PERFORMANCE:
TUNING-FORMULA:

engine *sees* the new fact, it must check whether that fact matches any antecedents of rules currently in the knowledge base. This process, known as matching, lies at the heart of every inference engine. To match a fact, the pattern of the rule clause must match a pattern in the knowledge base. Once the inference engine has matched a rule's antecedents, it will fire the rule by inserting the rule's consequent into the knowledge base.

Most rule-based systems reason using forward chaining, backward chaining, or a combination of two. The proposed fault-tolerant control system contains two expert subsystems: a real-time expert fault diagnosis subsystem and a controller reconfiguration subsystem. In the fault diagnosis subsystem, we use the forward chaining strategy to reason about the state of the process to be controlled. Later we use the backward chaining rules to reconfigure the controller based on the results of diagnosis and real-time simulation.

1. Failure Detection and Fault Diagnosis

A primary feature of any reconfiguration scheme is failure detection and fault diagnosis. From the point of view of industrial process control systems, a fault is understood as any kind malfunction in the actual dynamic system, the plant, that leads to an unacceptable anomaly in the overall system performance. Such malfunctions may occur either in the sensors, the actuators, or the components of the process. Failure detection and fault diagnosis are the first step before any corrective action can be taken. The design of a fault diagnosis strategy for a set of hypothesized faults involves several considerations. It must essentially be a fast system with minimum detection delay while also ensuring that false alarms are minimized. On the other hand it must be robust to modeling errors and take into account existing system redundancy.

Over the last decades, basic research on fault diagnosis has gained increasing consideration world wide. Several fault diagnosis approaches were proposed for industrial process control systems. This development was mainly stimulated by the automatic control system trend toward more complexity and the corresponding growing demand for higher availability and security of control systems. However, a strong impetus also comes from the side of artificial intelligence that has led to simplification of conventional systems and has made it possible to obtain control systems with new capabilities. The expert fault diagnosis strategy is a process of reasoning whether it is based on the sensitivity properties of processed signals with or without the fault. To do this, a fault–symptom (or pattern–fact) tree can

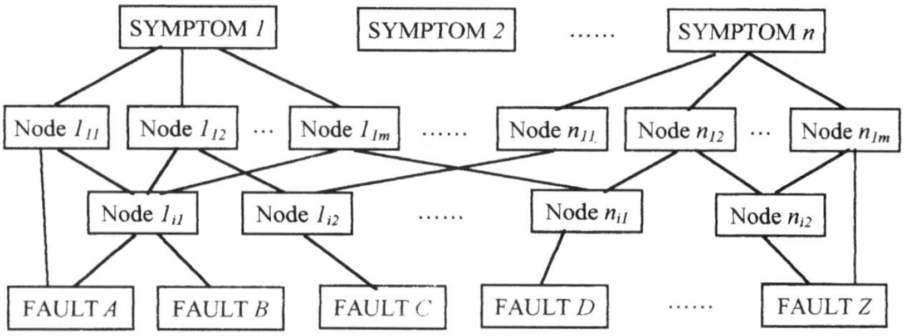

FIGURE 15 A form of fault-symptom tree.

be constructed, shown in Fig. 15. Each node in the tree is a frame. The nodes of different trees are frequently not independent, but directly related at the same instant. It needs to be noted that if the nodes of different trees are connected, several symptoms may appear at the same time or in a special sequence delayed with respect to each other.

In our application, forward reasoning techniques are used after a suitable means of knowledge representation has been established. The goal of the expert system is to infer the faults based on the observed symptoms. The inference engine is a program that applies rules from the rules base to the knowledge in the database to infer new knowledge. Given a fault symptom, the inference engine searches the rule base for a list of rules. These rules are selected so that, when applied in sequence, they infer new knowledge until the last rule provides a fault or faults. The search process implemented by the inference engine is called forward chaining, which means that the program works from an initial state toward some goals by successively applying the rules. The reference program consists of Diagnosis and Findout. Diagnosis is used to analyze rules and Findout is used to search the data they call each other. The diagrams are shown in Figs. 16 and 17.

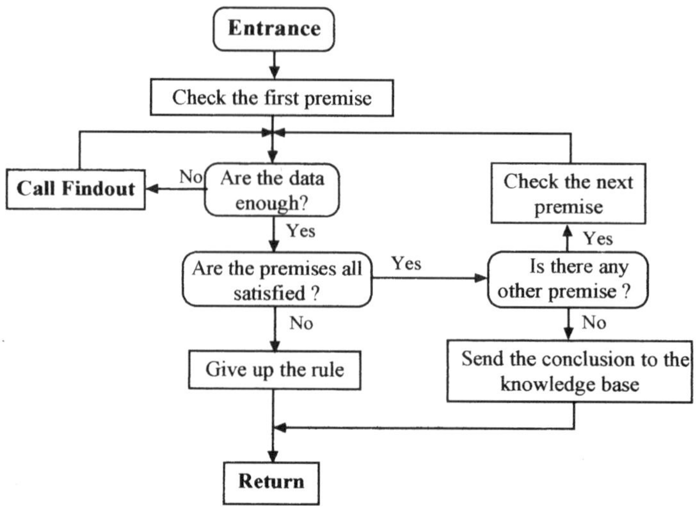

FIGURE 16 Diagnosis program.

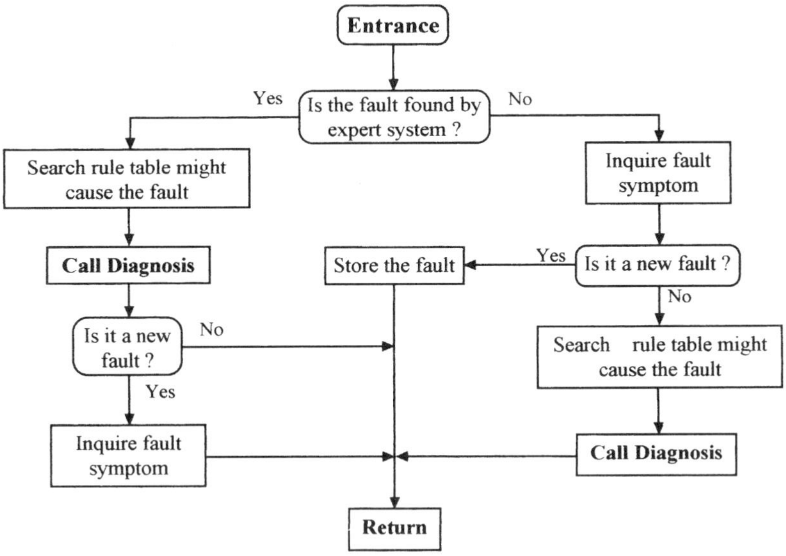

FIGURE 17 Findout program.

2. Controller Reconfiguration

Looking back on control technologies during the past 80 years, we have seen the field change dramatically. From ship steering in 1920s, where classical feedback control was used to keep the course, to the space probes and the automated manufacturing plants of today, control systems have played a key role in technological and scientific development. To meet the needs of a changing world, a number of control methods have been developed by engineers and scientists, including PID control, optimal control, robust control, adaptive control, and AI control of today. However, any control method has advantages and disadvantages over other methods. It is difficult to find a controller that can be used for industrial process control in any fault cases. Although some of techniques used in modern control theory are much more powerful and can solve more complex problems than can the classical method, there are often more restrictions when it comes to the practical applications of these methods. If the system failures are within an acceptable range, some process controllers, for example, an adaptive controller or robust controller, can still maintain the process at a satisfactory level by online adaptation of its own parameters. If the failures exceed the thresholds, the host controller must be switched from the initial structure to a particular structure that is predesigned to tailor itself the anticipated fault conditions by a decision-making algorithm.

In the following sections, the three main procedures for reconfiguring a controller are described. First, the selection of controller structure is addressed. Second, the expert system method is discussed mainly for tuning parameters of a PID controller. Finally, the real-time simulation strategy is presented, which determines whether or not the selected and tuned controller is to be started, replacing the initial controller.

a. Selecting the Structure of Process Controller

The control reconfiguration is to select a controller from the knowledge base for the anticipated fault conditions. Alternatively, the reconfigured control can use a pseudo-inverse approach to implement a feedback control law similar to that of the primary controls. For example, if there is partial loss of a control surface, reconfiguration could be implemented by increasing the gain to compensate for the partial degradation. The new feedback control is calculated by using a pseudo-inverse that tries to equate the product of the new control matrix (B_{new}) and the new control (u_{new}) with the product of the previous control matrix (B) times the control (u):

$$B_{\text{new}} u_{\text{new}} = Bu.$$

When there is a complete failure, the control influence matrix B_{new} is derived from B by eliminating the column, which corresponds to the failed control input. If there is redundancy in the actuators, the new control (u_{new}) to be applied to the system can be calculated by using the pseudo-inverse

$$u_{\text{new}} = \left(B_{\text{new}}^T B_{\text{new}}\right)^{-1} B_{\text{new}}^T Bu.$$

A slight modification can tailor the relation between the desired states and resulting controls. For example, there can be different weightings on the individual state and control variables [12].

However, in many cases, we must completely reconfigure the process controller; that is, the structure and parameters of the controller must be changed in order to retain stability and some key performance when some faults occur. If there is direct unique relationship between the controllers and faults, this can be classified as analytical knowledge. However, if there are no direct or no unique connections, heuristic knowledge has to be applied.

In the proposed strategy, the expert system monitors the process and control system for performance level achievement. If the control system performance is degrading or instability is detected, the expert system will first attempt to find out the most suitable structure of controller based on the interaction matrix that contains the relationship information between fault situations and controller structures. The interaction matrix can be obtained by observing the practice process or interviewing the control engineers. The number of candidate controller structures will rapidly increase with the increase in the numbers of inputs, outputs and faults. By turning and analyzing the controller in accordance with the control theory, the expert system can find the best controller structure from all candidates.

b. Controller Real-Time Tuning via Rule-Based Method

As mentioned previously, an expert-system-based fault-tolerant control system generally consists of the plant, a controller and a higher level knowledge base system that is used to diagnosis process faults, select the structure of the controller, and tune its parameters to achieve the required performance. The Ziegler–Nichols ultimate cycling or frequency response method is a well-known technique for tuning a PID controller manually. It is designed to give quarter amplitude damping for the load disturbance response. To use the Ziegler–Nichols ultimate cycling tuning formula to tune a PID controller manually, the first step is to switch off the

I (integral) and D (differential) parts of the controller to obtain a P (proportional) controller. The proportional gain is then gradually increased until sustained oscillation is obtained. This tuning method, however, is not very practical because of the difficulty in operating the process on the verge of instability. If sufficient care is not taken, the amplitude of the oscillation may grow unbounded, introducing a major upset to the plant operation. Even if a sustained oscillation is maintained, it may be difficult to control the amplitude of the oscillation. The long duration of tuning and the demand on the operator's close attention make this manual method unattractive.

Improvements to the Ziegler–Nichols tuning methods have also been made by several scholars. Astrom and Hagglund automated and improved the Ziegler–Nichols continuous cycling method. In their method, a low-gain PI controller is initially used to bring the process near the set point and then a relay replaces the PI controller so as to reduce the size of the oscillation. With proper adjustment of the relay output, a reasonable amplitude for the oscillations is obtained and, again, the frequency and the amplitude are used to tune the controller. Descriptions of several expert systems that perform PID controller tuning have appeared in the literature. Litt [19] described an expert system method for tuning the PID controller parameters. In his method, the expert system examines features of each transient response and corresponding controller parameters based on a three-dimensional tuning map. It determines a new set of controller gains to obtain a more desirable time response.

In this section, a rule-based controller parameter tuning strategy will be discussed, which can be regarded as an alternative approach to the design of expert process subsystem. The expert system also includes several functions for the analysis of the performance and robustness of the system. To tune the selected controller parameters, we construct a system, shown in Fig. 18, that consists of four parts:

- The *unknown plant*—If the fault diagnosis subsystem has detected that the ith fault has occurred, the unknown plant to be controlled can be represented by $G(q^{-1})$ relating the input $u(k)$ and the output $y(k)$ as follows:

$$y(k) = G(q^{-1})u(k).$$

- The *reference mode* $G_{mf_i}(q^{-1})$ is predefined, which describes that the dynamic performance should be achieved in the ith fault case. The mode is

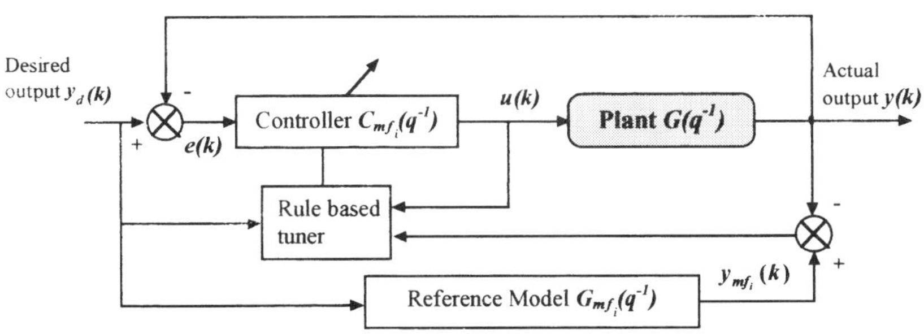

FIGURE 18 The expert tuning system scheme.

represented as follows:

$$y_m(k) = G_{mf_i}(q^{-1})y_d(k).$$

- The *controller* $C_{f_i}(q^{-1})$ is selected as a candidate controller by the expert system under the ith fault case, which relates the error to the control signal applied to the faulty plant as follows:

$$u(k) = C_{f_i}(q^{-1})e(k),$$

where

$$e(k) = y_d(k) - y(k).$$

- A *rule-based tuner* is used to find the best parameters for the selected controller matching the ith fault.

The selected controller may be P, PI, PID, or even ON–OFF structures toiling under the diagnosed fault conditions. The PID controller has no standard form and it can be represented in several ways [19]. A form common in industrial applications is used here, namely,

$$C_{f_i}(s) = K_P[1\backslash(T_I s) + 1 + T_D s].$$

In this form, K_P represents the proportional term, T_I is the reset time, and T_D is the derivative term.

This PID controller will be used as an example to illustrate the tuning process in the following sequence:

- *Online estimation*—For tuning a PID structure controller, the dead time K_U and sustained oscillation period T_U must first be determined. Here, they are estimated by the online LS method stated in Section IV.C with plant input $u(k)$ and output $y(k)$.
- *Basic point parameters calculation*—Once obtained the estimated values of $K_U$and T_U, the basic point parameters of the PID controller can be calculated by the Ziegler–Nichols tuning formula as follows:

$$K_P = 0.6K_U, T_I = T_U/2, \qquad T_D = T_U/8.$$

  The step response using these parameters settles rapidly; however, overshoot may be unacceptably high because of estimation errors and load disturbance. These parameters must further be modified to make the control system have good dynamic performance.
- *Extracting response features*—By comparing the desired model output $y_m(k)$ with the actual output $y(k)$, some important dynamic features, for example, dead time, rise time, settling time, and maximum overshoot, can be extracted.
- *Modifying the parameters*—Based on the differences between desired and actual response characteristics, one can infer general rules about how the changes in the controller parameters affect the features of the response, the

modifying process is similar to Litt's approach as follows:

1. Increasing K_P decreases period and vice versa.
2. Increasing K_P increases overshoot and vice versa.
3. Increasing K_P decreases rise time and vice versa.
4. Increasing K_P increases damping and vice versa.
5. Decreasing T_I increases overshoot and vice versa.
6. Decreasing T_I increases damping and vice versa.
7. Decreasing T_I decreases stability and vice versa.
8. Increasing T_I decreases overshoot and vice versa.
9. Increasing T_D increases stability and vice versa.
10. Increasing T_D decreases rise time and vice versa.

c. Real-Time Simulation

Generally, real-time systems and expert systems have a number of incompatibilities. The resources used in a real-time system are known and have predictable computation times; besides, the control problems must be solved in real time, including the knowledge-based parts, because the data is not static but changes as a function of time. In expert systems, there are no guaranteed response times and unknown resources will be used.

To deal with time-critical problems, the real-time simulation program is specially designed for industrial process control systems. Before the controller is completely tuned, the expert system only collects input data and output data from the running control process. Once the tuning process ended, the real-time simulation program is started, to indicate the dynamic performance of the process controlled by the tuned controller. The expert system has a signal base that can provide the system with different reference signals such as control noises and measurement noises for computer simulation. If the simulation results show that the performance is satisfactory, the new controller will replace the original controller to control a process with faults or malfunctions. Otherwise, the expert system has to find another controller structure and tune it again.

V. APPLICATIONS TO INDUSTRIAL PROCESS CONTROL

A. Case 1: Application to Steel Mill Soaking Pit Control

1. Steel Mill Soaking Pit Process Control

In one version of the steel-making process, the steel ingots, before they may be rolled at the rolling mill, typically pass through the soaking pit operation (another version—the continuous steel-making process, which does not utilize the soaking pit—is not considered here). The purpose of this operation is to equalize the temperature throughout the ingot masses at some prespecified level. Accurate description of the ingot temperature distribution would require the knowledge of analytical space–temperature relationships or of the temperature values at many points along the ingot side, top, and bottom surfaces, as well as throughout its mass. A typical soaking pit is shown in Fig. 19. The ingots (5–20 tons each, 5–15 ingots, per pit) come from the tripping yard, where they are stripped of their molds. At this time, the ingot surface and center temperatures are usually within the ranges of

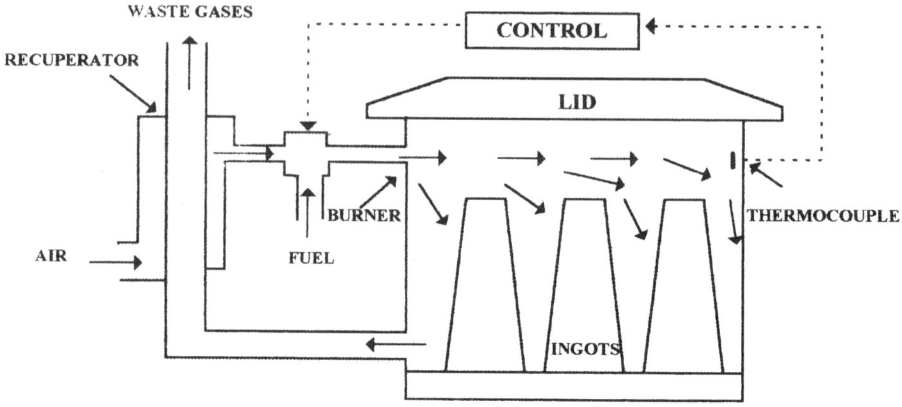

FIGURE 19 The soaking pit.

700–1000°C and 1100–1500°C, respectively. Sometimes, though, the ingots may come from cold storage, in which case their temperature will be the ambient temperature. To do the job (done today by the operator), the control system has to continuously estimate the current ingot temperatures, at least on the surface, and to stop the operation when these temperatures arrive at the prespecified levels (usually the level is the same for both temperatures). Underheating of ingots results in poor rolling mill performance or in returning the ingots to the pit for additional heating; overheating (which is often the case) results in a waste of energy. According to industry estimates, up to 15–20% fuel savings could be realized in this energy-intensive operation if an efficient ingot temperature estimation system is put into operation.

The soaking pit control process should guarantee the best performance at the lowest energy consumption. Early soaking pits did not have a good system of automatic control; the operator drove the process using experience gained over many years. Control actions and decisions were based on practiced knowledge, rules of thumb, intuitive feelings, and some other mysterious methods. The efficiency based on the conventional **PID** control is not good in this case. The main difficulty associated with the soaking pit process is in measuring the temperatures of the ingots that we are trying to control. Direct measurement of ingot temperature is not feasible because of the harsh conditions inside the pit. The distance between the walls and the ingots prevents contact measurements (using, e.g., optical pyrometers) inside the pit, so measurements inside the pit do not produce reliable results, according to industry sources. The only direct measurements available are the pit wall temperature, fuel and air flow, the waste gas temperature, several other indirect variables.

To improve the dynamic performance of the soaking pit control system, we designed a real-time expert control system. In the application, the online least square estimation algorithm is employed to estimate the temperature of ingots and an expert subsystem is used to tune parameters of the PID controller in real time based on the realistic circumstance of the process.

2. Controlling Effectiveness

An important feature of the designed control system is the ability to fine-tune the controller parameters in real time. Figures 20–22, show the dynamic tuning

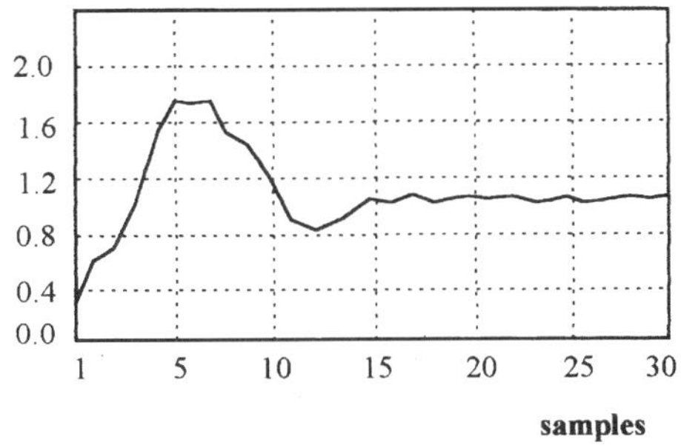

FIGURE 20 The dynamic tuning curve of the parameter T_I.

process for the three parameters of a PID controller. A Fibonacci sequence is used to determine the amount of change. It is an ordered set of numbers defined recursively as $f(n) = f(n-1) + f(n-2)$ for $n \geq 3$. The amount of change in each controller parameter is the reciprocal value of $f(n)$ times the sign of the sum of weighted errors associated with the controller parameters.

To determine the effectiveness of the proposed control strategy, we conducted experiments to test the setpoint tracking ability of the PID controller and online expert system PID controller. Each experiment was conducted over 500 samples with a sampling interval of 10 s. Figure 23 shows the outputs and the respective control signals of the two channels of the soaking pit due to change in the setpoints using the two algorithms. It can be observed that the PID controller performed much slower with overshoots in achieving the desired setpoints compared to the real-time expert PID controller.

We also conducted the experiment to study the ability of the two controllers when unknown load disturbances were imposed on the process. To ensure identical comparison between the two controller, artificial load disturbances of value 100°C were added to the outputs in the experiment. The performance of the two systems under the effects of the load disturbances is shown in Fig. 24 at the sampling period of interest. It can be observed that the real-time expert PID controller performed equally well with the ability to recover quickly from the effects of the positive load disturbance.

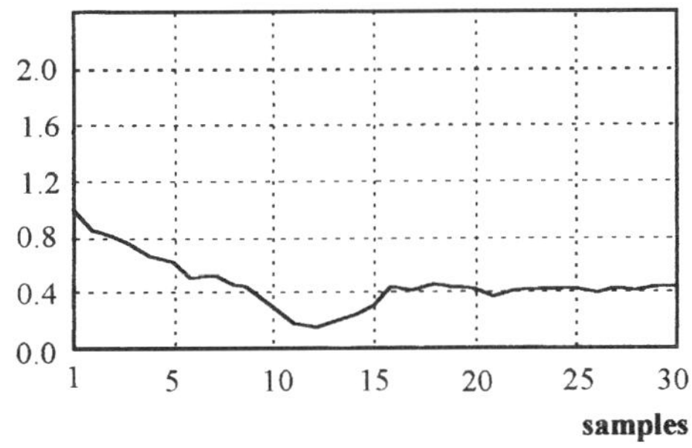

FIGURE 21 The dynamic tuning curve of the parameter T_D.

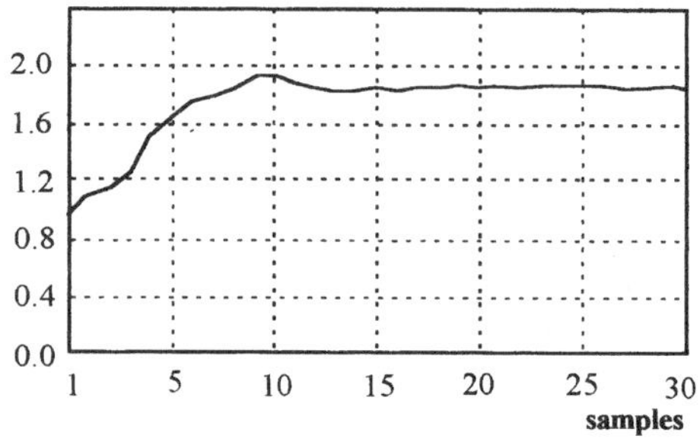

FIGURE 22 The dynamic tuning curve of the parameter K_P.

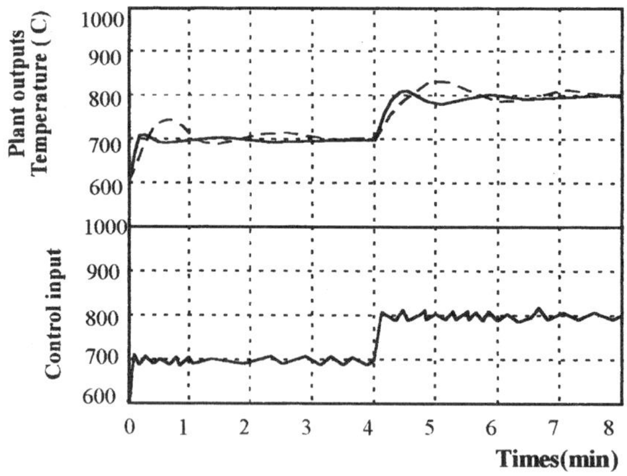

FIGURE 23 Temperature curves using expert system PID control (solid line) and PID control (dashed line).

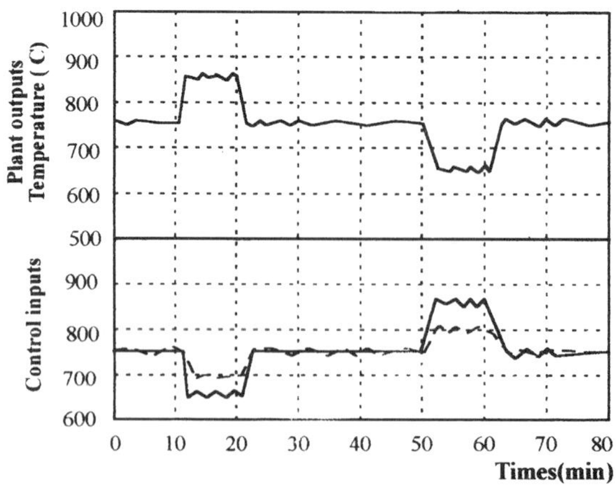

FIGURE 24 Temperature curves using expert system PID control (solid line) and PID control (dashed line) under the influence of load disturbances.

B. Case 2: Application to Batch Yeast Fermentation Process Control

1. Batch Yeast Fermentation Process

The example process is a batch yeast fermentation process, which consists of a fermentor and its peripherals: air compressor, agitation system, heat exchanger, control equipment for pH, temperature, dissolved oxygen, and foam leaves, shown in Fig. 25. The computer control system includes a sensor module, a parallel input–output (PIO) interface board, an actuator module, and a UNIX workstation to implement a real-time graphical interface for monitoring and controlling the process. The main control program is written using C++. The process has five feedback control loops where multiple variable optimum controllers were initially used [20]. The controllers keep the recycle flow rate, agitation rate, air compression, the pH level of the reactor, and the temperature of the reactor constant. Now, they are replaced by an expert-system-based fault-tolerant controller.

2. Experiment Results

Table 5 shows that faults or misoperations often occurred in the process control. To test the fault accommodation capability of the proposed control strategy, two experiments were designed to illustrate the behavior of the fermentation process control system in response to some failures. One was carried out when the fermentor pressure was higher than the limit value because the antifoam pipe was blocked. The other experiment was performed when a fault occurred in the heat exchanger. Fermentor pressure is an important parameter to be controlled, because a fermentation process is based on biological activity, which is an exhibition of interactive enzyme action. If fermentor pressure exceeds permissible limit over a long period, the whole reaction would be interrupted.

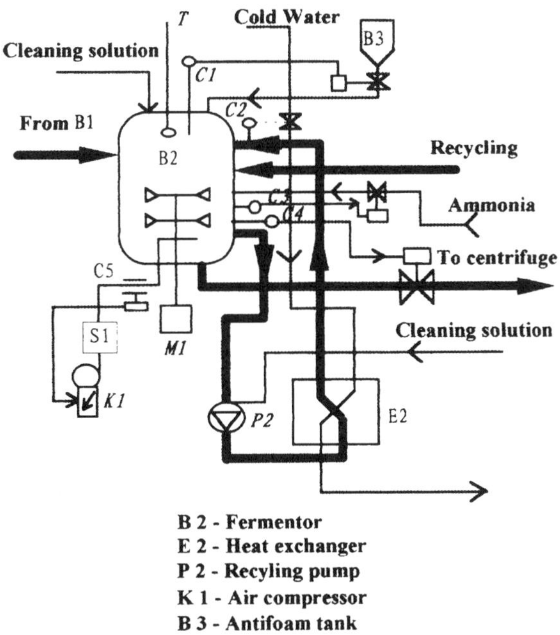

FIGURE 25 The yeast fermentation process.

TABLE 5 Selected Fault Situations

No.	Fault Description
1	Malfunction in air compressor
2	Cold water pipe partially blocked
3	Malfunction in recycling pump
4	Command position of air compressor abnormal
5	Fouled heat exchanger
6	Temperature control value stuck high
7	Malfunction in thermocouple
8	Command position of temperature abnormal
9	Leak flow in fermentor
10	Malfunction in flow meters
11	Command position of input flow abnormal

Figure 26 shows the experiment starting from a normal steady value for a 50% reduction in antifoam flow at approximately 5 min, which simulates the fault that the antifoam pipe is blocked. The reduction was achieved by placing the normal pressure controller in manual mode and the operator then closed the antifoam supply valve. After a small transient, the antifoam flow remained very steady at the reduced level for the duration of the experiment. Figure 27 shows that the controller for agitation rate is reconfigured as a PI controller with a dead space and the parameters are $K_P = 1.56$, $K_I = 0.64$, and $\theta = 0.45$ from the conventional PID controller, which makes the agitation rate descent. After 4 min the agitation rate is kept about 10 rpm. Figure 28 shows that the fermenting temperature is kept about 33°C after the temperature controller is reconstructed. The experiment results demonstrate that the system can be safely run for a longer period in the fault case. The control system can easily accommodate the failure of the antifoam pipe.

Figures 29–31 show the dynamic performance of the proposed control system while the fault in the heat exchanger occurred at approximately 4 min. The control law is changed into the isolated integral PID control from the multiple variable optimum control (the performance index is to make production maximum). The parameters of the controller are $K_P = 0.83$, $K_I = 2.17$, $K_D = 0.16$, and $A = 10$. After about 9 min, the reconfigured controller forces the agitation rate and the air compressor pressure to decrease to values in their safety ranges; that is, the ferment ratio is confined within necessary limits. Here, the fermentation production

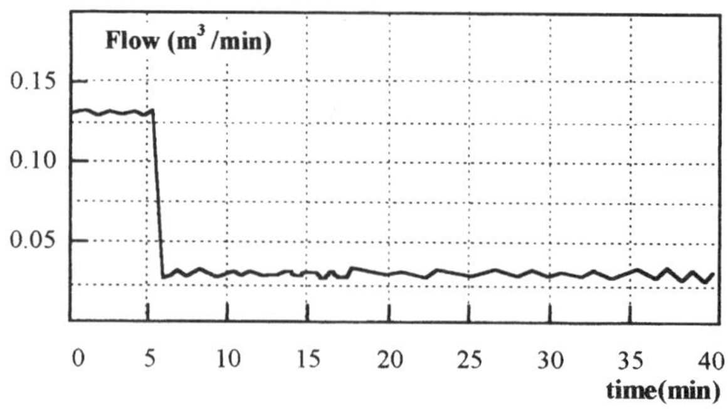

FIGURE 26 Dynamic curve of flow control in antifoam pipe fault case.

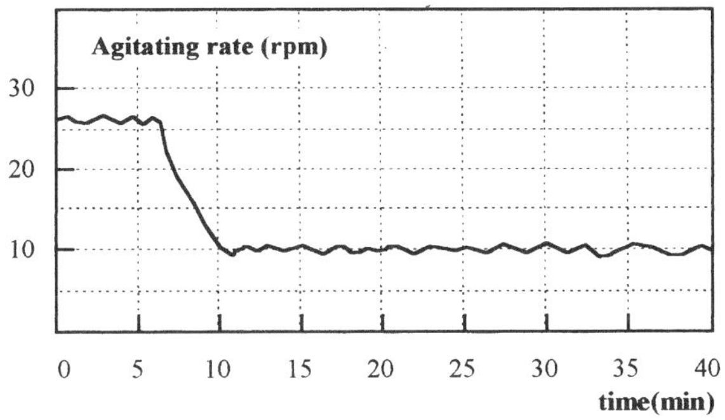

FIGURE 27 Dynamic curve of agitation control in antifoam pipe fault case.

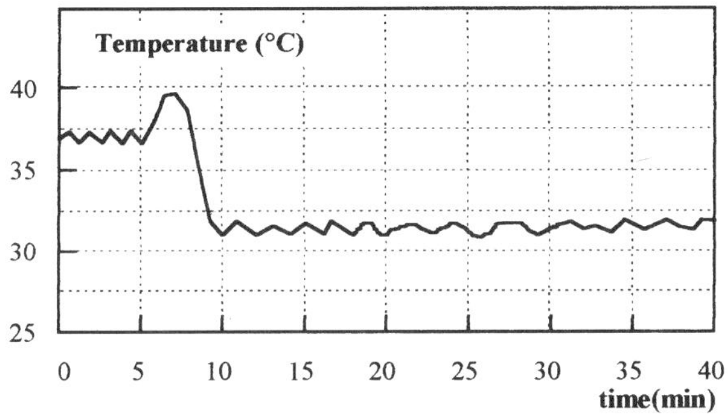

FIGURE 28 Dynamic curve of temperature control in antifoam pipe fault case.

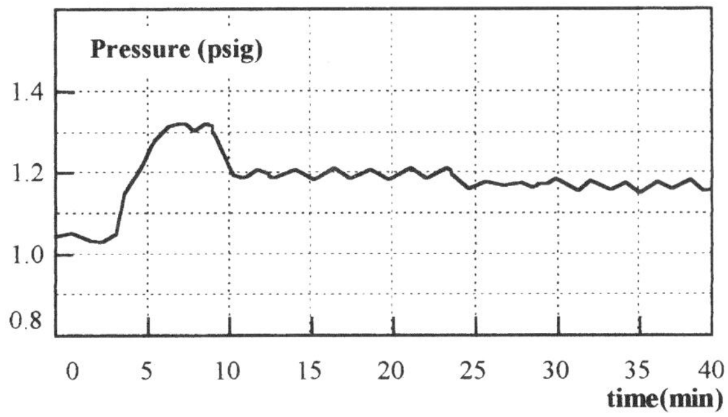

FIGURE 29 Dynamic curve of pressure control in heat exchange fault case.

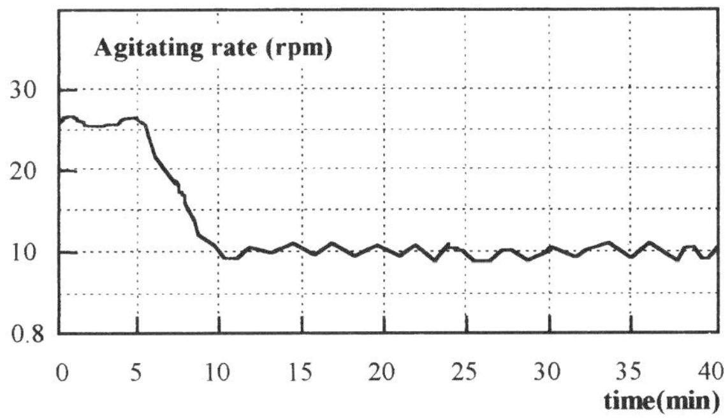

FIGURE 30 Dynamic curve of agination control in heat exchange fault case.

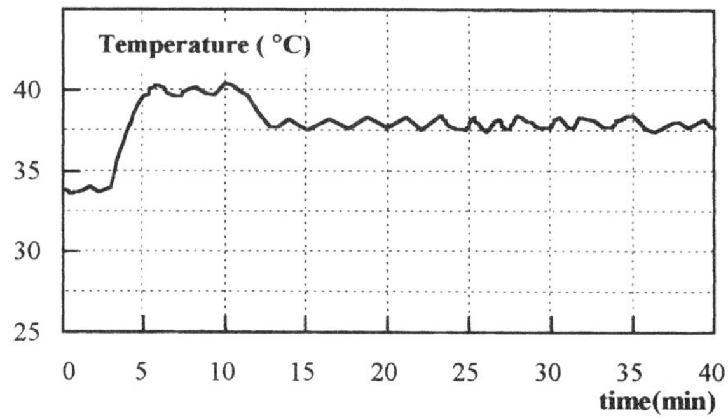

FIGURE 31 Dynamic curve of temperature control in heat exchange fault case.

is maintained for over 40 min in the failure case by using a reconfigurable control strategy. Otherwise, it can only be maintained for a few minutes. This demonstrates that the real-time expert-system-based fault-tolerant control provides a means of saving production costs.

VI. CONCLUSION

Application of expert systems to the control of technological processes is moving from the plane of theory into practice. This chapter presents a scheme for designing a real-time expert-system-based fault-tolerant control system (ESFTCS) for complex industrial process control. The system is capable of diagnosing faults and reconfiguring the controller and can accommodate different operating conditions (including failure circumstances) to accomplish the system task safely.

The applications to soaking pit and yeast fermentation processes have shown that ESFTCS can do much to improve the operating characteristics of the system. They also demonstrate that the approach proposed herein is suitable for industrial process control. It has advantages and disadvantages with respect to controlling dynamic processes. One advantage is that it is real-time, and it is almost possible for the control system to take the proper action for the instantaneous situation of the process, because it is based on observing the state variables of the process and diagnosing the faults or malfunctions of the control system. One disadvantage is that it depends upon a good knowledge of the plant, reliable control elements, and sufficient observability and controllability following failures. Future work should consider unknown fault diagnosis of the process. This was partly done for neural networks and they were shown to be able to cope with fault diagnosis of the process [21]. In such a case, a real-time neural network diagnostic subsystem would be added to the ESFTCS.

To extend these results, several directions can be pursued. First, the reconfiguration and simulation algorithms should be fully integrated and tested. Then, once other process control variables are operational, along with a new communication system supporting the variables, more sophisticated tasks involving fault accommodation can be envisioned. Besides, planning and execution tasks that require a longer planning phase are to be tested.

REFERENCES

1. IEEE CSS Report. Challenges to control: A collective view. *IEEE Trans. Automat. Contr.* 32(4):275–285, 1987.
2. Willsky, A. S. A survey of design methods for failure detection in dynamic systems. *Automatica* 12:601–611, 1976.
3. Isermann, R. Process fault detection based on modeling and estimation methods—a survey. *Automatica* 20(4):387–404, 1984.
4. Bassevile, M. Detection of changes in signals and systems—a survey. *Automatica*, 24:309–326, 1988.
5. Frank, P. M. Fault diagnosis in dynamic systems using analytical and knowledge-based redundancy—a survey and some new results. *Automatica* 26:459–474, 1990.
6. Isermann, R. Process fault diagnosis based on process model knowledge. In *Proceedings of '88 IFAC Software for Computer Control*, Johannesburg, S. Africa, 1988, pp. 53–65.
7. Wagner, J. and Shoureshi, R. A robust failure diagnostic system for thermofluid processes. *Automatica* 28(2):375–381, 1992.
8. Rychener, M. D., Ed. *Expert Systems for Engineering Design*. Academic Press, San Diego, 1988.
9. Mahmoud, S. M., Eid, S. Z., and Abou-Elsoud, A. A. A real-time expert control system for dynamical processes. *IEEE Trans. Syst. Man Cybern.* 19(5):1101–1105, 1989.
10. Krijgsman, A. *Artificial intelligent in real-time control*. Proefschrift, Technische Universiteit Delft, 1996, (in German).
11. Stengel, R. F. Intelligent failure-tolerant control. *IEEE Contr. Syst. Mag.* 11(4):14–23, 1991.
12. Rauch, E. H. Plenary speech from 1994 IEEE International Symposium on Intelligent Control (Intelligent Fault Diagnosis and Control Reconfiguration). *IEEE Contr. Syst. Mag.* 14(3):6–12, 1994.
13. Morari, M. and Zafiriou, E. *Robust Process Control*. Prentice Hall, Englewood Cliffs, NJ, 1989.
14. Barmish, R. B. *New Tools for Robustness of Linear Systems*. Macmillan Co., New York, 1994.
15. Farid, A. Z., Ioannou, P., Gousman, K., and Rooney, R. Accommodation of failures in the F-16 aircraft using adaptive control. *IEEE Contr. Syst. Mag.* 11(1):73–78, 1991.
16. Rauch, E. H. Autonomous control reconfiguration. *IEEE Contr. Syst. Mag.* 15(6):37–48, 1995.
17. Mistry, I. S. and Nair, S. S. Identification and control experiments using neural designs. *IEEE Contr. Syst. Mag.* 14(3):48–57, 1994.
18. Astrom, J. K., Anton, J. J., and Arzen, K. E. Expert control. *Automatica*, 22(3):277–286, 1986.
19. Litt, J. An expert system to perform on-line controller tuning. *IEEE Contr. Syst. Mag.* 11(3):18–23, 1991.
20. Liu, W., and Tian, S. B. Parameter estimation and optimal control of glutamic acid fermentation process. In *Proceedings of the 1988 IEEE International Conference on Systems, Man, and Cybernetics*, Beijing, 1988, 1: pp. 726–730.
21. Liu, W., Tian, S. B., and Lin, X. X. Neural networks in fermentation process fault diagnosis. In *Preprints of '95 IFAC Youth Automation Conference*, Beijing, 1995, pp. 699–703.
22. Liu, W. An on-line expert-system–based fault-tolerant control system. *Expert Sys. with Appl.* 11(1):59–64, 1996.
23. Liu, W. On-line expert system with application to steel mill soaking pit control. In *Proceedings of the 1997 IEEE International Conference on Intelligent Systems,* Beijing, 1997, Vol. 1, pp. 726–730.
24. Hein, F. Expert system using pattern recognition by real time signals. In *Proceedings of 1986 CIGRE*, Paris, 1986, pp. 39–45.
25. Ackermann, J. Robustness against sensor failures. *Automatica* 20(2):211–215, 1984.
26. Fu, M., Olbrot, A. W., and Polis, M. P. Comments on "Optimal gain for proportional–integral–derivative feedback." *IEEE Contr. Syst. Mag.* 9:100–101, 1989.
27. Litt, J. An expert system for adaptive PID tuning based on pattern recognition techniques. In *Proceedings of the 1986 ISA North Coast Conference*, Cleveland, 1986.
28. Liu, W., and Lin, X. X. Fault tolerant control with application. In *Proceedings of 1992 Chinese Conference on Control Theory and Application*, 1992, Vol. 2, pp. 701–706 (in Chinese).
29. Liu, W. Improved GMSM method and its application. *Adv. Model. Simul.* 28(2):35–43, 1992.
30. Liu, W. A fault tolerant control system based on expert system and its application in synthetic reaction process. *Contr. Instruments in Chemical Industry* 23(5):13–16, 1996 (in Chinese).

31. Liu, W., and Tian, S. B. A method of real-time fault detection and its application to biochemical process control. *Contr. Instruments in Chemical Industry* 24(2):13–16, 1997 (in Chinese).
32. Liu, W., and Tian, S. B. Current development of fault-tolerant control—a survey. *J. Hebei Inst. Technol.* 19(2), 1997 (in Chinese).
33. Martin, J. How to select controller modes and tuning parameters from simple process models. *ISA Trans.* 15:314–319, 1976.
34. Michal, J., Kminek, M., and Kminek, P. Expert control of vacuum pan crystallization. *IEEE Contr. Syst. Mag.* 14(5):28–34, 1994.
35. Penttinen, J. and Koivo, H. N. Multivariable tuning regulators for unknown systems. *Automatica* 16:393–398, 1980.
36. Pham, H. and Upadhyaya, S. J. Optimal design of fault-tolerant distributed systems based on a recursive algorithm. *IEEE Trans. Rel.* 40(3):375–379, 1991.
37. Rivera, D. E., Morari, M., and Skogestad, S. Internal model control. Chapter 4. PID controller design. *Ind. Eng. Chem. Process Des. Dec.* 25:252–265, 1986.
38. Kendra, S. J., Basila, M. R., and Cinar, A. Intelligent process control with supervisory knowledge-based systems. *IEEE Contr. Syst. Mag.* 14(3):37-47, 1994.